Nineteenth-Century Major Lives and Letters

Series Editor: Marilyn Gaull

This series presents original biographical, critical, and scholarly studies of literary works and public figures in Great Britain, North America, and continental Europe during the nineteenth century. The volumes in *Nineteenth-Century Major Lives and Letters* evoke the energies, achievements, contributions, cultural traditions, and the individuals who reflected and generated them during the Romantic and Victorian period. The topics encompass critical, textual, and historical scholarship, literary and book history, biography, cultural and comparative studies, critical theory, art, architecture, science, politics, religion, music, language, philosophy, aesthetics, law, publication, translation, domestic and public life, popular culture, and anything that influenced, impinges upon, expresses or contributes to an understanding of the authors, works, and events of the nineteenth century. The authors consist of political figures, artists, scientists, and cultural icons including William Blake, Thomas Hardy, Charles Darwin, William Wordsworth, William Butler Yeats, Samuel Taylor, and their contemporaries.

The series editor is Marilyn Gaull, PhD (Indiana University), FEA. She has taught at William and Mary, Temple University, New York University, and is Research Professor at the Editorial Institute at Boston University. She is the founder and editor of *The Wordsworth Circle* and the author *of English Romanticism: The Human Context*, and editions, essays, and reviews in journals. She lectures internationally on British Romanticism, folklore, and narrative theory, intellectual history, publishing procedures, and history of science.

PUBLISHED BY PALGRAVE MACMILLAN:

Shelley's German Afterlives, by Susanne Schmid
Coleridge, the Bible, and Religion, by Jeffrey W. Barbeau
Romantic Literature, Race, and Colonial Encounter, by Peter J. Kitson
Byron, edited by Cheryl A. Wilson
Romantic Migrations, by Michael Wiley
The Long and Winding Road from Blake to the Beatles, by Matthew Schneider
British Periodicals and Romantic Identity, by Mark Schoenfield
Women Writers and Nineteenth-Century Medievalism, by Clare Broome Saunders
British Victorian Women's Periodicals, by Kathryn Ledbetter
Romantic Diasporas, by Toby R. Benis
Romantic Literary Families, by Scott Krawczyk
Victorian Christmas in Print, by Tara Moore
Culinary Aesthetics and Practices in Nineteenth-Century American Literature,
    edited by Monika Elbert and Marie Drews
Reading Popular Culture in Victorian Print, by Alberto Gabriele
Romanticism and the Object, edited by Larry H. Peer
Poetics en passant, by Anne Jamison
From Song to Print, by Terence Hoagwood
Gothic Romanticism, by Tom Duggett
Victorian Medicine and Social Reform, by Louise Penner
Populism, Gender, and Sympathy in the Romantic Novel, by James P. Carson
Byron and the Rhetoric of Italian Nationalism, by Arnold A. Schmidt
Poetry and Public Discourse in Nineteenth-Century America, by Shira Wolosky
The Discourses of Food in Nineteenth-Century British Fiction, by Annette Cozzi
Romanticism and Pleasure, edited by Thomas H. Schmid and Michelle Faubert

Royal Romances, by Kristin Flieger Samuelian
Trauma, Transcendence, and Trust, by Thomas J. Brennan, S.J.
The Business of Literary Circles in Nineteenth-Century America, by David Dowling
Popular Medievalism in Romantic-Era Britain, by Clare A. Simmons
Beyond Romantic Ecocriticism, by Ashton Nichols
The Poetry of Mary Robinson, by Daniel Robinson
Romanticism and the City, by Larry H. Peer
Coleridge and the Daemonic Imagination, by Gregory Leadbetter
Dante and Italy in British Romanticism, edited by Frederick Burwick and Paul Douglass
Jewish Representation in British Literature 1780–1840, by Michael Scrivener
Romantic Dharma, by Mark Lussier
Robert Southey, by Stuart Andrews
Playing to the Crowd, by Frederick Burwick
The Regions of Sara Coleridge's Thought, by Peter Swaab
John Thelwall and the Wordsworth Circle, by Judith Thompson
Wordsworth and Coleridge, by Peter Larkin
Turning Points in Natural Theology from Bacon to Darwin, by Stuart Peterfreund
Sublime Coleridge, by Murray Evans
Longing to Belong, by Sarah Juliette Sasson
British Literary Salons of the Late Eighteenth and Early Nineteenth Centuries, by Susanne Schmid

FORTHCOMING TITLES:
Coleridge's Experimental Poetics, by J. C. C. Mays

British Literary Salons of the Late Eighteenth and Early Nineteenth Centuries

Susanne Schmid

BRITISH LITERARY SALONS OF THE LATE EIGHTEENTH AND EARLY NINETEENTH CENTURIES
Copyright © Susanne Schmid, 2013.

All rights reserved.

First published in 2013 by
PALGRAVE MACMILLAN®
in the United States—a division of St. Martin's Press LLC,
175 Fifth Avenue, New York, NY 10010.

Where this book is distributed in the UK, Europe and the rest of the world, this is by Palgrave Macmillan, a division of Macmillan Publishers Limited, registered in England, company number 785998, of Houndmills, Basingstoke, Hampshire RG21 6XS.

Palgrave Macmillan is the global academic imprint of the above companies and has companies and representatives throughout the world.

Palgrave® and Macmillan® are registered trademarks in the United States, the United Kingdom, Europe and other countries.

ISBN: 978–0–230–11065–6

Library of Congress Cataloging-in-Publication Data

Schmid, Susanne, 1964–
  British literary salons of the late eighteenth and early nineteenth centuries / Susanne Schmid.
      p. cm.—(Nineteenth-century major lives and letters)
  ISBN 978–0–230–11065–6 (hardback)
   1. Salons—Great Britain—History—18th century. 2. Salons—Great Britain—History—19th century. 3. Great Britain—Intellectual life—18th century. 4. Great Britain—Intellectual life—19th century. 5. English literature—18th century—History and criticism. 6. English literature—19th century—History and criticism. I. Title.
PR448.S3S36 2013
820.9′355—dc23   2012031260

A catalogue record of the book is available from the British Library.

This book is printed on paper suitable for recycling and made from fully managed and sustained forest sources. Logging, pulping and manufacturing processes are expected to conform to the environmental regulations of the country of origin.

Design by Newgen Imaging Systems (P) Ltd., Chennai, India.

First edition: February 2013
10 9 8 7 6 5 4 3 2 1

Contents

Acknowledgments vii

Abbreviations xi

1 Traditions and Theories 1
   Salons as Non-Places 1
   Traditions I: The French Salons 3
   Traditions II: The Bluestockings 7
   Private, Public, and Sociable Spheres 11
   The Theatricality of the Salon 15
   Sources and Source Problems 17
   Stages of Exploration 19

2 Mary Berry and Her British Spaces 23
   Mary Berry: The Life of a Conservative Feminist 24
   The Misses Otranto, Strawberry Hill, and Horace
      Walpole's Family Romances 29
   Anne Damer 35
   From the Closet to Drury Lane: *Fashionable Friends*
      (1801) on Stage 40

3 Mary Berry as a Learned Woman: Out of the Closet 51
   From a Parmesan Otranto to Malthus: Mary
      Berry's Reading 51
   In and Out of the Drawing-Rooms in North Audley
      Street and Curzon Street 55
   The Freedom of the Road in France and Italy 59
   Mary Berry as Editor and Historian 65

4 Holland House and Lady Holland 71
   Holland House and Whig Culture 72
   Lady and Lord Holland 76
   Reflections on Traveling: Italy and Spain 82
   Politics: Enthusiasm for Napoleon 88
   Spontaneous Versification 92

5	The Holland House Set	97
	The Circle and Its Oracle: The *Edinburgh Review*	98
	Three *Habitués*: Samuel Rogers, Sydney Smith, and Thomas Moore	104
	Byron and Holland House	109
	Amorous Entanglements and Caroline Lamb's *Glenarvon*	113
6	The Countess of Blessington as Hostess	119
	From Irish Country Girl to London's Outcast Queen: Lady Blessington's Life	120
	The *Conversations of Lord Byron*	126
	"Her Genius Lay in Her Tongue": The Salons at Seamore Place and Gore House	133
	Nathaniel Parker Willis: An American Connection	137
7	The Countess of Blessington as Writer and Editor	145
	Sociable Idlers in Italy	146
	Irishness: Female Idylls and an Irishwoman on the Loose	152
	London Society in Blessington's Silver-Fork Novels	158
	The *Book of Beauty* and Other Keepsakes	165
8	Epilogue	173

Notes	177
Works Cited	217
Index	243

Acknowledgments

This book would not have possible without many helpers, sociable and intellectual networks, and communications. My thanks go first and foremost to Claudia Brodsky, who generously invited me to Princeton on a two-year Lynen fellowship, and to the Alexander von Humboldt Foundation as well as Princeton University for funding me. Five follow-up visits to Princeton, only possible through Claudia Brodsky's unrelenting support and interest, were supported by the Humboldt Foundation, too. My thanks also go to Elinor Shaffer, whose project *The Reception of British and Irish Authors in Europe* taught me much about the sociable dimensions of reading.

I had many opportunities for debate, among them the Princeton Romanticism colloquium and panels at conferences of the Modern Language Association, the North American Society for the Study of Romanticism, and the American Society for Eighteenth-Century Studies in particular.

My thanks also go to the German Research Foundation (DFG), the German Academic Exchange Service (DAAD), the Humboldt Foundation, the English Department at the Ruhr-Universität Bochum, as well as the Philosophische Fakultät of the Ernst-Moritz-Arndt-Universität Greifswald, all of which funded trips to conferences in Britain and the United States. Besides, I want to thank the École normale supérieure in Paris/"Transferts culturels" and the English Department of the University of Zurich for inviting me to workshops. The Department of Book Studies at Mainz University kindly sponsored a research trip to Oxford.

I received many different kinds of support and feedback from individuals. In particular, I want to thank Uwe Böker, Fred Burwick, Angela Esterhammer, Michel Espagne, Ann Gardiner, Marie Hologa, Bettina von Jagow, Christian Lenz, Jon Mee, Uli Knoepflmacher, James McKusick, Franz Meier (†), Sophia Pasternack, Sandra Richter, Anson Rabinbach, Jonathan Rose, Michael Rossington, Sabine Sielke, and Michael Wood. I am extremely grateful to Marilyn Gaull, whose advice helped me finish the book, which she kindly accepted into her series.

I want to thank the staff at Firestone Library (Princeton), the Pforzheimer Collection and the Berg Collection of the New York Public Library, the British Library (London), the Bodleian Library (Oxford), the Pierpont Morgan Library (New York), the Lewis Walpole Library (Yale University), and the Staatsbibliothek (Berlin) for being extremely supportive and for digging deeply to satisfy my curiosity for books and manuscripts.

Early versions of this project appeared as contributions in books and journal articles, and I am grateful for the permission to reuse them. Parts of the chapters 1, 6, and 7 of my book are based on and develop ideas brought forward in "Lady Blessington und die Salons der englischen Romantik," in *Subversive Romantik*, ed. Volker Kapp, Helmuth Kiesel, Klaus Lubbers, and Patricia Plummer (Berlin: Duncker & Humblot, 2004), 153–164. My thanks go to Duncker & Humblot for kindly permitting me to reuse the material, especially pages 158–162. Some parts of chapter 2, 3, 4, and 5 develop ideas brought forward in "Holland House and Mary Berry's Drawing-Room: Salons, *Salonnières* and Writers," *The Wordsworth Circle* 35 (2004): 77–80. Some passages have been reused. Parts of chapter 6 and 7 reuse passages from "The Countess of Blessington: Reading as Intimacy, Reading as Sociability," *The Wordsworth Circle* 39 (2008): 88–93. The last part of chapter 2 reproduces the following article: "Mary Berry's *Fashionable Friends* (1801) on Stage," *The Wordsworth Circle* 43 (2012): 172–177. My thanks go to *The Wordsworth Circle* for permission to reuse the material. Besides, parts of the chapters 1, 6, and 7 of my book are based on and develop ideas brought forward in "Gespräch, Geselligkeit und Einsamkeit um 1800," in *Trianglulärer Transfer: Großbritannien, Frankreich und Deutschland um 1800*, ed. Sandra Pott and Sebastian Neumeister, special issue of *Germanisch-Romanische Monatsschrift* 56 (2006), 45–58, especially pages 53–55. Likewise, my book contribution "Einleitung: Einsamkeit und Geselligkeit um 1800," in *Einsamkeit und Geselligkeit um 1800*, ed. Susanne Schmid (Heidelberg: Winter, 2008), 7–16, summarizes some early findings; the chapter "The Countess of Blessington and the English Romantic Salon," in *Einsamkeit und Geselligkeit um 1800*, ed. Susanne Schmid (Heidelberg: Winter, 2008), 95–109, especially pages 95–107, have been reused in chapters 1 and 6 of this study. My thanks go to Universitätsverlag Winter for permission to reproduce the material.

Besides, my thanks go to the Pierpont Morgan Library in New York for permission to quote from a manuscript letter by Walpole (accession no. MA 494.41) and the Lewis Walpole Library for permission to quote from Damer's notebooks (LWL Mss Vol. 64), Courtesy of The Lewis Walpole Library, Yale University. I also want to thank the Lewis Walpole Library for providing me with the image on the title page: "Miss Damer and Miss Berry," artist unknown. Courtesy of The Lewis Walpole Library, Yale University.

Abbreviations

Throughout the text, the following abbreviations are used in citations.

BLJ *Byron's Letters and Journals*, ed. Leslie A. Marchand, 12 vols. (London: Murray, 1974–1982).

BP *The Berry Papers: Being the Correspondence Hitherto Unpublished of Mary and Agnes Berry (1763–1852)*, ed. Lewis Melville (London: Lane, 1914).

CB *Lady Blessington's Conversations of Lord Byron*, ed. Ernest J. Lovell (Princeton: Princeton University Press, 1969).

EHJ *The Journal of Elizabeth, Lady Holland (1791–1811)*, ed. Earl of Ilchester, 2 vols. (London: Longmans, Green, and Co., 1908).

FF Mary Berry, *Fashionable Friends* in *A Comparative View of Social Life in England and France, from the Restoration of Charles the Second to the Present Time, to Which Are Now First Added the Lives of the Marquise Du Deffand and of Rachael Lady Russell—Fashionable Friends, a Comedy, &c. A New Edition*, 2 vols. (London: Bentley, 1844), 2: 315–379.

I Marguerite Blessington, *The Idler in Italy*, 2nd ed., 2 vols. (London: Colburn, 1839).

JCB *Extracts from the Journals and Correspondence of Miss Berry from the Year 1783 to 1852* [1865], ed. Theresa Lewis, 2nd ed., 3 vols. (London: Longmans, Green, and Co., 1866).

MA Richard Madden, *The Literary Life and Correspondence of the Countess of Blessington*, 3 vols. (London: Newby, 1855; reprint New York: AMS Press, 1973).

R Marguerite Blessington, *Grace Cassidy; or, The Repealers*, 3 vols. (London: Bentley, 1833).

SJ *The Spanish Journal of Elizabeth Lady Holland*, ed. Earl of Ilchester (London: Longmans, Green, and Co., 1910).

TMJ *The Journal of Thomas Moore*, ed. Wilfred S. Dowden, 6 vols. (Newark: University of Delaware Press, 1983–1991).

WL *The Yale Edition of Horace Walpole's Correspondence*, ed. W. S. Lewis, 48 vols. (New Haven: Yale University Press, 1937–1983).

CHAPTER 1

TRADITIONS AND THEORIES

SALONS AS NON-PLACES

When the Countess of Blessington, who lived in Naples between 1823 and 1826, ventured on an excursion to the ruins of Paestum with her friends, the company found instructive entertainment, later chronicled in Blessington's travelogue *The Idler in Italy* (1839):

> A collation, that would not have shamed the Sybarite inhabitants said to have once possessed Paestum, was spread in the temple of Neptune; to which, after ample justice had been rendered, succeeded a highly intellectual treat, as Mr. George Howard complied with the pressing request of the company to recite a poem, written by him when at college, on the ruins we were then contemplating. The poem was admirable, and so spirited as to convey an impression that it must have been written on the spot, and under the inspiration which the actual scene, and not merely a classical description of it, had created. (I 2:181)

In the 1820s, the notorious Marguerite Blessington presided over a fairly informal "traveling" salon in Italy, which is well documented through her *Conversations of Lord Byron* (1832–1833) and *The Idler in Italy*, and this was later followed by several more formal and acknowledged salons in London in the 1830s and 1840s. British salons, veritable hothouses of political and cultural agitation, often cosmopolitan in their outlook, were gatherings of mixed-gender conversation and resembled earlier, similar formations like the bluestocking circles and the French aristocratic salons. They were headed by hostesses. Blessington's circle of wits and literati, likewise Holland House, the Whig political and cultural center, and Mary Berry's drawing-room, a meeting-place for famous as well as neglected conversationalists, were well-known landmarks in and around London. These three salons spanned more than 60 years, from the Berrys' first sociable encounter with Horace Walpole in 1788 to Blessington's death in 1849, and counted Lord Byron, Thomas Moore, Joanna Baillie, and George Canning, writers, editors, reviewers, painters, scholars, and politicians among their guests. Whereas scholarship on French and German salons is blooming,[1] English Romantic salon sociability is regrettably under-researched, possibly because the lonely subject often dominates the "mental theatre"[2] of the major Romantic poets, who relished a cult of male solitude exemplified in poems such as Percy Bysshe Shelley's *Alastor* (1816). However, 1798, the publication of the *Lyrical Ballads* and the beginning of Romanticism proper, meant no caesura in terms of sociability, which was all-important to cultural alliances. Sociability not only enabled the production of these "lonely" poems but also a cultural exchange that did not necessarily have the great literary text at its center but rather a chain of communicative acts, some of which have left traces in print, whereas others have disappeared for good.

Research into salons faces a methodological problem because their central activity, conversation, is elusive: The spoken word evaporates immediately. The leftovers, sketchy diary entries, letters, dedicatory poems, or episodes in novels, resemble the ruins where our party finds itself, which inspire intellectual as well as culinary treats, a poetry recital and a picnic, all of which are ephemeral and perishable, too. Marc Fumaroli's famous essay about French conversation as a site of cultural memory, published in Pierre Nora's *Lieux de mémoire*, the *grand récit* of French cultural history, begins with the reflection that his project of writing a history of conversation is condemned to be considered as foolish as maybe "a history of tears, farewells, or first encounters."[3] If the French salon, despite Fumaroli's gesture of modesty, has been considered the cradle of French thought, academics as well as literati have been surprisingly silent about its English counterpart. If, in France, conversation and thus the salon, is a "lieu de mémoire," a major site of memory, has been allocated space, in fact constitutes a space, hardly anyone would list the British salon among the nation's formative cultural sites. However, as salons, mixed-gender gatherings presided over by women, existed in Britain, my study aims to remedy this omission by restoring British salon sociability to the pantheon of culturally relevant sites, which has hitherto displayed coffeehouses, museum spaces, theaters, clubs, associations, and churches. It will also show that the

Traditions and Theories 3

bluestocking tradition continued well into and beyond the Romantic period. Oscillating between historical and theoretical reflections, this introductory chapter will define salon space, explore its traditions in France, link it to the eighteenth-century bluestocking tradition, map out its place between the public and the private spheres, consider its fundamentally theatrical dimension, and reflect on the methodological paradoxes of research into a "non-place."[4]

Why do the Countess of Blessington, Lady Holland, and Mary Berry merit further investigation? Mary Berry (1763–1852), a conservative feminist, introduced into society in 1788 through her friendship with the then nearly octogenarian writer Horace Walpole, ran several salons and is close to the British bluestocking tradition, both through her learning and her ideals of female companionship. She was famous for her "drawing-room" sociability, which she conducted on a comparatively small scale. Elizabeth Vassall Fox, Lady Holland (1771–1845), was the hostess of Holland House, one of London's leading cultural and political hothouses, gathering Whig politicians, reviewers, and writers around her. She was famous not as an author but as a Whig hostess presiding over one of the most prestigious London salons of her time. Marguerite Blessington (1789–1849) ran an informal traveling salon in Italy in the 1820s as well as several London salons after 1830 and is known today because of her friendship with and her publications about Byron, her silver-fork novels, and her editorial work for the *Book of Beauty* and other annuals. All three women stand in varying degrees in the bluestocking tradition and emulated the sociability they had encountered on their journeys to the continent, particularly to France. Since their salons were linked to larger publishing ventures, like Holland House to the *Edinburgh Review*, these cosmopolitan institutions also contributed in a much wider sense to Romantic-era culture.

Traditions I: The French Salons

One of the few early books on the English salon is a study dating from 1915 by Chauncey Brewster Tinker, who argues that the eighteenth-century bluestockings ran salons in imitation of the French model, a proposition that Deborah Heller has contested.[5] Although some English literary hostesses were aware of Parisian salons,[6] the French *salonnières* were not the bluestockings' immediate institutional or intellectual grandmothers, nor was the French salon the sole root of the English bluestocking circle, yet the French salon, even if no major influence, serves as a point of comparison, first because critics have frequently applied the term "salon" to English formations, and second because numerous English guests to and organizers of "salons," among them the famous hostess Elizabeth Montagu, or Horace Walpole, who later befriended the Berry sisters, likewise Lady Holland, and the Countess of Blessington, had traveled to France, had moved in elite Parisian circles, and had brought knowledge and news about the "salon" to Britain.

The great time of French salon sociability, which was situated at the intersection of the private and the public spheres, of orality and writing, were the seventeenth and eighteenth centuries,[7] while the nineteenth century is generally regarded as a period of decline. Initially founded in Paris as an alternative to the power of the French court, salons were nevertheless at the very center of "le monde," of the French elite. In the salons of the Ancien Régime, the Marquise de Rambouillet, the Marquise du Deffand, Julie de Lespinasse, Marie-Thérèse Geoffrin, and Suzanne Necker became the influential organizers of circles that were essential to cultural production. The salonnière invited guests and directed conversations, which might focus on literature, music, the fine arts, or politics. She was the center yet not the object of conversation. The gatherings occurred regularly, on a specific day of the week, the "jour fixe," and were usually bound to one location, the salonnière's private home, often a specific room like the Marquise de Rambouillet's famous "chambre bleue." Centered on the ideals of "honnêteté," "bienséance," and "l'art de plaire,"[8] salons encouraged visitors from different social and national backgrounds, likewise authors and patrons, to mingle, creating coherence through conversation. Conversation, the chief activity, had numerous functions: exchange of ideas and information, education, acquisition of refinement, and display of politeness. As the salon was the backdrop for formal and informal writing, for example, epistolary exchange, the reading of one's own manuscripts, or the debates surrounding new books, it was situated at the intersection of orality, writing, and publishing. If some critics like Dena Goodman argue that women and their salon activities were at the very center of all cultural exchange and essential for the understanding of the Enlightenment, others, for example, Jolanta T. Pekacz, question the women's power but still see a major role for them within the context of this formation. Critics often declare that with the caesura of the French Revolution, the women lost their power, likewise the salon its greatness.[9] However, due to their social, cultural, and sometimes political importance, salons did not come to an abrupt end with the French Revolution, neither in

France nor elsewhere, even if their power to cause social and political change waned.

While in seventeenth-century France, the nobility metamorphosed into an aristocracy, its medieval code of valor was substituted by interaction, speech, and gesture, in short: social deportment was mounting in importance. As elite culture was based more and more on interaction, one's behavior and the ability to interpret another's became crucial for advancement.[10] Those who wanted to climb up the social ladder or retain their place on it had to know how to move in elite circles and how to interact with those on the same, on a lower, or on a higher social level. Hence, conduct books and model letters instructed individuals about sociable politeness, as Elizabeth C. Goldsmith's study *Exclusive Conversations* shows. Triumph in the salons, where conversation stood at the center, was decisive for social success in the wider world.

While the term "salon" originally denotes a large and richly decorated room, built for reception, the use of "salon" meaning an institution only became current in the nineteenth century when the great pre-Revolutionary "salons" had become history; it is a nostalgic term applied in retrospect.[11] To contemporaries, a Parisian salon ran under the labels of "cercle," "chez elle," "société," or "soirée." Since it is hard to retrace the exact activities of any salon and since no detailed documentation of conversation exists, research into French salons has used conduct books, instructive dialogues, letters, memoirs, even novels, thereby setting a model for any study on similar formations in Britain. Although the bluestockings themselves did not necessarily consider French salonnières as their primary models, twenty-first-century researchers into sociability should be aware of scholarship on French salons, especially of its sources and methods.

Even though French salons were not copied in Britain, where court and crown were less domineering in the seventeenth and eighteenth centuries than in France, the English were nevertheless aware of a special type of French sociability. In a comparison of English and French sociability between 1660 and 1715, Lawrence E. Klein shows that the English, while regarding France as "the nation of sociability par excellence,"[12] nevertheless began to claim a distinct English type of sociability built around a critique and mockery of French manners, while English plainness, moral fiber, and a subsequent lack of alienation were advocated as healthy alternatives by prominent Whig writers such as the Third Earl of Shaftesbury, Joseph Addison, and Richard Steele. Needless to say, this type of English sociability was not primarily woman-defined, whereas it was in France. Michèle Cohen's seminal study *Fashioning Masculinity* shows that although English practices of sociability were frequently modeled on French ones, sociable women, be they French or English, appeared as ambivalent: as civilizing forces on the one hand, as superficial products of an overrefined society on the other. On March 17, 1711, *The Spectator*, for example, contrasted urban women's Frenchified luxuries—splendid equipages and clothes—with the plain and reasonable lives of women who prefer their "own Walks and Gardens" in rural England, and five weeks later on April 21, 1711, criticized French women's levity as well as their lack of restraint in conversation.[13] If, in the popular perception, Frenchified manners not only were detrimental to English womanhood but also turned English men into effeminate fops, it is understandable why French salon sociability did not force itself as a model onto English bluestockings such as Hannah More, who was famous for her censorious view of fashionable female accomplishments.[14]

Among the European influences on women-headed circles in Britain were also Italian sociable circles. They stood at the intersection of the academy and the salon and were often hosted by erudite women, who made knowledge circulate, for example, through translation.[15] Mary Berry's *Journals and Correspondence* (JCB 1: 70) mentions that she was invited to such a "conversazione," a large gathering of people, while she was staying in Rome. A number of eighteenth-century English travelogues found them so unusual that they remarked on them. The Italian word "conversazione," meaning an evening gathering for conversation, occasionally appears in English texts to denote modish urban sociability, as in Samuel Hoole's satire "A Conversatione" (1781), which through its use of the Italian word in the title demonstrates an awareness of a continental fashion, which, the author insinuates, is alienating in its superficiality.[16] Hoole's rhymed epistle contrasts the plain and male English speaker with the absurd demands imposed on him by vain women laboring under the dictate of foreign fashion, demonstrating that the guests lack the gift of cultivated speech and likewise the cosmopolitan outlook suggested by the Italian title. The "conversatione" eventually climaxes in the threat of a duel over a trivial issue: the speaker's lack of respect for a cucumber. Despite their reservations and their fears that foreign banalities might wreak havoc on English common sense, the majority of readers and writers considered Italian conversation to be a worthy model, as the translation of Stefano Guazzo's *La Civil conversatione* (1574) into English in 1738 exemplifies.[17]

In Germany, the use of the term "Geselligkeit" ("sociability") became inflationary after 1750, especially in weekly magazines and philosophical texts,[18] while its institutionalization set in. Notable women headed regularly meeting circles in Berlin and Vienna, but also in smaller towns and on country seats. In the wake of Jewish emancipation and during the growth of Berlin's urban spaces, Jewish women like Rahel Levin (later Rahel Varnhagen) and Henriette Herz became fashionable hostesses. As in France, the term "salon" was rarely used; and the visitors attended "aesthetic teas" ("ästhetische Tees") or "evenings" ("Abende"). Nevertheless, today's critics frequently employ "salon" as an auxiliary term to denote this kind of formation.[19]

The institutionalization of sociability in salons ran parallel in Europe. Among the characteristics of these women-headed circles, which cultivated conversation, was the fact that despite their frequent marginality in terms of political power, they were often central to a country's or a city's intellectual life, had male as well as female visitors, and were situated at the intersection of the public and the private spheres. It is regrettable that so much research has focused on salons as national sites, neglecting the internationality of these institutions,[20] which is another of their central features. Many sociable circles had international visitors: The Hungarian composer Franz Liszt and the American journalist Nathaniel Parker Willis attended Blessington's salon.[21] Journeys helped to form networks: As Willis was traveling from Italy to Britain, he found himself the carrier of a manuscript by Walter Savage Landor, which he had to deliver to Blessington and which provided him with a reason for his first visit to one of London's famous hostesses.[22] Sources that testify to multilingual interaction are scarce and scattered. In Ottilie von Goethe's salon in Weimar, the guests conversed in several languages and published in the salon's own trilingual journal, *Chaos*.[23] Blessington's Italian household saw a heated argument between Charles Mathews and the Count D'Orsay through an exchange of French notes, which culminated in the challenge to a duel.[24] If cosmopolitan salons shared a common linguistic ground, it was the centrality of the spoken word as well as the multiplicity of quickly changing verbal styles and modes, ranging from argument to raillery, from sincerity to wit and satire.

Traditions II: The Bluestockings

> Was there ever a man who was married so sorry?
> Like a fool, I must needs do the thing in a hurry.
> My life is reversed, and my quiet destroyed;
> My days, which once pass'd in so gentle a void,

> Must now, every hour of the twelve, be employed;
> The twelve, do I say?—of the whole twenty-four,
> Is there one which I dare call my own any more?
> What with driving, and visiting, dancing, and dining,
> What with learning, and teaching, and scribbling, and shining,
> In science and art, I'll be cursed if I know
> Myself from my wife...
> (Byron, "The Blues: A Literary Eclogue")[25]

Sir Richard Bluebottle alias Lord Holland, who sees his very identity threatened by his wife's desire for social success among the literati, bitterly complains in this satire written in 1821 by Lord Byron, himself a frequent guest at Holland House between 1812 and 1816. The bluestockings, women like Elizabeth Montagu, Elizabeth Vesey, Hester Chapone, Elizabeth Carter, Hannah More, Hester Lynch Thrale, and others who ran salon-like formations from the mid-eighteenth century onward, have received mixed receptions. They were often felt to be too intellectual, too public, or too political and began to attract satirical and pejorative remarks very early on.[26] Among the most famous caricatures of intellectual women are the conservative Reverend Richard Polwhele's satirical poem *The Unsex'd Females* (1798), which heaped ridicule on "a female band despising nature's law," among whom he counted radical intellectuals like Mary Wollstonecraft, and Thomas Rowlandson's print "Breaking up of the Blue Stocking Club" (1815),[27] which depicts a turbulent fracas of females exchanging blows instead of rational ideas. If the term "bluestocking" has been a popular coinage, decrying intellectual women, the historic bluestockings received little attention in the first half of the twentieth century. Only in the last few decades have academics, mostly women at universities, started to rediscover individual bluestocking women, their writing, and their sociable activities. Most of the nineteenth and twentieth century was only aware of these women as "minor" eighteenth-century writers, if at all. The available editions had been compiled in the nineteenth century, sometimes, as in the case of Elizabeth Montagu's letters, by a relative eager to present an appropriate public image at the cost of accuracy. Tinker's already mentioned volume of 1915, which casts the bluestocking circles as imitations of French aristocratic salons, has its merits because he saves them from oblivion, describes them as a group, and links them to the male literary mainstream. Only the last decades have seen groundbreaking research: Sylvia Harcstark Myers's important study, published in 1990, Gary Kelly's six-volume collection of 1999, as well as the exhibition "Brilliant Women" at the National Portrait Gallery in London in 2008 are among the milestones of a rapidly growing academic interest, as is Elizabeth Eger's seminal exploration of the bluestocking women and their writing.[28] The British bluestockings can lay claim to being the mothers of Romantic women's sociable activities. From about 1750, Montagu, Vesey, Thrale, and others created circles, quasi-salons, and assemblies, both in London's drawing-rooms and outside the capital, on estates like Streatham. Unlike French salons, these circles were fairly informal yet gradually established themselves as quasi-institutions as the meetings occurred on a regular basis. They document the middle classes' and the gentry's growing awareness of themselves as carriers of taste and culture, an awareness that also cultivated deliberate anti-courtly gestures, as the anecdote surrounding the bluestockings' name shows: Benjamin Stillingfleet, a visitor to Mrs. Vesey's circle, appears to have worn the blue worsted stockings associated with the city or with workers, thus giving the circle its name, which soon came to denote only intellectual women.[29] Although less formal, less aristocratic, and less rigidly structured, the bluestocking circles shared central ideals with French salons and attached particular value to politeness and conversation. Hannah More, a frequent guest at various bluestocking gatherings, called those circles "conversation-parties."[30] Her long poem *The Bas Bleu* (1786) praises verbal exchange:

> Enlighten'd Spirits! you, who know
> What charms from polish'd converse flow,
> Speak, for you can, the pure delight
> When kindred sympathies unite;
> When correspondent tastes impart
> Communion sweet from heart to heart.[31]

If conversation had to conform to the demands of propriety through being "polish'd," tastes had to be "correspondent," that is, of equal measurement. Notions of symmetry and equality expressed through such metaphors were at the very heart of bluestocking social and intellectual companionship.

Because, in terms of quality, most of the bluestockings' literary output is nowhere near Jane Austen's novels or the fairy tales of French aristocratic women like Marie-Catherine d'Aulnoy, the tendency prevails to categorize them as "minor" writers and to marginalize them. Kelly, however, has pointed out that the women could only write in acceptable feminine (and that is minor) genres like conduct books, essays, or domestic poetry. Not only would contemporaries have considered an open display of knowledge negative, but they would have associated a woman who was public or, even worse, published for money, with prostitution.[32] Although Mary Wollstonecraft's name sometimes appears in bluestocking contexts, for example, during the exhibition in the National Portrait Gallery in 2008, bluestocking women were no radicals; on the contrary, they were content with and thriving within the boundaries of the established customs. Many were "conservative feminists,"[33] in line with the Church of England, and they differed from radical intellectuals like Wollstonecraft by *not* wanting to overthrow the societal order through their mode of living or their manner of writing. Unlike some French salonnières, the majority of the English bluestockings did not help to spread daring philosophical ideas. Thus, it is not surprising that the Berry sisters as well as other later London salonnières followed in the conservative footsteps of their intellectual mothers and grandmothers through striving for social acceptance rather than intellectual upheaval.

Central to the bluestockings was sociable, intellectual companionship among women and men, likewise female friendship, which could range from prosaic offers—a dish of roast rabbit[34]—to elaborate letter-writing in celebration of friendship. Although the correspondence between Montagu and Carter constructs an egalitarian friendship, Montagu was wealthier and socially more powerful so that the offer of food can also be considered an act of patronage. Research has tended to idealize such woman-to-woman interaction while overlooking hierarchies, rivalry, gossip, verbal biting, scandalmongering, or exploitation, all of which could occur in the interaction between the women, their friends, and their guests. If the Berry sisters, who befriended the sculptor Anne Damer and the playwright Joanna Baillie, were fairly close to the bluestocking ideals of female companionship, other salonnières were further removed from them. Due to her status as runaway wife and former mistress of her later husband, throughout her career as salonnière, Marguerite Blessington was more or less ostracized by the ladies of the *bon ton*, who would not stoop down to visiting her. Blessington took revenge by depicting society women in her fiction as vain, superficial, and ignorant.[35] Caroline Lamb, bitterly disappointed by Byron, turned Lady Holland alias "the Princess of Madagascar" into one of the satirical targets of her novel *Glenarvon* (1816) and represented Holland House, which she dubbed "Barbary House," as the epitome of verbal combat.[36]

Blessington's professional activities, especially her editorship of the *Keepsakes*, popular anthologies, for which many of her guests wrote poems or stories, shows that interaction between the women could go further than personal friendship or rivalry. The poetess Letitia Landon contributed to these annuals, which could yield huge profits for those writers who were already famous. If in 1828, the poet laureate Robert Southey was offered 50 guineas by Charles Heath for any poem he might contribute to the *Keepsake* for 1829, Mrs. Crosland ("Camilla Toulmin"), another contributor yet barely known, in a difficult financial situation, and a woman, would be paid less. Although Blessington sent her a note of encouragement in 1838, she did not strive to ameliorate the social and economic wrongs from which she was herself suffering.[37] Professional cooperation could stretch even further, as the parallel marketing of tainted reputations by Blessington and Caroline Norton exemplifies.[38] If, in the bluestockings' applied philosophy, virtue was a central issue, some of their successors, who followed in the footsteps of intellectual exchange and companionship, stopped short when it came to keeping up the public image of the virtuous woman because it was hardly possible for a writing salonnière to create a high public profile and to be simultaneously considered as immaculate and pure. If women's sociable intellectual activities consist not only of the companionable reading of plays and the writing of letters about friendship but also of the skillful and subversive use of scandal as a commodity, it may well be time to say goodbye to the ideal of the literary woman as a sentimental being. Mary Berry, Marguerite Blessington, and Lady Holland conducted their writing as well as their sociable activities as professionals and thus succeeded in conquering their own spaces while participating in the public sphere.

Private, Public, and Sociable Spheres

English salons are closely connected to what the German philosopher Jürgen Habermas termed the emerging "public sphere" of the eighteenth century, which he saw linked to urban meeting-places such as the coffeehouse and the tavern.[39] The terms "public," "private," and "sociable" appear to be clear concepts yet become murky and overlap when critics apply them to individual case studies. Habermas's much-cited work *The Structural Transformation of the Public Sphere* (1962), which had enjoyed cult status among the German Left over many years, locates the emergence of a bourgeois public sphere in the eighteenth century. Strictly speaking, Habermas's "public" is situated between "private" and "state" and is part of an urban republic of letters, yet by no means a mass audience. His "public" consists of a small urban group of educated and mostly male individuals. After years of unquestioned canonical status, Habermas's study, like other much-read books, eventually has been exposed to harsh criticism for its conceptual shortcomings, especially his Marxist concept of "bourgeois," which fails to differentiate between middle class and gentry, in fact ignores the gentry, his traditional Marxist framework, his belief in the enlightened rationality of intellectual exchange, the disregard of gender issues, and the neglect of the Romantic period.[40] Although his former devotees have found much that is at fault, the study has remained one of the most authoritative in its field.

A lucid article by J. A. Downie, who summarizes some of the criticism, shows to what extent Habermas's reception has been complicated by the laissez-faire use of the terms "public" and "private" through critics who have regarded these concepts as fundamental oppositions in Western culture and, moreover, as gendered opposites. That the male public sphere is not only in opposition to but privileged over the female private sphere has been a major feminist claim, as Downie explains, and has structured a number of studies on women's history, which have replicated an unspecified notion of "separate spheres."[41] Thus, some of the research on French salons, which attempts to reclaim the public sphere for women, upholds the fallacy it aims to demolish: an oversimplified public–private dichotomy. A very informative article by Lawrence E. Klein demonstrates that although the distinction between "public" and "private" was common in the eighteenth century, each term held a variety of meanings. Klein identifies four "modes of public life": the "magisterial public sphere," the broader public life, the economic public sphere, and finally the associative public sphere of cultural production,[42] and explains that the concepts do not always coincide with the actual use of the terms: "What people in the eighteenth century most often meant by 'public' was sociable as opposed to solitary (which was 'private')."[43] Concluding his article on a list of examples, he shows that the theories and practices of applying these terms varied significantly.

If much of the 1980s research into women's history contrasts a male public sphere (clubs, coffeehouses) with a female private and domestic sphere (the family), more recent studies have proved that these spheres, as Klein states, were "less exclusively gendered than they are sometimes represented to be."[44] Amanda Vickery's *The Gentleman's Daughter* attacks this binary concept and presents a list of late eighteenth-century urban institutions, among them the royal court, the opera, the theater, the criminal court, the assembly, the pleasure garden, and the church, that allowed female involvement. She shows that although women's participation differed from men's and although the access to the public sphere they enjoyed was much more narrow, they did not move in an entirely separate sphere. As an alternative to the misleading public–private dichotomy she argues for a "social sphere," a term she borrows from C. Dallett Hemphill.[45] This social sphere is situated between public and private and constitutes a sphere of mutual visiting, of conversation. Sociable gatherings in and around the home attracted both sexes and were frequently but not solely organized by women. Even though this social sphere was no separate female realm, it was often governed by women, whereas the meetings in taverns and coffeehouses were not. The salon sociability my study aims to analyze is what happens in an in-between space of mutual visiting and conversation, in a "Third Space" situated between the private and the public sphere, where, as in Homi Bhabha's "Third Space," seeming opposites merge creatively.[46]

Recent studies like Gillian Russell and Clara Tuite's volume of essays *Romantic Sociability* (2002),[47] likewise Russell's *Women, Sociability and Theatre in Georgian London* (2007), emphasize the significance of sociability to any analysis of urban late eighteenth- and early nineteenth-century culture. Russell defines sociability as "the practices, behaviours and sites that enabled social interaction that was oriented toward the positive goals of pleasure, companionship or the reinforcement of family, group and professional identities."[48] Many eighteenth-century writers mused about sociability and conversation. Among the numerous contemporary reflections Shaftesbury's stands out; it links sociability to politeness, free speech, humor, and in a wider sense to the formation of the gentleman in a changing cultural and social environment.[49] At the center of all sociability are conversation and exchange. If the eighteenth-century term "conversation" carried economic overtones because it could be employed in the sense of "commerce," trade, the very heart of London, it thus became linked to sociability and politeness,[50] while middle-class and aristocratic values began to fuse. The early periodicals *The Tatler* and *The Spectator*, which through their structure alone imitate conversations, testify to the fact that urban commercial culture was deeply sociable. Yet by no means was sociability a stable concept: It consisted of a set of practices that changed over time and that were realized in different ways. Peter Clark's study *British Clubs and Societies, 1580–1800*

(2000), for example, follows transformations of urban sociability. He identifies the "private" sociability of the home, the "old-style" male-centered sociability of the coffeehouse and the tavern, and, from about 1760, a new type of fashionable sociability, which complemented the "old-style" male sociability, namely the sociability of the public park, the elegant theater, and the Pantheon, all spaces in which women played a much more important role than before.[51]

Much of this new-style sociability evolved around cultural interests, which, in the course of the eighteenth century, gradually became a marker of the middle and upper classes,[52] until the final decades of the century saw the formation of what Roy Porter termed an "Enlightenment intelligentsia,"[53] which privileged intellectual pursuit over political power. Poets, antiquarians, travelers, musicians, editors, and artists socialized in salon-like formations. The sociable formations under scrutiny in this study all take a shared interest in culture as a starting point. If circles around major poets like Shelley and Byron have received attention, other groups with cultural interests, for example, the circle around Joseph Johnson, or the self-styled Society of Gentlemen at Exeter, may be less famous but are important, too, for the dissemination of culture.[54] Salon sociability possessed a smaller degree of organization than a club yet has a shared interest in exchange and culture as its center, toward which regular visitors gravitate.

Salons are both places and non-places. They are not only situated between public and private but also lack a definite space: sociable activities create their own spaces while they last. If the British Museum is a fixed location, Blessington's salon, the court she held on her Italian journeys and in her London venues, is not. The salon as space is of a dual nature, both a "material site" and a discursive "formation,"[55] a real and a virtual space. If at all continuously tied to a fixed location, this tie can be of varying duration: While Holland House was a sociable landmark for decades, Blessington's Italian salon might occupy a space only once, like the above-mentioned ruins, eternal reminders of a past empire yet also ephemeral backdrop for a single picnic. If older research looks upon the salon as a formal institution that can be grasped, it implicitly and sometimes wrongly assumes that sociable circles must have one fixed architectural center like the "chambre bleue." It is the nostalgic look back and the desire for an ideal past that facilitate such visions of stability. If the salon is an auxiliary concept and its location vague, it is a "non-place" in the sense of Marc Augé, a French anthropologist, who provides an entire list of such contemporary non-places, which are temporal and ephemeral: "airports and railway stations, hotel chains, leisure parks, large retail outlets," likewise "means of transport,"[56] places where performances of self take place, which resemble one another. And in that sense, the salon would also be a non-place, defined not through stable architectural surroundings but through accessibility and visibility, in which the performances of the self took place.[57]

The Theatricality of the Salon

In line with what is sometimes called the "performative turn" in Cultural Studies, I want to look at salon interaction, likewise at the stagings of the self, as a series of cultural performances. Recent years have seen an inflationary use of the terms "theatricality," "performance," and "performativity" in the humanities by scholars who have expanded these concepts beyond the institution of the theater to include cultural "performances" such as festivals but also human behavior and the social order in a wider sense.[58] The salon, occasionally used for private theatricals, is a *theatrum mundi*, visited by guests who were both actors and spectators for one another's activities and utterances. Elin Diamond's observation that every performance "embeds features of previous performances"[59] finds its application in salons, too, where guests could have similar conversations during subsequent meetings. If, according to Erving Goffman, all everyday activities have a theatrical dimension, so have the salon rituals of visiting, conversation, politeness, gossiping, gazing, and exhibiting oneself. Salons are, to use Joel Haefner's words, "creative spaces,"[60] allowing visitors not only to observe but also to participate in what Russell and Tuite have called the "performative dimensions of sociability."[61] While Stephen Greenblatt's concept of "self-fashioning" constructs a rather unfree individual,[62] this study aims to challenge his notion by showing that the very act of performing held liberating potential.

Many of the texts upon which this study will draw show a marked awareness of the perceived theatricality of everyday life as opposed to the desire for authenticity.[63] If many sources relating to Blessington show her as the skilled mistress of her own performances of self, others emphasize her sincerity, her emotional authenticity when dealing with protégées like Mrs. Crosland. Blessington's *Conversations of Lord Byron* oscillate between presenting the poet's two personae: the melancholy, hapless outcast, whose authentic desire for social recognition had failed, stands in contrast to the gossipy, superficial poser and socialite. Or: After a visit to Lord Holland on August 31, 1821, the poet Thomas Moore, a frequent guest, entered into his journal: "Found Lord Holland in high spirits, and reciting verses in all languages while he tore up his bills & letters" (TMJ 2: 482). Moore describes him as bursting into an impromptu performance. Lord Holland's spirited disregard for documents raises the question as to whether the bills had been paid and the letters answered. The lightheartedness with which Holland discarded what could have been serious and time-consuming paperwork is underlined by the recital of poetry in several languages: art and playfulness can supersede all necessities, Moore seems to be saying. The episode testifies to an atmosphere in which spontaneity is cultivated over the sincerity one would associate with the payment of bills. Age, class, and gender are invented and reinvented. The autobiography of Charles Mathews, an actor's son, describes the Blessington entourage dressed up in fancy costumes during the sojourn in Italy: "Lady Blessington was dressed as an old lady in an embroidered silk gown, a cap, and a quantity of curls in front, powdered...I was disguised as a nice old doctor...bald and powdered, with black net breeches, white silk stockings, and large buckles."[64] As these games allow their participants to explore new identities, age and gender become variable masks. Class is disposed of when Mathews pretends to be Count Lieven, as he later describes in a letter to his mother: "If you had seen Lady Blessington's elegant curtsy to me you would have died."[65] Performances could also help to test out gender roles, ranging from courtship and married life to same-sex desire, as in Mary Berry's comedy, *Fashionable Friends*, which was performed privately before a circle of friends and neighbors at Strawberry Hill in 1801, later in Drury Lane.

No sociable formation is ever stable, fixed, finite, or monolithic. Roger Chartier's model of cultural history, in which "representations" and "practices" are central terms,[66] is congruent with a performative model because "practices" are geared more toward processes than toward results. The use of a performative concept also entails a shift from the authority of a single narrative voice to a multiplicity of voices and effects,[67] thus providing an academic method suited to the very phenomenon of the salon. Thus, salons are no authoritative centers of artistic, scholarly, or journalistic power, but they collect many voices, some of which come from the margins. Wolf Lepenies attributes the cultural activities of salons to a "melancholia" and "boredom" that arise from the lack of political power and participation.[68] This political marginalization went hand in hand with a geographical one: although they were culturally influential, British salons were frequently situated on the outskirts or outside the fashionable quarters, or even outside London, like Blessington's traveling salon, her later salon at Gore House in Kensington, the Berry sisters' first circle in Strawberry Hill, or Holland House, also in Kensington.

Sources and Source Problems

> Forgot to mention that one of these days young Murray (son to "Bibliopola Tryphon") wrote to me to say that Miss Berry, having got a glimpse of me in the street was anxious to catch me for a lunch-party she was to have next day at Richmond. He added that she had commissioned him to bring down Borrow, the Gipsy, and he would be glad to take *me* down also. What a catch for the Blue—a bard and a Gipsy!— but I wasn't able to contribute to the Menagerie. (TMJ 6: 2334)

Enigmatic in its briefness, Moore's journal entry, dating from June 8, 1843, exemplifies some of the methodological problems research into salons and sociability encounters. Who are the people? "Bibliopola Tryphon" is not only a bookseller mentioned by the Roman author Martial but also a nickname for the publisher John Murray.[69] George Borrow was the writer of novels and travelogues, which expressed his fascination with gypsies. The nickname suggests that he may be straying from socially accepted values and circles. How do they interact? Moore's witticisms turn Miss Berry, the "Blue," into a huntress for a "menagerie," a zoo of guests—was that her preferred method of achieving social success? Her diaries are kept in a tone very different from Moore's satirical biting, whom she much more kindly named "Anacreon Moore," or, with a brush of irony, "Little Moore" (JCB 2: 345, 3: 460). Whose perspective is more adequate? And what happened at the lunch party, who were the other guests? If any records of the table-talk survive, they will be as sketchy as Moore's. Only the careful piecing together of fragments reveals the wider picture. Byron, who met all three salonnières gathered in this study, occasionally dropped remarks about them, some of which are negligible but—like many other writers'—contribute pieces to the huge jigsaw puzzle and therefore merit attention. Digging up 200-year old gossip about someone's acquaintances is time-consuming, and the amount of data necessary for drawing at least a sketchy picture is immense. The available material is uneven: the further one goes back in time, the fewer items one finds. The evidence about the Berrys' early career before 1800 is far more scarce than later sources from the 1820s and 1830s about Holland House or Blessington, whose whereabouts are easier to trace.

Since orality, the hallmark of the salon, is as fugitive as a gesture, critics need written sources, which carry their own weaknesses, like the reliability of an edition. Older biographies, letters, and diaries are important printed material for establishing the hostess's and the guests' movements, biographies, and networks. Since many editions were compiled in the nineteenth century, their editorial standards differ from today's. R. R. Madden's three-volume edition of 1855, *The Literary Life and Correspondence of the Countess of Blessington*,[70] is largely based on holdings that today are in the Pforzheimer and Berg Collections of the New York Public Library as well as Princeton University's manuscript collection. In the face of Blessington's not always too legible handwriting, Madden's efforts are heroic, his results admirable, and without his edition we would know even less about this circle, yet a comparison of some manuscripts with the printed edition shows that Madden freely omitted what he saw as irrelevant or indiscreet and got dates as well as names wrong.[71] To a nineteenth-century editor, especially to a friend of the deceased like Madden, or to a relative, it was acceptable, even mandatory, to erase private issues in order to protect the writer from the curious gaze of the public. Researchers working with the printed version of Blessington's and the Berrys' correspondences must be aware of certain shortcomings. The academic community urgently needs more scholarly editions like Kelly's collection of bluestocking writings or Harriet Devine Jump's six-volume set *Silverfork Novels*.[72]

A large number of different types of texts give information about networks, interaction, activities, and opinions. Among those are imaginary or recorded dialogues like Blessington's *Conversations of Lord Byron*, conduct books, which Kelly dubs a "culturally less prestigious form" of philosophy,[73] *Keepsakes*, popular reading matter, which mirror social contacts, and the women's own writing. *A Comparative View of the Social Life of England and France* and its sequel (1828–1831)[74] situate Mary Berry in the antiquarian tradition and show how her journeys and her reading influenced her views about French versus English manners. Blessington, in contrast, poured her views, or rather misgivings, about some contemporaries into her silver-fork novels, which point out the disturbing sides of the "good" society on whose margins she stood, like *The Victims of Society* (1837), an epistolary novel in which intrigues destroy an innocent young woman. The novels testify to the author's very own personal fears embodied by false friends, gambling husbands, and malicious gossips. Blessington, a notorious London figure, also appeared as a character in silver-fork novels like Rosina Bulwer's *Cheveley* (1839), a revengeful roman à clef aiming to expose her husband, Edward.[75] Lady Holland was immortalized as "the Princess of Madagascar" in the novel *Glenarvon*,[76] which cast anything but a favorable light on her activities as hostess. Not all silver-fork novels provided keys to let readers establish the identities of those under scrutiny, yet the urban scenarios they describe and the types they depict (the dinner party, the literary hostess) make them rewarding sources. Another useful genre are travelogues like those by Willis, the American dandy-journalist, who conveyed his fascination for the Old World and its aesthetics to his New York readership, making Blessington appear far more aristocratic than she was. His example proves that no salon text reflects this institution in a neutral way because everyone who wrote about it was aiming to make a point, and therefore, no reader should take the sources at face value. Much material belongs to minor and forgotten genres. Little known today but informative all the same are nineteenth-century collections of literary worthies, exemplary men's and women's biographies, like Henry F. Chorley's *The Authors of England: A Series of Medallion Portraits* (1838),[77] expensive editions with portraits, useful because of their biographical information but also as reflections of networks, tastes, and publishing ventures. Material that has fallen into oblivion is juxtaposed with texts by literary giants like Byron, yet since cultural history has questioned the emphasis on high culture for a considerable time,[78] this study will not distinguish between more and less valuable artifacts, between better-known or less known characters, and therefore, Sydney Smith's hidden antics will be as relevant as the blasé Lord Byron's famous witticisms.

STAGES OF EXPLORATION

Since this study spans over 60 years, which were marked by major political upheavals, technical innovation, demographic alterations, and changes in print and media culture, it will treat sociable encounters, damaged reputations, cultural commodities like private theatricals, or publishing ventures such as the *Edinburgh Review* individually in the context of each salon. This book falls into seven chapters: After this introductory first chapter, which links traditions and theories, two chapters are devoted to each of the three salonnières, Mary Berry, Lady Holland, and the Countess of Blessington. As women who hosted salons often led unusual lives, each salonnière will be introduced by a brief biography, factual descriptions of her whereabouts, and reconstructions of her social networks. It is not surprising that for all three, traveling, the exploration of space, and the liberty to explore themselves happened early in their careers and shaped later sociable activities. Two of the three, Berry and Blessington, authored plays, novels, and poetry, worked on history and compiled editions, while Lady Holland, not known for her literary output, supported a major critical institution, the *Edinburgh Review*, through her salon.

Chapter 1 has mapped out the English salonnières' two main traditions: European, especially French, salons and English bluestockings, and has established a theoretical framework by resorting to debates around the public versus private spheres and the concept of performativity. After a sketch of Berry's vita, chapters 2 and 3 will look at her friendships with her patron Walpole and the sculptor Damer, her journeys through France and Italy, and her sociable circles (Strawberry Hill, the London "drawing-rooms" in North Audley Street and Curzon Street). The section about Berry will situate her in the bluestocking tradition and contextualize her writing, little known today, for example, her *Life of Lady Russell* (1819). Her play *Fashionable Friends* deserves particular attention because it exemplifies the status of women playwrights in the context of private theatricals. Chapters 4 and 5 will focus on Lady Holland, hostess to one of the Whigs' cultural centers. After a look at her and her husband's biographies, the chapters will treat her role as a hostess and the non-literary works she helped to create, like the cult around Napoleon. They will also pay attention to the rhetorics of describing a culturally powerful woman: unlike the other two salonnières, Lady Holland was continuously characterized through her guests' disparaging remarks. Since Holland House was a Whig cultural and political center, these chapters will also consider the collaborative efforts involving the *Edinburgh Review*. Case studies of important guests (Samuel Rogers, Smith, and Moore) as well as Byron's feud-turned-friendship will highlight the sociable turbulences, rounded off by the storms that Lamb's revengeful novel, *Glenarvon*, caused. Chapters 6 and 7 will describe Blessington's activities, whose first traveling salon in Italy in the 1820s was of a rather fluid nature and is documented in her travelogue *The Idler in Italy* and the *Conversations of Lord Byron*. Later in London she held court at Seamore Place and Gore House, creating international social networks that were essential to literary London in the 1830s and 1840s. Herself a prolific writer of novels and editor of annual gift books such as the *Book of Beauty*, she became so well-known—partly through her writing, partly through scandals—that she appeared in other authors' silver-fork novels.

Whether William Hazlitt's claim that "the conversation of authors is better than that of most professions"[79] is true remains to be seen. The salons elicited enthusiastic praise as well as biting criticism, often from the same guests. The huge number of documented reactions, be they positive or negative, show that these three women made a major contribution to London's intellectual life through sociability, through the running of their circles and salons.

Chapter 2

Mary Berry and Her British Spaces

A very few years since, I knew familiarly a lady, who had been asked in marriage by Horace Walpole, who had been patted on the head by George I. This lady had knocked at Doctor Johnson's door; had been intimate with Fox, the beautiful Georgina of Devonshire, and that brilliant Whig society of the reign of George III; had known the Duchess of Queensbury, the patroness of Gay and Prior, the admired young beauty of the court of Queen Anne. I often thought as I took my kind old friend's hand, how with it I held on to the old society of wits and men of the world. (William Thackeray, *The Four Georges*)[1]

Although she was not old enough to have met George I, Mary Berry, Thackeray's "lady," knew everyone of renown, was a veritable London institution for decades, and lived to a very old age. Mary and her sister Agnes were born in 1763 and 1764 respectively and both died, aged nearly 90, in 1852. While the sisters were virtually inseparable, Mary, who was a prolific writer, an avid reader, an energetic hostess, a daring traveler, and a famous conversationalist, attracted her contemporaries' attention, whereas Agnes, noted for her pencil drawings, remains shadowy. Despite the reputation she enjoyed during her lifetime, Mary Berry is little known today. Her learning firmly situates her in the intellectual traditions of the eighteenth-century bluestockings, some of whom, such as Hannah More, she had met in person. Her journals brim with descriptions of sociable encounters in London, Paris, Rome, Genoa, and elsewhere. While they retained a life-long connection with Horace Walpole's Strawberry Hill, the Berrys took residence in North Audley Street in Mayfair, an abode far less splendid than Devonshire House and other aristocratic houses they visited. However, their famous "drawing-room" continuously attracted the fashionable world, members of the *bon ton,* literati, actors, and politicians. The following two chapters will explore Mary Berry's life, her interaction with Walpole, who was flirt, friend, and patron alike, her companionship with the notorious sculptor Anne Seymour Damer, her successful private theatricals at Strawberry Hill followed by a failure in Drury Lane (chapter 2); her extensive reading, her sociable activities in London and elsewhere, Berry's travels to the continent as grand tourist, and finally her activities as editor and historian (chapter 3). While chapter 2 presents Berry's rehearsals of gender roles as a participant in good society, as a companion, and as a woman of the theatrical world in social spaces in and around London during the years up to 1802, chapter 3 shows her entering a larger stage: as a reader of literary and historical works that span continents and centuries, as a hostess to the literati and the bon ton, as a traveler through Italy, France, Germany, and Switzerland, and as a cultural historian and editor of English and French writing.

Mary Berry: The Life of a Conservative Feminist

Mary was born on March 16, 1763, in her grandmother's house in Kirkbridge, North Yorkshire. The Berrys' early family life is overshadowed by the loss of an inheritance, which would have rendered them not only financially secure but wealthy. Mary's father, Robert Berry, angered his rich unmarried uncle, the Scottish merchant Robert Ferguson, through a love match with Elizabeth Seton, who died in childbed in 1767; he then alienated the old man even more by refusing to remarry and to produce a male heir. In the meantime, William, Robert's younger brother and presumably the better businessman of the two, formed an alliance with a woman more agreeable to the old uncle, gained his trust, and eventually inherited most of his money when Ferguson died in 1781. Since Robert only received the comparatively small sum of £10,000, his brother William settled an annuity of £1,000 on him so that their father's death in 1817 left the sisters Mary and Agnes badly provided for.[2] Right after Ferguson's death, the new income made them more independent and enabled them to tour the continent from 1783–1785, the first of many journeys abroad. In 1788, they rented a house in Twickenham Common and met Walpole, who installed them at Little Strawberry Hill (or "Cliveden") in 1791. In his will, Walpole left Little Strawberry Hill to Mary and Agnes as well as £4,000 each, thus rendering them financially more secure because they could rent out the house.[3] Mary Berry's journals occasionally voice frustration over what she considered her father's "neglect" (JCB 1: 377). A short essay, "On Poor Marriages" (1808, JCB 2: 373), reflects on the disadvantage of a small fortune on a family's happiness and shows that her awareness of how wealthy and influential she could have been may have kept her from marrying. To the dismay of her friends, the practical-minded Mary occasionally considered taking up an occupation (1794, JCB 1: 447–455; 1805, JCB 2: 296–297). The father seems to have left many important decisions in his oldest daughter's hands, who declared: "I soon found that I had to lead those who ought to have led me; that I must be a protecting mother, instead of a gay companion, to my sister; and to my father a guide and monitor, instead of finding in him a tutor and protector" (JCB 1: 12). Until Robert's death in Italy in 1817, sisters and father, who shared a large circle of friends, lived together. The Misses Berry remained unmarried, but both of them were engaged at one time: Mary to General O'Hara, the recently appointed Governor of Gibraltar, in 1795, Agnes to her cousin Robert Ferguson in 1804; yet both engagements were broken off.[4] A letter by Joanna Baillie to Mary Berry in December 1805 mentions a widower, "a certain Gentleman of Yorkshire," unfortunately not identifiable, another suitor of Mary's. Baillie wrote: "You wish for employment, and you wish to be useful in the world: as the Wife of a man of fortune you will have this much more in your power than you are ever likely to have by remaining single."[5] Yet after her disappointment with O'Hara, who, while already engaged to her, kept two mistresses in Gibraltar, the 42-year-old Mary preferred the freedom of her sociable circles and of the road over matrimonial bonds.

The Berrys' geographical mobility is striking: Many journeys took them abroad, mostly to Italy, France, Switzerland, and Germany, in the years 1783–1785, 1790–1791, 1802, 1802–1803, 1816, 1816–1818, 1819–1821, 1822–1823, 1827, 1828–1829, 1830, 1834, and 1836. Tours in Britain led to the seaside, to Scotland, Wales, and Yorkshire, yet most of these shorter trips receive less attention in Mary's journals. The Berrys spent much of their lives in or near London in houses they rented. In 1790, they moved to North Audley Street, where they stayed until 1824, and in 1825 to Curzon Street. It was at these two addresses in Mayfair as well as at Strawberry Hill where the famous sociable evenings were conducted. Their traveling facilitated the friendships documented through epistolary exchange. In their early years in society, Walpole and Damer were among the most important contacts. In later years, when the circle of friends grew wider and wider, the Berrys were on the fringe of high society circles. Mary's diary mentions repeated visits to and from the Princess of Wales. She was also close to the Devonshire House set, probably through Damer, and attended sociable events in Carlton House. Her journal, which abounds with famous names of writers, members of the bon ton, and politicians, proudly mentions Sir Walter Scott's attendance at a breakfast party in 1809, during which Baillie's *Family Legend* was read (JCB 2: 381). Contacts were cultivated both at home and abroad.

The Misses Berry were an institution, yet without the permanent space that goes with our concept of culturally relevant sites because their sociable activities were not restricted to a single place; they rather occurred in a series of locations, over a long time-span. One reason for their fame was that they were so long-lived: in March 1845, *The Quarterly Review* praised the 82-year-old Mary Berry for having "experienced and enjoyed the pleasures of fashionable as well as literary intercourse more and longer than any living author."[6] Her intellectual interests were art and literature; moreover, she considered herself as the defender of Walpole's reputation. While her journal reflects an interest in political events, she is rarely concerned with the philanthropic issues so important to other Victorians. Unlike the more radical Mary Wollstonecraft, the deeply conservative Mary Berry did not shock her contemporaries by situating herself deliberately outside the confines of propriety. She felt that women's intellectual endeavors should receive more appreciation but never seriously considered questioning the power of the privileged or provoking the elite.[7]

Compiling the facts of Mary Berry's life, or of any *salonnière*'s life, is a task that necessitates the consultation of rarely considered and often scattered sources. If, throughout the last two centuries, male writers have monopolized critics' and biographers' attention, the more recent interest in female intellectuals has called attention to a deluge of relevant material that awaits publication. All accounts of women's lives entail descriptions of printed and unprinted sources and their limitations. The main source on Mary Berry are the three volumes of her *Journals and Correspondence*, edited in 1865 by Theresa Lewis.[8] In order to ensure that she remained the main architect in the construction of her posthumous persona, Mary Berry took an active part in the preparation of the material before passing it on to Lewis. For example, Walpole's letters to Berry, which are today among the manuscript holdings of the Pierpont Morgan Library, are published in volumes 11 and 12 of the Yale edition of Walpole's correspondence; some of them also appear in Berry's *Journals and Correspondence*, either fully or abbreviated.[9] The manuscripts themselves bear the marks of Berry's and Lewis's editorial work in their respective handwritings: crossed-out passages and footnotes with biographical details about the acquaintances paraded in the letters. Lewis had distinguished herself as the compiler of a historiographical work, *Lives of the Friends and Contemporaries of Clarendon* (1852),[10] which had met with Berry's approval. Her editorial work comes with all the enthusiasm and problems of older editions and conforms to the standards of her time: unidentified omissions, mistakes in names, dates, and spelling, as well as a Victorian urge to respect privacy. Thus, a comparison between the Walpole letters in the Yale edition and in the 1865 *Journals and Correspondence* paradigmatically exposes the shortcomings of published nineteenth-century lives.

The three volumes of the *Journals and Correspondence*, over 1,600 pages long, are organized by years and consist of several textual layers: Sparse editorial comments by Lewis introduce and link passages. Most space is taken up by Mary Berry's day-to-day journals, brief entries that cover only some periods, especially journeys abroad, periods of remarkable sociable activities, and political events; moreover, letters both by and to Berry are added. Her main correspondent in the first and second volume is Walpole, among the other correspondents are Anne Damer, Joanna Baillie, Germaine de Staël, John Playfair, Richard Keppel Craven, and William Gell. The selection of letters rarely serves to exhibit sentiments; on the contrary, Berry and her female friends appear as women of reason, far less gossipy than Walpole, and embedded into intellectual and sociable networks. Occasionally, events are described from several angles, for example, when Berry, Damer, and Walpole (JCB 1: 217–219, 348, 297) each mention the French National Assembly. The space given to individual years varies greatly. The first 20 years of Berry's life are summarized; most of the years after 1823 are sketched on a few pages each, while the 41 years between 1783 and 1823, approximately half of her life, fill most pages. Tours to the continent and sightseeing especially in Italy and France, likewise sociable events, particularly in London and Paris, take up more space than journeys in Britain or provincial encounters. If the first volume and the beginning of the second volume leading up to Walpole's death focus on the Berrys' intense friendship with him, the rest of the second and third volumes deals with Mary Berry's social life, her journeys, and her activities as a writer. Large-scale political events ranging from the French Revolution to the 1830 July Revolution in Paris, and also Lord Nelson's funeral in 1806, the Peterloo Massacre as well as London's politics of the day find their way into the journals. Occasionally, news from abroad are presented in the shape of long letters: an eyewitness account of the eruption of the Vesuvius in 1822 by William Gell complements the journal Berry kept during her sojourn in Rome in the same year. A complementary volume, *The Berry Papers*, edited by Lewis Melville in 1914, retells the Berrys' story, partly recycling already published letters and partly using new manuscripts, especially letters by Damer.[11] *The Berry Papers* testifies to Damer's and Berry's intense friendship, thereby implicitly defending it from nasty rumors, and devotes more space to female voices, whereas especially the first volume of the *Journals and Correspondence* is a monument to Walpole. Moreover, Melville is more accurate in his uses of sources, as the following example shows: Both the *Journals and Correspondence* and *The Berry Papers* contain a letter by Hartington, the Duke of Devonshire's son, to Mary Berry, dated January 30, 1803, the former in an abbreviated version, with omissions marked by ellipses, whereas the latter has the full text, as a comparison with the manuscript, today held by the British Library, shows.[12] What is striking is the type of information omitted in the earlier publication: The 12-year-old future Duke muses about his sister ("I have given your message to Mama, and will to G. when I write to her, who, instead of being in Hill Street playing with my nephew, is now dancing at all the Paris balls, while little George is now with us at Devonshire House," BP 223), the death of an acquaintance in childbed, a woman's sudden loss of memory at whist, and the impression left by an opera singer. The haphazard juxtaposition of undigested events that must have been upsetting to a 12-year-old conveys the impression that the offspring of peers was not raised with the consideration due to a child. Both versions retain Hartington's political reflections about Napoleon. Thus, the earlier publication focuses on the future leader while whitewashing those responsible for his upbringing. Since Mary Berry was proud of her contacts with Devonshire House, she may have cut the text to let Hartington's aristocratic family appear as more caring.

Further manuscripts and printed sources throw additional light on Berry. If the letters she included in the *Journals and Correspondence* present her as an exemplar of rational Victorian modesty, Damer's four autograph notebooks in the Lewis Walpole Library, believed to contain passages from Berry's letters, tell a different story. They are striking because of their personal and urgent tone. Other sources are scattered: Berry is mentioned in numerous writers', artists', and politicians' correspondences and diaries: Hannah More liked her, whereas Byron felt uneasy about "blue" women (BLJ 3: 228). The painter Joseph Farington, a Twickenham neighbor, was skeptical and cultivated a dislike of Damer, about whom he occasionally made nasty comments in his diary: "Exhibition I went to at 12. Mrs. Damer & two Miss Berrys...The observations of Mrs. Damer did not seem to me to prove that she has any exact knowledge of painting, whatever she may have of Sculpture; and she did not make intelligent remarks on the latter."[13] Such short diary entries help to establish women's sociable networks as well as the kinds of support or opposition they encountered. Additional sources are literary texts, for example, Damer's novel *Belmour* (1801), or satires like Charles Pigott's *Female Jockey Club* (1794), which mentions "two delicate virgins of the name of B-rry" in a chapter entitled "The Blue Stocking Club."[14] These references are parts in a huge jigsaw puzzle; a researcher into women's lives needs to find and combine the interlocking pieces to obtain a complete picture.

Mary Berry herself became a prolific writer and editor. Like other bluestockings, she was no Jane Austen yet found an interested readership. After Walpole's death, she effectively became his literary executor and editor of the five-volume edition of his work (1798),[15] likewise the editor of Mme du Deffand's *Letters* to Walpole (1810),[16] his friend and mentor during his time in Paris. Moreover, she wrote a play, *Fashionable Friends*, which premiered in 1801, and another play, *The Two Martins*, which never seems to have seen a stage or a publisher.[17] With her *Comparative View of the Social Life of England and France, from the Restoration of Charles the Second to the French Revolution* (1828) and *Social Life in England and France, from the French Revolution in 1789 to that of July 1830* (1831), she entered into the male domain of historiography and, despite her obvious conservatism, transgressed "generic frontiers" drawn up not by but for women.[18] As a historiographer, she ventured into the seventeenth century by authoring her *Life of Lady Russell* (1819), which was accompanied by an edition of her letters.[19] Berry's fascination for the seventeenth century probably received its earliest stimulation through her intense friendship with Walpole, who built his own historical and genealogical fantasies of past centuries into the mock Gothic villa of Strawberry Hill.

The Misses Otranto, Strawberry Hill, and Horace Walpole's Family Romances

"Pray, do the Misses Otranto still live in that house?" Cleveland, the brilliant fictitious politician in Benjamin Disraeli's novel *Vivian Grey* (1826–1827), enquires while reminiscing about Lord Byron and Horace Walpole.[20] The famous "Misses Otranto," who—of course—are "blooming as ever," were the sisters Mary and Agnes, by then over 60, who had been close friends of Walpole's, the eighteenth century's most gossipy chronicler but also very influential man and patron of the arts. He first met Mary and Agnes Berry, his "grand fusses" (WL 11: xxv) as Damer bluntly stated, in 1788, when the two women were in their mid-twenties, whereas Walpole was over 70, and aided their launch into society. The Berrys, who had been on the grand tour from 1783 to 1785, continued to travel during the years of their friendship with Walpole, both in Britain and abroad: In 1790–1791, they went once again to the continent; or they spent time in London when Walpole was at Twickenham, and vice versa. It is their absence, much-lamented by Walpole, that produced the correspondence that fills volumes 11 and 12 of the Yale edition of his letters. When the Berrys were not on the road, they lived in various rented houses in London and Twickenham, until in 1791, Walpole eventually installed them as tenants at his own house, Cliveden, later named "Little Strawberry Hill." When he died in 1797, he left Little Strawberry Hill to Mary and Agnes Berry for their lives, while giving Strawberry Hill proper to Anne Damer, also for life, thus enabling the women to continue to live in each other's vicinity.

Walpole, who remained unmarried and cultivated friendships, repeatedly created his own "family romances," as Marcie Frank stated, of which the companionship with the Berrys constituted yet another episode.[21] His famous Gothic novel *The Castle of Otranto* bears witness to a complicated family history, to problems arising from rules imposed by concepts of family and inheritance, which are then in turn crossed by illicit desires working against the family. *Otranto* exemplifies on the one hand what can go wrong with families and genealogies, on the other hand shows a world that cannot do without family ties. The construction of Walpole's Gothic manor, the imaginary castle of the novel, was a collaborative project, in which the "Strawberry Committee,"[22] made up of his friends, aided him; Strawberry Hill served as an "extension" of his body into architectural fantasies.[23] Not only his advisers but also Walpole's collections of objects functioned as a family substitute. Into the range of thematically arranged portraits, many of which were paintings of kings and statesmen, Walpole would occasionally slip his own portrait, thus situate himself beside royalty, and pretend to be of royal descent. Likewise, his collection of heraldry and weapons reveals his desire for a genealogy, for the descent from an ancient family, yet it is an ancient military item, a helmet, that crushes a new family life in

Otranto before it can even start. The names he gave to some of his rooms, for example, the "State Apartment," underline this theatrical attempt at "fictive history,"[24] his desire to reinscribe himself as belonging to the highest circles. Strawberry Hill's "architecture of the 'as if,'" to borrow a term coined by Dianne S. Ames, is reflected by Walpole's "as if" family life. Walpole, who remained unmarried, collected friends and family alike.[25] When he met the Berrys, he was over 70, many of his old friends had died, and by setting the Berrys up he ensured that they would be around him. Walpole collected contemporary women and added them to his Gothic fantasies of earlier centuries. Neither his objects nor his women were ever securely fixed. He enjoyed promoting women artists, none of whom were unusually gifted, like his old friend and first cousin Henry Seymour Conway's daughter, Anne Damer, whose terracotta sculpture "Two Sleeping Dogs" was on display in the Little Parlour. To Walpole, the Berrys were a substitute family, whom he generously provided with accommodation, new friends, entertainment, and, after his death, financial support. He produced *Reminiscences Written by Mr Walpole in 1778 for the Amusement of Miss Mary and Miss Agnes Berry* and inscribed a copy of his *Description*, the catalogue of artifacts at Strawberry Hill, to them in 1789.[26] Mary Berry, in turn, made it her task to keep his memory alive and to defend him, for example, against Thomas Babington Macaulay's attack in the *Edinburgh Review* in 1833.[27]

Of the epistolary exchange documenting this peculiar friendship, 164 letters by Walpole to Mary and Agnes Berry, one by Walpole to Robert Berry, and 11 by Mary Berry to Walpole have survived. He was one of the eighteenth century's most prolific letter writers, and part of his literary legacy consists of a huge correspondence, the 48-volume Yale edition. His epistolary style adheres to the gentlemanly ideals of ease, grace, and wit,[28] while promoting an aesthetic of the "small particular," as Patricia Meyer Spacks put it in her study *Gossip*.[29] The eighteenth-century letter is a key medium of business, political, and personal interaction, situated at the intersection between public and private, between print and manuscript culture, and is, to use Clare Brant's term, as "impermanent" as conversation.[30] While Walpole's letters to the Berrys treat similar topics as his other letters— great and small events, politics, art, and trivial ephemera—they contain more gossip and are thus closer to conversation, possibly because Walpole had become too old to move around. He loved to exhibit his newly found friends like the objects in his collection. "I have made a much more, to me, precious acquisition," he wrote to Lady Ossory on October 11, 1788 (JCB 1: 151). A description of the two young women followed:

> They are exceedingly sensible, entirely natural and unaffected, frank, and, being qualified to talk on any subject, nothing is so easy and agreeable as their conversation, nor more apposite than their answers and observations The eldest, I discovered by chance, understands Latin, and is a perfect Frenchwoman in her language. The younger draws charmingly, and has copied admirably Lady D.'s Gipsies, which I lent, though for the first time of her attempting colours. They are of pleasing figures; Mary, the eldest, sweet, with fine dark eyes, that are very lively when she speaks, with a symmetry of face that is the more interesting from being pale; Agnes, the younger, has an agreeable sensible countenance, hardly to be called handsome, but almost... I must even tell you, Madam, that they dress within the bounds of fashion, though fashionably; but without the excrescences and balconies with which modern hoydens overwhelm and barricade their persons—in short, good sense, information, simplicity, and ease characterise the Berrys. (151–152)[31]

He found an opportunity for conversation: "I sat next to Mary, and found her an angel both inside and out" (152). Soon, Walpole and the Berrys were on visiting terms, and poems as well as letters were exchanged.

Walpole began to style his epistolary persona as lover and husband, not of one but of both young women, thereby foregrounding the theatrical dimension of his fictitious, his "as if" family life: Walpole, the "husband" (WL 11: 14) repeatedly addressed Mary and Agnes as his spouses, his "wives," while idealizing their companionship as a "honeymoon" (7).[32] He was basking in his "double love" (14), his "matrimonial vows" (6), threatened to "sue for divorce" (21), divided his "jealousy" (37) between them, and suffered terribly when they did not find time to write. This playful fantasy of himself as the doting husband of not one but two wives and his comic love declarations continue throughout their correspondence. The rumors of a proposal were emphatically denied, both by Mary Berry and Walpole, yet a letter by Joanna Baillie, dating from around 1842,[33] reveals that Mary confided in her friend about Walpole's offer of marriage! The attraction Walpole felt for the young women achieved yet another expression through a pun that the Berrys' family name in combination with that of Walpole's abode invited: the strawberries. In his letter of April 11, 1789, he addresses them as "Mes très chères Fraises," "my very dear Strawberries" (WL 11: 7) and through linking their name to his "as if" place of heritage incorporates them once again into his collection. Repeatedly, their letters and poems play with the Berrys' name. When they visited Strawberry Hill for the first time, Walpole composed a poem and had it printed at his own Strawberry Hill Press:

> To Mary's lips has ancient Rome
> Her purest language taught,
> And from the modern city home
> Agnes its pencil brought.
> (October 19, 1788, JCB 1: 153)[34]

"Albion's old Horace," as he boldly styles himself in the poem, admires the young women's learning and their accomplishments: Mary's knowledge of Latin and Agnes's skillful drawing. Further poems followed, and even a Twickenham neighbor, Richard Owen Cambridge, joined in the playful versifying.[35] On November 1, 1788, Mary contributed a 30-line eulogy in praise of the strawberry:

> Far in a wood, not much exposed to view,
> With other forest fruit two Berries grew;
> Unheeded in their native shade they lay,
> Nor courting much, nor too much shunning day.
> A wandering sage, whose footsteps oft had roam'd
> Out of the beaten track that fashion own'd,
> Observ'd these Berries half-concealed from sight,
> And, or from chance, or whim, or his delight
> Of bringing unregarded worth to light,
> Tasted the fruit, and in a lucky hour,
> Finding it neither vapid yet, nor sour,
> ...
> The new-found fruit with partial care he prais'd,
> And so the Berries' reputation raised. (155)[36]

The poem praises the berries/Berrys as modest, unpretentious, and therefore pleasing. Strawberries were no exotic fruit and, unlike peaches and nectarines, were not cultivated in hothouses.[37] If they grew in woods, they were smaller but also tastier than today's produce. In the hierarchy of culinary pleasures, the strawberry signifies pleasant and unpretentious refreshment. Berry's poem celebrates Walpole, the true arbiter of taste, the discoverer of hidden treasures, who stands above ephemeral fashions—all roles he had prescribed for himself. Berry cast him as a private and public man of taste, a fair judge, who would help the women to receive the recognition they deserved.

Flirtatious writing did not originate from Walpole alone. When, on April 29, 1789, Mary acknowledged the receipt of Erasmus Darwin's *Botanic Garden*, she was treading on erotic ground because eighteenth-century poetry on botany, which dealt with procreation, was considered improper for women. Mary took an active part in the "as if" game of a married couple's interaction by owning up to previous experience:

> I must at last own with blushes what I have hitherto concealed, perhaps improperly, from my husband, but as I *am* married, it must at last come out, that I was early initiated into all the amours and loose manners of the plants by that very guilty character Dr. Solander [a Swedish botanist], and passed too much time in the society and observance of some of the most abandoned vegetable coquettes. (162–163)[38]

The "concealed" experience is that of reading, expressed in an image of sexuality. Berry implies that she is Walpole's partner, albeit in educated conversation. The combined codes of chivalry, libertinage, and intellectual debate are daring and highlight the peculiar nature of their friendship: The persona Berry constructs of herself throughout her writing is that of a woman of reason, yet she undermines it in her correspondence with Walpole. Such flirtatious skirmishes with a much older patron look ambivalent. Mary Berry certainly did not have to turn herself into an object; she rather seems to have enjoyed the game of matrimonial illusion as well as the intellectual intimacy.

Even though the Yale edition constitutes a monument of scholarly achievement, a look at the manuscripts provides information otherwise not available. A letter by Walpole, dating from January 9, 1791, is addressed to Mary Berry in Pisa. The manuscript letter, kept in the Pierpont Morgan Libary[39] and reprinted in the Yale edition (WL 11: 177), begins in a spidery hand, Walpole's own, with the words "I am unfortunate," leading on to a description of the gout from which he was suffering on that day. The second paragraph, in Kirgate's hand, as the editor points out, begins "Now I have satisfied you that my handwriting is alive, I shall act by proxy." What is remarkable is that the handwriting on this page increases in size. The final sentence on this first page of the letter runs: "It is a novelty to me that you have put up some learned Men/[there]." "Men" is the last word on the first page of the manuscript. On the following page, the names of the two men whom the Berrys have met, "Pinkerton" and "Parsons," are encircled and thus highlighted. These additional graphic elements are not mentioned in the Yale edition. Was Walpole sizing himself up? Was he jealous? Why did he need to tell his female friends that he knew what they were doing in such large handwriting? And was Walpole calling for emotional backup through employing another man, Kirgate, to ensure that the Berry sisters knew that he knew what they were up to? Walpole's letters to the Berrys deal with many more topics. He turned the latest additions to his collection of "as if" family members into an audience for his collections of portraits, books, and the printed ephemera produced at his own press in Strawberry Hill, such as Hannah More's poem "Bishop Bonner's Ghost" (1789). Their interaction became even more intense when the Berrys were abroad. While the Berrys were touring France and Mary was chronicling their day-to-day activities in her journal, Walpole remained at home. As he was fearing for his friends, he wrote long letters about the dangers of traveling through Revolutionary France so that the *Journals and Correspondence* offer two perspectives side by side and constitute a double travelogue, one by the actual traveler Mary Berry, and one by Walpole, who was in England but had access to first-hand information about the political and military situation in France. Walpole's letters to the Berrys also deal with events in Britain, politics, art, theater, his own increasing health problems, as well as acquaintances and neighbors. One frequently mentioned friend is the sculptor Anne Damer.

Anne Damer

Anne Seymour Conway, the only child of the Field Marshal and Whig politician Henry Seymour Conway, Walpole's cousin and companion on the grand tour, was born in 1749 and died in 1828.[40] In 1767, she married the wealthy dandy and gambler John Damer, who ran up immense debts and shot himself in 1776. Widowed at 26, Anne Damer was left with comparatively little money, never remarried, and turned to sculpture, but because of her sex underwent no formal training. Henceforth, her public persona was that of an amateur artist. In addition, she also made herself a name in the context of private theatricals. Damer had very influential friends, among them Georgiana, Duchess of Devonshire, with whom she participated in canvassing for the 1784 Westminster Election to get Charles James Fox into Parliament. Another good friend was Walpole, her godfather, who bequeathed Strawberry Hill to her. Like the Berrys, she repeatedly traveled to the continent, visiting Germany, France, Italy, Portugal, and Spain. Before her death in 1828, she burnt most of her papers, including Walpole's letters to her; her notebooks, however, have survived.

As an acknowledged sculptor, who presented 32 of her works at Royal Academy exhibitions, Damer remained within the artistic boundaries of her time. She worked in marble, bronze, and terracotta and created mostly animals and neoclassical busts of people she had met, occasionally statues: among her works were busts of Elizabeth Farren, Mary Berry, Lord Nelson, and Princess Caroline, a statue of George III, and the keystones of the bridge in Henley-on-Thames.[41] A bust of Charles James Fox, the Whig politician, was presented by her to Napoleon in 1815.[42] If Walpole, who displayed her eagle and her kittens at Strawberry Hill, was proud of his godchild and praised her as talented in his *Anecdotes of Painting*,[43] his tribute for what many considered as a female amateur may have been motivated by his desire to criticize the standards of the academy.[44] Damer was no Angelica Kauffmann. Fanny Burney looked at the sculptress's work with far less enthusiasm than Walpole,[45] while Farington, the painter and Twickenham neighbor, continuously raged in his diaries over what he considered as an undue intrusion into his own field. He found Damer's model of the keystone representing the Thames "ill executed," criticized her busts of Fox and Nelson as "not very good likenesses" but conceded that they "might be known," and explained at a dinner party that women artists were "feeble and wanted the masculine energies."[46]

Apart from pursuing her artistic work as a sculptor, which contemporaries regarded as masculine, Damer did not engage in activities that would have been considered improper or unusual for an upper-class woman. However, from the late 1770s onward, the young widow was repeatedly accused of "sapphism," of entertaining illicit sexual relationships with women. Two recent studies by Andrew Elfenbein (1999) and Emma Donoghue (2010)[47] have tracked down the libelous attacks on her. Among them was William Combe's 38-page satire *The First of April: or, The Triumphs of Folly* (1777),[48] which merely hints at forbidden sexual pleasures, while the more explicit and anonymous *Sapphick Epistle, from Jack Cavendish to the Honourable and Most Beautiful Mrs. D***** (?1778) blames her for her husband's suicide ("You are a pattern of a wife,/That could resign a husband's life,/To raise a Sapphick name")[49] and again hints at affairs with women. The rumors, brimming with juicy details, continued and were refueled by Damer's friendship with Elizabeth Farren, one of the most famous actresses of the 1780s and 1790s, who was courted by the Earl of Derby. Farren's relationship with Derby was famously asexual until 1797, when his wife's death eventually left him free to marry Farren. *The Whig Club* (1794), a satire by Pigott, aiming to humiliate Whigs, insinuates that Farren was sexually disinterested in men because she preferred the "more exquisite delight from the touch of the cheek of Mrs. D——r."[50] In the context of political attacks aiming to portray the elite as immoral, charges of deviant sexual mores such as "sapphism" were not unusual. Marie Antoinette, too, was accused of taking an active interest in her own sex. It is hardly surprising that Farren's and Damer's careers and lifestyles excited some satirists' imagination: Instead of becoming a kept woman, the actress kept an Earl at bay until he married her, while the attractive young widow refused to remarry and pursued male artistic endeavors instead. Both women opted for independence. Surprisingly, Damer's later friendship with Berry, whom she met in 1789, did not lead to any further libelous attacks by anonymous satirists, yet rumors seem to have persisted. Farington's diary suggests more than mere companionship:

> The singularities of Mrs. Damer are remarkable—She wears a Mans Hat, and Shoes, and a Jacket also like a mans—thus she walks abt. the fields with a hooking stick... The extasies on meeting, & tender leave on separating, between Mrs. Damer & Miss Berry, is whimsical. On Miss Berry going lately to Cheltenham, the servants described the separation between Her & Mrs. Damer as if it had been parting before death.[51]

The male clothes, the phallic walking stick, and the "extasies" imply that Damer may have acted as Berry's substitute husband in other areas, too.

Since no explicit eighteenth-century accounts of sex between women exist—only derogatory texts like satires, probably by men who aimed to discredit such sexual practices—we cannot be sure what went on behind closed doors and whether Damer had affairs with women or not. If her sculptures prove that she was a successful competitor in a male environment, her one novel, *Belmour* (1801), lets us glimpse another side of her, the closeted artist, whose desires may have led her astray from the path of heterosexual righteousness. *Belmour* was written between 1791 and 1797 and probably begun while she was traveling through Portugal and Spain. Like Damer herself, the characters explore regions around the Mediterranean. The story, dealing with courtship and mostly unhappy marriages, conforms to the literary fashions of its day: formulaic elements like Byronic melancholy, a damsel in distress, Gothic scenarios, and emotional extravaganza in the style of sensibility go hand in hand. The central hero Belmour, "haunted" by the woman he loves, is, as Jonathan Gross argues, "a cross-dressed version" of Damer herself.[52] Emily, one of the main female characters, is introduced as an object of desire early on—for men and women. It is striking that another young lady, Clementina, expresses utter fascination with "that beautiful creature" at their very first encounter.[53] Such passages, however, are rare: the novel's focus is on heterosexual love, frustration, and fulfillment.

Anne Damer and Mary Berry met through Walpole, who had known the sculptress since her infancy.[54] After the Berrys had been introduced to Damer and her mother, Lady Ailesbury, in early 1789 (JCB 1: 159), they visited Park Place, where Damer had grown up, for the first time. Many more visits followed, while Damer also frequently stayed at Strawberry Hill during the 1790s until, with Walpole's death, she was chosen to guard his treasures, the house and the collections. Damer continued Walpole's famous hospitality, for example, the garden parties,[55] and began to conduct her own private theatricals in Twickenham. She also spent much time in London and was Mary Berry's close friend and confidante. During Mary's love affair with O'Hara, kept secret from Walpole, Damer acted as a go-between. That the two women went traveling together several times, for example, in 1799 to Malvern and in 1802 to Paris, proves that they must have been close to another. A drawing shows them in a library, presumably at Strawberry Hill: Damer, who is looking up from a book, on the left, and Berry, holding a book in her hand, on the right, deeply engaged in conversation.[56] Their epistolary exchange reveals varying degrees of closeness. Berry's journals contain numerous brief and impersonal entries on Damer as well as her correspondence, especially the letters from her tour of the Iberian peninsula. Most of the epistolary exchange in the 1865 edition of the *Journals and Correspondence* is rather unemotional, whereas the 1914 *Berry Papers*, which contain a large amount of Damer's letters, invite the reader to witness an intense friendship. Damer wrote to Berry on October 10, 1790:

> I have not, it is true, been accustomed to the charm of real friendship, but my own heart has taught me its value. Rest assured that, could you know to what degree you contribute to the comfort, even the repose, of my mind, your utmost good nature would be more than satisfied. (BP 24)

The tone throughout signals trust and friendship, yet, despite the apparent closeness of the two correspondents, the letters reprinted in *The Berry Papers* make it difficult to uncover a hidden erotic subtext. Another source reveals an even more personal tone: The Lewis Walpole Library keeps four manuscript notebooks, which the editors of Walpole's correspondence as well as Elfenbein, Donoghue, and Gross believe to contain passages from Berry's letters to Damer. The handwritten excerpts are emotionally more intense than the published letters, sometimes urgent, sometimes playful, but in any case different from the assumed modesty on display in the three-volume *Journals and Correspondence*. Here is one example:

> You left your fan here last night, a sentiment of honesty once prompted me to return it, but another sentiment not so easily defined prompted me to keep it—farewell, we are just setting off and I am as melancholy as a cat—but I have been happy and I shall be happy—can we ever say more?—remember all your kind promises last night—farewell, farewell
>
> (no exact date, only "1789–90–91")[57]

These lines are far more intimate than the erotically tinged versifying quoted earlier on. A fan was an object eighteenth-century women used for flirtation. Yet what is the "sentiment not so easily defined"? What promises were made? Not a lot is said, much is left open. As the handwritten excerpts seem fragmentary and are often undated and as at least some of them seem to be Damer's own journal entries, for example, quotations from classical authors, it is difficult to extract a narrative from them. Even their authorship is unclear. Elfenbein's and Donoghue's meticulously researched articles use the manuscript notebooks to support their arguments that Mary Berry was aware to what extent rumors threatened the women's friendship. However, without the contexts provided by dates, places, and names, the notebook entries are of limited value. One example:

> I can see no reason whatsoever why I should deny myself the joy of embracing you upon our <u>first</u> arrival _..... but as we parted with you & Mr. W. together, for heaven sake let us have the infinite pleasure of meeting you together, and as the last moments of our stay were passed with you, so let the first of our arrival be as my affection for both you & him <u>owes</u> me all the pleasure I expect, in meeting up with you, for what I suffered when we parted.[58]

As the first notebook probably covers the early 1790s, Mr. W. may be Walpole. The feeling that an embrace needs justification indicates, like other passages, the writer's feeling that the women's friendship needed to be defended. "Infinite pleasure," "affection," and "suffering" all point at strong emotional involvement yet not necessarily at a sexual liaison. What kind of relationship did they have under Walpole's eyes? Did he understand? Rumors of a homosexual affair surrounded Walpole and Conway, Damer's father. Since Walpole was apparently jealous of the friendship between the women, Mary Berry, whose public persona was built on her closeness to her patron, may have decided to present him rather than Damer as her major social contact of the 1790s. Walpole, however, generously acknowledged their deep friendship when he left Little Strawberry Hill to the Berrys and Strawberry Hill to Damer, thus enabling them to remain neighbors. Donoghue's recent historical novel *Life Mask* (2004)[59] uses Damer's notebooks to map out the friendship and, eventually, the love affair between the two women. Her fictitious ending, a happy lesbian vision, a successful coming-out story, makes Damer and Berry goddesses in the pantheon of fulfilled same-sex desire. No matter what they were up to in private, they cooperated successfully in many fields that were open to a wider sociable circle, for example, theater.

From the Closet to Drury Lane: *Fashionable Friends* (1801) on Stage

Mary Berry's play *Fashionable Friends*, first successfully staged as a private play at Strawberry Hill toward the end of 1801, while six months later a failure at Drury Lane, was originally written and performed in the fashionable context of private theatricals, significant sociable endeavors, which gave women a role the major patent theaters around 1800 failed to provide.[60] Well-known women writers of the Romantic period such as Hannah More, Elizabeth Inchbald, and Fanny Burney are today remembered for other genres although they also authored plays. If female dramatists like Joanna Baillie found that they were by no means always welcome in the institution of the theater, that they had to struggle, one reason was that their male competitors had secured the territory for themselves. Women could be celebrated and achieve stardom if they appeared on the stage as actresses, like Sarah Siddons or Elizabeth Farren, yet in the public opinion such professional activities were often linked to prostitution: public women took the risk of being considered scandalous.[61] In contrast, private performances, dubbed "theater of the closet" by Catherine Burroughs,[62] enabled women to explore the world of the theater while suffering fewer attacks on their reputation. Private theatricals, fashionable in the late eighteenth and early nineteenth century,[63] were, as Burroughs points out, no "avant-garde movement,"[64] rather, to use Gillian Russell's phrase, "a key social ritual"[65]; they could be exclusive but were not necessarily as private as the label denotes. They often occurred beyond the immediate circle of the family, included friends and neighbors, and, as the reviews some of them received in print publications like *The Times* or *The Morning Post* document, could be brought to the attention of the public. The costly performances staged at Richmond House in the later 1780s, for example, drew fairly large audiences yet remained socially exclusive, aiming to attract members of the bon ton only. As part of salon sociability, these theatricals were situated between public and private and thus in the same in-between space as assemblies and dinner parties. Private theatricals enabled their female participants to be creative, to move between the roles of author, actress, producer, manager, and hostess. Sociable female networks were central to such endeavors. That private theater was not above reproach is obvious from the best-known and most frequently cited performance of this kind, the fictitious staging of August von Kotzebue's *Lovers' Vows* (1791) in Jane Austen's novel *Mansfield Park* (1814), where acting disrupts domesticity. Joanna Baillie's comedy *The Tryal* (1798) also deals with one such private performance and the upheavals it causes.

Mary Berry's own play *Fashionable Friends* owed much to two close friends: the playwright Joanna Baillie and the sculptor Anne Damer. Berry has been considered as one of Baillie's closer friends, as Slagle's edition of the Baillie letters shows. Unfortunately, hardly any letters of Baillie predating the year 1804 have survived so that any written communication concerning *Fashionable Friends* remains in the dark. Those of Baillie's letters to Mary Berry that have recently been edited, 23 in number, written between 1804 and 1844, are kept in a very personal tone.[66] They deal with topics as various as mutual friends (especially Damer), suitors, family, bereavement, other authors, reviewing, plans for traveling, practical issues like the letting out of houses, the two women's literary production, religion, or, simply, the weather. The letters show that the women collaborated in the field of theater and frequently communicated about the literary scene as well as about London's performance spaces: "Mrs Damer tells me in her note which came to my hand yesterday that there are some corrections you have to make on the last acts of my Family Legend" (1806), "What do you think of your friend Mr Moores intended duel with that tremendous man Mr Jeffrys [sic]?" (1806), "I thank you for recommending Child Harold to me" (1812), "my Constantine was produced as a Melo Drama at the Surry Theatre this summer, and had a run to good houses of 34 nights" (1817).[67] To what extent Mary Berry influenced Baillie's self-awareness as a writer is shown by the fact that the latter left an autobiographical manuscript (1831) because the former asked her to.[68] Judith Slagle, the editor of Baillie's letter, points at some striking biographical similarities between Baillie and

Berry: They were both born in nearly the same year (Baillie in 1762, Berry in 1763), both had sisters (named Agnes), who were supportive yet remained in the background.[69] Both spent much of their lives in or near London. Around 1784, Joanna Baillie, her sister, and her mother settled in London and eventually, in the late 1790s, moved to Hampstead, while the Berrys lived partly in Twickenham, partly in the center of London. Both Baillie and Berry were lucky enough to command over an income that granted independence. Neither of them got married. Despite all setbacks, they exerted a fair amount of social and cultural power. If Baillie has frequently (and correctly) been presented as the victim of machinations within the predominantly male theater establishment, she nevertheless was acquainted with and supported by well-known literati: Lord Byron, Samuel Rogers, or Sir Walter Scott. Both Baillie and Berry were voracious readers: Baillie's letters, like Berry's journals, abound with references to the literary production of the day but also to classics. As no documents of their conversation, which must have far exceeded the letter-writing, survived, we can only guess how much the two women, who were friends, must have spoken about theater.[70]

Baillie's dramatic texts attracted Berry's interest very early: After Baillie had published the first volume of the *Plays on the Passions* anonymously in 1798, she sent a copy to Berry, who enthusiastically wrote into her journal: "Everybody talks in the raptures (I always thought they deserved) of the tragedies, and of the introductions of a new and admirable piece of criticism" (March 12, 1799, JCB 2: 88). The diary entry goes on to praise *Basil* and *De Montfort* (March 21, 1799, 90), arguing intuitively that the presentation of female dramatic characters proves the unknown author to be a woman herself. Baillie felt Berry's support was the reason why this volume of plays was spoken about, "got into circulation," and eventually attracted John Philip Kemble's interest.[71] Before Baillie's identity as the author of *De Montfort* was uncovered on April 30, 1800, only a few people knew about her as a playwright.

The second friend important to the gestation of Berry's comedy was the notorious Anne Damer, who mentioned a play (presumably *Fashionable Friends*) in a letter as early as 1793 (BP 119). Damer was not only a successful sculptor but also a sought-after participant in private theatricals in Brandenburgh House and Richmond House, was renowned for her acting style and dresses, and staged plays herself.[72] Damer moved in the elite social circles of theater enthusiasts: She knew the Margravine of Anspach, who hosted the performances at Brandenburgh House, the Duke of Richmond was her brother-in-law, and she struck up a friendship with the actress Elizabeth Farren, the later Lady Derby. A painting by Daniel Gardner of 1775 depicts Damer together with Elizabeth Lamb, Viscountess Melbourne, and Georgiana, Duchess of Devonshire, as the three witches in *Macbeth*. Thus, Damer appears as a devoted participant in private theatricals but also as participating in ambitious political power games.[73] Baillie also was among her thespian friends: it was through Damer that Baillie originally received the idea for the plot for her *Family Legend* (1810) in 1805.[74]

The history of this fashion for private theater is tied to the 1737 Licensing Act, which imposed severe control on British theater and had far-reaching consequences. In the Romantic period, spoken drama, which had to obtain the censor's approval, remained an elite affair and was confined to the patent theaters, while other London performance spaces resorted to music and melodrama, or pantomime, in which the censor took less interest. Another way to circumvent the censor was to stage plays in private houses. Private theatricals were not restricted to one social class, yet those that got the most attention in the late eighteenth century were private theatricals organized by members of the upper class, for example, by the Margravine of Anspach in Brandenburgh House or by the Duke of Richmond in Richmond House. Especially these latter two places saw theatricals that were very expensive and socially very ambitious: the Prince of Wales attended Richmond House as well as Brandenburgh House. Among the plays staged were pieces that belonged to the classical repertoire, plays especially written or adapted for the occasion, with musical accompaniment, and imports from abroad.[75] The actors were partly family and friends, partly professionals hired for such occasions, who would occasionally vent negative opinions. The *Memoirs of Miss Mellon*, an actress who later through marriage became the Duchess of St. Albans, explain: "Her services were sometimes required for the private theatricals with which the nobility occasionally disported themselves."[76] When *Fashionable Friends* was staged at Strawberry Hill, she "undertook the character of stage-manager, besides being privy-councillor in all matters relative to costume and other little etceteras known only to the initiated in Thespian mysteries." However, this appointment was no undiluted pleasure: "That her office of manager was no sinecure may be inferred from a remark she afterwards made, and which, at this distance, we may venture to repeat—that 'there never was such a stupid task as drilling fine people!'"[77] The performances staged at Brandenburgh House and Richmond House, which attracted gatherings of the social elite, received much attention in the press. Reviews remarked on the aristocratic actors, the sumptuous costumes and designs, the audience, the musical accompaniment, and also on the plays themselves. Parallels between salon sociability and private theatricals certainly existed: both focused on interaction, both occurred at the intersection between the public and the private spheres. When Damer opened a performance space at Strawberry Hill, after Walpole had bequeathed it to her, she may have simply taken her turn in providing the sort of entertainment she enjoyed as actress or member of the audience elsewhere in London.

The comedy *Fashionable Friends*, probably no major contribution to the literary canon, nevertheless exemplifies what was at stake in women's private theatricals. *Fashionable Friends* is a comedy of manners and closer to the traditions of late seventeenth-century Restoration Comedy than to Baillie's Romantic *Plays on the Passions*. Like Richard Brinsley Sheridan's *School for Scandal* (1777), another late exemplar of Restoration Comedy, it satirizes the manners of people of fashion, as already the title indicates: The coinage "fashionable friends," which carries an ironic ring, occasionally appeared in the press of the day, for example: "The Prince, and many of his fashionable friends at Brighton, wear short green jackets. They have a very aukward [sic!] and indelicate appearance."[78] The phrase "fashionable friends," two words linked by alliteration but not by semantic closeness, implies that the principles of true friendship such as mutual support and understanding no longer apply in surroundings where companionship is based on the superficialities of dress and appearance rather than on any deeper feelings. Berry's comedy exhibits several such fashionable friendships, their superficiality, and their ultimate failure. *Fashionable Friends*, set in London, is a social satire and presents a cynical world, in which expressions of sentiment are calculated and rarely true. The plot—several interwoven stories of amorous adventure, love, seduction, intrigue, greed, and generation conflict—is conventional: Mrs. Lovell, recently married, is a close friend of the emotionally dishonest Lady Selina, who has just arrived in town. What Mrs. Lovell does not know is that her husband has an amorous interest in this Lady Selina, who, however, just seems to have had an affair with Mr. Lovell's friend, Sir Dudley Dorimant. Although Sir Dudley still retains feelings for her, he plans to marry the wealthy Miss Racket; yet in order to succeed, he must first overcome the reservations of her guardian, Sir Valentine Vapour, who also happens to be Mr. Lovell's uncle. To complicate matters even further, it is Sir Dudley's prospective mother-in-law, Mrs. Racket, who has cast an eye on her daughter's suitor, intending to marry him herself. Sir Dudley is resolved to marry the daughter, not the mother, yet considers alleviating the impending burden of matrimony by turning to Mrs. Lovell. The intrigues, which gradually unfold, culminate in the fifth act, a huge private masquerade, where the various couples try to meet in disguise. Eventually, two couples are united: Mrs. and Mr. Lovell, already married, confess their mutual affection, while Sir Dudley manages to elope and return with Miss Racket, leaving the mother, Mrs. Racket, as well as the guardian, Sir Valentine Vapour, to acquiesce the status quo. Lady Selina, ostentatiously left on her own, will no longer be Mrs. Lovell's confidante and announces her departure from London.

As in a Restoration Comedy, many of the characters are flat, not individuals but types, as a number of telling names, especially of minor characters, shows: The fashionable physician is called Doctor Syrop, Sir Valentine Vapour, absorbed by obscure scientific projects, carries a name reminiscent of the recently invented steam engine, while the noisy heiress and her loquacious mother go by the fitting family name of "Racket." Mr. and Mrs. Lovell's name indicates that the couple will learn to love one another, not with an abundance of "passion" or "sentiments" but with the affection necessary for a happy marriage. The characters' actions lack in psychological depth and are often motivated by sexual appetite, financial greed, or the desire for social climbing. Some of the characters are outright caricatures such as Sir Valentine, whose schemes for improvement range from violet soap to the use of electricity to charge up housemaids. The satire is also prominent in the scene in which Sir Valentine reads through the bills for Miss Racket's education:

> *Sir Valentine.*—Why, what the devil! here's the income of many a moderate fortune gone in the education of one girl. (*Looking over the accounts.*) To Mr. Parallel, the drawing-master, five guineas entrance; to three sets of prints, picteresque [sic!] views on the Brentford Road— picturesque views on the Brentford Road! nine guineas: papers, colours, brushes, preparing drawings, mounting drawings, finishing drawings... To Signor Celestini, ten guineas entrance: to six sets of sonatas, dedicated to Miss Racket. (FF 354–355)

In addition, two dancing masters, a teacher of the art of filigrain as well as philosophical lectures, and painting on velvet are listed. To Mary Berry, who valued serious reading, such trivial accomplishments, also severely criticized in Hannah More's writing, must have been anathema.

What makes the play such an interesting document is the performance of love and marriage, domesticity, and women's roles.

Fashionable Friends, staged five years after Berry's broken-off engagement with O'Hara, attacks the "marriage à la mode" immortalized in William Hogarth's biting satire of the same name. In act I, Mr. Lovell apologizes for entering his wife's apartment ("It is then generally that the visits of a husband require the most apology," 323), while Mrs. Lovell, who leaves soon afterwards, gives voice to her fear that she might be an "interruption." A politeness that consists of avoiding one another has replaced companionship, and it is hardly surprising that Mr. Lovell complains about his disenchantment. Sir Dudley, in contrast, has more realistic aims when it comes to marriage: he wants money, not love, and therefore wishes to enlist Mr. Lovell's help in obtaining the wealthy Miss Racket's hand. Miss Racket is Sir Dudley's equal in wishing a marriage of convenience—that is, an arrangement suited to her own needs, a fashionable life based on status symbols: "a chair with tassels," "two monstrous tall, handsome footmen," "horses to ride in the Park," "a villa to give breakfasts in the spring," "a phaeton and four," etcetera (340). Words like "delicacy", "sentiment", "love," and "passion" appear continuously yet are meaningless and only serve to hide emotional insincerity. Thus, *Fashionable Friends* satirizes fashionable couples, who were not to be seen together, as an exchange of ideas between Miss Racket and Sir Dudley shows:

> *Miss Rac.*—Then I will have a husband as soon as I can, that I may lose no time in getting a lover. I want somebody that will sit by one at an opera, and dance with one at a ball, and call for one's carriage, and hand one out, and—
>
> *Sir D.*—Lord, child! how much you expect of a lover! where could you get such antiquated ideas? (338–339)

Being fashionable is not compatible with caring for one another. The play rarely focuses on domesticity, which is the area of life from which the characters are trying to escape. Only Miss Racket's education, expensive and inefficient, lets the audience guess what life at home is like: trivial and superficial, like the characters' social life. That mother and daughter are rivals for the same man testifies to the extent of domestic disorder.

Among the gender roles tested is the figure of the married women. If Miss Racket and Mrs. Lovell are eventually rewarded through finding partners of their choice, Lady Selina, the woman of fashion, seductress, and intruder into her best friend's marriage, is left alone. Since Mrs. Lovell was played by Mary Berry while Anne Damer took the role of Lady Selina, Berry is symbolically returned to a secure place in society, while the notorious Damer remains on her own. Andrew Elfenbein astutely argues that the play "devalues same-sex friendship for supposedly more satisfactory heterosexual pairings."[79] In the face of accusations of a supposed lesbian love affair, the two women may have opted for a "strategic deflection of the rumors"[80] simply by holding up the ideal of heterosexuality. Elfenbein analyzes several lesser-known plays in which Damer acted, for example, Henry Seymour Conway's *False Appearances* (1789), to show that these create "a space for lesbian representation."[81] Lady Selina's and Mrs. Lovell's friendship is indeed very close. At the beginning of act II, they appear together, "arm-in-arm":

Mrs. Lovell.—The charm of seeing you thus unexpectedly—

Lady S.—Can only be guessed by those who, formed to pass their lives together, have *suffered* separation for a long month! (328)

Later, Mrs. Lovell asks: "Where are the moonlight walks, and the strolls in mossy woods, that we were to have had together?" (329). The thrill of unforeseen encounters and nocturnal walks evokes notions of sentimental friendship if not lovers' business. In the light of the accusations leveled against Berry and Damer, the comedy may well allude to same-sex desire. On the other hand, declarations of sentimental feelings between women were not out of the ordinary in the eighteenth century. Since *Fashionable Friends* aims to dismantle the concepts of sentimental love and friendship per se, showing reason and affection to be better alternatives, passages like the above may simply serve to emphasize the pitfalls of misguided sentimentalism.

Furthermore, Berry's comedy concerned itself with the dangers of acting. Nearly all the characters try to deceive someone, their current or future partner in marriage, parent, guardian, or master. Acting is not restricted to one sex or one social group. Lady Selina pretends to like Mrs. Lovell more than she does, Sir Dudley feigns an interest in Miss Racket's plans for a fashionable married life while planning to spend her fortune on himself, Mrs. Racket appears as motherly while attempting to steal her daughter's suitor, and Mr. Lovell declares his love for Lady Selina although he already has a mistress. The tensions between pretended and real emotions become noticeable through a number of asides, utterances directed only at the auditorium, not at any of the other characters. All this acting is motivated by self-interest. The masquerade in the final act, a type of event one could attend at Ranelagh Gardens, symbolizes the theatricality of social interaction: no one is what he or she appears to be; acting is a lifestyle, an attitude, a necessity.

How did contemporary audiences perceive of the play? As a dramatic text, *Fashionable Friends* is fairly conventional and, unlike Baillie's drama, does not attempt to conquer new aesthetic ground. Like *The School for Scandal*, Berry's play criticizes fashionable society, yet without Sheridan's sarcastic bite. Neither Mrs. Racket nor Lady Selina command over the stage presence of a Lady Teazle. The plot is stilted, the speeches are witty but also wordy. The reactions to the two different types of performances, private and public, varied greatly. The first private performances took place at Strawberry Hill, where Damer had opened an "elegant little theatre."[82] *The Lady's Monthly Museum* and *The Monthly Mirror* give November 28 and December 12, 1801, as the dates of performance. As attendance was by invitation only, the audience was comprised of the social elite: "the noblemen and the gentlemen's families round the country."[83] The hiring of Mellon as stage manager and advisor proves that this production ranked among the major sociable events at Strawberry Hill. That the review in *The Monthly Mirror* praises the tasteful scenery and masquerade shows that the producers' efforts went beyond the mere acting. The actors were friends and acquaintances, among them Earl Mount Edgcumbe as Sir Dudley, Damer as Lady Selina, Berry herself as Mrs. Lovell, Agnes Berry as Miss Racket, and their father as Sir Valentine, as the cast list in Berry's journal shows (JCB 2: 116). Surprisingly, Harriet Mellon, professional actress and assistant manager, is omitted from the brief description as well as the cast list, possibly because Berry or her editor tried to make the production look as the artistic product of an elite social circle alone. As was customary in private plays, prologue and epilogue were written by another member of this circle, a writer, here Joanna Baillie. Such paratexts were considered worthy of attention in themselves and were therefore sometimes published separately: the British Library holds a copy of this epilogue as a separate private print on laid paper.[84] The framing of a play with prologues or epilogues by well-known writers was an act of legitimization.

Private theatricals are a prime example of how the "third space" between public and private spaces was linked to sociable activities. The public figure of a literary character often had a private dimension, too, known only to the initiated audience. One such example is the character Dudley Dorimant, the calculating man-of-the-world, pursued by mother and daughter alike. In the correspondence between Damer and Berry of the year 1792, "Dorimant" is a code name for a Mr. Fawkener, then Damer's suitor (BP 104). Presumably, the dialogues on stage contained a fair number of allusions to past events, known to some members of the audience, which, after all, was comprised of friends and acquaintances. Percy Noble's biography of Damer contains a friend's poem in praise of the amateur actors, reminiscent of the earlier versifying that went on between the Berrys and Walpole.[85] In this respect, the plays resemble the silver-fork novels of the 1820s and 1830s, which were romans à clef. Moreover, watching this comedy of manners must have resembled a look into a mirror because the characters on stage were acting out the roles the audience knew through frequenting society.

A few months after the success of the private performances, on April 22, 1802, *Fashionable Friends* premiered in Drury Lane, with a cast that included some of the most famous actors of the day, Kemble as Sir Dudley and Mrs. Jordan as Miss Racket, yet was hissed off the stage after only two performances.[86] A review in the *Universal Magazine* criticized the play's immorality and found "desires the most loose and abandoned" in the character of Selina, thus possibly alluding to the rumors of "sapphism" surrounding Damer. While Berry kept her authorship secret, the advertisement to the subsequent publication explains that the manuscript had been found among the papers of the late Lord Orford.[87] Maybe it is Walpole's play with a fictitious author in *The Castle of Otranto* that Berry imitates. Although the author of *Fashionable Friends* was not identifiable as a woman, those who condemned the play must have had access to the reviews that provided the information that the comedy had previously been staged at Strawberry Hill, now inhabited by Damer. What were the reasons behind this failure? Like Baillie, Berry experienced rejection when she left the closet behind and went public. *The Critical Review* states that the "great disapprobation" with which the play was received stemmed from "causes which we are unable to fathom," and: "Play-house politics are however too deep for our plummet to fathom." In other words: unsavory machinations caused the failure at Drury Lane. Mary Berry continued to be interested in theater yet seems to have written only one other play, a farce entitled *The Two Martins* (BP 208), of which no surviving manuscript is known. The reasons for Berry's failure as a dramatist are not clear. As in the case of Baillie, the male-dominated world of the theatrical establishment, where women playwrights were feared as competitors, may have muted her as it had previously muted Baillie.

Chapter 3

Mary Berry as a Learned Woman: Out of the Closet

From a Parmesan Otranto to Malthus: Mary Berry's Reading

"Inter folia fructus"—between the leaves (pages) is the fruit—is the Latin motto on Mary Berry's bookplate, which features strawberries framed by leaves (WL 11: 150). Text and image once again pun on her name and emphasize the joys of reading. If uttered by a woman, any such endorsement of the pleasures of intellectual pursuit might be frowned upon in the late eighteenth century, especially in the context of debates about women's education and the dangers of reading, particularly of novels. "It has been advised, and by very respectable authorities too, that in conversation women should carefully conceal any knowledge or learning they may happen to possess,"[1] is the famous beginning of Hannah More's essay "Thoughts on Conversation" (1777), which refutes such male "authorities" and argues in favor of women's learning. It is her interest in books that situates Berry firmly in the tradition of the bluestockings, to whom learning was not for solitary use and who believed that sociability was educational and beneficial. Berry's journals are frequently concerned with her current reading, debates about new releases, and occasionally, women's education.

Germaine de Staël declared Mary Berry to be "by *far* the cleverest woman in England" (JCB 3: 13). Berry's education, however, was not the result of parental foresight; she acquired her learning through her own initiative.[2] Her journal complains that due to her father's financial restrictions, her education was neglected: "Every expense of education in the acquirement of talents was denied us" (JCB 1: 4). Mary's and Agnes's schooling more or less came to an end in 1775 when their second governess left to get married: "My extreme precocity, both mental and physical, helped to lead him [the father] to suppose that the expense of another governess might be spared, and we were thus left, almost children, to our own devices" (JCB 1: 7). Although she complains that idleness and desultory reading were the consequences, her *Journals and Correspondence* prove the opposite. Berry became a keen reader and retained a life-long awareness of the shortcomings of the instruction available to her sex: "Considering the education given to women...I am only astonished that they are not more ignorant, weaker, and more perverse than they are" (JCB 2: 313). In 1799, she read Hannah More's *Strictures on the Modern System of Female Education* (1799) as well as an unspecified text by Mary Wollstonecraft and concluded: "It is amazing, or rather it is not amazing, but impossible, they should do otherwise than agree on all the great points of female education. H. More will, I dare say, be very angry when she hears this, though I would lay a wager that she never read the book" (91–92). Berry quickly realized that, despite their different political views, the conservative More and the radical Wollstonecraft resembled one another in their ideas about female education, advocating moral responsibility and intellectual learning over mere accomplishments such as making oneself pleasant. Although she shared More's conservative outlook, Berry criticized her friend for being too overtly religious in her writing ("a principle radically false," 191). Berry had a keen eye when it came to recognizing the spirit of intellectual independence in other women. Of Annabella Milbanke, Byron's famous "Princess of Parallellograms" (BLJ 4: 48), she wrote: "Lady Milbanke's daughter appears to have a great deal of mind, and she is said to have a good deal of information, and is not at all affected" (JCB 2: 505). Berry herself never voiced the opinion that her own knowledge made her superior or even influential.

Her diaries and her epistolary exchange abound with references to books and learning. Mary was not only fluent in French and Latin, quoting from Latin inscriptions in her account of Pompeii, but also employed a tutor to improve her Greek (90). If a knowledge—often only a smattering—of modern languages, especially of French and Italian, was among the accomplishments a young lady ought to acquire, Latin and Greek, considered to be more rigorous, were not. In Tobias Smollett's satirical novel *Roderick Random* (1748), the hero's new employer, a stately, ugly, and ridiculous lady, the caricature of a learned woman, welcomes Roderick with incoherent quotations from classical literature. A woman who knew Greek might find herself thus exposed to public ridicule.[3] Science was not among Berry's interests. In Florence she looked at Lord Cowper's devices for scientific tests ("electricity," "optics," "hydraulic experiments," 1784, JCB 1: 122), yet as such topics are rare in her journals, it seems to have been the social occasion rather than the gain of knowledge that took her fancy. Throughout her life, Mary Berry was an avid reader of many sorts of texts: classics, eighteenth-century fiction, contemporary writing, philosophy, political theory, history, and newspapers.[4] Berry read English and European literature alike and was, as her comments on Joanna Baillie show, aware of women writers. When she began to work on Lady Rachel Russell's life and letters, her interest in manuscripts grew. Some of her diary entries merely name authors or books, some sketch her impressions. After Walpole's death, she became more confident in her own judgment. Among the many, many books Berry read were Pope's translation of Homer, Milton's *Paradise Lost*, and Shakespeare's works. She found *Tristram Shandy* diverting (JCB 2: 80) and advised a friend to read Kotzebue's *Lovers' Vows* (72), discussed Roscoe's translations from the Italian (82–83), considered Staël's novel *Delphine* too autobiographical (233–234), criticized Godwin's *St. Leon* ("it was written for bread...written as the printers wanted it," 111), praised Moore's poems, was familiar with Byron and Scott, delighted in Thackeray's and Balzac's "brilliant pen" (BP 438) but managed to steer clear of Jane Austen until the 1840s ("totally uninteresting," "long-drawn-out details," "tedious," ibid.). Novels were the genre she held in lowest esteem, fearing that their perusal would induce idleness (JCB 2: 262). Philosophy appeared more useful to her: Berry knew Montaigne's essays and had varied views on Rousseau's passions while she also concerned herself with contemporary political thought, purchasing Malthus's much-debated "Essay on the Principle of Population" in 1798. She was so impressed by his ideas that she wrote a short essay on them (73–77); 13 years later she found herself sitting next to him at a dinner party, where they enjoyed "a good deal of conversation" (475).

The silent and solitary perusal of books was not the only method of reading, which could also be a communal activity. On March 9, 1808, Berry wrote: "I went in the evening to Mrs. D[amer]. Read 'Marmion,' just come out, to her" (342). Soon afterwards, in April and May, they read Ashe's *Travels in America* together. During her sojourn in Raith in 1814, Berry entered into her diary: "Lord Rosslyn read to us 'Lara,' Lord Byron's new tale" (JCB 3: 34). As these books were expensive and new releases, the journal shows that Berry and her friends spent a fair amount of money on contemporary writing.

Many other accounts testify to the pleasure of joint reading in the evening, which could also take the form of play-reading. In the winter of 1797–1798, the famous actress Mrs. Siddons "read 'Hamlet' to us one evening, in N. Audley Steet, which was to me a great treat" (JCB 2: 70). Reading was not necessarily solitary but cohered with other sociable activities. Berry hosted and attended numerous breakfast and dinner parties, where she met writers like Baillie or Scott, with whom she conversed about their writing as well as her own.

Visits to libraries, bookshops, museums, and art galleries also served the accumulation of knowledge, as Berry's travel journal reveals. She took a lively interest in libraries at a time when many of these institutions restricted their access and were by no means open to the general public. She went to see the library at Mannheim (JCB 1: 25), the Vatican library (64), the Laurentian Medicean Library at Florence (331), the Bibliothèque Nationale in Paris (JCB 2: 184), which in 1802 was open to the public, as she points out, the library at Cambridge (401–402), and many others. Her comments, rarely longer than one page, show an avid reader's sensibility, focusing not only on architecture and artwork but also on the layout of the rooms, the number of volumes and manuscripts, accessibility, conditions for studying, and the history of ownership. Berry also communicated with booksellers while traveling, with varying success. When she was at Liège, she entered a bookshop, which, to her regret, stocked only "libertine and profligate tales and novels" (JCB 1: 20). Other visits to bookshops, for example, in Basle, or to the French bookshop in Darmstadt, were more to her liking. A journal entry in November 1790 mentions that she went to a printing-office in Parma, where 300 copies of *Otranto* were produced for the London bookseller Edwards. As Walpole was her main correspondent during the journey, she thus linked his fantasy of *Otranto*'s Italian origin to her own sojourn. Soon afterwards, he wrote to her: "I am glad you did not get a Parmesan Otranto. A copy is come so full of faults, that it is not fit to be sold here" (268).

Art exhibitions, both in London and abroad, were another source of attraction for Berry. No matter whether her brief journal entries deal with a provincial art gallery in Cassel, where she discovered a Rembrandt, or a visit to the Louvre, Berry shows immense awareness of art and artists. Her friendship with Damer must have increased her interest, especially in sculpture: in 1820, she saw Canova's studio in Rome and, while in Florence, visited the sculptor Bartolini, who was then working on a statue of Venus (JCB 3: 230–233) for the Duke of Devonshire, by whom Mary Berry had been commissioned to act as a deputy. The Elgin Marbles and other antique artwork brought to the

British Museum also attracted her curiosity. Despite her obvious preference for classical and neoclassical sculpture as well as older paintings, Berry would muster up interest in contemporary art: "Agnes and I went to Mr. Blake's, to see his drawings, which are admirable. He sketches in every style, and always well. I never saw a more perfect amateur" (1811, JCB 2: 486). Another, much more popular type of entertainment were panoramas, circular paintings of cities, landscapes, or military fields of action, with much attention to accurate detail.[5] Berry visited such panoramas of Cairo and Dublin, and of the Battle of Vittoria. All these trips to institutions of popular and high art, undertaken with friends, were extensions of the sociable events the Berrys hosted and visited.

In and Out of the Drawing-Rooms in North Audley Street and Curzon Street

Research into salon sociability encounters a methodological problem: much of the interaction consists of words, which literally evaporate once they have been uttered, or linger in memory and survive imperfectly. As textual records of sociable activities and conversations are usually produced in retrospect, they often summarize and abbreviate drastically. The account of a convivial evening is often merely a terse diary entry or a short passage in a letter:

> Last night we had a comfortable quiet game at whist here with only Mr. and Mrs. Burn, Jerningham, Mrs. Damer and myself, and Mme de Coigny the latter part of the evening as a looker-on with Agnes. News there are none, French or English, public or private, or between Mr. Burn and Mme de Coigny we should have heard it. (Letter to Mrs. Cholmeley, December 16, 1799, JCB 2: 107)

Such brief sketches usually provide the names of some visitors, the central activity (here: whist), and one or two topics of conversation (here: the lack of a topic). Longer texts are rarer and are often written years after the hospitable events they document. Kate Perry's 12-page booklet *Reminiscences of a London Drawing-Room* (c. 1860) centers on the old Misses Berry in Curzon Street,[6] the period between January 1849 and Mary Berry's burial in November 1852, and chronicles some conversations in detail but otherwise condenses the sociable events. Another, better-known example of this genre of the recorded conversation is William Hazlitt's essay "My First Acquaintance with Poets" (1823), which recounts meetings with Coleridge and Wordsworth that occurred in 1798, 25 years before the publication of his piece.[7] As Hazlitt's text follows its own poetological program in describing an initiation into a new Romantic way of thinking, it cannot be taken at face value because the conversations he outlines are meant to support his argument. Even if they aim at accuracy, the authors of longer texts about previous sociable encounters have a story to tell, must create narrative coherence, and will restructure their material accordingly. Epistolary exchange is another useful source, yet as letters are written during times of absence, they often inform about more relevant topics than the previous evening's conversation, though, if they do, they will often be as brief as the passage above. Moreover, a socialite like Berry tended to write more about events she attended than those she hosted.

In order to establish the nature of the sociability Berry cultivated, it makes more sense to look at patterns: types of sociable events, places, and acquaintances. If Petra Wilhelmy-Dollinger's profound study of the Berlin salons of the Romantic period aims to provide a complete picture, with lists of *habitués*, my study is less concerned with the exact comings and goings of guests and more with types of interaction. Mary Berry attended breakfast parties, dinners, suppers, balls, parties with card games, assemblies, went to church with others as well as to exhibitions, museums, libraries, the theater, and the opera, and enjoyed walks in public gardens. As a hostess, she restricted herself to events on a smaller scale than the entertainments she frequented in the large aristocratic houses. She went out and entertained both in London and during her frequent sojourns in Paris, where she keenly observed the organizational details of French urban sociability, for example, when she remarked on a host's *jour fixe*: "Went to the Greffulhes, who receive every Wednesday evening" (1816, JCB 3: 75). Her most sociable years lay between the late 1780s and the late 1820s.

Among the largest sociable events were so-called assemblies: "I went to Lady Caroline Lamb's. An immense assembly" (1808, JCB 2: 346). Sometimes, during such occasions, several rooms were opened to the guests, for example, at Lady Cork's on July 11, 1811: "a great assembly in her upper rooms, which are very prettily furnished, particularly the boudoir, opening into the conservatory" (483). The entertainment might consist of music and cards.[8] When attending large sociable events in post-Revolutionary France, Berry sometimes made a point of remembering the Paris she had known before the Revolution. A journal entry in 1802, which distinguishes between "the manners of the *old* and *new world*" (174), finds its application a few pages later when Berry attends an assembly at the Duchesse de Luines', where she finds three rooms with card games and only one with refreshments (176), to her an example of "the old world," that is, pre-Revolutionary Paris. A somewhat curious highlight among large invitations was a "Venetian breakfast," hitherto unknown to the experienced socialite: "The garden looked pretty, filled with young and gaily-dressed people dancing, some of them in masks, and many in dominoes, for this was the notion of a Venetian breakfast! The eating part of it was luckily quite à l'Anglaise, good bread and butter, tea and coffee" (1810, 419). Another such "Venetian *déjeuner*" offered "tents, lotteries, and fortune-tellers" as entertainment (1812, 502). These, however, seem to have been exceptional. A further diversion were balls, also restricted to the great aristocratic places like Devonshire House.

Parties at her own home, especially breakfast and dinner parties, were smaller. Obtaining reliable information about the numbers of guests invited is difficult because it remains unclear whether the journal entries give complete lists of names. On March 30, 1814, Berry had "a small party at home in the evening, consisting of about ten ladies and twenty-six gentlemen" (JCB 3: 8). 36 guests seems a huge number for a "small" invitation, particularly if one considers that her journal usually only provides a handful of names on similar occasions. It was unusual for men and women to encounter separate seating arrangements, as Berry's comment on a small evening party at Mr. Grattan's in 1811 shows: "But they don't understand society in their own house...In this very small party all the women were sitting round the door of one of the two rooms, and all the men in the other" (JCB 2: 467). Berry did not like parties that were dominated by female guests: "To Mrs. Sotheby's where was a sort of blue-stocking assembly, misses and their mammas without end, so pleased to carry them to a rational house, and unite pleasure and wisdom together!" (1811, 454). Other small-scale sociable occasions were visits to friends, church attendance, or watching a play from somebody's box: Mrs. Kemble's (454), Prince Staremberg's (406), or the Duke of Devonshire's (JCB 3: 9). Sharing a box with a well-known public figure indicated social prestige. As the Berry sisters grew older and more sedate, the number of lively evening entertainments they attended or organized seems to have decreased, yet they continued to act as hostesses well into their eighties. In 1825, the venue of their sociable evenings, which had been in North Audley Street for over 30 years, moved to Curzon Street. Toward the end of their lives, the Berrys acquired the reputation of an institution that linked the Victorian present to late eighteenth-century and Regency London. Perry's nostalgic *Reminiscences of a London Drawing-Room* evokes Mary Berry's accounts of Horace Walpole, the victory of Waterloo, and the Duke of Wellington. That she foregrounds the invitation of "Poodle Byng," one of the Prince Regent's former friends, on Christmas Day 1851, shows the slightly anachronistic aura this salon must have had during its last years for some of the visitors.

What did people do at these evening entertainments? If larger events offered the opportunity for dancing, smaller parties could attract musical and literary activities: "In the evening, a large party at home. Gow, the Scotch fiddler, a second fiddle, and a harp, came to us at half-past nine, and played some Scotch airs to my father" (1808, JCB 2: 343), or "Went to Devonshire House. Catalani singing in the saloon, Sapio accompanying" (339), or "In the evening at a pleasant party at Lady Donegal's. Anacreon Moore sang a great deal—his old things, all the prettiest" (345). The boundary between entertainers and guests was fluid. Authors read their work:

> Mrs. Cholmley and two of her daughters and Walter Scott breakfasted with us. Shortly after came Sir G. and Lady Beaumont, Robert Walpole and Lady Louisa Stuart, and Sir W. Pepys and F. Cholmley. Somebody was to read Joanna Baillie's tragedy, 'The Family Legend;' this somebody was obliged to be me, as nobody else knew her hand, or had ever seen the play. I read the first three acts, Cholmley the fourth, and I again the fifth. It had a vast effect upon Walter Scott, and one that was very pleasing, from the evident feeling of one poet for another. (June 7, 1809, 381)

The story had first come to Baillie via Damer in 1805, that is, through sociable networks she shared with Berry. When *The Family Legend* was performed in Drury Lane in 1815, Mary Berry saw the play in Lady Hardwicke's box (JCB 3: 50). Berry, both audience to and producer of writing, was a member of an inner literary London circle, which she had helped create and which was situated between public and private, where it thrived on intellectual exchange.

The host of people she knew was legendary. Among her closest friends were Horace Walpole, Anne Damer, Joanna Baillie, but she also counted among her friends and guests Germaine de Staël, William Thackeray, Hannah More, Samuel Rogers, Sydney Smith, Thomas Lawrence, Lord Brougham, the Starembergs, Thomas Moore, Sir Walter Scott, Lady Charlotte Lindsay, William Gell, Richard Keppel Craven, and Lady Donegal (BP 288). She and Damer were repeatedly visited by the Princess of Wales, the hapless Caroline of Brunswick, whose trial in 1820 is recorded in great detail and with much sympathy in the *Journals and Correspondence*. Both the *Journals and Correspondence* and *The Berry Papers* have a tendency to emphasize connections with the aristocracy (e.g., the Duke of Devonshire) and sometimes the court. During and immediately after the Revolutionary years, through such name-dropping, the Berrys avoided suspicions of Revolutionary sympathies; later it would serve to heighten their social prestige. Adickes astutely argues that Mary Berry's "intense identification with the ruling class" may have been a reaction against her father's failure to succeed.[9] That Ann Radcliffe and Harriet Martineau, who had both met Berry, are not mentioned by her in the *Journals and Correspondence* or *The Berry Papers* confirms the hypothesis that Berry and her editors omitted some names, probably to reduce the overload of information.[10] However, it is also possible that Radcliffe, of whose passionate narratives the rational Berry would not have approved, likewise the social critic Martineau, then very young, simply did not meet her expectations of a woman writer.[11] Therefore, it comes as a slight surprise that Berry emphasized her acquaintance with the Princess of Wales, an act many might have considered as an implicit criticism of the Royal Family.[12]

The question remains how "blue" the Berrys were. As their sociable activities only commenced in the late 1780s, they were too young to be part of the bluestocking matriarchs' circles but they knew, for example, the famous hostess Elizabeth Montagu, as a letter by Agnes shows, who, plagued by migraine, declined an invitation because her sister had not yet returned from a visit to the country (c. 1800, BP 200). Byron cheekily decried them as "blue" (BLJ 3: 228), while Martineau considered them as "rather blue," but not as "express 'blue,'"[13] unfortunately without explaining the exact nature of her nomenclature. By the early nineteenth century, the term "bluestocking" had become derogatory if not funny and was no label an educated woman would aspire to. Through aligning herself with the social elite, Berry escaped the narrow identification with a group of women, who, however, were her intellectual and sociable forebears.

The Freedom of the Road in France and Italy

"It is now quite as impossible to judge from appearances in France as it was formerly, though from directly opposite reasons" (JCB 2: 135–136), the truly conservative traveler Mary Berry remarked with regret in 1802.[14] Although women were not advised to undergo the hardships of traveling, she was one of the many who left England to experience the grand tour. Parts of her three-volume *Journals and Correspondence* constitute a minute itinerary of numerous journeys, mainly to France and Italy, though occasionally also to Germany and Switzerland. She went to the continent 13 times between 1783 when she was 20 and 1836 when she was 63 years old. This section will look at Berry's journals in the context of travel writing, her changing aesthetics (the regular as opposed to the sublime), and her predilection for theatricality, especially in Italy.

While traveling through France in 1790, Mary Berry received a fair amount of letters from Walpole, who disapproved of her prolonged absence. The general eighteenth-century view was that women did not need to travel, yet they did: they often went as daughters or spouses like Mary Wortley Montagu, who accompanied her husband on a diplomatic mission to Constantinople and whose *Turkish Embassy Letters* (1763) are among the first travel narratives by women to be published in Britain. Women rarely commanded over an income large enough to enable them to go abroad on their own; moreover, the grand tour, an educational journey for British aristocrats, was largely restricted to men. If, before 1800, only about 20 travelogues by women appeared in print,[15] their number increased in the nineteenth century. Brian Dolan's entertaining study *Ladies of the Grand Tour* reveals how women travelers went to educate themselves through journeys to France and Italy in the later eighteenth century.[16] One aim was "to secure a considerable degree of emotional as well as intellectual freedom denied by social constraints at home," as John Wilton-Ely explains.[17] The Berry sisters traveled with their father, who, as a young man in expectation of a large fortune, had done the grand tour himself. Since, with Ferguson's death, an annuity had been settled on Robert, father and daughters could now afford the long stays abroad. Like other women travelers (and travel writers), Mary Berry defined herself not by her sex but by her nationality:[18] she was an English traveler, not a woman traveler. It is sometimes argued that women who went traveling thereby carved out an individual space for themselves, yet it is evident that Mary Berry did not aim to develop an individualism that would set her apart, that she rather shrank from reporting very subjective encounters or emotions, let alone radical views. If contemporary academics take other women writers as a point of comparison—Wollstonecraft, Radcliffe, and Helen Maria Williams—to Mary Berry, they were not. When she went to the continent for the first time in 1783, she traveled in the golden age of the grand tour and of the elite tourist, whereas at the time of publication of her *Journals and Correspondence* in 1865, she was catering to a reading (and traveling) public that conceived particularly of Italy as a destination for mass tourism. A reference to *Murray's Handbook*, a popular guidebook (JCB 1: 356), in a footnote reveals Berry's awareness of a posthumous audience who might read her published journals alongside travel guides.

The passages in the three-volume *Journals and Correspondence* relating to traveling in Europe are constructed as a many-voiced, panoramic view. The primary textual basis is Berry's own detailed itinerary, kept during her journeys abroad. The terse entries covering her first tour of the continent between 1783 and 1785 are later followed by more elaborate descriptions of towns, cities, landscape, art, sociable encounters, religious ceremonies, and political events. Some of her earliest travel journals, today in the British Library, are small, slim booklets filled with occasional drawings and kept in a minute handwriting that claims as little space as possible. One reason for her early reticence may be lack of self-confidence in the face of norms that did not expect women to travel, let alone write about the experience. The published *Journals and Correspondence* are not one person's account but offer a variety of perspectives: The description of the Berrys' second trip to Italy and France (1790–1791) is complemented by Walpole's letters, written in London and Twickenham, which mirror and legitimize Berry's voice. Walpole provides extra information about the Revolutionary turmoil but also news about the weather abroad: "I am glad you are going to Pisa; Florence is too cold for you" (276). If Mary Berry frequently mentions the opera and the theater in Italy and France, Walpole, the tycoon of fine arts, writes to her about the opera in London or the opening of the Haymarket Theater (165, 288) so that England's cultural life is embedded into international contexts. Throughout the three volumes, Berry's accounts of France, Italy, Germany, and Switzerland are complemented by reports from further regions, for example, by Damer's letters from Portugal and Spain. Although Berry is concerned with practical matters—the quality of accommodation, sociable gatherings, and obstacles such as bad roads—she avoids styling herself as a subjective traveler. In contrast, Smollett's *Travels Through France and Italy* (1766), which brought its author a reputation for extreme ill humor, is a prime example of a travelogue that foregrounds the traveler's personal views. Most of Berry's travel writing is so impersonal that she even refrains from venturing detailed information about her companions. The 70-page account of her one-month trip to Paris in 1802 mentions her fellow traveler Damer merely six times. Father and sister remain shadowy throughout; occasionally, Agnes's drawings are mentioned.[19] Other English travelers in Italy, whom the Berrys encountered, are named but rarely described in detail. Yet it is her impersonal style that enables Berry to present herself with the authority of an objective chronicler.

On her early tours, Berry did not warm to Romantic aesthetics. In her description of towns, she voices regret about what other travelers welcome as picturesque and attractive. Among German towns, Mannheim with its geometrically constructed city center elicited her approval: "Dined at Manheim, the capital of the Elector-Palatine's dominions. It is by far the prettiest town I have seen in Germany; all the streets are broad and at right angles, and all the houses white" (1783, 25). On her early tours, she favored criteria like regularity, cleanliness, and propriety, yet when she visited Edinburgh in 1814, she was fascinated by its aesthetics of unevenness: "Nothing is more picturesque than the irregularity, the height, and the grotesque form of its buildings" (JCB 3: 40). The hundreds of pages of her early travel journal rarely praise sublime landscape. An account of a journey in the Swiss Alps from Geneva to Chamonix and other popular Alpine destinations in 1783 (JCB 1: 28–36) is concerned with hardships and obstacles, especially the bad weather. One of the few comments on the landscape runs: "The road from Bonneville to Sallenches beautifully wild, winding along the valley of the Arve, in some places so narrow as only to admit the river and a narrow road for a carriage, walled in on each side by immense mountains" (28). Berry's brief scenic descriptions, here as elsewhere, recycle stock elements of other travel narratives portraying the sublime Alps and are obviously compiled with little emotional involvement. Walpole, in contrast, was basking in his exposure to the lofty scenery, as his famous letter to Richard West on September 28, 1739, demonstrates:

> Precipices, mountains, torrents, wolves, rumblings, Salvator Rosa— the pomp of our park and the meekness of our palace! Here we are, the lonely lords of glorious desolate prospects…
>
> But the road, West, the road! winding round a prodigious mountain, and surrounded with others, all shagged with hanging woods, obscured with pines or lost in clouds! Below, a torrent breaking through cliffs, and tumbling through fragments of rocks! Sheets of cascades forcing their silver speed down channelled precipices, and hasting into the roughened river at the bottom! Now and then an old footbridge, with a broken rail, a leaning cross, a cottage, or the ruin of an hermitage! This sounds too bombast and too romantic to one that has not seen it, too cold for one that has. (WL 13: 181–182)

The most striking difference between the two descriptions is the degree of emotional involvement and the intensity with which the beholders find or do not find themselves reflected in their exalted surroundings. Walpole is overwhelmed but remains aware of the artistic conventions that structure his ecstatic perception. When Berry traveled across the Simplon Pass in 1818, she took more notice of her environment, faithfully recording all she saw, yet again without Walpole's enthusiasm:

> One magnificent fall of the torrent by the side of the road, separated by a rock of enormous size...The road winds through certainly the highest and most perpendicular masses of rock I ever beheld, till at last, where two torrents meet and occupy the whole space of the narrow cut in the rocks over which they pass, a stone bridge of a single handsome arch is thrown over one of them...Blasted pines and enormous inaccessible masses of bare rock seem to record the passage of the Great Destroyer rather than the creation of a Beneficient Being. (JCB 3: 165)

Remaining true to her aesthetics of order, Berry conscientiously catalogued individual elements without being overwhelmed. Eighteenth- and nineteenth-century women not only wrote no tracts about the sublime and the picturesque but were, as Elizabeth A. Bohls states, marginalized in "the practices of taste."[20] Berry's brief verbal sketches of landscape assimilate the concepts and vocabulary of male authorities. That she adapted her portrayals of places of touristic interest to her reading is also illustrated in the section of the *Journals and Correspondence* that chronicles a tour of the Lake District in 1808, where she visited a cottage:

> The one we now entered was that of a mere labourer, with a young wife and three children; it had every necessary comfort. The good woman was making girdle-cakes of oatmeal (here the bread of the poor) over a fire of fern...she and her sister-in-law would hardly accept a trifle for their hospitality. (JCB 2: 360)

Rousseau and Wordsworth are lurking round the corner: the young family, the frugal meal, and the happy and simple life are stock elements of the Romantic rural idyll, while the waterfall on the next page situates the description in the wider context of literary effusions about the Lake District.

Mary Berry's voice becomes more individual when she turns to things theatrical. During her sojourns in French and Italian cities, she loved to attend theaters and operas, and her astute comments deal with acting styles, interiors, architecture, the dress and the manners of the audience, the plays, and the music. She was captivated by the spectacular quality of Italy,[21] especially of religious events, and described her presentation to the Pope on January 1, 1784, and the celebration of a mass by him in unusual detail (JCB 1: 67, 57–61), listing the dominant colors of the spectacle ("crimson," "gold," and "green"), the cardinals' seating arrangements, as well as the reactions among the select congregation:

> The emperor's deportment was the most serious and respectful that can be imagined; he spoke very little, was attentive to what was going on, knelt when the rest of the people knelt, crossed himself twice, and had every external mark of decent devotion. The King of Sweden talked a great deal, was more eager to see every part of the show, knelt more awkwardly, and bowed less low. It is impossible for me to remember in their order, or to attempt to describe, the various manœuvres of the grandest and best-acted pantomime that can be imagined. (58)

The church is the Italians' theater. Other ambivalent comments on the Catholic Church follow; yet Berry's attitude to Catholicism is a product of her time. Texts ranging from Matthew Lewis's Gothic novel *The Monk* (1796) to the Swiss Protestant writer Léonard Simonde de Sismondi's *History of the Italian Republics in the Middle Ages* (1807–1818) are all critical of Catholicism.[22] Throughout the three volumes, the accounts of Italy are interspersed with descriptions of church-related events: processions, illuminations, masses, all fascinating spectacles and performances that appeal to the senses but are rarely intended as sincere acts of devotion. In November 1817, she attended a Florentine church:

> There was a very grand feast, or rather function, at the Church of Sta. M. Novella, for the repose of the soul of a certain Sigr. Ventini, who died some weeks ago. The whole church was hung with crimson velvet and gold fringe, quite new—very brilliant and magnificent. The high altar was glittering with gold and silver stuff; and all was lighted up between four and five o'clock by about 5,500 wax-lights distributed in all parts, and in large lustres hanging from the ceiling of the church. Numbers of people began to go there from eight o'clock in the morning, and from three o'clock till past five, when all the lights were lighted, and the Archbishop gave the benediction. The crowd became too dense for us to penetrate. (JCB 3: 148–149)

Her fascination stands in contrast with her uneasiness about the apparent lack of interest in the deceased. The church service in remembrance of a member of the community is a beautiful spectacle, like the carnival to whose description Berry turns a few pages later. Unlike Alpine landscapes, these religious events touch Berry's emotional side so much that she wants to fuse with the multitude. This fusion of subject and object is one of the central psychological criteria of the Romantic sublime, which she transfers from reflections about landscape to the pleasures of watching a feast of light and mingling with a crowd in search of religious ecstasy, thus demonstrating her own authorial voice.

MARY BERRY AS EDITOR AND HISTORIAN

In referring to late eighteenth-century and Romantic women writers, we often mean Fanny Burney and Jane Austen. Susan Staves's comprehensive *Literary History of Women's Writing in Britain, 1660–1789* (2006), however, rejects the notion that women writers had to be novelists or poets and concentrates on semi- and nonliterary genres such as historiography, correspondence, advice literature, and literary criticism, while showing how precarious the position of women was who claimed to be critical authorities.[23] Bluestockings, she explains, studied so that they would benefit from their education but did not necessarily consider themselves as "deliberate producers of literary works."[24] Their sociable activities and intellectual debates, rather than any idealizations of the solitary genius, helped them find the topics they wrote about. That female authorities were in a much more precarious situation than male authors, received less support, and sported less self-confidence becomes obvious from the many anonymous publications by women. Mary Berry's journals indicate that her authorship was known to her friends and acquaintances, yet she did not seek public recognition as a writer. The 1798 publication of Walpole's *Works*, many of which had first been printed at Strawberry Hill, was nominally undertaken by Robert Berry, while his daughter Mary spent about a year doing the actual work (WL 11: xxviii; JCB 2: 21).[25] The title page and preface mention no editor's name. As the advertisement to Berry's next publication, *The Fashionable Friends* (1802), claims that the comedy had been found among Orford's papers, public recognition of her authorship was avoided again. Her four-volume selection of Madame du Deffand's letters (1810), a continuation of her earlier edition of Walpole's works, carries no editor's name on the title page; the preface is left unsigned. Likewise, the edition of Lady Russell's life and letters (1819) fails to have Berry's own name on the title page, which assigns the authorship of the volume to "the editor of Madame du Deffand's Letters," whereas "His Grace the Duke of Devonshire," who owned many of the manuscripts, is explicitly named. The unknown female writer thus positions herself under the tutelage of a well-known aristocratic patron. The two volumes of *Social Life in England and France* (1828, 1831) also name the editor of Deffand's letters as the author, as does the 1844 omnibus edition of several of her works.[26] She only used her own initials "MB" in an essay in 1840, which was prefixed to the sixth volume of the edition of Walpole's letters and which defended Walpole against Macaulay's vitriolic attack in the *Edinburgh Review* (1833).[27]

Mary Berry's editorial activities, which commenced with her friend and patron Walpole's works, were by no means unusual: other women also edited male writers, for example, Anna Laetitia Barbauld, who published Samuel Richardson's correspondence in 1804. Walpole had left "a box, marked O, containing MSS." to Mr. Berry and his daughters, effectively appointing Mary as his editor "without the necessary publicity attached to the name" (21). It is not entirely clear to what extent she merely followed Walpole's instructions and where she made her own editorial decisions. The last volume, selections of the huge correspondence, must have made the most demands on her time and judgment. The unsigned preface, supposedly by Robert Berry, explains that "in the arrangement of the last two volumes...the editor has been materially assisted by a daughter," who appears as a helpmate, inferior to the father's intellect and achievement.[28] That Mary Berry presented Hannah More with a copy of Walpole's *Works* shows that she strove for recognition.[29]

The next editorial project were Deffand's letters to Walpole, which she had bequeathed to him. Deffand, his senior by 20 years, famous Parisian *salonnière*, friend of Voltaire's, blind, and Walpole's intimate attachment, was one of the most important French letter-writers of the eighteenth century. Berry was well-suited to the task because she was fluent in French, had visited Paris several times, and was familiar with its society, yet by asking one female friend to select from another's papers, Walpole posthumously created a new episode in his family romance of tentative "as if" connections. Moreover, while the edition contains Deffand's letters to him, Walpole wished his own letters to her to be destroyed after Berry had made use of them (WL 3: xxxi).[30] A number of journal entries between 1807 and 1810 show how she progressed with her work, which she debated with friends and acquaintances, among them Joanna Baillie and Sydney Smith. Eventually, Berry received the fairly large sum of £ 200 from Longman (JCB 2: 422). On September 8, 1810, she took a set of the volumes to the Princess of Wales, who thanked her "in the most gracious manner possible" (425). The four volumes, which combined an English preface and a selection from the letters in French, received ambivalent recognition in France: they were edited four times in 17 years, yet Berry's preface was soon replaced. This somewhat moralizing biographical sketch conveys a fascination with a woman who ran her own life yet also voices regret over her irreligious views and the "profligacy of French manners" that had prevailed during her youth.[31] Nevertheless, all further editions of Deffand's letters made use of Berry's early editorial work.

This edition of a salonnière's correspondence prepared Berry well for her next book, Lady Rachel Russell's life and a selection of her letters. Staves explains that "history offered a much less claustrophobic discursive space"[32] to women than the domestic novel did. One might ask why Berry never considered writing a novel. The answer would be that, first of all, Berry criticized novels for promoting idleness. Yet another reason might be that editing and history writing was preferable because it allowed a look at the wider world of politics and society; besides, it carried more prestige and brought more money.[33] Although the genre of history was not considered as female,[34] Catharine Macaulay's extremely successful eight-volume *History of England* (1763–1783), devoured by radicals and dissenters in Britain, France, and America during the Revolutionary years, had set an example other women could emulate. The bluestockings' general attitude to women's education, favoring—in Hannah More's words—the "useful" and reasonable over the purely "ornamental,"[35] made it easier for women like Berry to justify supposedly male activities like editing and history-writing. That she was aware of Walpole's creative reinventions of genealogies, Baillie's interest in historical themes, as well as Scott's literary popularizations of history must have increased the genre's appeal to her. Berry herself owned and read history books, while her travel journals testify to a strong sense of the past. Yet if male history has traditionally focused on great men and great public events, Berry's *Life of Lady Russell* of 1819 combines a consideration of political actions and private matters.

By turning to Lady Rachel Russell, Berry, the daughter of a Whig, was contributing to the writing of Whig history. Lord Russell was generally considered to be a martyr and therefore a symbol to the Whig cause: he had been executed for participating in the Rye House Plot in 1683, which aimed at assassinating Charles II to keep

Roman Catholicism out of Britain. As Lord and Lady Russell had led an exceptionally happy marriage and had three surviving children, she did everything in her power after her husband's arrest to avert the execution, but without success. With the Glorious Revolution of 1688–1689, she regained her social status and her influence. Her letters and other documents testify to numerous activities centering around her children, who, with her help, made extremely advantageous matches. Her daughter Rachel married William Cavendish, later the Second Duke of Devonshire, and became great-grandmother to the current Sixth Duke, who granted Berry access to the manuscripts and was named on the title page of her book. Lady Russell was an influential "Whig matriarch,"[36] an ancestress of the Duke, to whose house Mary Berry was frequently invited. Berry cast Lady Russell as a devoted wife and tragic heroine, affectionate and pious but also clever and influential, an astute businesswoman with a head for financial arrangements, and a brilliant hostess. It may have been Lady Russell's status in London society that made her so attractive to Berry: "Yet her devotion separated her in no degree either from the affections, the interests, or the amusements of the world. She appeared at a court, in the profligacy of which she did not participate; and amused herself in a society, whose frivolity she avoided."[37] The attached letters partly deal with the happy marriage, family life, politics, and her grief after her husband's death. Her successful combination of domesticity, sociability, and piousness make her appear as the virtuous opposite of Deffand, whose morals, Berry insinuates through the term "profligacy," were not always above reproach. Berry's achievement in this volume that combines biography and edition partly rests on her use of manuscripts.[38] According to her journals, Berry worked on Russell's biography and letters between 1814 and 1819 and made sure to read the original letters herself, which, at a time before the existence of scholarly archives, means that she had to ask for access to her source material. Since women were not meant to work as scholars and were often not well-connected in the world of learning, they rarely found themselves in a position to edit from original manuscripts. As during her work on the edition of Deffand's letters, Berry discussed her progress with her literary friends but did not divulge her name to the reading public.[39] In recognition of her achievement, the *Journals and Correspondence* proudly present several letters, one of them by the Duke of Bedford, praising the quality of her work. Baillie, also cited, applauded Lady Russell for being "an edifying example to the young woman of the day" (JCB 3: 176). Berry's final works were *A Comparative View of the Social Life of England and France, from the*

Restoration of Charles the Second to the French Revolution (1828) and *Social Life in England and France, from the French Revolution in 1789 to that of July 1830* (1831), which combine a mixture of political history, often in anecdotal form, reflections about past literary achievements and the present cultural as well as social life with a strong focus on the upper class. These were followed by a two-volume edition of most of her previous work in 1844.

* * *

Mary Berry is one of the women writers of the Romantic period who simply vanished. Elizabeth Eger's much acclaimed study *Bluestockings: Women of Reason from Enlightenment to Romanticism* maps out this phenomenon by looking at Elizabeth Montagu, Elizabeth Griffith, and Charlotte Lennox, who were acknowledged Shakespeare critics during their lifetimes but were literally written out of the critical canon in the nineteenth century and eventually fell into oblivion as cultural authorities on the most enduring national poet.[40] Montagu first published her work anonymously yet received so much encouragement that she eventually had her name printed on the title page. Griffith openly admitted her authorship, while Lennox chose to appear as the author of her novel *The Female Quixote*. In the case of Berry, one central reason for posthumous oblivion is the lack of openly acknowledged authorship. Her journals testify to a wide circle of friends and acquaintances who read and discussed her texts, recognized her achievements, praised her hard work, but as she was not seeking any acknowledgement before the eyes of the reading public, maybe because of the early failure of *Fashionable Friends* in 1802, she eventually disappeared from sight and survived as the icon of a brilliant, if somewhat anachronistic, Regency hostess. Berry was an author of the social sphere, between private and public, and therefore had little chance to survive as a literary brand name beyond her death.

Chapter 4

Holland House and Lady Holland

Apropos to Lady Holland, in addition to all her former insults upon the town, she has set up a huge *cat,* which is never permitted to be out of her sight, and to whose vagaries she demands unqualified submission from all her visitors. Rogers, it seems, has already sustained considerable injury in a personal affair with this animal. Brougham only keeps *him* or *her* at arm's length by snuff, and Luttrell has sent in a formal resignation of all further visits till this odious new favorite is dismissed from the Cabinet.[1]

Thomas Creevey's diary entry, dating from December 23, 1822, captures what contemporaries considered as the true spirit of Holland House in Kensington. Numerous guests described the playful interaction of this major literary and political salon as often bordering on the ridiculous, if not insane. It was frequented by members of an inner circle, *habitués* like the poet Samuel Rogers, occasionally visited by many others like the politician and reviewer Henry Brougham, and run by an imperious hostess who demanded absolute obedience, ordered her guests around, and aspired to rule not only over her own domestic space but also her husband's, Lord Holland's, political affairs ("Cabinet"). The imperious Lady Holland, whom her guests often described as imposing on them in any imaginable (and unspeakable) way, was the frequent subject of anecdotes. In Creevey's parodistic account, the cat's unprohibited physical assaults on the guests symbolize female sexuality and power, rendering Lady Holland a witch who cares more for her pet than for her guests.[2] Brougham's use of snuff appears as a last, desperate measure to keep masculinity intact on a physical as well as symbolic level. Masochistically, they all returned for more real and imagined humiliation at her hands. *The Creevey Papers* document that their author, the Whig politician Creevey, likewise Luttrell and Rogers, two of the three men he cast as victims of feline aggression, had continuous and in fact friendly contact with Lady and Lord Holland over the years. Like other regular visitors, Creevey relished gossip, thus contributing to the halo of communication that created the myth of Holland House, a powerful cultural and political center between 1797 and 1840, the most prestigious of the three salons described in this study. The following two chapters will describe Holland House and its place in Whig culture, introduce hostess and host, and explore some of their manifold "works": Lady Holland's travel writing, especially her *Spanish Journal,* the cult of Napoleon she shaped, and networks of impromptu poetry, (chapter 4); the Holland House circle and the *Edinburgh Review,* three male habitués (Samuel Rogers, Sydney Smith, and Thomas Moore), Lord Byron, and finally a female guest's, Caroline Lamb's, amorous entanglements, which motivated her novel *Glenarvon* (chapter 5). If chapter 4 focuses on the house, the hostess, and the host, chapter 5 explores the brilliant intellectual circle ruled by Lady Holland alias "Old Madagascar"—a nickname derived from Lamb's novel.[3] Both chapters will predominantly deal with the cultural side of this salon and the communication that happened at the intersections of the private and the public spheres, of the spoken and the printed word.

HOLLAND HOUSE AND WHIG CULTURE

None of the three sociable circles dealt with in this study was tied to one location only, yet of all three, Lady Holland's salon was the one that possessed most continuity in terms of place: a story of this salon is a story of Holland House. Its reputation was identified with this location, and the fact that its sociability declined and never regained its previous quality after the Third Lord Holland's demise in 1840 heightened its posthumous aura. Holland House, originally Cope Castle, was built around 1605 and inhabited by 1606,[4] leased to Henry Fox in 1746, and acquired by him (then already Baron Holland) in 1768.[5] In 1774, he was succeeded by his son Stephen, the Second Baron Holland, who died six months after his father, thus making the one-year-old Henry Richard the Third Baron Holland. Subsequently, the house was let, and in 1797, a few months after his wedding, Holland moved in. Holland House was already famous before it became one of London's cultural centers under the Third Baron Holland: Joseph Addison had lived there for three years; another famous inhabitant was Charles James Fox, the Whig politician, second son of the First Baron, brother to the Second, and uncle to the Third. It was a country house when first built and retained that quality even in the nineteenth century, when it was part of suburban London and surrounded by a small park.

Soon after their marriage in 1797, Lady and Lord Holland settled down in their residence, and, apart from time spent on journeys within Britain or abroad (e.g., to France and Spain, 1802–1805), lived there for most of their lives until Lord Holland died in 1840. According to the Dinner Books, some days saw up to 50 visitors. The central sociable events were the dinners, to which an invitation was needed. Although the couple and their entourage occasionally resided in town, they expected their friends to travel to Kensington at a time when the ritual of mutual visiting was an important part of urban sociability. Thomas Babington Macaulay described his first visit in a letter to his sister Hannah on May 30, 1831:

> Well, my dear, I have been to Holland House. I took a glass coach, and arrived, through a fine avenue of elms, at the great entrance towards seven o'clock. The house is delightful,—the very perfection of the old Elizabethan style,—a considerable number of very large and very comfortable rooms, rich with antique carving and gilding, but carpeted and furnished with all the skill of the best modern upholsterers. The library is a very long room,—as long, I should think, as the gallery at Rothley Temple,—with little cabinets for study branching out of it, warmly and snugly fitted up, and looking out on very beautiful grounds. The collection of books is not, like Lord Spencer's, curious; but it contains almost everything that one ever wished to read.[6]

Like most guests, he was invited for "a most excellent dinner," which took place "in a fine long room, the wainscot of which is rich with gilded coronets, roses, and portcullises."[7] Further visits followed. The dinners were so popular and so crowded that many guests complained about the lack of elbow space.[8] Some visitors came for the library, which held 13,000 volumes in 1816, like Robert Southey, who used it for his *Cid*.[9] The hostess and host of Holland House do not seem to have encouraged gambling inside the walls of their residence.

The great time of Holland House as a major cultural center spanned more than 40 years, which stood under varying political auspices. It was a focus for the Whigs, who had little or no political power until 1830 when Grey became Prime Minister; its dinners were meeting points for those who shared Whig political ideas but also for literati, reviewers, members of the *bon ton*, and artists. If, according to Wolf Lepenies, the cultural activities of a salon may be the result of "boredom" and frustration over lack of political power,[10] the cultural climax of Holland House may be linked to the political marginalization its host and its visitors felt so keenly—yet "boredom" was certainly not among the sensations recorded by the numerous guests. If after 1830, Holland House stood at the center of political decision-making and hosted dinners that constituted impromptu cabinet meetings, its cultural side grew less visible, yet when Melbourne became Prime Minister in 1834, its political influence declined once again. After Lord Holland's demise in 1840, Lady Holland, who died in 1845, occasionally entertained there, as did others after her, yet Holland House never again achieved its former splendor. In 1940, much of the building was destroyed in consequence of an air raid. Today, it is a youth hostel.

Approaching the history of sociability at Holland House involves sifting through a deluge of primary material. If, in the case of the Berrys, the unearthing of sources that often merely devote a few lines to the sisters can be slow and painstaking, a different situation arises when it comes to Holland House. A large number of texts focuses on this center of Whiggery, ranging from edited correspondences and memoirs by family members to journals kept by guests as varied as the poet Moore and the politician Creevey. The British Library owns the *Holland House Papers*,[11] among which, for example, one finds the famous Dinner Books, which record visits to Holland House. Another source are the letters by Caroline Fox, the Third Baron's sister, which give insight into sociable interaction, scandals, family matters, and questions of housekeeping. Some of Lord Holland's papers were edited posthumously by his son: the *Memoirs of the Whig Party* (1852) and the *Foreign Reminiscences* (1850).[12] Marie Liechtenstein's account, the two-volume work *Holland House* (1874), provides detailed descriptions of the entire house: the grounds, the rooms, interiors, art objects, paintings, and books.[13] In the twentieth century, the Sixth Earl of Ilchester, by then the owner of Holland House, began to dig into the history of this institution and made much primary material available in the shape of editions and book-length studies, for example, Lord Holland's *Further Memoirs of the Whig Party* (1905), *The Journal of Elizabeth, Lady Holland (1791–1811)* (1908), Lady Holland's *Spanish Journal* (1910), *The Journal of the Hon. Edward Fox (Afterwards Fourth and Last Lord Holland), 1818–1830* (1923), and the collection of letters *Lady Holland to Her Son, 1821–1845* (1946).

He also authored *The Home of the Hollands, 1605–1820* (1937) and *Chronicles of Holland House, 1820–1900* (1937), in fact a two-volume history of the house.[14] Derek Hudson's brief and entertaining book *Holland House in Kensington* (1967) is mainly based on Ilchester's work. Ilchester did not consider himself primarily a chronicler of the Whigs but of Holland House, its inhabitants, and its cultural and sociable life. If he occasionally omitted passages and corrected what he found, he nevertheless worked meticulously to produce reliable editions and survey studies, on which much current research is built. A more recent edition is Abraham D. Kriegel's *Holland House Diaries, 1831–1840* (1977).[15] Moreover, the salon interaction left traces in novels, newspaper articles, and travelogues written by relatives, guests, friends, or enemies.

The Whigs of the late eighteenth and early nineteenth centuries have a political as well as a cultural side to them. If much academic criticism by historians has focused on politics,[16] two studies by Leslie Mitchell, *Holland House* (1980) and *The Whig World, 1760–1837* (2005), concentrate on the cultural side of Holland House and Whiggery.[17] During most of the great time of Holland House, the Whigs were in opposition. Yet they contributed to the Ministry of All the Talents in 1806–1807, and the governments between 1830 and 1841 are called "Whig." Who were the Whigs? It is difficult to keep Whigs and Tories apart with any precision. Mitchell astutely argues that in the period in question, the Whigs were at best an unsuccessful and loosely structured political party, at worst merely an outmoded label.[18] Rather than talk about a Whig political program or a Whig party, he suggests a "Whig state of mind" and a "Whig lifestyle" as categories more suited to further explorations of Whig culture.[19] In the late eighteenth and early nineteenth centuries, the Whigs were a social elite, a coterie of aristocrats, owners of property, wealthy, and aware of their privileges, which they did not wish to share with everybody. The aura and the splendor of Holland House must have appeared daunting to a young man like Macaulay, then already an MP but without the advantage of an aristocratic background. Aristocrats who belonged to Whig circles lived in London and participated in the season.[20] Mitchell credits them with rather liberal views of marital fidelity and a very good culture of conversation. Among their major centers were Holland House and Devonshire House. Whigs moved in circles of acquaintances usually made up of people with similar backgrounds. For example: in February 1792, when Lady Webster (the later Lady Holland) visited Nice, she made the acquaintance of the Duchess of Devonshire (EHJ 1: 5), who henceforth was one of her contacts.

Urban, fashionable, and Francophile, Whigs cultivated their contacts with Paris and spoke and read French. A diary entry by Lady Holland in 1799, a comment on Voltaire, highlights the quality of this French connection. Although she was critical of Voltaire, she also feared that an "anti-conspiracy" against his ideas would lead to "the ruin of all taste, literature, and civil liberty" (EHJ 2: 16). In contrast to her, the more conservative British critics of the post-Revolutionary era emphasized the "moral disease of France."[21] Lady Holland's statement contains two key terms in the value system of Whiggery: "taste" and "liberty." "Taste" could mean a refined, expensive lifestyle only possible through inherited wealth. "Liberty" was a political key ideal, frequently called upon yet only vaguely defined, which found one outlet in the cult around Charles James Fox (the Third Baron's uncle) but also in the support for the abolition of slavery or the endorsement of political reform.[22] Lady Holland's interest in Voltaire went hand in hand with a marked disinterest in religion, which played hardly any role for the Whigs, who felt uneasy about the nineteenth century's growing religious revival.[23] Whig political positions and Parliamentary activities always had a cultural or a lifestyle side, which were reflected in the salons. As a Whig hostess of renown, Lady Holland managed to combine the political and the cultural sides of Whiggery while, for example, engaging in her acts of veneration for the tragic fallen hero Napoleon after 1815.

Lady and Lord Holland

Macaulay's letter also gives insight into the communicative styles cultivated by the hostess and host:

> She is certainly a woman of considerable talents and great literary acquirements. To me she was excessively gracious; yet there is a haughtiness in her courtesy which, even after all that I had heard of her, surprised me. The centurion did not keep his soldiers in better order than she keeps her guests. It is to one "Go," and he goeth; and to another "Do this," and it is done. "Ring the bell, Mr. Macaulay." "Lay down that screen, Lord Russell; you will spoil it." "Mr. Allen, take a candle and show Mr. Cradock the picture of Buonaparte." Lord Holland is, on the other hand, all kindness, simplicity, and vivacity. He talked very well both on politics and on literature. He asked me in a very friendly manner about my father's health, and begged to be remembered to him.[24]

The contrast between Lady Holland's imperious, masculine self-fashioning and Lord Holland's friendly and polite chats with his guests are remarked upon in many diaries and correspondences and were in fact among the major attractions of Holland House: those who could complain about the treatment they had suffered through this "centurion" belonged to an in-group. Joseph Jekyll sarcastically characterized host and hostess as "the different ends of a magnet, attractive one and repulsive the other."[25] Politicians and studies about political Whig contexts tend to consider Lord Holland as the central figure, while women, for example, the Countess of Granville and others, even if they did not like Lady Holland, nevertheless mention her more frequently. These two chapters will try to remedy this situation by focusing more on the hostess without, however, ignoring the host's activities.[26]

Elizabeth Vassall was probably born in London on March 25, 1771, the only child of Richard Vassall, and was to inherit several West Indian sugar plantations.[27] As her father and her maternal grandfather were in possession of a considerable fortune, Elizabeth must have grown up with the self-confidence of an heiress, and when her father died in 1795, she inherited an income of more than £ 10,000 a year.[28] In 1786, aged 15, Elizabeth Vassall was married to Sir Godfrey Webster, aged 38, with whom she had five children, three of whom reached adulthood. Between June 1791 and November 1796, she toured the continent (apart from a brief period spent in England), visited famous sites in France, Italy, and Germany, and went to see Prague and Dresden. Her journal complains about her unhappy marriage, about the "very cruel usage from the unequal and ofttimes frantic temper of the man to whom I had the calamity to be united," and therefore she avoided being "in a journey alone with him" (EHJ 1: 6). Instead, she socialized and made numerous friends, many of whom visited her later when she had become mistress of Holland House. In February 1794, she met Lord Holland, her junior by two years. At first she was not overwhelmed but liked him: "Ld. H. is not in the least handsome; he has, on the contrary, many personal defects, but his pleasingness of manner and liveliness of conversation get over them speedily" (117). In June she wrote: "He is exactly what all must like, esteem, and admire" (121). Her journal entries show that throughout the years 1794, 1795 (when Sir Godfrey finally returned to England without his wife), and 1796 they met regularly, yet it avoids detailing this relationship or the events that led to her pregnancy in 1796. They dined together, went out, met at social functions, or he visited and read to her. In March 1795, he composed a poem on her birthday (130). When she was pregnant, she returned to England, gave birth to a son in November 1796, and was divorced by Sir Godfrey, who could not possibly have fathered the boy. After her marriage had been annulled by an act of Parliament on July 4, 1797, she married Lord Holland on July 6. "My own individual happiness is so perfect, that I can scarcely figure to myself a blessing that I do not possess," she wrote into her journal (148). Still, getting rid of Sir Godfrey was forbiddingly expensive because she had to hand the bulk of her fortune over to him and was left with a mere £ 800 pounds per annum, while Sir Godfrey could enjoy £ 7,000 a year from her estate.[29] She was not granted access to her surviving children.[30] When Sir Godfrey shot himself in 1800, probably because of his losses at gambling, she had her fortune restored to her.

Shortly after their wedding, in autumn 1797, Lord and Lady Holland moved into Holland House. In her new position, Lady Holland was influential, yet as her divorce rendered her unacceptable in elite circles, she was not presented at court, and some aristocratic women seem to have ostracized her, that is, they excluded her from the ritual of mutual visiting, even if their husbands were guests at Holland House. As a reaction, Lady Holland established her own society within society, a veritable republic of letters intertwined with a political center (Creevey's "Cabinet"), and soon, her journal, previously devoted to descriptions of her journey, became an account of guests they entertained, from "Monk" Lewis to His Royal Highness, the Prince. The couple had met through sociable gatherings in Italy, and their marriage thrived on managing and extending sociability. Although host and hostess resided most of the time in Kensington, they occasionally went traveling, for example, to visit Scotland in the summer of 1798, or to tour Germany in 1800. A trip to Paris in 1802, during which they were presented to Napoleon, was continued further South to Spain, where they stayed until 1805.[31] More journeys followed, for example, another stay in Spain in 1808–1809. Lady Holland had five more children born in wedlock by her second husband, two of whom reached adulthood, which makes her a mother of 11, not unusual in her days. It also means that between 1789 and 1809, she was pregnant at least 11 times. Throughout the years, the intensity and the warmth of her relationship with her children varied. From the 1820s onward, her income declined to an extent that Lord Holland's sister Caroline ironically spoke of "poverty on 5,000 a year."[32] Decisive factors for the diminishing finances were the abolition of the slave trade in 1807 and the liberation of slaves in the West Indies in 1833. Eventually, her health deteriorated, and by the early 1830s, both she and her husband were chronically ill and severely restricted in their mobility yet continued to entertain.

The host of Holland House, Henry Richard Fox, born on November 21, 1773, became the Third Baron Holland at the age of one.[33] After his mother's death in 1778, he was sent to his uncle, Lord Upper Ossory, and in his own words later "went through Eton and Oxford without disgrace and without distinction."[34] He traveled to the continent for the first time in 1791, visited Paris, and encountered Talleyrand. In 1792 he visited Germany and Denmark, in 1793 Spain, and then Italy, where he met Lady Webster in Naples in early 1794. Although his *Memoirs of the Whig Party* provide some biographical information, they belong to the genre of the political chronicle and present him as a man of state while marginalizing private issues. Of his time in Naples, during which he met his future wife, he merely says: "I travelled with Lord Granville Leveson (afterwards Lord Granville) through Florence and Rome, to Naples, where the society, though agreeable, was chiefly English."[35] Lady Webster remains unmentioned.

Holland never held a major office yet was very influential, partly because he was Charles James Fox's nephew. After his maiden speech in Parliament in January 1798 he soon became an important Whig speaker; his protests, brief political statements, were posthumously published as *The Opinions of Lord Holland* (1841).[36] While he was interested in the post of Foreign Secretary, he was made Privy Councillor in August 1806, then in October Lord Privy Seal, but when the short-lived Ministry of All the Talents came to an end in March 1807, he no longer held an office and only returned officially in 1830. By then he was too old and unwell to take up a major post and became Chancellor of the Duchy of Lancaster. His continuous interest in foreign affairs led to his activities in Spain, his concern for Napoleon after 1815, and his support for the abolition of slavery (although much of his income derived from the West Indies). He died on October 22, 1840, followed five years later, on November 17, 1845, by his wife. Lord Holland authored a number of texts with a political focus, some of them edited posthumously, for example, the *Memoirs of the Whig Party* and *The Opinions of Lord Holland*. His fascination for Spain resulted in his *Life of Lope de Vega* (1806).[37] Spontaneously created poems, not great literary works yet part of the communicative network of Holland House, were a pastime he delighted in. Much of his writing was motivated by his political and sociable contexts.

If Lord Holland followed the usual educational path for a young male aristocrat of his time, Lady Holland bitterly complained about the lack of systematic teaching, not unusual for girls, which resulted in what she later called "so strange an education": "My principles were of my own finding, both religious and moral, for I never was instructed in abstract or practical religion, and as soon as I could think at all chance directed my studies" (158). Not only her moral education but also her writing skills were neglected: "Till lately I did not know the common principles of grammar, and still a boy of ten years old would outdo me." She resorted to self-education and "devoured books" (159). Her journals prove her fascination with historiography and travel writing. If she lacked the bluestockings' sometimes missionary zeal to educate and improve others as well as themselves, she was nevertheless well-read, as an entry in June 1798 shows:

> I have read since Xmas the D. of Marlbro's *Apology*, Burnet's *History*, ye *XIII. Satire of Juvenal*, Hearne's *Travels into N. America*, Smith on ye figure and complexion of ye human species, Bancroft on dying, some desultory chemistry, *Roderick Random*, *Lazarillo de Tormes*, Leti's *Life of Sixtus V.*, various German and French plays, novels, and trash, Cook's *Third Voyage*, Wolf's *Ceylon*, part of Ulloa's *Voyage*, and some papers in ye memoirs of ye Exeter Society. Frequent dippings into Bayle, Montaigne, La Fontaine, Ariosto. Read ye three first books of Tasso; Ld. Orford's works. (192)

This list is striking because it is so varied. To this she added an interest in Rousseau (EHJ 2: 101) and Voltaire, and, inspired by Napoleon's Egyptian campaign, turned to "Volney's account of Egypt and Syria" (EHJ 1: 199). Despite her obvious predilection for French and Spanish texts and topics, she moaned about "French literature of a desultory sort," which she considered as "pernicious to the mind" (206), presumably meaning novels, a genre she viewed in an ambivalent light: "During my confinement I have been reading among other things multitudes of novels, most of them sad trash, abounding with the general taste for spectres, hobgoblins, castles, etc., etc." (January 1800, EHJ 2: 41). Science was more interesting: she read about chemistry and attended chemical lectures in Turin, London, and Florence (EHJ 1: 7, 97, 130). Her visits to places like the Vatican, where she mused about the famous statue of Laocoon, well aware of its significance, or her quotation from Milton in a description of Tuscany (130) prove her cultural awareness and her erudition. Since Lady Holland—unlike Berry and Blessington—did not write to publish, she was less visible as an intellectual woman. Like Berry, she frequented the theater and the opera, yet often merely mentioned her visits without naming plays, maybe because she preferred the sociable to the literary and artistic pleasures. Only her *Spanish Journal* gives details of performances.

Avid reader, scandalous divorcée, mother of 11—yet in the public awareness, Lady Holland survived as the imperious hostess, the "centurion," "Old Madagascar," the witch with a cat. Why was she represented in such a negative light? Maybe the gossips around her simply expressed an anxiety that only a strong and influential woman could raise. Lady Jersey, one of the patronesses of Almack's, another powerful elite woman, seems to have elicited similar reactions.[38] It is impossible to establish in retrospect whether Lady Holland was a tyrant or the victim of slander. Certainly, the conversationalists at Holland House cultivated the art of verbal combat, in which she, like many of her guests, excelled, as chapter 5 will show. If the majority of those who wrote about her emphasize her acts of domination, others appreciated her skill in arranging sociable events, like the physician Henry Holland (no relative), who found her "remarkable" and retained positive memories of the iron hand that ruled this salon:

> Supreme in her own mansion and family, she exercised a singular and seemingly capricious tyranny even over guests of the highest rank and position. Capricious it seemed, but there was in reality *intention* in all she did; and this intention was the maintenance of power, which she gained and strenuously used, though not without discretion in fixing its limits. No one knew better when to change her mood... Her management of conversation at the dinner table—sometimes arbitrary and in rude arrest of others, sometimes courteously inviting the subject—furnished a study in itself. Every guest felt her presence, and generally more or less succumbed to it.[39]

He credits her with the strengths of a good hostess. Moreover, the question arises why Lady Holland should be saved from being decried as an eccentric. What is wrong with being cast as an imperious and manly woman, or an efficient organizer? Her critics implied that she lacked in demureness and modesty, virtues expected of young women out on the marriage market. Married upper-class women, however, could literally afford a self-fashioning that highlighted qualities like independence and power.

As Lady Holland did not lay any claims to literary fame, it was her personality that helped her to leave impressions and imprints. Of the following three achievements she was involved in, none conforms to the usual concept of "works": her unpublished journal with travel writing about Italy and Spain, her admiration for Napoleon, and coterie poetry of dubious textual status, partly unpublished and not even written by her. If one takes Susan Staves's *Literary History of Women's Writing* one step further, then the activities of *salonnières* like Lady Holland also qualify as a sort of minor genre, as culturally relevant "works." The remainder of chapter 4 will deal with these "works," which again stand at the intersections of the private and public spheres, of the spoken and the printed word.

Reflections on Traveling: Italy and Spain

Lady Holland's travel writing about Italy, France, Spain, and Germany was part of the journal she kept, not intended for publication and only printed in 1908 and 1910, that is, over 60 years after her death. Unlike Berry and Blessington, she did not write for a readership in search of cultural guidebooks. Although not authored as a travelogue, most of her journal up to her second marriage in 1797 deals with traveling, sociable encounters abroad, and sightseeing. In the words of Brian Dolan, one of the few who included her journal into his analysis of women's travel writing, she was yet another "lady of the grand tour."[40] If Italy was a space that also invited other English writers in the eighteenth century, her *Spanish Journal* is unique because until around 1800, Spain was terra incognita for most British travelers.

The journal of her extended journey to the continent, which lasted from 1791 to 1796, faithfully records her stations, among which were Paris, Lausanne, Nice, Turin, Milan, Tyrol, Munich, Dresden, Prague, Vienna, Venice, Naples, Rome, Florence, Parma, Schaffhausen, Frankfurt, Cologne, Brussels, and Valenciennes. She briefly returned to England in 1793 but soon left again to visit and revisit Ghent, Brussels, Stuttgart, Florence, Rome, Naples, Lucca, Genoa, Ferrara, Dresden, Berlin, and Hamburg. A fair amount of time was spent in various places in Italy, the region that interested her most. The young Lady Webster was a fast if not hectic traveler, who quickly passed through places and returned later to see more of them.[41] Her writing about Italy is more personal than the sketchy entries provided by the emotionally much more restrained Mary Berry. Lady Webster not only recorded the places she saw but also detailed her own emotional reactions. About a ride near Terni she wrote:

> We went to the foot of the mountain to look up at the cascade, a magnificent sight. We rode upon *somarelli* through a delicious grove of orange and lemon trees, and afterwards through a small wood filled with nightingales. I was enchanted: the melody of the birds, the tranquillity and perfume of the air, and the beauty of all the objects around, suspended for a moment my habitual discontent, and I felt even happy. We dined in a little wood of myrtle and ilex, but when we assembled together the illusion of happiness vanished. (EHJ 1: 42)

In this and in comparable passages, the beautiful landscape induces momentary peace and happiness. A view from the Convent of the Camaldoli near Naples effects a similar response: "I never in my life experienced the degree of happiness enjoyed: it was the gratification of mind and sense" (26). If the momentary, solitary basking in sights, smells, and sounds renders her happy, it is usually followed by an awakening, an awareness of other humans, of her own suffering, presumably in an allusion to her unhappy marriage.

In her entries on her Italian journey, she highlights sociability, even flirts, as central, often detailing sociable encounters, naming traveling companions, summarizing conversations. As she frequented the Countess of D'Albany's salon in Florence, she wrote of excursions and balls. In Nice, Naples, Florence, and other towns she met communities of Anglo-Italian travelers like herself, who toured the continent for longer periods of time and became near-residents in order to enjoy the warmer climate, yet without planning to become expatriates forever. Italy was also a space of flirts: "Ld. Digby fell in love with Ly. Bruce, who only coquets with him," and "Mr. A. fell in love with me and Mrs. W.; he was most in love with the one he last saw. We went to balls, and were very gay" (122, 129). Both entries date from 1794, the year when she made Lord Holland's acquaintance and subsequently grew closer to him through sociable encounters. Being married, upper-class, and very wealthy, Lady Webster could afford to be more outspoken about love matters than Mary Berry. She also voices awareness of sexual matters in one of the few passages critical of the Catholic church, which describes the acts of repentance of "many a debauched fair one in the comely attire of matronly humility" (125). Her journal indirectly serves to justify her own conduct, that is, her love affair with Holland. At the very beginning, she complains: "I was left *alone* at twenty years old in a foreign country without a relation or any real friend" (5), thereby excusing her emotional trajectory into another man's arms. Unlike Berry, she did not bask in the sensuous religious experience, nor did she seek any spiritual growth through religious assistance.[42]

If Lady Holland's journey to Italy was essentially a private matter, the involvement of Holland House in Spain was much more far-reaching, both politically and culturally.[43] While Italy was one favorite destination of the English elite, Spain, which had been a commercial and territorial rival to England from the sixteenth to the eighteenth centuries, was little known to English tourists. In 1808, the Spanish uprising against Napoleon saw England and Spain united on a political and military level in the Peninsular War, which lasted until

1814.[44] Subsequently, a refashioning of Spain, hitherto neglected, occurred.[45] A large body of anti-Spanish writing before 1800, the so-called "Black Legend,"[46] cast the Spanish as superstitious, servile, and hierarchic, yet with the onset of the Peninsular War, a more differentiated image of Spain began to appear in British Romantic writing, for example, in Canto I of Byron's *Childe Harold* (1812) and in *Don Juan* (1819–1824), or in Felicia Hemans's *England and Spain* (1808). Lord Holland had first visited Spain in 1793.[47] The journey of 1802–1805, which led him and his wife to Spain via Paris, was partly motivated by major building work in Holland House and partly by the need to take their son Charles to a healthier climate. The second journey, between 1808 and 1809, happened at the time of the military campaigns. As Lord Holland had not been appointed to any position by the British government but acted like an "unofficial ambassador,"[48] he was in effect interfering with another country's politics, likewise with British foreign affairs. To Holland the Whig, it was all-important that the Spanish resistance against Napoleon could be interpreted as a popular movement and therefore in need of logistic support, which he felt called upon to provide.[49] While he and his wife gathered the Spanish dignitaries around them for sociable activities such as dinners, his influence grew: for example, he was asked to act as a go-between for bank loans.[50] In 1809, he and John Allen drafted a constitution, which they sent to Spain. Such activities were meant to be helpful but also expressed a huge amount of condescension, "patronage verging on a cultural imperialism," as Mitchell stated.[51]

If historians like Mitchell focus on the political and military side of Lord Holland's Spanish involvement, Lady Holland's *Spanish Journal* is often overlooked or merely considered an auxiliary source. As it remained unpublished until the beginning of the twentieth century, it had no power to move the Spanish cause but reflects her journey and Whig attitudes in a wider sense. Like the eighteenth-century letter, it stands at the intersection between public and private, between print and manuscript culture.[52] Despite its belated publication, it holds a firm position in the body of texts published about Spain in the 1810s and 1820s. If Lady Holland's reflections about Italy show her as following in earlier travelers' footsteps, her writings about Spain could draw on far fewer models. The English popular imagination had thrived on the uncivilized horrors of Matthew Lewis's Gothic novel *The Monk* (1796), which transports an image of Spain as violent and hierarchic, firmly in the grip of a church that is a safe haven only for those who wish to abuse their power. Lady Holland's diary about Spain documents genuine interest in another culture and its people. As both she and her husband were fluent in Spanish, they gained firsthand experience of a country with which most British were unacquainted. If Lady Holland is more concerned with culture and the people during her first journey (1802–1805), the journal of her second journey (1808–1809) retells the military and political turmoil during which it took place.

As liberty was a key ideal to any Whig leader, her reflections on women's subjugation, religion—seen as superstition—and outmoded court ceremonies reeking of medieval hierarchies are among the most remarkable passages of the entire *Spanish Journal*. While her fashion ideal was that of the woman "dressed to the utmost of her taste" (SJ 61), she criticized the strict dress codes ruling women's appearance in Spain: it was "not only unpleasant but positively unsafe for a woman to appear without the *basquiña* and *mantilla*" (19). The blame for this, she felt, lay with the men and the church: "I walked about and experienced what I could never have believed otherwise, the extreme derision and scorn with which a woman is treated who does not conform to the Spanish mode of dressing"(5), and: "Just as I was entering the inner door of the church *del Colegio,* a rough ill-tempered priest stopped and turned me back because I had not a thick *mantilla* of cloth wrapped round my body" (35). Here, Lady Holland cultivates her individual female version of liberty, the liberty to dress as one pleases, to present oneself as sexually attractive through clothing. Most churches are deemed hideous, and worship, especially if tied to relics, appears as superstition: "Churches heavily laden with golden ornaments, bad taste, outside mean, and without any pretentions even to architecture" (5). In Barcelona, she is amused about a popular legend concerning a saint's preserved body, which, when newly clad, actually stood up to facilitate the process of dressing (10). The theatricality of religion becomes most noted in a puppet show in Lent:

> In the evening not having yet seen the Lent diversions of the Passion, Birth of Christ, Bible histories, &c., we went to a representation of the first. It was well performed by tolerably large sized puppets; the decorations were good and the voices well managed; before the stage cords hung perpendicularly to confound the sight with those by which the puppets were suspended. Several women cried, and demonstrated by sighs and groans how much they were affected by the representation. The whole audience appeared to feel especially for the sorrows of the *Virgen.* (33)

The Passion is a spectacle for the masses but does not offer any spiritual guidance or consolation. If the puppet show is entertaining, it is nevertheless also a metaphor for the status of religion and the church in Spain: the masses identify with well-presented and popularized emotions without taking note of the strings that are being pulled. In a similarly critical vein, the journal scrutinizes the ceremonies of the Spanish court, renowned for its inflexible hierarchies:

> King and Q., and even the little *Infantes*, served with drink by the gentlemen-in-waiting on their knees. Old custom retained of tasting what the King is to drink and eat. When the cup is carried through the apartments or corridors of the palace, every one by whom it passes must take off his hat. (156)

The passage highlights the spectacular quality of Spanish court etiquette as well as its utter impracticability. The method Lady Holland follows is not the explicit voicing of criticism; instead, she tells a series of anecdotes, thus drawing attention to what she considers as absurdities. Another story concerns an officer who had dared to carry a parasol and was repeatedly denied promotion over the next 30 years (167). Her representation of hierarchies, which are nonsensical, oppressive, and in need of amelioration, corresponds to Lord Holland's view, who felt that he had been called upon to initiate and support future reforms.

Lady Holland, who enthused about the experience of reading *Don Quixote* in the original (31), sketched a far more positive image of Spain when writing about its literature and culture. She was also full of praise for libraries she had visited. If her descriptions of theater in London and during her previous journeys rarely go into details about plays and playwrights, let alone interiors and acting styles, her observations on Spanish theater are much more specific. She attended Spanish plays, for example, by Calderon (42), but also translations, both in terms of language and of culture. As the kiss, central to a French play, was forbidden on the Spanish stage, "love is demonstrated by the lady lousing the lover" (27), she observed, thus comically endowing erotic intimacy with a tinge of the absurd. Or, in a Spanish version of Shakespeare, Lady Macbeth was given a six-year-old son—not to care for but to murder in bed, "enabling her to run upon the stage with bloody hands" (119). When staying in Madrid in October 1803, she invited Mouravieff, a minister from Russia, who had translated Sheridan's *School for Scandal* for the private theater of Catherine II (103). In December of that year, she attended a performance at a private theater: "Went to a private play at the Marqués de Peñafiel's. The *dramatis personae* consisted of the persons most distinguished for their birth and youthful brilliancy"; Belloy's *Gabrielle de Vergy* was performed (127). A more negative experience was a bullfight

(63-66), which she did not enjoy because of the brutality inflicted on the animals; it was the butchering of the horses that annoyed her most. If, on the one hand, Lady Holland was highly critical of the status accorded to women, of outmoded hierarchies, and of popular forms of religious worship, she enjoyed, on the other hand, the spectatorial side of contemporary Spanish culture, the sociable encounters, and the overall gain of knowledge. Among the topics on which she reflected in her journal are architecture, landscape, agricultural methods, and the local economy. Problems in finding accommodation loom large; visitors to her Anglo-Iberian dinners are proudly named. The entries she made during her second journey to Spain abound with military news about troop strength, vessels, supplies, and success as well as failure in battles and skirmishes.

Since her journal was not published during her lifetime, it could not influence the English image of Spain directly in the way *Childe Harold* did. However, it would be wrong to assume that her unprinted ideas remained without impact because her salon provided the communicative framework for further exchange about Spanish culture and politics. Lord Holland, one of the first British Hispanists, published his *Life of Lope de Vega* in 1806 and cultivated his contacts with major Spanish intellectuals such as Gaspar Melchor de Jovellanos; Spanish visitors often came to Holland House.[53] Lady Holland's diary mentions a dinner of Spanish deputies at Holland House on August 16, 1808, shortly before their second journey to Spain (EHJ 2: 245-246). In 1810, José María Blanco White, a priest of Irish descent, fled from Spain and was welcomed in Holland House, where he soon played an important role as an authority on Spanish cultural and political issues[54] and from where he edited his own journal, *El Espagnol*, between 1810 and 1814, which informed the English about Spain and advised the Spanish on future developments in their own country. As Holland himself had a hand in editorial matters, the Spanish-language journal, read both in Britain and Spain, was yet another attempt at shaping foreign policy from Holland House. Colburn's *New Monthly Magazine* was reorganized in 1820-1821 and, again under the influence of Holland, began to publish writing on Spain, for example, Blanco White's *Letters from Spain by Don Leucadio Doblado* and other contributions on Spanish historical and cultural themes. The library of Holland House, renowned for its collection of Spanish books and manuscripts, attracted readers, writers of poetry and fiction, as well as scholars. When the American academic and Hispanist George Ticknor stayed in London in 1819, he frequented Holland House and praised Lord Holland for being "a good scholar."[55] Romantic authors who treated Spain sooner or later encountered the Holland House circle, its positions, and maybe its books. If Southey was able to use the Holland House library for his research, Mary Shelley was given the cold shoulder although Thomas Moore interfered on her behalf.[56] Byron, who chose the Iberian peninsula as the setting for Canto I of *Childe Harold,* adhered to Whig principles in his praise of liberty, yet without aligning himself too much with the exact positions and reform ideas of Holland House. One early version of Canto I contains some ironic lines about Lord Holland's Spanish involvement and his wife's divorce and remarriage, which the poet later removed, presumably because he began to move in Whig circles:

> Yet here of Vulpes mention may be made
> Who for the Junta modelled sapient laws,
> Taught them to govern ere they were obeyed—
> Certes fit teacher to command, because
> His soul Socratic no Xantippe awes,
> Blest with a dame in Virtue's bosom nurst,
> With her let silent admiration pause!
> True to her second husband and her first
> On such unshaken fame let Satire do its worst.[57]

Byron wrote the first two cantos of *Childe Harold* before he started to frequent Holland House. Planning his political career, he was well aware of its centrality and did not wish to offend anyone, especially after the episode involving his satire *English Bards and Scotch Reviewers.*[58]

No doubt, Holland House played a prominent role in mediating an alluring image of Spanish culture to British readers after a long period of negative stereotyping. What is less known is that Lady Holland also took very practical steps. That she not only cared for a better understanding of a foreign culture but also demonstrated awareness of economic questions is obvious in her journal. Her reflections on the local economy, especially her praise for the quality of the fine wool on the Iberian peninsula (SJ 37, 83, 362), testify to her interest in the production of textiles, which eventually led to the acquisition of a flock of Merino sheep in Spain, which Lord and Lady Holland imported to Kensington.[59]

Politics: Enthusiasm for Napoleon

If the creation of awareness for Spain's culture and politics is one of the major achievements of Holland House, the cult of Napoleon, manifest after 1815, is yet another, although it took place on a smaller scale. The worship of Napoleon was by no means isolated from the veneration for Charles James Fox, whose statue stood in the entrance area of Holland House, where he had the status of a "household deity."[60] Other portraits of Fox were placed around the house and ensured that the visitors were continuously aware of the political environment in which they were moving. Holland House considered itself as a kind of forum for Fox's ideas, during his life and after his death. In this, Lord and Lady Holland were not alone: Fox clubs were formed, Fox dinners held, and children in Whig families were named after him. The Third Baron Holland, Fox's nephew, made it his task to defend his uncle, to spread his political creeds, and to share his friends as well as his foes. The Whigs' need for an icon was linked to the frequently evoked catchword "liberty," and Fox was credited with having spent his entire life fighting for it.[61] As the Whigs were out of power with the brief exception of the Ministry of All the Talents, many of Fox's ideals remained without application. Despite the prevailing fear of radicalism in the years during and after the French Revolution, Holland House and the Foxites made a point of linking their ideal of liberty to a criticism of the executive, as Mitchell points out,[62] that is, in a wider sense, the power of the state.

As at least some of the Whigs' self-fashioning as a political opposition centered on Fox as the hero-martyr, it is striking that the cult around Napoleon, which was by no means confined to Holland House, began with his final defeat in 1815. What made him so attractive to Holland House? Particularly Lady Holland was renowned for a veneration that lasted beyond the great man's death: "Napoleon's voice was inimitable: so melodious that no heart could resist," she disclosed by letter to her son Henry Edward in 1826.[63] Not all her contemporaries shared her quasi-erotic admiration. On May 5, 1822, the first anniversary of Napoleon's death, the poet Thomas Moore paid a visit: "Irving walked about with me—called together at Lady Blesinton's, who is growing very absurd—'I have felt very melancholy & ill all this day,' she said—'Why is that?' I asked—'Don't you know?'—No—'It is the anniversary of my poor Napoleon's death'—" (TMJ 2: 560).[64] Blessington, not recognized by major hostesses like Lady Holland, was taking revenge by parodying her rival's overflowing emotions. Since Moore belonged to the Holland House set, he was a suitable target for a joke only the initiated could appreciate.

If eighteenth-century English society was essentially Francophile, matters changed with the bloodshed of the Revolution and Napoleon's military actions. British fears that the French Revolutionary spark would ignite in Britain led to a popular reassessment of Anglo-French relations, which resulted, for example, in an anti-Voltairism cultivated especially among the middle classes.[65] As Whig families were Francophiles and stood, merely through their devotion to all things French, in an eighteenth-century tradition, any nineteenth-century critique of France and French manners could be understood as a critique of the great aristocratic Whig families and their world view. Although the Whigs resented the bloodshed of the French Revolution, they were also critical of the autocratic pre-Revolutionary government.[66] The pre-1815 Whig views on Napoleon varied. Many admired his reforms yet feared him as a powerbroker and warmonger.[67] Still, even during his wars, he was credited with having brought the idea of liberty to remote parts of Europe. If many considered Napoleon's complete removal from power as a must, Holland House took a more positive view of him and of his influence on France and Europe as a whole, especially after 1815 when his teeth had been taken out. The ties of Holland House with France went back much further. Both Lady Webster and Lord Holland had visited Paris in 1791, independent of one another; both had taken an interest in the changes the Revolution had effected. They had always entertained French guests, but after the peace with France in 1802 more French names appeared in the Dinner Books.[68] During a visit to Paris in 1802, the current and the future Whig deities met. Charles James Fox, who was traveling with Lord and Lady Holland to collect material for his *History of the Reign of James II*, was presented to Napoleon, who gave a speech pointing out that Fox "was the greatest man of one of the greatest countries" and praised him fervently for his beneficial effect on peace, justice, and humanity (EHJ 2: 150).[69] Lord Holland also had occasion to speak to him, and Lady Holland was presented to the First Consul a few days later.[70] The Hollands' unfettered enthusiasm for the martyr Napoleon, however, seems to have set in fairly late, around the time when his enforced stay on St. Helena began. Now that the former monster was arrested, a popular cult around the fallen hero began, which was by no means restricted to Kensington.[71]

In Holland House, the support for the tragic Napoleon took various forms. In 1816, Lord Holland, for example, wrote a protest against Napoleon's exile into the Lords' Journal, reprinted in *The Opinions of Lord Holland,* in which he complained about the "repugnant" treaties enforcing action against "a foreign and captive Chief."[72] Here as elsewhere, his openly avowed pro-Napoleonic stance alienated the Duke of Wellington as well as the Prince Regent.[73] Help was also made available materially: clothing, fine linen, wine, and Eau de Cologne, likewise reading matter, were sent by Lady Holland. Keppel estimates that by the time of his death in 1821, she had presented Napoleon with 475 books. The purchase and delivery of a newly invented machine for the production of ice, however, failed.[74] While Lady Holland's pro-Napoleonic activities achieved notoriety, she also drew members of his family into her circle through epistolary exchange and invitations to dinner. In 1816, for example, she began a correspondence with Lucien Buonaparte. Moreover, Holland House helped to spread information about the captive Napoleon through the *Edinburgh Review*.[75] The most visible sign of the veneration of Napoleon was Canova's bust in the Dutch garden, which carried an inscription by Homer.[76]

When Napoleon died, he bequeathed a snuffbox to Lady Holland, which Count Bertrand and General Montholon delivered to her four months later in full uniform,[77] thus displaying the insignia of a diplomatic mission. A locket with his hair, a gold ring, and a sock he had worn in the hour of his death followed.[78] Especially the snuffbox, today in the British Museum, highlights the intersection between politics and culture, between orality and writing, because its symbolic value created a sequence of poems. Moore recounted the following dinner conversation in his diary on July 30, 1821, while he was staying in Paris:

> Lady H. showed me some verses Lord Holland had written to her in English & Latin upon the subject of Napoleon's gift—some lines of Lord John's, too—she said *I* must do something of the same kind, and wished she could have a few lines from Lord Byron too to add to her triumph—Lord Holland's verses chiefly turn upon the circumstance of the box having been originally given to Napoleon by the Pope for his clemency in sparing Rome. (TMJ 2: 473)[79]

Moore, one of the habitués of Holland House, who enjoyed parodying gestures of exaggerated demureness, began to compose the next morning before even leaving his bed. On August 8, he wrote down his poem, presumably "To Lady Holland, on Napoleon's Legacy of a Snuff-Box," which begins with the words "Gift of the Hero, on his dying day," emphasizing Napoleon's loneliness and celebrating her acts of kindness.[80] The gift, however, was not undisputed: A few months later, in November 1821, the Earl of Carlisle published a poem of eight stanzas in *The Gentleman's Magazine*, "To Lady Holland, on the Legacy of a Snuff-Box, Left to Her by Buonaparte," asking her to refuse the gift:

> Lady, reject the gift! 'tis tinged with gore!
> Those crimson spots a dreadful tale relate:
> It has been grasp'd by an infernal Power:
> And by that hand which seal'd young Enghien's fate.[81]

The box, he set out to explain, had "magic power to raise/Spectres of myriads slain" in Russia and Egypt and therefore should be unceremoniously thrown into the ocean. Byron, in turn, replied with a four-line poem to Carlisle and admonished Lady Holland to accept the gift.[82] Further anonymous verse followed. This episode shows how conversations and literary production were flowing into one another to create an open-ended sequence of poetry, which documents the veneration for the fallen hero, to which Lady Holland contributed so avidly.

Spontaneous Versification

Although numerous published poets—famous like Byron, forgotten like Luttrell—frequented Holland House, host, hostess, and guests were occasionally involved in the impromptu production and rendering of the kind of poetry glorifying Napoleon's relics. If our notions of original genius demand that the difference between author and non-author/audience is clearly marked, likewise that between "major" work and "minor" ephemeral text, or between writing and conversation, the concept of "coterie" poetry deviates from this norm because it is tied to notions of community and communication.[83] No coterie poet writes in isolation. If salon interaction is a continuous performance, then the communal processes of conversation and production are as important as individual authorship and cannot be separated from it. Some texts such coteries create are ephemeral, "minor," poems of the kind that Horace Walpole, the Berry sisters, and their Twickenham neighbors had crafted. The question arises whether such poems are "works" in our sense. As they are often improvised and not always committed to paper, a lot of them are irretrievably lost. It is unknown how many such texts, which came to life in the salon, ever acquired an afterlife in print and how faithful the recordings are, which survive not necessarily through the author's own effort but maybe in another person's documentation, for example, a diary. Such production takes the shape of an open-ended sequence of poems, or an expanding network of conversations, of which the poems constitute only one part. The following parody of Rousseau exemplifies the status of such impromptu poetry in the salon. Lady Holland's *Journal* mentions that when one evening in 1800, Etienne Dumont read the description of the Isle de St. Pierre from Jean Jacques Rousseau's *Rêveries du promeneur solitaire* at Holland House, Lord Holland, who disliked the French philosopher, penned down a doggerel:

> Rousseau was so charmed in his island St. Pierre
> With walking and rowing about;
> I agree with heartily when he was there
> 'Twas a pity he ever came out. (EHJ 2: 101)

If Rousseau's autobiographical *Rêveries* is a great canonical text, Lord Holland's reply is not. Two criteria for a poem are fulfilled, the use of rhyme and meter; otherwise, from an aesthetic viewpoint, it is negligible. Unfortunately, Lady Holland's *Journal* omits all details of the performance and the response this spontaneous poetic outburst encountered—most likely laughter because it parodies Rousseau's intense emotional experience of nature. What was the function of this and other such poems, some of which were noted down in Lady Holland's diary and thus found at least a belated way into print? As they constituted part of an ongoing communication, an intellectual game, the performance aspect was far more important than the ephemeral text itself. If some exchanges of poetry like the versification surrounding the snuffbox are well documented, in other cases, our imagination must substitute the missing applause, criticism, or the spontaneous parody of the parody. Such poetic endeavors are hard to trace: Some poems written or recited in the context of Holland House are reprinted in Ilchester's editions and studies, or they appear in letters by guests like Macaulay, in journals like Moore's, in manuscripts, or they are irretrievably lost. Or the poems could be outside: In the Dutch garden of Holland House, Macaulay found a spot called "Rogers's seat," adorned with poetic inscriptions by Lord Holland and Luttrell.[84] Holland's brief poem runs: "Here Rogers sat, and here forever dwell/With me, those Pleasures that he sings so well. Vll. Hd. 1818," to which Luttrell replied in a poem of 24 lines, playfully regretting his own inferior skill as a poet. Liechtenstein's chapter on the grounds cites several poems and shows that even the garden constituted part of the network of coterie poetry and social interaction. Occasionally, an impromptu poem was deemed important enough to be passed on to posterity. Shortly before his death, Holland wrote these lines:

> Nephew of Fox, and friend of Grey,—
> Enough my meed of fame
> If those who deign'd to observe me say
> I injured neither name.[85]

Ilchester states that the poem circulated and that he had seen a printed sheet with a slightly different version as well as parodies and replies. One of the central textual features of such impromptu poetry is that the text never comes to an end. This type of coterie poetry is not a series of closed and finished texts but an open sequence because responses, comic or serious, are always possible. If one considers that Holland House was a major cultural center for literati, then the fragmentary and spontaneous poetic mocking stands in an odd contrast to the official culture that was made, debated, and reviewed there.

The host and hostess of Holland House certainly lived with a strong awareness of poetry. Like other young aristocrats, Lord Holland had been taught to produce rhyme and verse. After the Countess of Ossory had sent Walpole some poetry by the adolescent Lord Holland, then 16 years old, Walpole replied on December 30, 1789: "I am extremely pleased with his variety of metres, and if I may decide, prefer his heroics: if I may criticize, his trochaics are not always perfect, now and then wanting a syllable" (WL 34: 91). Poetry writing served to display knowledge of classical meter, was a marker of a gentleman's education, a display of his learning and wit. If an improvising poet and the audience both had a classical education, then the art of casting spontaneous emotions into meter and rhyme demonstrated shared cultural awareness. Although Lady Holland complained about her lack of structured education, she had acquired a profuse knowledge of poetry. During her trip to Germany in 1800, she visited the poet Klopstock in Hamburg: "His *Messiah* is his greatest work. He talked to us of English literature, especially of Pope's Homer" (EHJ 2: 111). His work she described as being "in the sublime, incomprehensible style."

Much of the coterie poetry of Holland House is anything but sublime and mocks poetic conventions. When Pierrot, Lady Holland's spaniel, died in 1799, Lord Holland dashed off an impromptu poetic obituary:

> Pierrot of race, of form, of manners rare,
> Envied alike in life and death lies here.
> Living he proved the favourite of the fair,
> And dying drew from beauty's eye a tear. (19)

The dog is endowed with a courtier's distinctive features ("manners rare," "favourite") and envied for his closeness to his ruler, Lady Holland, whose reaction—she apparently cried—is poetically exaggerated ("drew...a tear"). Her *Journal* mentions other poetic parodies, for example, Canning's recital of his own comic imitation of Lewis's "Alonzo the Brave," a ballad from *The Monk* (EHJ 1: 239). This comic imitation, in which Lewis's "A Warrior so bold, and a Virgin so bright"[86] becomes "A Parson so grave and a Baron so bold," alludes to the host (the Third Baron Holland) and is again part of an ongoing conversation, particularly as Lewis himself was a frequent guest. Such parodies were not restricted to the genre of poetry. A letter by Macaulay, written shortly after his first visit to Holland House, contains a 14-line untitled dramatic sketch of his arrival and initial welcome through two footmen:

> *Second Footman.*—And art thou come to breakfast with
> our Lord?
> *Macaulay.*—I am: for so his hospitable will,
> And hers—the peerless dame ye serve—hath bade.
> *First Footman.*—Ascend the stair, and thou above shalt find,
> On snow-white linen spread, the luscious meal.[87]

"Take it dramatically in the German style," Macaulay advised his sister, to whom the letter was addressed, while caricaturing the grandeur of Holland House through the choice of words like "ascend," "peerless," or the obsolete "hath."[88] One of the key characteristics of these improvised poetic reactions in the context of Holland House is that they all have a marked tendency toward parody. Although playfulness and performance were important to all three salons described here, the Holland House circle seems to have had more than the usual share of mocking and mimicking.

Chapter 5

The Holland House Set

"Life is a difficult thing in the country, I assure you, and it requires a good deal of forethought to steer the ship when you live twelve miles from a lemon."[1] The famous witticism by Sydney Smith links life in the countryside—particularly undesirable to a Whig—to the lack of a luxury good available only in town. Smith had been one of the *habitués* of Holland House before he was forced to move to Foston-le-Clay in Yorkshire, where he held the position of rector. This chapter attempts to portray the Holland House set, the group of individuals who frequented this location over a time-span of more than 40 years, and also suggests methods of research. As a cultural hothouse of this size attracted thousands of visitors over the years, the question arises how one can represent the set of people who belonged to this salon, to its inner and outer circles. The materials considered here are in particular biographical data, gossip, and select publications involving the visitors.

Salon research cannot do without biographies. If most conversations are irretrievably lost or survive only in the form of condensed diary entries, have left traces in poems, travelogues, and newspaper articles, salon guests, in contrast, can be tracked down more easily, and their biographies can be established. Yet a mere listing of names cannot suffice. The most comprehensive older study, Lloyd Sanders's *The Holland House Circle* (1908), solves this problem by grouping the visitors ("Some Men of Letters," "Authors and Wits," "Men of Science"),[2] providing biographical sketches of varying length depending on the guests' importance, and thereby producing a veritable *Who's Who* of the British Whigs in the Regency period, although, unfortunately, marginalizing female guests. Moreover, practically all books that deal with Holland House—by Sanders, Ilchester, Hudson, and Mitchell—use gossipy anecdotes, which not only add flesh to the skeletons of the biographies but also highlight interaction: power games, insider jokes, and the making of cult figures. Patricia Meyer Spacks has pointed out that among the attractions of gossip are "an aesthetic of surfaces" and a delight in "specific personal particulars."[3] It provides those who spread it with a sense of power[4] and is a reaction against various kinds of marginalization. As tattling, bad-mouthing, and idle talk were essential to the unique type of verbal combat cultivated at Holland House, a consideration of this conversation, which departs from the polite model associated with the salon, is necessary. If interaction is to be mapped out, publications involving several guests at once can illuminate sociable activities: a number of visitors to Holland House participated in the collaborative efforts that led to the making of the *Edinburgh Review* and in turn received patronage of various kinds. A completely different print product that concerned the hostess and her friends is Caroline Lamb's scandalous novel *Glenarvon*, a piece of extended and fantastic gossip, which provided Lady Holland's famous nickname "Old Madagascar." This chapter will deal with types of guests and rites, explain their involvement with the *Edinburgh Review*, then focus on several members of the inner circle (Samuel Rogers, Sydney Smith, and Thomas Moore), map out the interaction of Holland House with Byron, and finally examine the storms created by Caroline Lamb.

THE CIRCLE AND ITS ORACLE: THE *EDINBURGH REVIEW*

Although not situated in the fashionable center of London, Holland House was a much-frequented location, had many regular guests, an inner and an outer circle, key rituals, and its own idiolect. On April 12, 1799, Lady Holland noted that 50 visitors came in the course of one day (EHJ 1: 236). Among the most important sources for the comings and goings of people are the Dinner Books, which commenced in 1799 and were kept by John Allen after 1806,[5] and letters as well as journals by family members and guests. The frequency of visits varied: Holland House knew occasional visitors, who dropped by every now and then, maybe over a time span of several years, like Byron, who first visited in 1812, left London in 1816, yet wrote the snuffbox poem in reaction to the interaction in the Holland House circle although he was already in Italy. Since this salon was geographically on the periphery, guests sometimes stayed overnight. In this respect, Holland

House differed from the Berrys' and Blessington's circles. At the occasion of his first visit to Holland House, Thomas Macaulay was asked "to dine and take a bed" yet declined.[6] Holland House had its own internal hierarchy, in which places were awarded according to merit. Among the highest-ranking were a number of frequent guests, habitués like Sydney Smith, or semi-residents like Thomas Moore, who also belonged to the inner circle. Another key figure was Dr. John Allen, a Scotsman, who had been recommended by Smith, went to Spain with the Hollands from 1802 to 1805, and after his return began to live at Holland House, where he acted as a sort of secretary-cum-librarian, kept the Dinner Books, helped Lord Holland write his speeches, contributed to the *Edinburgh Review,* and, according to Macaulay, lent himself to being treated like a "negro slave" and a "footman."[7] When Charles Greville joked about the "inmates" of Holland House in 1832,[8] he meant those who belonged to the inner circle, frequently stayed overnight, knew one another by nicknames, and took delight in exchanging endless anecdotes about abusive treatment received at the hands of "Old Madagascar." This Whig custom of giving nicknames to one another, a practice that held up a linguistic boundary between insiders and outsiders,[9] is documented in *The Creevey Papers,* which contain a three-page list of them (e.g., "Pie and Thimble" for Lord John Russell, "Cupid" for the Viscount Palmerston, "Little Vic" for Queen Victoria, and "Madagascar" for Lady Holland).[10]

The activities visitors primarily engaged in were politics, writing, publishing, and traveling. If Blessington predominantly attracted writers and editors in the 1830s and 1840s, Holland House was a political as well as a literary salon. During some periods—the involvement with Spain, the Ministry of All the Talents, Grey's premiership—politics dominated. The earlier years saw many of Charles James Fox's political allies, for example, Thomas Erskine and Richard Brinsley Sheridan, in Holland House; in some years guests involved with Spanish political and military affairs arrived; between 1830 and 1834, some dinners had the character of impromptu cabinet meetings. Although most politicians who flocked to Holland House were understandably Whigs, the Tories visited, too: In 1806, Sir Walter Scott dined at Holland House; in 1822, Lord Eldon came. In 1800, the Dissenter Benjamin Hobhouse dined there, to whose intellectual background the hostess devoted a detailed journal entry.[11] The majority of guests, however, had Whig backgrounds. Although Holland House did not aim to attract primarily artists, the sculptor Richard Westmacott, an occasional guest, whose bronze statue of Fox graces Bloomsbury Square, remarked that "there was no House at which Artists were received with more respect."[12] Writers came: Moore, who had already made himself a name, Lord Byron, little known when he first visited in February 1812 a few weeks before the publication of *Childe Harold,* or Henry Luttrell, the author of *Advice to Julia,* a verse satire on Regency London, which appeared in 1820, went into several editions, and is forgotten today. For his initial visit, Byron came as a politician, not as a poet. Men of science called: the German geographer and explorer Alexander von Humboldt, or Count Rumford, an American who had been in the service of the Bavarian Elector and then helped to set up the Royal Institution in Albemarle Street.[13]

Although many visitors belonged to the upper echelon of society, members of the middle classes could gain entry as well, like Thomas Macaulay or Charles Dickens. For an aspiring author, it was necessary to be lionized in salons, which could be daunting if social prejudice prevailed. Benjamin Haydon's diary tells an anecdote about Dickens's planned journey to America, of which he informed Lady Holland: "She hated the Americans, and did not want Dickens to go. She said, 'Why cannot you go down to Bristol & see some of the third or fourth class people, & they'll do just as well!'"[14] Far fewer women than men figure in the diaries and academic studies about the Holland House set. Because of Lady Webster's scandalous divorce, many wives did not want to visit, especially in the early years, yet Holland House was by no means an all-male salon. As most chroniclers of Holland House were men, they may not have considered women as important guests, which would explain their lack of visibility. The letters by the Countess of Granville, for example, mention more female acquaintances of Lady Holland than other comparable collections by men. Among the women who frequented Holland House was Lady Bessborough, the sister of the Duchess of Devonshire, who belonged to an earlier generation of great hostesses and also visited herself occasionally; Lady Bessborough's daughter, Caroline Lamb, was another guest. Germaine de Staël dined at Kensington several times. Before she followed an invitation on December 8, 1813, she contacted Byron, who commented: "This morning, a very pretty billet from the Staël about meeting her at Ld. H's to-morrow. She has written, I dare say, twenty such this morning to different people, all equally flattering to each" (BLJ 3: 235).

Holland House had its own regular events and rites. At the center were the dinners, to which an invitation was needed. They usually started at six or six-thirty and allowed the participants little space: "15 at dinner each day at a table that holds only nine."[15] Or: "For once, to my delight, plenty of elbow-room," Creevey remarked in 1836, showing that elbow room and leg space were indeed exceptional.[16] When Lady Holland changed the dinner time to 5 o'clock in 1832, Greville complained about the inconvenience of "shortening the day" and of the "lengthening of the evening."[17] If the Dinner Books give the exact names and numbers of all visitors, Lady Holland's journals and letters talk of "large party," "a good deal of company" (EHJ 1: 251, 249), or even "a most brilliant assembly," often mentioning merely some names, possibly those that carried most prestige.[18] Although the dinners were the very heart of Holland House sociability, some guests would come for breakfast, or could arrive after dinner, have separate conversations with the host in the library, or take a stroll in the garden, especially during the summer. As visitors had to travel to Kensington by coach, the approach to and departure from the house and the verbal interaction on the way were among the rituals, as was the overnight stay, which effectively meant that the previous evening's conversations were continued the next morning. On November 26, 1818, Thomas Moore went to Holland House, where the evening began with a predinner conversation with Lord Holland about politics and with Lord Russell on publishers and on Mary Berry's edition of the Russell letters. During dinner, additional guests (Tierney, Sharp, Wishaw, Wilbraham, Rogers, and Mrs. Smith) joined in a conversation touching on numerous topics related to the theater, politics, society, and history. Moore's entry, a sketchy summary of the table talk, ends on the sentence: "Slept at Holland House" (TMJ 1: 91). The following day began with a stroll in the garden, during which Moore, Rogers, and Tierney read Luttrell's poetry before joining Lord Holland for breakfast, who discussed politics with them. In these ongoing conversations, Holland House differs from other circles, where the end of an evening party marked the end of a conversation. Not everyone was asked to stay overnight. Although Macaulay had at first declined the offer of a bed, he was an overnight guest in August 1832 and slept in the room formerly occupied by the recently deceased historian James Macintosh.[19] Macaulay thus symbolically inherited his position as well as his space.

The atmosphere at Holland House was characterized by an odd mixture of restraint and liberty, which manifested itself in the gossip that surrounded it. One already mentioned rite, "almost an art form," as Mitchell declared, was being snubbed by Lady Holland.[20] Many guests' stories took the cliché of the eccentric hostess to the extreme, whose imperious manner constantly seemed to threaten disciplinary measures. Creevey in particular relished malicious anecdotes:

> Sefton was very good fun about a morning call on Lady Holland... Amongst other things she talked about ages, and observed that Lord Sefton and Lord Holland were of the same age—about 56. "For myself," said she, "I believe I am near the same;" and then the page being called, she said: "Go and ask Mr. Allen how old I am." As the house is so small and the rooms so near, they heard Allen holloa out in no very melodious tones—"She is 57." But Lady Holland was not content with this, and said it was too old for her, and made the page go back again; and again they heard Allen roar in a much louder voice: "I tell you she's 57."[21]

While Creevey sarcastically points at the shortcomings of a woman who does not even know her own age but wants to be younger and—this is the implicit allusion—sexually more desirable than she is, he also uncovers a male alliance, consisting of himself, Sefton, and Allen, who, by exposing the hostess, unwittingly lay open their own need for gossipmongering. It was the liberty to play and to laugh about one another that constituted a key feature of the Holland House circle. Sometimes a sarcastic tone prevailed, sometimes it was benign and lighthearted irony, or playful mockery. Many guests found the latter embodied by their host. In September 1819, Moore recorded that Lord Holland "once kept a journal for a week of the conversations at Holland House, and that he read it himself with much effect, being such an excellent mimic" (TMJ 1: 214). No one escaped. In 1800, Lady Holland recorded a conversation with the Duke of Somerset: "I suspect that he has a love of fun in him, for he told me that he was occupied in persuading Lewis [the author of *The Monk*] to write a book on moral philosophy, as he was certain from the opinions he heard from Lewis that it would be at least entertaining" (EHJ 2: 45). These anecdotes—Creevey on Lady Holland, Moore on Lord Holland, or Lady Holland on Lewis—share the propensity to create laughter. If they reflect a value system, it is a denial of strict rules ("moral philosophy"), an emphasis on wit, and a love of verbal combat as an art form. This style of interaction is far from the ideal of politeness cultivated in French salons, but it is compatible with the rather relaxed "Whig state of mind" outlined by Mitchell.[22] Moreover, such insider jokes created social coherence within the Holland House set.

Holland House was also by far the biggest and most powerful salon because it was a major political center. In addition, it cultivated close connections with one of the period's most important journals, the *Edinburgh Review*, which Newman ironically termed "the oracle of Holland House."[23] The entanglements of English patrons and Scotch reviewers deserve a closer look. If studies like Biancamaria Fontana's (1985) and George Pottinger's (1992) situate the *Edinburgh Review* in the context of the Scottish Enlightenment, others like Mark Schoenfield's (2009) analyze its impact in a broader literary and intellectual field.[24] Founded in Edinburgh by a circle of young Whigs—Henry Brougham, Sydney Smith, Francis Horner, and Francis Jeffrey—it was an immediate success. After the first issue had appeared in 1802, the sales figures went up rapidly, and the magazine soon exerted a huge influence on literary and political culture in Scotland and England. It offered its readers a daring combination of intellectual fields: politics, economics, contemporary literature, history, philosophy, religion, and travel writing. While Jeffrey, its long-time editor between 1803 and 1829, stayed in Scotland for much of the time, Smith, Brougham, and Horner went to London to further their careers, where Holland House was among the sociable places they frequented. Some visitors to Holland House were substantially involved in the making of the *Edinburgh Review*. William Christie points out that the articles were often products of collaboration, for example, between Jeffrey, Allen, and others.[25] The memoirs of John Whishaw, a frequent visitor, occasionally identify contributors to the *Edinburgh Review*, who belonged to the Holland House set.[26] By far not all Reviewers were habitués, yet of those who lived in London, Smith was probably one of the closest to Holland House before he left for Yorkshire in 1809. Brougham, in contrast, did not belong to the inner circle, had problems adapting to the Holland House style of politics, and in 1810 more or less broke off his contacts with the Kensington coterie. Allen, a resident in Holland House and another contributor to the *Edinburgh Review*, held the contact with Jeffrey, who profited through such communication but did not belong to the inner circle himself and did not want Holland House to influence the *Edinburgh Review* too much.[27] When Jeffrey, who was in touch with many contributors from the inner circle or at least the periphery of Holland House, was in London, he dined with the Hollands, who in turn supported him; when they visited Scotland in 1810, they met Jeffrey in Edinburgh (EHJ 2: 257–258). They helped him to sustain and extend his network: when Creevey took his ailing wife to Brussels in 1814, Lady Holland wrote to her about an impending visit of Jeffrey, "that very dear little man, who has the best heart and temper, although the authors of the day consider him as their greatest scourge."[28] Holland House and the *Edinburgh Review* shared many positions: They were pro-French, took an interest in Spain, believed in progress and liberty, agreed on their dislike of the Lake poets, and watched Napoleon's fate after 1815. Allen, for example, reviewed the *Letters from St. Helena* in 1816 as part of the ongoing campaign to improve the conditions of Napoleon's exile.[29] The captive Napoleon read the article, added pencil notes, and when his copy of the *Edinburgh Review* was eventually returned to Holland House, it remained in the Yellow Drawing Room together with the other Napoleonic relics.[30] Reviewing, patronage, and hero worship coincided in and through the *Edinburgh Review*. With the Whigs' return to political power in 1830, the *Edinburgh Review* moved closer to the government. A posthumous tribute to the Whig politician and host was paid by Macaulay, a contributor since the 1820s, who published his famous review essay on *The Opinions of Lord Holland* in 1841.[31]

Three *Habitués*: Samuel Rogers, Sydney Smith, and Thomas Moore

Rogers, Smith, and Moore, writers and poets, all contributors to the *Edinburgh Review*, were well-known during their lifetimes yet, with the exception of Moore, have fallen into oblivion. Frequent guests at Holland House, they made use of and contributed to its sociability but at times also went their own way. All three belonged to the inner circle. Rogers, who appears in nearly all memoirs and correspondences, was famous for his acerbic wit and for being disagreeable: "What a sour, snarling beast this Rogers is, and such a fellow for talking about the grandees he lives with," Creevey moaned in 1828.[32] Even the diplomatic Mary Berry complained: "Rogers never liked me much, and seldom called on me except once a year, on his and my birth day which happened to be on the same day."[33] When she found out that Rogers's visits were followed by snarling remarks comparing his and her fading looks, she was truly annoyed. Considering that the Holland House circle cultivated the art of verbal combat, Rogers's sarcasms are part of an ongoing conversation, an exchange of insider jokes. Although Lady Holland occasionally snubbed him, the two got on well, and his well-cultivated sarcasms probably had the function of indicating his high rank within the coterie.

To his contemporaries, Rogers was a renowned poet and writer, decidedly on the literary and not the political side of the Holland House gatherings. His posthumously published *Table-Talk* (1856), a series of anecdotal encounters, presents him in conversation with Lord Holland about topics like Fox's edition of Virgil, Horace's verse, and Spanish theater.[34] Apart from poetry, Rogers published a two-volume work about Italy in 1822 and 1828, reissued with illustrations by Turner and Stothard in 1830,[35] which went into numerous editions. He benefited from the close contacts between Holland House and the *Edinburgh Review*. In November 1813, John Whishaw described this network in a letter:

> Pray mention to the Smiths that the new number of the *Edinburgh Review* (just published) contains two articles by Mackintosh, on Rogers and Madame de Staël. Three by Brougham—on Dumont, the Abuses of the Press, and a translation of Cicero. There is also an article by Playfair on Dr. Hutton's tracts; by Allen of Holland House, on the ancient legislation of Spain...Jeffrey will be much surprised on his return from America, where he has gone to be married, that the *Review* has changed his character.[36]

Most writers and reviewers named in this passage can be traced as guests at Holland House at one time or another. The issue of October 1813 contained a long review of Rogers's new collection and enthusiastically hailed him as one of "the classical poets of his country."[37]

Roger was not only a frequent guest at Holland House but headed his own sociable circle. As he had inherited a bank, he was fairly well off (but not rich) on 5,000 a year and could afford to live in a beautiful house praised for its collections of books, art objects, paintings, and antiques.[38] He usually invited his friends for breakfast, not so much for dinner, possibly because this meant less preparation. Many of the Holland House guests like Byron and Moore could also be found under his roof. When Moore challenged Jeffrey to a duel over an article in the *Edinburgh Review*, Rogers helped to reconcile the two men.[39] He did not share the dislike for the Lake poets that prevailed in Holland House but counted Wordsworth among his friends, whom he even introduced to Fox, albeit without success.[40] It is striking that, despite his closeness to Holland House, Rogers retained his independence when it came to choosing members of his own circles, which only partly overlapped with that of Holland House. His interest in American literature led him to invite a number of American authors over the years, among them Washington Irving, James Fenimore Cooper, Nathaniel Parker Willis, Henry Wadsworth Longfellow, Lydia Sigourney, and William Cullen Bryant.[41] Today, Rogers is only remembered as a minor poet if at all.

"Sydney, ring the bell," Lady Holland decreed, to which Sydney Smith is reported to have replied: "Oh yes! and shall I sweep the room?"[42] In the Holland House circle, Smith was renowned for a wit that was more benign, less acerbic than Rogers's, but still had bite. Lady Holland's reaction to Smith's quick-witted repartee is not know, yet since his correspondence documents a long-standing friendship with Holland House and a sincere concern for its "inmates," one can assume that his cheek did not destabilize his position. Smith was the only clergyman who belonged to the inner circle of a salon run by a hostess who was considered an agnostic and whose librarian, Allen, was nicknamed "Lady Holland's Atheist."[43] Smith, who briefly lived in Edinburgh, was one of the founders of the *Edinburgh Review* and a devoted contributor for many years. Between 1803 and 1809, he dwelt in London, where he frequented Holland House. In 1806, he gained the position of rector of Foston-le-Clay without becoming a resident, yet eventually had to move to Yorkshire with his family in 1809, hence his regretful definition of life in the countryside as a state of being "twelve miles from a lemon." Lady Holland had been the prime force behind his appointment:

> When Erskine was made Lord Chancellor, Lady Holland never rested till she prevailed on him to give Sidney Smith a living. Smith went to thank him for the appointment. "Oh," said Erskine, "don't thank me, Mr. Smith. I gave you the living because Lady Holland insisted on my doing so: and if she had desired me to give it to the devil, *he* must have had it."[44]

Rogers's anecdote from the *Table-Talk* confirms all preconceptions about the crony mafia reigning from Holland House, where livings and positions were secured for those who submitted to an influential hostess, whose infernal powers might even induce a pact with the devil. Lady Holland's support shows to what extent those involved with the *Edinburgh Review* could benefit from Whig patronage while promoting Whig ideals.

During as well as after his time in London, Smith was in contact with Jeffrey, whom he kept informed about political and intellectual life, disputes and alliances, and with whom he debated about contributors, their work, rival magazines, and reactions to the *Edinburgh Review* of which he became aware. In other words, Smith was an important source of informal information through his London contacts. In a letter presumably dating from October 1805, Smith expressed irritation about "a very anti-Christian article" and admonished Jeffrey: "I need no other proof that the Review was left on other hands than yrs, because you must be thoroughly aware that the rumor of infidelity decides not only the reputation, but the existence of the

Review."[45] In August 1819, he declared: "I write for the London, not for the Scotch market, and perhaps more people read my nonsense than your sense,"[46] sketching the difference between the urban London as opposed to Jeffrey's Scottish readership. Some articles by Smith deal with social issues—the chimney-sweepers' suffering, the injustice of the Game Laws, the treatment of prisoners, the status of Catholics in Ireland—and usually side with the weak. Travel writing also interested him. He contributed literary criticism, for example, on Matthew Lewis's dramatic output (which he liked), Staël's *Delphine* (which he disliked), and Hannah More's *Coelebs in Search of a Wife* (which he also disliked). Smith was a severe critic of the Methodists, whom he saw as too zealous, too righteous, and too emotional.[47] His entertaining and polished kind of Christianity went well with the Whig style but also with political Whig principles such as liberty and the fighting for the weak and disenfranchised.

Smith, who returned to London regularly after 1809, was not only a guest at Holland House but also frequented other circles, for example, Rogers's breakfasts. Moore's diary records an anecdote that Smith, the Whigs' favorite clergyman, told about Allen at such an occasion:

> Sydney very amusing about Allen—said that there was a dark place with bars to it at Holland House which people did not know the use of, but it appears that Allen keeps a clergyman there whom he torments occasionally...giving him a poke occasionally, crying to him "blaspheme, blaspheme." (TMJ 5: 1972)

This is one of the many anecdotes about the Holland House circle from the *Journal* of Thomas Moore, the singing Irish poet, who was a major Whig literary figure. Even though many critics concentrate on Moore as Byron's friend or as the literary champion of the Irish cause, the extent of his involvement with the Kensington circle is frequently overlooked. From about 1812 onward, Moore often dined and slept at Holland House, where during some periods his status seems to have been that of a semi-resident.[48] After the comic duel with Jeffrey, he became one of the *Edinburgh Review*'s contributors. While he prepared his *Memoirs of the Life of Sheridan* (1825),[49] another demi-God in the Whig pantheon, Moore was using the Holland House circle to gather serious and frivolous data. If Lady Holland ventured the indiscreet bit of information that Sheridan took "a bottle of wine & a book up to bed" but only used the former, repeated conversations with Lord Holland and others helped him to collect further detailed material otherwise not available (TMJ 1: 62, 199). Another project were the memoirs that Byron had given to Moore, who was meant to publish them after Byron's death. Initially, Moore had received the huge sum of 2,000 guineas from Murray, but when he realized that Lady and Lord Holland, whom he had shown the manuscript, objected to some passages, partly on moral grounds, the contract with Murray was changed.[50] "Was not your showing the Memoranda to ** [Lady Holland?] somewhat perilous?" (BLJ 8: 164) Byron admonished his friend. When Byron died in 1824, legal confusion ensued, until finally the memoirs were burnt and Moore wrote a biography of Byron, which appeared as part of his edition of Byron's poems and letters.[51] Opinions on the exact nature of the offensive passages of the destroyed memoirs vary. Byron, who met Henry Edward Fox, Lady Holland's son, in Genoa in 1823, did not play them down but explained that "he offered L[ad]y Byron to read them and add whatever she chose in the shape of note or observation" but that she had "declined to inspect them."[52] Henry Fox's diary alone shows to what extent the Holland family and the Holland House circle were involved in the discussions surrounding Byron's memoirs.

Moore was also a skilled chronicler of the inner circle's sociable interaction. He got on well both with Lord and Lady Holland: "As I was about to take my place next Lord Holland at dinner, my Lady said 'No—come up here'—ordering me to another seat—'So you have taken Moore from me' said Lord Holland, with the look of a disappointed school-boy" (TMJ 3: 1250). In his descriptions, the verbal fights gain a theatrical quality, even with references to corporeal aspects, albeit in metaphorical form: "Allen, too, sometimes growls at Lady Holland through his muzzle" (TMJ 1: 45). If Allen, usually subservient but sometimes protesting noisily, is depicted as a dog, Rogers is endowed with the qualities of a snake. According to Moore, Lady Holland once commented on her most acerbic guest: "How remarkably well he is to-day! he is in full venom" (TMJ 2: 479). The grand style associated with Holland House gains a sordid dimension in the description of Allen's living quarters: "Allen has got the room that is called 'the Chapel' in the Hollands' new residence" where he "makes all sort of filth & mess" (461). These vivid images, which cast the habitués as animals, take the concept of the "inmates" one step further. Lady Holland's regime is compared to slavery: when she mentions that her page Antonio had eloped with the kitchen maid, Moore suggests that the couple may have made their way to Wilberforce, who was one of the leading abolitionists (TMJ 1: 138).

Writing and the conditions of publishing were frequently debated topics. Moore found a fervent critic in the hostess, whose opinion on *Lalla Rookh*, for example, was: "She had two objections to reading it—in the 1st place it was Eastern, & in the 2nd place it was in Quarto...Poets, inclined to a Plethora of vanity, would find a dose of Lady Holland now & then very good for their complaint" (187). Lord Porchester, about to publish a poem, received the following advice: "I am sorry to hear you are going to publish a poem. Can't you suppress it?" (TMJ 2: 810). Despite much support and patronage, from which Rogers, Smith, and Moore profited, authors who did not or not yet belong to the Holland House circle could find the treatment they received disconcerting, like Byron, whose *Hours of Idleness* was torn apart in the *Edinburgh Review* before he joined the gatherings in Kensington, became a regular visitor, a sufferer at "Old Madagascar's" hands, and a posthumous celebrity guest.

Byron and Holland House

> Why does Lady H. always have that damned screen between the whole room and the fire? I, who bear the cold no better than an antelope, and never yet found a sun quite *done* to my taste, was absolutely petrified, and could not even shiver. All the rest, too, looked as if they were just unpacked, like salmon from an ice-basket, and set down to table for that day only. When she retired, I watched their looks as I dismissed the screen, and every cheek thawed, and every nose reddened with the anticipated glow. (BLJ 3: 226)

Lady Holland, 17 years older than Byron but no nurturing mother, seems to have scared the poet stiff in a very literal sense. His vision of metamorphosing from a graceful antelope into an item of food, that is, of consumption, mirrors his constant fear of being devoured by domineering women.[53] Byron, whose complaint about the hostess signals closeness to the salon in Kensington, was one of the heroes of Holland House, especially after his death, although he never belonged to the inner circle. On his second visit to Holland House in 1831, Macaulay was led into Lady Holland's own drawing-room, which was decorated with miniature paintings: "Among them I remarked a great many,—thirty I should think,—which even I, who am no great connoisseur, saw at once could come from no hand but Stothard's. They were all on subjects from Lord Byron's poems."[54] The entry into the hostess's inner sanctum, not granted to every visitor, was followed by an account of how Byron himself had given the paintings to her so that they would not fall into the bailiffs' hands. This devotion to Byron, whose relationship to Holland House had its ups and downs, was more personal than the cult around Napoleon or Fox and happened on a smaller scale. Although he was counted among the literary heroes in Kensington after his death, his interactions with Holland House also had a political side. Byron is an interesting salon guest through his tentative relationship to the Kensington coterie alone: not every visitor was as close as Allen, Moore, Smith, or Rogers. Byron's case highlights how guests could drop into and out of the Holland House circle. If the most famous occurrence linking Byron's name to Holland House is his attack in *English Bards and Scotch Reviewers* (1809), other activities are less known: the help he received for his maiden speech, his poem for the reopening of Drury Lane, communication on various minor artistic and political matters, as well as advice for his settlement with Lady Byron in 1816.

Byron's verse satire *English Bards and Scotch Reviewers* (1809) with its famous attack on Jeffrey, the *Edinburgh Review*, and Lord Holland's "hirelings," was originally written in 1807–1808 as *The British Bards: A Satire*.[55] When the volume *Hours of Idleness* (1807) received an unfavorable review,[56] Byron wrongly believed it to have been written by Jeffrey, while its author, in fact, had been Brougham. Byron subsequently rewrote *The British Bards* and added revengeful passages. In its published form, *English Bards and Scotch Reviewers* deals blow after blow at contemporary writers, among them Wordsworth, Southey, Moore, and Scott, ridicules the Gothic mode and the modern stage, and claims that the current literary products fail to live up to previously achieved standards. Jeffrey was ridiculed through the retelling of the story of his duel with Moore. Byron castigated the Scottish reviewers and, in a wider sense, the powers of the market for print products, which he felt had treated him unfairly. He saw its most abusive mechanisms—patronage, reviews written as favors, and lack of moral control—at work in Holland House, of whose importance as the London center of the Reviewers he was well aware:

> Illustrious HOLLAND! hard would be his lot,
> His hirelings mentioned, and himself forgot!
> HOLLAND, with HENRY PETTY at his back,
> The whipper-in and huntsman of the pack.
> Blest be the banquets spread at Holland House
> Where Scotchmen feed, and critics may carouse!
> Long, long beneath that hospitable roof,
> Shall Grub-Street dine, while duns are kept aloof.
> See honest HALLAM lay aside his fork,

> Resume his pen, review his Lordship's work,
> And grateful for the dainties on his plate,
> Declare his landlord can at least translate!
> Dunedin! view thy children with delight,
> They write for food, and feed because they write:
> And lest, when heated with the unusual grape,
> Some glowing thoughts should to the press escape,
> And tinge with red the female reader's cheek,
> My lady skims the cream of each critique;
> Breathes o'er the pages her purity of soul,
> Reforms each error, and refines the whole.[57]

Byron's satire expresses unease about this intersection of the public and the private spheres, the "third space" of sociable encounters, which was not accessible to newcomers like him and which, in Byron's view, facilitated Holland's dubious acts of patronage, hidden by a smoke screen of evening entertainments. Byron's acerbic pen labels the Reviewers as Holland's "hirelings," bought by exquisite dinners ("banquets," "dainties on his plate") and maybe worse, who were under the influence of alcohol ("grape"), and whose impaired powers of judgment led to absurd acts of adulation: "Declare his landlord can at least translate."[58] The final lines of this passage mock the hostess, who was rumored to participate in the literary debates and to help even with the proofreading of the *Edinburgh Review*. Byron also aimed to deal a blow at Lady Holland's morals by insinuating that the scandalously divorced hostess had the cheek to pose as the guardian of propriety. The pun on the dual meaning of "error" (moral and typographic) anticipates his later digressive style. To anyone aware of her first marriage, the words "purity of soul," "reforms," and "refines" would be a joke. Byron launched another, similarly crude attack on her in a stanza about Holland House, which he later omitted from the published version of Canto I of *Childe Harold*.[59] At some stage, Byron recognized his mistake and, as he wished to make peace with Holland House, suppressed further editions of *English Bards and Scotch Reviewers*. Since the publication of this long satirical poem marks "Byron's emergence on the public stage,"[60] as Schoenfield argues, the controversy with the literary market proved to be a major step, and by no means one into the wrong direction. Despite the early skirmishes, the *Edinburgh Review* not only praised Byron's later poetry but devoted attention to his new poetic style in reviews about *Childe Harold, The Bride of Abydos, The Corsair*, and others.[61]

When Byron first visited Holland House, he was a young politician, seeking a leading figure's support for his maiden speech on the Frame

Work Bill in February 1812.[62] After Holland had sent him "indirectly a kind of pacific overture" (BLJ 2: 128) in late 1811, Rogers acted as a go-between a few months later (160–161). One reason for Byron's interest in Lord Holland was that the rioting workers were in Nottingham and that Holland was the Recorder of Nottingham. On February 25, Byron wrote him a letter, which mapped out the frame-breakers' position and is deferential in its style, far from the previous aggressive satire. Byron concluded: "I am a little apprehensive that your lordship will think me too lenient towards these men, & *half a framebreaker myself*" (166). He met with friendly encouragement: "Ld. H[olland] tells me I shall beat them all if I persevere" (167). On March 5, Byron sent him an advance copy of Cantos I and II of *Childe Harold*, thanked him for his forgiveness, and accused himself of "boyish rashness" (168). He later dedicated *The Bride of Abydos* to Holland, sent him proofs of *The Giaour*, and wrote a long letter to debate the poem with him (BLJ 3: 167–169). The tone of Byron's correspondence, friendly throughout, suggests that he had come to consider Lord Holland, 14 years his senior, as a mentor.

Other cooperations—literary, private, political, and social—occurred, which, because of Byron's fame, are better documented than those with other guests. Again in 1812, Lord Holland invited Byron to enter into a poetic contest and to contribute a poetical address for the opening of the new theater in Drury Lane.[63] Byron, hardly the type of public poet who wished to grace the opening of an institution with his metric effusions, first tried to back out but then, because he was asked again, submitted a poem. Although Lord and Lady Holland liked to have a celebrity poet in their midst, Byron's literary output was, strictly speaking, not the kind of writing they were striving to make more visible. Between 1812 and 1816, Byron repeatedly dined at Holland House, where he met other writers.[64] In 1816, Lord Holland again acted the mentor's part when he became involved in the arrangements of Byron's separation from his wife and advised him on the settlement. After Byron had left England, he refueled his contact with the Hollands every once in a while. In 1817, while in Venice, he asked Rogers to thank them for Lord Holland's book on Lope de Vega, which he was then expecting (BLJ 5: 206) and which he used for his work on *Don Juan*, as a diary entry on January 6, 1821, shows (BLJ 8: 14). In March 1823, he wrote to Lord Holland, recommending Count Rasponi (BLJ 10: 122). It was around that time in Italy that Henry Edward Fox, the son and heir of Lord Holland, met his idol Byron once more. A letter dating from late 1823 recommends the Greek deputies to Lord Holland (BLJ 11: 59–60). Maybe Byron had hoped that Greece might become the Hollands' second

Spain but did not live long enough to coordinate their support with his actions. All these latter activities show that Byron was in contact with this cultural hothouse in Kensington for more than one reason: he gained political, intellectual, as well as personal support and made contacts, while Lord Holland acted as a kind of mentor. Even after Byron had stopped frequenting the Holland House circle, he stayed in touch through letters, made the odd request, was happy to invest into a renewed friendship with the Hollands' son, and thus in a wider sense remained part of the Holland House circle.

Amorous Entanglements and Caroline Lamb's *Glenarvon*

The genesis and reception of Caroline Lamb's scandalous novel *Glenarvon*, a fantasy of her affair with Byron and an attack on the society that condemned her for it, are closely linked to Holland House, which she frequented regularly. From a very early age, Caroline Ponsonby, later Caroline Lamb, the daughter of Lady Bessborough, a friend of Lady Holland's, developed a habit of unconventional self-fashioning and quickly acquired a corresponding reputation. Her biographer Paul Douglass diagnoses her with "a disastrous personality fragmentation".[65] She was highly strung, lived through intense emotional ups and downs, and struggled to express the emotions that were tearing her apart. With Lady Holland, she created a complex friendship-cum-rivalry even before *Glenarvon*. After she had started an affair with Sir Godfrey Webster, Lady Holland's son from her first marriage, in 1810, she wrote a condescending letter of advice to her.[66] That Caroline's grandmother was worried about this association with Holland House shows that the coterie was hardly the place where a young married woman caring about her reputation should be seen.[67] A number of letters kept in a rather personal tone, dating from 1811, document that Caroline gradually moved closer to Lady Holland, her senior by 14 years, whom Caroline cast into the role of motherly confidante.[68]

In early 1812, Rogers lent her an advance copy of *Childe Harold*, which made her wish to meet the author;[69] soon afterwards, Byron introduced himself to her at Holland House. The fatal attraction resulted in an affair, which lasted from March to September until her family removed her to Ireland. Her mother-in-law, Lady Melbourne, was not alone in wanting to end the scandalous relationship to prevent further damage. If Byron soon became disinterested, Caroline continued to be obsessed with him. Both the liaison and Caroline's attempts to win him back, likewise her acts of revenge, happened before the eyes of the Holland House circle: "Several women were in love with Byron, but none so violently as Lady Caroline Lamb. She absolutely besieged him," Rogers commented, and: "But such was the insanity of her passion for Byron, that sometimes, when not invited to a party where he was to be, she would wait for him in the street till it was over!"[70]

The emotional upheaval created by the affair and its end caused Caroline Lamb to recreate the events and to fantasize about possible different outcomes in the novel *Glenarvon*, on which she worked over a period of at least two years and which was published only weeks after Byron had left England in 1816.[71] This work of fiction was a reenactment in more than one sense: With her Gothic fantasy, she recreated her own liaison with Byron while also imitating his style of writing, as she later did again in her *New Canto*, a satirical reaction to Byron's *Don Juan*. As the initial attraction had been literary,[72] she forced him to consider her literary works, thereby mirroring and reversing the constellation of their first encounter. Moreover, as she had been stigmatized for the scandalous affair, she took revenge on London society through painting a satirical image of her own social environment and of Holland House in particular. The novel was published by Colburn, who specialized in romans à clef, and went into four editions with substantial textual variants. The author's careful revisions prove her incapability to relax her imaginary grip on the interlude with Byron.[73]

Glenarvon, set in Ireland, is a story of rebellion, into which a melodramatic love plot is embedded. Past and contemporary critics have agreed that the construction of plot and character are flawed and that the novel is extravagant and at times incoherent. However, the real importance of *Glenarvon* lies in the fact that it was a roman à clef. Caroline inscribed her affair into the text by creating an amorous triangle: Calantha (herself), married to Lord Avondale (William Lamb), is seduced by the wicked libertine Glenarvon (Byron). The romantic subplot of the novel loosely follows the events of the actual liaison. Moreover, she punished the audience who had condemned the spectacle of her affair by casting its members as literary characters. In many cases, it is possible to identify the originals, those women at whose hands Caroline had suffered most. Her pen ensured that they were castigated: Lady Mandeville (Lady Oxford) and Lady Buchanan (Lady Melbourne) were among the most unpleasant characters. Her former lover Sir Godfrey Webster reappeared, too, under the name of Buchanan. Even more offensive was her rendering of the Holland House circle in chapter XXVIII of volume I, which famously presents the "Princess of Madagascar" (Lady Holland).[74] Her residence, "an old-fashioned gothic building, called Barbary House, three miles beyond the turnpike," was easily recognizable, especially as its guests were "reviewers, poets, critics, and politicians."[75] The description of Holland House oscillates between fascination and repulsion:

> At the end of a long gallery, two thick wax tapers, rendering "darkness visible," the princess was seated. A poet of an emaciated and sallow complexion stood beside her; of him it was affirmed that in apparently the kindest and most engaging manner, he, at all times, said precisely that which was most unpleasant to the person he appeared to praise. This yellow hyena had, however, a heart noble, magnanimous and generous; and even his friends, could they but escape from his smile and his tongue, had no reason to complain. Few events, if any, were ever known to move the Princess from her position.[76]

The atmosphere is eerie: The wax tapers, the phrase "darkness visible," a quotation from Milton's *Paradise Lost* that describes hell, together with the name "Barbary house" mock the circle's inherent belief that its members were the harbingers of enlightenment ideas. The "yellow hyena" by the name of Fremore is the acerbic Rogers, who was often described as looking rather ill. Caroline Lamb softened his portrait in the second edition.[77] Lady Holland's regal posture as well as her immobility (she was in fact ill) become symbols of power and inflexibility. Caroline's pen orientalized Allen by turning him into the servile "Hoiaouskim." If Hoiaouskim is deferential, the reviewers, in contrast, are ferocious. When Calantha asks why they "wear collars and chains around their necks," Fremore explains: "Observe that the chairs are well gilded; that the tables are well stored; and those who bend the lowest are ever the best received."[78] The reviewers (or rather, Reviewers) are a pack of dogs Lady Holland may set lose any minute, dangerous because they inflict pain with their mouths, that is, through the (spoken, and ultimately, written) language they produce. Imagery relating to the mouth reflects Caroline Lamb's ambivalent attitude to salon conversation. The charge she levels against the contributors to the *Edinburgh Review* resembles Byron's accusation in *English Bards and Scotch Reviewers*: in exchange for exquisite dinners and other forms of remuneration, they become creatures of Holland House and attack at random. Moreover, she criticizes cant, that is, hypocrisy and gossip, as Byron himself did later.[79] This is one example of the textual strategies through which she ensures a Byronic position for herself.

Caroline Lamb also expressed her very personal frustration about Lady Holland: The chapter ends on an outcry when the narrator accuses the Princess of having "taught Calantha to love" her, of supplying her with "sugared poisons" while refusing to help the heroine when she "fell into the mire." Such hypocrisy on the side of the Princess of Madagascar is punished by Calantha: "The sun may shine fairly again upon her; but never, whilst existence is prolonged, will she set foot in the gates of the Palace of the great Nabob, or trust to the smiles and professions of the Princess of Madagascar."[80] It is symptomatic of Caroline's lack of balance that she mingled the personal and the public, Lady Holland's supposed lack of maternal care for her friend's daughter and her power as a hostess. Implicitly, Caroline contrasts Lord Holland's help for Byron with the support she had been denied by Holland's wife. This fantasy, a combination of childish helplessness and empowering revenge, is taken even further at the end of the novel where the Princess of Madagascar, who lives to an old age, is described in her moment of death, when she suddenly repents her previous lack of faith. After her demise, her reviewers "died in the same year as the princess, of an epidemic disorder."[81] They are like an apparition that dissolves, a specter that disappears from sight.

It is hardly surprising that *Glenarvon,* which added further damage to Caroline's reputation, was much debated for a few months, by critics as well as by those who unwittingly found themselves on its pages. Several keys exist, one of them by Lady Holland, who, in a letter to Mrs. Creevey, commented on the presentation of herself in the novel:

> Where every ridicule, follery and infirmity (my not being able from malady to move about much) is portrayed. The charge against more essential qualities is, I trust and believe, a fiction... There is not much originality, as the jokes against me for my love of *aisances* and comforts she has heard laughed at by myself and *coterie* at my own fireside.[82]

It is hard to imagine that the hostess of Holland House was completely unaware of the gossip behind her back. As long as it remained informal and inside the Holland House set, no damage was done. Caroline Lamb's image of the hostess is not outrageous because it is unflattering—so were Creevey's and Moore's comments—yet as it was situated outside the coterie through publication by its author, it was freely available to anyone and therefore much more offensive than many an insider joke.

* * *

Knowledge about Spanish culture, the cult of the tragic Napoleon, impromptu poetry—Lady Holland's sociable activities left traces and imprints, to which her contemporaries added unflattering descriptions of the "centurion," the witch with a cat, or "Old Madagascar." However, as the physician Holland was wise enough to see, she ran together with her husband one of the most successful salons of the period for over 40 years. Her own voice is audible in her travel writing, where she appears as genuinely interested in people and places, customs, and ideas. Since, unlike Berry and Blessington, she did not publish plays, poems, novels, or historical works, her public persona rests on what others said and wrote about her. If the activities relating to the popular cults around Charles James Fox and Napoleon usually found their way into print straightaway, gossip of the sort Lady Holland attracted is situated at the intersection of public and private and belongs to the realm of spoken language. Such acerbic comments are lost or appear in print after a long delay because memoirs and correspondences are often published posthumously. *Glenarvon* documents the scandalmongering in the third space of sociability in an exceptional way because a print version of the negative image of Lady Holland as "Madagascar" became available to her almost immediately. This negative typecasting is linked to the art of verbal combat cultivated at Holland House. Although, if one trusts diaries, correspondences, and table-talks, much of the interaction was in fact peaceful and friendly, some habitués developed the art of verbal fighting, of snubbing and of being snubbed, and of sparring in conversation. These cult activities centered on Lady Holland. Her guests' unfettered enthusiasm in collecting her tactless remarks, the crazy conversations of the madhouse in Kensington, point at the existence of a unique conversational style hardly in line with ideals such as politeness, a cult of gossip, an art of verbal biting that included the use of nicknames and allusions for the initiated. If previous criticism has identified the male cult figures of Holland House—Napoleon and Fox—it is time to redeem verbal biting *à l'hollandaise* as an achievement, a cult activity, and to award to Lady Holland the status of a Regency cult figure. Being seen in the act of submitting to her, being able to tell an anecdote about the famous snubs, meant membership in an elite club: the Holland House set. The ability to gossip about her was a trophy signaling closeness to the inner circle. And in this respect, the satire of *Glenarvon* is not only an act of revenge but also a fantasy of belonging.

CHAPTER 6

THE COUNTESS OF BLESSINGTON
AS HOSTESS

My first sight of Lady Blessington was connected with circumstances sufficiently characteristic of her extraordinary personal beauty at the period in question—about five or six and twenty years ago—to excuse my referring to it somewhat in detail... It was on the opening day of that Royal Academy Exhibition which contained Lawrence's celebrated portrait of Lady Blessington—one of the very finest he ever painted, and universally known by the numerous engravings that have since been made from it...

Presently, on returning to this portrait, I beheld standing before it, as if on purpose to confirm my theory, the lovely original. She was leaning on the arm of her husband, Lord Blessington, while *he* was gazing in fond admiration on the portrait. And then I saw how impossible it is for an artist to "flatter" a really beautiful woman.[1]

Thus P. G. Patmore's "Personal Recollections of the Late Lady Blessington," published shortly after her death in 1849, introduces the notorious Countess, who was also a renowned hostess, visited by famous men but shunned by most women. Sexual scandal offended those who wished to uphold moral standards because Lady Blessington had been the Earl's mistress before marriage; but maybe, her biographer Michael Sadleir suggests, she was just too attractive to be popular among women, particularly as she had caught one of the wealthiest eligible men in London, to whose hand her humble origins as an Irish commoner had not predestined her.[2] Marguerite, Countess of Blessington, was no modest "strawberry" in the style of Mary Berry, no wallflower, but highly visible, an expert at self-marketing, who enjoyed standing in the limelight. Born 26 years after Berry, Blessington, simultaneously central and marginal to good society, hosted several salons in London and in Italy, acquired notoriety for her wealth as well as her financial problems, suffered from scandal, and gained through its successful marketing. If most of her guests celebrated her as a gifted conversationalist, other contemporaries found her too outspoken and dubbed her the "Countess of Cursington."[3] Nearly all twentieth-century critics ignored her, apart from a few Byron scholars, whose main interest in dealing with her has been the reconstruction of the great poet's whereabouts. Yet nineteenth-century diaries, biographies, travelogues, and correspondences mention her frequently: the Countess of Blessington knew everyone, and everyone knew her, or of her and her literary activities as travel writer, novelist, and editor. Her salons in St. James Square (1818–1822), Seamore Place (1831–1836), and Gore House (1836–1849), as well as her traveling sociable circles in Italy (1823–1828), especially in Naples (1823–1826), made her a famous institution. The following two chapters will focus on her notorious life, her well-known *Conversations of Lord Byron* (1832–1833), her salons, and one exemplary guest, the American aesthete and dandy traveler Nathaniel Parker Willis (chapter 6); her literary activities—travelogues, keepsakes, and novels—her own appearances in her contemporaries' silver-fork novels, and the marketing of scandal (chapter 7).

From Irish Country Girl to London's Outcast Queen: Lady Blessington's Life

To understand the inner workings of Lady Blessington's salons, it is necessary to explore her life, including the scandals surrounding her. Margaret (later Marguerite) Power was born in Knockbrit in County Tipperary in Ireland on September 1, 1789,[4] one of five children of Edmund Power, a moderate Catholic and a magistrate, who was much hated by his Irish neighbors. Power, violent and financially in dire straits, married or rather sold his daughter Margaret to a Captain Farmer in 1804, whom she left after a period of only three months to return to her parents. From 1807, she lived with a Captain Jenkins, possibly for some time in Dublin, then in Hampshire, until the rich Irish widowed nobleman Lord Mountjoy, later Earl of Blessington, an old friend of Jenkins's, more or less bought her, offering £ 10,000 in compensation for previous expenses. The rich and extravagant Blessington, who commanded over an income of £ 30,000 per annum and was renowned for his hospitality and his theatricals at Mountjoy in Ireland, took his new possession to London and set her up in

Manchester Square. In late 1817, Farmer conveniently fell to his death from a window while drunk, and four months later, in February 1818, Lord Blessington and Marguerite Farmer got married. While the keeping of a mistress was not unusual for a wealthy aristocrat, such a connection nevertheless happened according to certain "etiquettes," which usually did not include a later marriage.[5] After a brief honeymoon in Ireland, Lord and Lady Blessington set up a house in St. James's Square, one of the most fashionable London addresses, where they entertained. Soon Marguerite Blessington realized that her past history as a runaway wife and kept mistress hindered her from achieving the elite social status she desired. Throughout the three decades of her career as a hostess, the fashionable ladies of the *bon ton* more or less ostracized her. Among her female friends were women of lower social status like Mrs. Charles Mathews, the actor's wife, and, possibly, the poet Letitia Landon.[6] From 1818 to 1822, she and her husband had a hospitable house, which, in theory, was open to men and women alike but in practice was frequented only by men. Among their guests were politicians like the Viscount Castlereagh and George Canning, the poets Thomas Moore and Samuel Rogers, the classical scholar Samuel Parr, and the painter Thomas Lawrence, whose acclaimed portrait of the hostess attracted Patmore's attention.

Between 1822 and 1829, the couple lived in France and Italy, where they met Byron in 1823. Because of the death of his only legitimate son in the same year, Lord Blessington added an ill-advised codicil to his will, which led to scandal as well as pecuniary problems and eventually contributed to his widow's financial ruin. This codicil made the dazzling French dandy Alfred D'Orsay, who had been introduced to the couple in 1821, the main beneficiary of Lord Blessington's will, provided he married Blessington's daughter, who was to inherit the bulk of the fortune. D'Orsay's subsequent marriage to the 15-year-old Harriet in 1827 fueled rumors about a *ménage à trois* between Lord and Lady Blessington and their dandy friend, thus adding to Lady Blessington's scandalous reputation. If some observers insinuated that D'Orsay was sleeping with his own mother-in-law, they may have overlooked the attraction between D'Orsay and Lord Blessington, newly wed husband and father-in-law.[7] The two *dramatis personae* who had no amorous interest in one another were Alfred and Harriet, husband and wife. After Lord Blessington's untimely death in Paris in 1829, Lady Blessington and her entourage returned to London in 1830, where Harriet left her husband in 1831, while the deceased Lord Blessington's family took legal steps to contest the will in order to secure the fortune. The scandal that was brewing seriously impeded

Lady Blessington's attempts to position herself as a major hostess.[8] Nevertheless, she opened her salon at Seamore Place in 1831 before, in 1836, she moved to Kensington to establish herself in Gore House. Continually surrounded by gossip, she was never acknowledged by London's major hostesses and received no visits from them but could enlist a large number of male visitors: politicians, literati, travelers, and artists. When her finances finally collapsed and her belongings were sold at a widely publicized auction in May 1849, she removed to Paris, where she died shortly afterwards, on June 4, 1849.

As Lady Blessington's pecuniary ups and downs motivated not only many of her activities as *salonnière* and author but also incited her contemporaries' envy and their subsequent schadenfreude, they are essential to any analysis of her salon. If she grew up in modest surroundings, her union with Lord Blessington catapulted her into fairy-tale-like wealth. Patmore takes the bedroom in her Parisian residence as an example of the luxury with which she surrounded herself: her bed "rested upon the backs of two exquisitely carved silver swans," while the recess in which it stood was lined with silk and lace, adorned with expensive pieces of furniture and fanciful objects.[9] Although Lord Blessington had an income of £ 30,000 per annum, his odd will stipulated that his widow would have only £ 2,000 a year, enough for a quiet and withdrawn existence but not for the sociable activities she envisioned. If she wrote her first books in the 1820s probably to entertain herself, her literary and editorial activities after her husband's death were necessary to secure additional income. She earned a lot in some years, as William Jerdan, editor of *The Literary Gazette*, explained: "I have known her enjoy from her pen an amount somewhere midway between £ 2,000 and £ 3,000 per annum, and her title as well as talents had considerable influence in 'ruling high prices.'"[10] During his sojourn in London in 1835, the gossipy American traveler Willis compared the royalties paid to novelists, among whom Lady Blessington ranked high: "Do you know the *real* prices paid now for books? Bulwer gets *fifteen* hundred pounds— Lady B. *four* hundred, Honourable Mrs. Norton *two* hundred and fifty, Lady Charlotte Bury *two* hundred, Grattan *three* hundred, and most others below this."[11] In the late 1840s, however, several financial problems coincided: D'Orsay's extravagant spending as well as his gambling, the potato blight, which reduced the income from Ireland, and the editor Charles Heath's death in 1848, which left the £ 700 he owed Blessington unpaid. The creditors began to move closer, the number of sociable evenings declined, and eventually, Blessington's belongings were sold at an auction, which lasted for 12 days.

To the reading public, Blessington was a noteworthy writer, who authored three travelogues, a conversation, 11 novels, numerous poems and short stories, and who edited a large number of keepsakes. Her first publications are two collections of short texts, *The Magic Lantern* (1822) and *Sketches and Fragments* (1822), stories and sketches of fashionable life in London, followed by a brief travelogue, *Journal of a Tour through the Netherlands to Paris* (1822) and the poem *Rambles in Waltham Forest* (1827).[12] If these early publications were anonymous, those that appeared after her husband's death, commencing with the *Conversations of Lord Byron* in 1832–1833, boldly carry her name and title, "by the Countess of Blessington," at a time when many women writers preferred to remain anonymous. Her literary self-fashioning, the exhibition of her authorship, was built on her aristocratic status. Many of the 11 novels she wrote, likewise her shorter fiction, are set in the present time and frequently depict protagonists who belong to or try to make their way into fashionable society. Blessington is sometimes listed among the "silver-fork school" of the 1820s and 1830s, together with the young Disraeli and Bulwer.[13] Silver-fork novels, often romans à clef, portray scenes from high life and are structured along plots of courtship and marriage. Blessington repeatedly pointed out the disturbing sides of this good society, as in her epistolary novel *The Victims of Society* (1837), in which a young woman is driven to death through the intrigues of a seemingly well-meaning friend—another woman. The novels express Blessington's personal anxieties: matchmaking mothers, gambling, loss of one's income, loveless marriages, and intrigue, which often has a female face. Unexpected deaths frequently put things right. The social satire, only thinly veiled, is developed in the dialogues. The 11 novels are: *The Repealers* (1833), *The Two Friends* (1835), *The Confessions of an Elderly Gentleman* (1836), *The Victims of Society* (1837), *The Confessions of an Elderly Lady* (1838), *The Governess* (1839), *Meredith* (1843), *Strathern* (1845), *The Memoirs of a Femme de Chambre* (1846), *Marmaduke Herbert* (1847), and *Country Quarters* (1850).[14] Among the settings are rural England, London, Ireland, France (especially Paris), and various regions in Italy, the space in which some of her protagonists find peace and harmony, like Marmaduke Herbert in the novel of the same name, who, heavily weighed down by misfortune, regains some happiness in Sorento's beautiful surroundings. Her travelogues *The Idler in Italy* (1839) and *The Idler in France* (1841) are thematically linked to her fiction.[15] Most of her writing was done for financial reasons, which was also the impetus behind her time-consuming editorial work for *Heath's Book of Beauty* (1834–1850) and *The Keepsake* (1841–1850). Ironically, one of Blessington's earliest texts, "The Auction," sketches the sale of a distinguished but ruined family's belongings,[16] the kind of event that put a visible end to her own career as a London hostess.

The large amount of available source material shapes the descriptions of Blessington's sociable activities. Since Blessington was more than 25 years younger than Berry and had her most active sociable phase in the 1830s and 1840s, that is, several decades later than Berry, her self-fashioning was far more noticeable in a mass print culture that was constantly on the lookout for celebrities. More and longer printed texts exist. That she published under her own name at least in the last two decades of her life also contributed to the public's growing awareness of her as a brand name. She seems to have kept a journal, which has not survived and which served as a basis for some publications, namely the *Conversations of Lord Byron, The Idler in Italy,* and *The Idler in France.* She may have rewritten the passages she used to meet her readers' expectations. Besides, a huge correspondence has survived. Immediately after her death, a number of obituaries and recollections in the style of Patmore's appeared, one of which was a memoir written by her niece, Miss Power, and prefixed to the posthumously published novel *Country Quarters.*[17] The first biography-cum-edition proper was a three-volume work by Blessington's old friend of 27 years, Richard Madden (MA 1: 3), entitled *The Literary Life and Correspondence of the Countess of Blessington* (1855), which combined biographical narrative, quotations from and summaries of Blessington's travelogues, documents relating to her family, various reminiscences including the author's own, and quotations from journal articles, autobiographies, and correspondences by other acquaintances. Madden, who aimed to present his long-standing friend as a well-connected hostess and writer, was very Victorian in carefully circumscribing events that his contemporaries would have considered scandalous. Unfortunately, the quality of his edition does not conform to today's standards. A comparison between some manuscript letters and Madden's edition shows that he omitted names as well as entire passages, or assigned wrong dates. One example is a letter by the former Lord Chancellor Henry Brougham to Blessington, dating from November 28, 1843, that runs: "I wish you would tell your clever, and, I believe honest friend of the Paper, that I have given up both my prosecutions before he said a word" (MA 3: 128). A look at the manuscript reveals that the original letter has not only been abbreviated by Madden but that the

"Paper" is in fact the *Examiner,* whose editor Albany Fonblanque was one of Blessington's regular guests.[18] Maybe Madden wished to present the *habitués* as a harmonious group, while the threat of a legal battle would have endangered this image. Another edition of additional letters, mostly addressed to Blessington, was undertaken by Alfred Morrisson in 1895, who, unlike Madden, was very exact in his editorial approach, as a comparison between some manuscript letters and the printed text shows.[19] These additional manuscripts were among the material J. Fitzgerald Molloy used for a new biography, *The Most Gorgeous Lady Blessington* (1896), which employs the strategies of a novel in laying open the characters' innermost feelings. One example: Molloy describes the devastating effect of Farmer's marriage proposal on the young Margaret in detail and through her eyes: "She heard in silence, scarce believing he was serious...she escaped from the room and blindly sought her own, situated at the top of the house, a dingy little apartment sacred to her as a sanctuary...Here she gave vent to the grief which shook, to the fear which overwhelmed her."[20] Molloy's book was followed by Michael Sadleir's excellent biography (1933), well-written and exact in its use of sources. Sadleir saw no need to Victorianize his subject, did not mince his words when it came to sexual matters, and contributed astute suggestions about the entanglement between the amorous, financial, and legal aspects of Lord Blessington's will on the one hand and the ensuing scandals on the other. Despite their vastly different approaches to their subject, all three major biographies (Madden, Molloy, and Sadleir) went into several editions or reissues.

Biographical information was also conveyed through the medium of short sketches in compendiums like Henry F. Chorley's *Authors of England* (1838), a magnificent representative volume with gilt edging, which presents a literary pantheon of 14 contemporary authors: Felicia Hemans, Sir Walter Scott, Lord Byron, Robert Southey, the Countess of Blessington, Samuel Taylor Coleridge, Edward Bulwer, Lady Morgan, Percy Bysshe Shelley, Thomas Moore, Charles Lamb, Mary Russell Mitford, Thomas Campbell, and William Wordsworth. The four pages devoted to Blessington situate her in a tradition of French salonnières and bluestocking hostesses, delineate a brief biography, praise her literary achievements, and show a medallion portrait.[21] Another example is "Fraser's Gallery of Illustrious Literary Characters," a series in *Fraser's Magazine,* which ran between 1830 and 1838 and devoted one page of text and a drawing to the Countess.[22] Such publications, featuring contemporary "worthies" of both sexes, contributed to sometimes reductionist images of well-known persons while fueling the celebrity cult, which Blessington herself was skillfully using when she began to publish her *Conversations of Lord Byron*.

THE CONVERSATIONS OF LORD BYRON

Blessington, one year younger than Byron, met and befriended the poet during her sojourn in Genoa in 1823 and published her *Conversations of Lord Byron* nearly ten years later, first in serialized form in the *New Monthly Magazine* (1832–1833) and then as a book (1834),[23] thereby fashioning herself as celebrity hostess and literary salonnière. These *Conversations*, which dramatize her encounters with Byron, belong to the genre of the printed conversation, popular around 1800, which has a unique tradition.[24] Printed conversations need to be considered in the context of advice books on conduct and education, which found their readers from the sixteenth century onward. In early modern Europe, a text prescribing polite discourse and appropriate conduct could gain immense popularity, like Castiglione's famous *Il Libro del Cortegiano* (1528), which ran into nearly 60 Italian editions in the sixteenth century alone. Numerous books on conversation were published, some of a general nature, some aiming at specific instruction such as Fenne's *Entretiens familiers pour les Amateurs de la Langue Françoise* (1690), which simultaneously teaches the French language and polite sociability.[25] Some of these texts assign particular roles to women, like the German *Frauenzimmer Gesprächsspiele (Women's Conversation Games*, 1641–1649) by Georg Philipp Harsdörffer, whose playful conversations have no immediate practical purpose but train the participants to sharpen their minds. It is the women's task to check the men: they are the skeptical audience the men have to convince, and they ensure that the conversations get neither too scholastic nor too pedantic.[26] The genre remained fashionable well into the nineteenth century. Blessington knew Walter Savage Landor's *Imaginary Conversations* (1824–1829), a series of fictitious dialogues by historical and contemporary figures such as writers, statesmen, and philosophers, men and women.[27]

All printed conversations, fictitious dialogues, and manuals of polite etiquette stand between the two poles of conversation as performance and conversation as sincere articulation of self. Although no conversation is pure performance or pure self-expression, the emphasis can either lie on the performative side, the awareness of the theatricality involved in successful self-fashioning, or on sincere and authentic self-expression. To use the vocabulary of speech act theory: all printed conversations oscillate between the "constative" and the "performative" poles.[28] One of the central oppositions in the *Conversations of Lord Byron* is that between speech as performance and speech as search for truth, between the performative and the constative side of his utterances. Blessington's Byron rapidly goes through a variety of poses but also seeks sincerity and lets his partner in conversation and, ultimately, his reader know what he is "really" like and how he feels. Through this publication, Blessington aimed to cast herself as a celebrity alongside Byron and thus raise her reputation (and of course her income). One of her models were Thomas Medwin's best-selling *Conversations of Lord Byron* (1824), which appeared in numerous editions, were quickly translated into French, German, and Italian, and contributed to the rise of Byronism.[29] Byron, who had died in Greece in 1824, was surrounded by an aura of literary fame, scandal, and gossip. His posthumous reception was fueled by rumors about his memoirs, burnt by well-meaning friends. The world was dying to know what Byron had "really" said in the last months of his life. It is important to note the circumstances of publication: Like Medwin's, Blessington's *Conversations* were taken on by Colburn, who first serialized them in his *New Monthly Magazine* between 1832 and 1833 and then published them in book form in 1834. Colburn held a unique place in the landscape of early nineteenth-century publishing because his publishing endeavors were part of a huge celebrity machine. He specialized in society novels, the already mentioned silver-fork novels. One of Colburn's advertising techniques consisted in writing to members of the aristocracy, inviting them to subscribe to gossipy books about their own acquaintances. Colburn focused on elite authors, whom he puffed and had reviewed in his periodical *New Monthly Magazine*. Occasionally, his marketing strategies caused his own authors to drop sarcastic comments: Benjamin Disraeli compared himself to "a literary prostitute" and called his publisher "Mother Colburn," insinuating that Colburn was as unconscionable as the proprietor of a brothel.[30] It was Samuel Carter Hall, assistant to Bulwer, the new editor of the *New Monthly Magazine*, who persuaded Blessington to write down her personal reminiscences of Byron.[31] Thus, the staging of a seemingly personal tête-a-tête occurred for a large readership and served to introduce Lady Blessington as a literary hostess.

Blessington's *Conversations* incorporate a threefold salon: (1) First, the conversations themselves, mainly between Blessington and Byron, are sociable activities. (2) Byron and Blessington constantly evoke their friends (and enemies) with such vivacity that they seem to participate in an imaginary salon. (3) The serialized *Conversations* invite the readers to feel as the guests, the habitués, of yet another salon, possibly Blessington's own. These different levels of sociability are linked.

(1) Blessington and Byron: The *Conversations of Lord Byron* are a retrospective first-person narrative, similar to a diary, sometimes akin to a novel, and related by Blessington. Among the major features is closeness to spoken language. Authentication is provided through the insertion of dates and details. The *Conversations* begin like a diary: "Genoa, April 1st, 1823. Saw Lord Byron for the first time" (CB 5). Blessington continues with Byron's appearance: "His head is finely shaped, and the forehead open, high, and noble" (5). Through the use of the present tense, her description creates immediacy. Much of the book consists of Byron's speech, to which Blessington's occasional comments are added. Unlike the plot of a novel, the structure of the *Conversations* is not linear but made up of a string of anecdotes and observations like the following:

> I observed that when, in our rides, we came to any fine point of view, Byron paused, and looked at it, as if to impress himself with the recollection of it...He told me, that from his earliest youth, he had a passion for solitude; that the sea, whether in a storm or calm, was a source of deep interest to him, and filled his mind with thoughts. "An acquaintance of mine," said Byron, laughing, "who is a votary of the lake, or simple school, and to whom I once expressed this effect of the sea on me, said that I might in this case say that the ocean served me as a vast inkstand: what do you think of that as a poetical image?" (84)

It is comic to imagine Byron, famous for his witticisms, considering a grave and unwieldy poetic image. After observations on landscape, the sublime, and literature, he continues to talk about the military. The recurrent topics—traveling, periodicals, London life, Napoleon, his numerous acquaintances, contemporary writing, etcetera—are not treated systematically. The famous digressions, stylistic features of his verse narratives, are also a marked element of the *Conversations*. The movement from one topic to the next is usually abrupt, the tenses change within a few lines. Often, one observation flows into the next, occasionally sudden breaks occur. As the *Conversations,* due to their lack of linearity, resemble spoken interaction, the reader becomes a guest who has just arrived and can join whenever he wishes. One need not read the *Conversations* from beginning to end: the book may be opened on any page. Interruptions occur, as in a real conversation, when a person or a letter arrives.

Although the *Conversations* do not possess the linear plot of a novel, they have one central character, Byron, whose style is convincingly reproduced and who takes up most of the space, while Blessington's thoughts and feelings only surface as she muses about him. Performance and essence are constantly at war with one another. In the earlier parts of the *Conversations*, Byron repeatedly emphasizes how much he misses his wife, from whom he had separated in 1816. The exact circumstances surrounding the breakdown of his marriage and his last months in London are unknown. In the eyes of "good" society, he had lapsed morally, possibly through an affair with his half-sister Augusta, possibly through his bisexuality, certainly because of the treatment to which he had exposed his wife. Accused of heartlessness, Byron represented himself as the jilted lover, but, within a very short time, he was cut by members of his own circle, left England, and never returned. In Blessington's *Conversations*, he figures as a true sufferer ("the old wounds are still unhealed," 73), cruelly mistreated by unfeeling people—handled roughly, like Blessington herself, who makes him talk a good deal about London society, which had rejected them both. The other Byron of the text performs, as Blessington remarks: "Ridicule is his play" (120). Byron repeatedly criticizes English "cant" (29) but constantly gossips about his acquaintances.[32] The insecurity as to who is the "real" Byron is heightened through frequent references to conversation, speaking, ridiculing, or gossiping. The text reflects the fundamental instability of all language, be it spoken or printed, like the text the reader of the *New Monthly Magazine* has before his eyes.

(2) The imaginary salon: For most of their conversation, Byron and Blessington are alone, although some communication is accompanied by sociable gatherings, mostly in the early part, for example, when Blessington describes Byron's cordial relationship with her husband. As Byron and Blessington converse, a second salon, an imaginary salon, gradually takes shape before the reader's eyes, London literati and those who belong to the bon ton, virtual guests, who are the topic of conversation. Germaine de Staël, famous salonnière and writer, who had visited London, is frequently talked about. They discuss her conversational behavior, by which Byron—who was scared stiff of her— felt dominated:

> Talking of literary women, Lord Byron said that Madame de Staël was certainly the cleverest, though not the most agreeable woman he had ever known. "She declaimed to you instead of conversing with you," said he, "never pausing except to take breath; and if during that

interval a rejoinder was put in, it was evident that she did not attend to it, as she resumed the thread of her discourse as though it had not been interrupted." (22)

Still, she repeatedly figures as a virtual guest of this imaginary salon, like Thomas Moore, Percy Shelley, and other authors. The descriptions can be vivid, especially when communicative peculiarities are under scrutiny. Like her silver-fork novels, Blessington's *Conversations* gossip about contemporaries, especially women at whose hands she had suffered exclusion. Among the readers of the serialized *Conversations* were in all likelihood two of Lady Blessington's old enemies, the famous hostesses Lady Jersey and Lady Holland, or at least their salon guests. In the first installment, she makes Byron describe the "imperious" Lady Holland, with whom she was rivaling for Byron's attention, as a domestic tyrant (11–12). Lady Jersey does not fare any better in the second installment:

> "But," said he, "my friend, Lady [Jersey], would have talked them all out of the field. She, I suppose, has heard that all clever people are great talkers, and so has determined on displaying, at least, *one* attribute of that genus; but her ladyship would do well to recollect that *all* great talkers are not clever people." (36–37)

This critique, conveniently uttered by Byron, depicts Blessington's rival as deficient in conversational and social skills. Men, in contrast, were judged more kindly: Moore's "social attractions" are "unrivalled" (10), Shelley is "most amiable" (52). The stereotyping of the great hostesses was an act of revenge for the rejection Blessington had suffered.

(3) The serialization and the readers as guests: The readers of the 1832–1833 serialization are the guests to yet another, a virtual salon, headed by Blessington, who assumes the role of the salonnière in mediating between the reader and Byron. The 1832 public was yearning for more information about Byron, "mad—bad—and dangerous to know,"[33] who had been dead for eight years. His reputation made him even more interesting. Although Blessington refrains from indiscrete disclosures of too personal details, she appeals to the reader's curiosity by inserting titbits: what Byron thought of his acquaintances, what he had stipulated in his will, and why. She gossips not only with Byron but also with the reader. Among the most detailed passages are attacks on the hypocrisy of English society, which she addressed through this publication. Blessington's status,

like Byron's, was problematic because she not only tried to build up a reputation but also had to refute malicious gossip.

After her return to England, Blessington struggled to combat a scandal that had arisen from her deceased husband's will: The rumors that the marriage between D'Orsay and Harriet was merely meant to cover up D'Orsay's affair with his mother-in-law were growing more audible. In 1831, anonymous attacks in the press, which had started as early as 1829, recommenced, Harriet left her husband, and Blessington's family took legal steps.[34] These events seriously damaged Blessington's reputation and destroyed her plans of joining fashionable society. Therefore, the *Conversations* not only served to justify Byron. When Blessington made Byron criticize English hypocrisy and cant, she saw not only the poet but also herself as a victim. Her critique disguises a demand for another, a fairer treatment of herself. In order to save her reputation, the key to all elite circles, Blessington tried to entice her readers into a reevaluation of her own case and thus suddenly became a performer in her own right. Among those she indirectly addressed was, for example, Lady Byron: Blessington made Lord Byron voice his regret that Staël, who he felt possessed too much imagination, was lacking "a mathematical education" (23). Lady Byron, known to be interested in mathematics, may have felt flattered. Friendly and unfriendly reviews of the *Conversations* testify to lively debates surrounding the serialized version and the book publication: the *Examiner* praised it as "clever and interesting," while *The Metropolitan Magazine* was wondering whether the author had a "most retentive memory" and asked if Byron had known "that the lady took notes," implying that it was risky to trust her.[35] It is not known to what extent exactly the *Conversations* helped Blessington succeed in reducing the scandal.

Blessington's own performance is an underrated yet central element of the *Conversations*, which through their serialization become part of an enlarged salon that includes the London reading public, friends, future allies, and old enemies. While the 11 installments appeared between July 1832 and December 1833, the actual communication surrounding the more or less monthly publication was powerful enough to change the structure of this printed salon conversation: The relationship between hostess and star guest deteriorated. In the last installments, Blessington seems to lose her patience with Byron, whose fascinating contradictions have turned into nuisances. While Blessington was finishing the writing of her *Conversations*, some friends may have told her that Byron had spoken of her in less than admiring tones.³⁶ Byron had even denied their friendship in a letter to Hobhouse on May 19, 1823: "Lady Blessington, with whom I have merely a common acquaintance" (BLJ 10: 177). She took revenge. At the end of the last installment, she complains about his "flippancy," his lack of tact, and his "incontinence of speech on subjects of a personal nature" (CB 228). This example demonstrates that printed conversations lead to spoken ones, which find their way back into the printed text. Writing feeds back into orality, orality feeds back into writing.

Serialization added further shades of meaning. Periodicals like the *New Monthly Magazine* are a "literary form" in themselves,³⁷ composed of separate but thematically related textual entities, which cohere through the "power of juxtaposition,"³⁸ as Deborah Wynne states. The October issue of the *New Monthly Magazine* (1832) can serve as an example. The fourth installment of the *Conversations* centers on Byron's temper, his sensitivity, his love of solitude and then turns to his poetological concepts, his dislike of the Lake School, the imagination, and the contrast between authors and men of fashion.³⁹ Embedded are remarks on conversational style, Napoleon, Staël, and Constant. The structure of Blessington's text, neither linear nor systematic, resembles a real-life conversation. The other articles contained in this issue of the *New Monthly Magazine* mirror Blessington's themes, for example, the sequel of *The Life of Shelley* by Thomas Jefferson Hogg, which elaborates on poetry, liberty, and literary performances of a very different sort: as Hogg muses about the "highest effort of his art,"⁴⁰ the contrast with the blasé Byron is huge. Another piece, "Private Hints to a Juvenile Physician," signed by "M.," is a satire on advice literature and carries the self-fashioning, so important to Blessington's *Conversations,* into a new area of life. "M." advises a young physician to wear the right dress and attend the right church in order to climb up the social ladder: "The greatest test of medical ability are solemnity of mien and mysteriousness of manner."⁴¹ The patients' welfare, in contrast, seems less important. A further article laments the lack of proper judgment in public opinion, also a recurrent theme between Blessington and Byron. As a literary form, the group of texts in any one issue of a nineteenth-century periodical may not support or refute an argument but add various angles of observation. What contributes to uniting the texts embedded into this cultural intertextuality are the readers, who peruse them and talk about them. As every issue of a Victorian periodical had several readers, Blessington's *Conversations of Lord Byron* led to ever-widening circles of communication, linking orality and writing.

"Her Genius Lay in Her Tongue": The Salons at Seamore Place and Gore House

"Hesitating, Humming, and Drawling, are the three Graces of our Conversation," Edward Bulwer unflatteringly stated in his classic survey *England and the English* (1833) and continued with the satirical imitation of a conversational style that is vague and inarticulate:

> We are at dinner:—a gentleman, "a man about town," is informing us of a misfortune that has befallen his friend: "No—I assure you— now err—err—that—er—it was the most shocking accident possible—er—poor Chester was riding in the Park—er—you know that grey—er—(substantive dropped, hand a little flourished instead)—of his—splendid creature!—er—well sir, and by Jove—er—the—er (no substantive, flourish again)—took fright, and e—er."[42]

Bulwer's point is that the gentleman's lack of fluency, regarded as characteristic of English upper-class speech, especially of Tory speech, in the early nineteenth century, prevents him from telling even a simple anecdote, and so "poor Chester's" fate must remain obscure.[43] When *England and the English* appeared in 1833, its author, then also editor of the *New Monthly Magazine*, had recently befriended Blessington, in whose circle he encountered a very different communicative style. Many contemporary voices testify to the vivacity and the brilliance of the conversations at her gatherings in Seamore Place, later in Gore House. "Her genius lay (so to speak) in her tongue," Patmore reminisced about her salon: "Talking, not writing, was Lady Blessington's forte."[44] Madden admired her brevity, her "particular turn for cramming a vast deal of meaning into an exceeding small number of words" (MA 1: 156); Henry Crabb Robinson found her talk "very pleasant"; Mrs. Crosland dubbed her "quite the best *raconteuse* I ever heard"; other guests dropped similar comments.[45] The genuine pleasure caused by her conversation was of magnetic force to her visitors.

All in all, Blessington ran four salon-like formations, three of them in London, which happened in several places and under varying pecuniary auspices: in St. James Square between 1818 and 1822, in Seamore Place between 1831 and 1836, and in Gore House between 1836 and 1849. During her time in Italy, she kept an open house in Naples and other places and was continuously visited by many Englishmen so that these sociable activities resemble a traveling salon, dealt with in chapter 7. Her first salon is by far the worst documented. It was visited by politicians like Canning and Castlereagh and writers (71–72) but seems to have caused far fewer ripples than her later sociable activities. When she returned to London after her husband's death, the mansion in St. James Square was too expensive for her to keep up. She needed the additional income that came from writing and editing, and that may be one reason why her salons at Seamore Place and Gore House eclipsed her earlier one. The house in Seamore Place in Mayfair, which she rented for five years, was much more central and closer to Hyde Park than Gore House, which was situated in Kensington. Sadleir muses that the move in 1836 was not only motivated by the lapse of the five-year lease but had two other reasons: The continuing lack of recognition on the side of the social elite made her no longer wish to live in their vicinity. Moreover, she needed quiet surroundings for her full-time work as an author.[46] Despite financial worries, both houses were fitted out luxuriously when she moved there. Visitors would be asked to meet the hostess not in the drawing-room but in the library, which in many nineteenth-century households was considered to be the gentlemen's retreat.[47] The writer Mrs. Crosland describes a large, splendid room at Gore House with walls "almost entirely covered with books," enamel white shelves with small ornamental mirrors, two fireplaces, and white-gold-green furniture, where Blessington, with a hairstyle in "lady-abbess fashion," reigned: "Summer and winter Lady Blessington always occupied the same seat, a large easy-chair near the fireplace, with a small table beside her, on which was probably a new book with the paper-knife between the leaves, and a scent-bottle and a fan."[48] If nineteenth-century descriptions of interiors often served to present women as domestic, this account fuses intellectual with asexual connotations: contrary to all rumors, Blessington appears as pure in her devotion to the higher good of literature. The grandeur of her salons was further enhanced by a tall, powdered footman, a status symbol of the wealthy.[49] Like Walpole, Blessington collected and exhibited objects: portraits and glassware, souvenirs from her journeys, but also artifacts that had belonged to the famous, thus creating an imaginary circle of celebrities around her through items like "a ring with a black pearl found in the East by Lord Byron," a vinaigrette that had belonged to Napoleon,[50] a clock "enamelled in medallions of Cupids" that had been Marie Antoinette's.[51] Despite its initial splendor, Blessington's last salon in Gore House was weighed down by pecuniary problems, which eventually made most sociable activities come to a halt.

Being a renowned salonnière meant competition: Once she was back in London, Blessington soon found herself engaged in territorial fights with other major hostesses. Many a habitué attended several salons, like Joseph Jekyll, lawyer and politician, who wrote on June 20, 1831: "Within this fortnight I have also dined with no less than three immaculate Countesses—she of Cork and Orrery, she of Blessington, and she of Harrington."[52] Jekyll, who was in his seventies, was sought after; he also knew the Berrys: "The Misses Berry tell me they have dined with the Speaker and wife, who have thrown my Blessington overboard" (July 18, 1831).[53] Jekyll meant Charles Manners-Sutton, the speaker of the House of Commons, who was married to Ellen, Lady Blessington's sister. On November 24 he complained that Lady Cork, another well-known hostess, had scolded him "for leaving her to visit Lady Blessington, whom she called the worst of women."[54] Such unfriendly reactions were probably connected to the scandals surrounding Blessington in 1831. Other rivaling hostesses were Lady Holland, Lady Jersey, Lady Charleville, and Lady Morgan; Jekyll, who read the serialized *Conversations of Lord Byron* in the *New Monthly Magazine*, was amused by Blessington's hostile comments on Lady Holland and Lady Jersey.[55] The cult of female friendship, sometimes nostalgically evoked in salon research, had no place among the London hostesses of the 1830s.

Who went? The table of contents of Madden's three-volume biography-cum-edition reads like a who's who of nineteenth-century literary life. Among the regular guests were Edward Bulwer, Benjamin Disraeli, Charles Dickens, Henry Crabb Robinson, Thomas Moore, Albany Fonblanque, Joseph Jekyll, William Makepeace Thackeray, Walter Savage Landor, Samuel Rogers, and other well-known literati, writers as well as editors. When the Hungarian composer and pianist Franz Liszt became involved with Gore House in 1840, he complained about the lack of aristocratic visitors from whom he had hoped to gain patronage.[56] Politicians of varying affiliations passed through her salon: If she played hostess to Castlereagh as Lord Blessington's wife in St. James Square, the widowed salonnière was less sought after by major politicians. According to the painter Benjamin Haydon, one of the nineteenth century's most prolific diarists, Blessington wished "to be considered the female rallying point of the Liberals" in June 1834.[57] The careful wording suggests that her attempt to become a political hostess did not lead to triumph. One can only muse about whether she seriously planned to rival Holland House. In 1838, Louis Napoleon, then unsuccessful claimant to the French throne yet nevertheless an internationally known figure, came to live in London and began to frequent Gore House before he made another attempt to gain the throne in 1840. To Blessington, herself on the periphery of good society, he must have appeared equally marginalized, Romantic, and therefore interesting. Barely any women were among the habitués. William Archer Shee praised the "brilliant" and "*recherché*" society at Lady Blessington's but added: "I am speaking of male society."[58] As the once runaway wife, mistress to a nobleman whom she later married, and now reputed mistress of a French dandy, who lived in or close to her household for most of the time after their return from the continent, Blessington was shunned by other women of the bon ton. Archer Shee joked that the mentioning of Lady Blessington's name in Lady Morgan's presence was "like shaking a red flag in front of a bull."[59] Hall remarked: "Ladies were rarely seen at her receptions." His own wife visited during daytime but did not attend in the evening because the Halls could not afford to risk their reputation: "We were not of rank high enough to be indifferent to public opinion."[60] Among those who avoided her was Lady Holland, who, as a divorcée, received similar treatment and had more male than female visitors. Of course, Blessington was visited by some women, like her sister Ellen, the speaker's wife, while her niece Ellen Power lived with her. Women who wrote for her *Keepsake*, like Mrs. Crosland or Letitia Landon, came to talk about work. Mrs. Mathews, the actor's wife, whose son had worked with Lord Blessington on architectural schemes, was a friend. And the Countess Teresa Guiccioli, notorious through her affair with Byron, another tainted woman, came, too. The guests Blessington surrounded herself with stood somewhere between celebrity and notoriety.

Talking, eating, and drinking were among the main activities during Blessington's evening parties. As Hall's statement exemplifies, the men went in the evenings, often to debate literature and gossip about acquaintances. They cherished the combined pleasures of intellectual conversation and good food, as an account given by Jekyll of a dinner party in January 1832 shows:

> George Colman, James Smith of the "Rejected Addresses," Rogers of the "Pleasures of Memory," and Campbell of the "Pleasures of Hope" dined with me yesterday at a Parisian repast of much refinement given us by the Countess of Blessington. There was wit, fun, epigram, and raillery enough to supply fifty county members for a twelvemonth.[61]

Numerous other diary entries or biographical sketches, many written after her death, praise Blessington's evenings and sometimes (unlike most texts about the Berrys) account for the conversation in greater detail, like several sections in Haydon's diary, or the anonymous essay "Gore House," which takes the auction in 1849 as an occasion for a nostalgic look back.[62] Another reason for attending Blessington's salon was that up-and-coming authors were waiting to be "lionized." A "lion" was a minor celebrity who had gained renown through one literary work and was hoping to achieve more fame.[63] Young writers desired to make contacts, or meet publishers and reviewers. Some expected help in obtaining an ordinary job: in 1848, Blessington tried to get Thackeray a position in the post office but did not succeed.[64] One such "lion," who gained through his contacts with Blessington, was the American journalist Willis, the self-styled chronicler of British upper-class lifestyle.

NATHANIEL PARKER WILLIS: AN AMERICAN CONNECTION

Blessington's salon was not only a London institution but also known in other countries, partly because of the success of her *Conversations of Lord Byron* but also because of the friends she had made abroad. When Nathaniel Parker Willis, an American journalist who traveled through Europe in the early 1830s, visited London in 1835, one of his aims was to meet the capital's social and intellectual elite, and therefore, he paid Blessington a visit soon after his arrival.[65] The following description, one of the most detailed of the library at Seamore Place, appeared in an article in the *New-York Mirror* soon after his visit and emphasized his supposed familiarity with European patrician mores for a wider American readership. Willis, who carried a letter from their mutual friend Landor, was fascinated by what he mistook to be the epitome of an aristocratic style of sociability:

A friend in Italy had kindly given me a letter to Lady Blessington, and with a strong curiosity to see this celebrated lady, I called on the second day after my arrival in London. It was "deep i' the afternoon," but I had not yet learned the full meaning of "town hours." "Her ladyship had not come down to breakfast." I gave the letter and my address to the powdered footman, and had scarce reached home when a note arrived inviting me to call the same evening at ten.

In a long library lined alternately with splendidly-bound books and mirrors, and with a deep window of the breadth of the room, opening upon Hyde Park, I found Lady Blessington alone. The picture to my eye as the door opened was a very lovely one. A woman of remarkable beauty half buried in a fauteuil of yellow satin, reading by a magnificent lamp, suspended from the centre of the arched ceiling; sofas, couches, ottomans and busts, arranged in rather a crowded sumptuousness through the room; enamel tables, covered with expensive and elegant trifles in every corner, and a delicate white hand relieved on the back of a book, to which the eye was attracted by the blaze of its diamond rings. As the servant mentioned my name, she rose and gave me her hand very cordially, and a gentleman entering immediately after, she presented me to her son-in-law, Count D'Orsay, the well-known Pelham of London, and certainly the most splendid specimen of a man and a well-dressed one that I had ever seen. Tea was brought in immediately, and conversation went swimmingly on.[66]

Although salons were places of social interaction, they nevertheless also opened possibilities of intimate tête-a-têtes. Willis renders Blessington as the solitary queen residing over an orientalizing and erotic space, as the convener of a sociability that furthered intimate encounters. It is interesting to note that a similar surrounding, the library at Gore House, made Mrs. Crosland compare its owner to an "abbess," that is, a female ruler without erotic claims. Blessington's employment of a powdered footman is—to borrow Homi Bhabha's term—an instance of a "mimicry" of aristocratic mores, which is then doubled by Willis himself, who, in an act of what Sandra Tomc calls "Old World mimicry," not only (wrongly) presents the marginalized Countess of Blessington as an icon of British aristocratic spirit but also emphasizes his own "sameness,"[67] thus appearing as a paragon of British aristocratic mores to his American readership.

Willis is an early mediator of English and American literature and culture, a go-between, and little known today. During the nineteenth century, Willis's journalism helped to build up the cult of celebrities in America, which is the main motivation behind his interest in British life and in the notorious Lady Blessington. Born in the district of Maine in Portland in 1806, Willis grew up in a strictly evangelical family and was educated at Yale. Among his first literary products was scriptural verse, poetry that dealt with Biblical and religiously inspired topics and deliberately imitated Byron's style. Even though young Willis quickly found an enthusiastic readership, his poetic endeavors were highly problematic from a religious viewpoint because, in American evangelical circles, style and beauty were not considered as relevant. On the contrary, it was upheld that piety should not be judged by appearance.[68] Eventually, Willis fell victim to Boston's church discipline, and in 1829, was expelled from church fellowship for attending the theater and for failing to go to communion. Since this meant the end of his religious career, Willis subsequently converted to dandyism and turned to journalism as a source of income. He soon became the editor of the *American Monthly Magazine* and styled himself as a dandy after the model of Pelham, the main character of Bulwer's novel *Pelham* (1828), which was popular on both sides of the Atlantic. Between 1831 and 1834, Willis traveled through France, Italy, and Britain as a freelance foreign European correspondent. He wrote a series of articles for the *New-York Mirror*. In 1835, he published a compendium of travel writing, *Pencillings by the Way*,[69] that became very popular and was reprinted several times in Britain and America. He also wrote short fiction on topics related to his journeys through Europe.

Willis, whose early poetry was influenced by Byron, was charmed by Blessington's celebrity status. To him, she represented the heart and soul of British refinement and of London's sparkling society, to which he devoted several articles. His initial description sets the tone for later encounters. The passage above abounds with words like "splendid," "lovely," "magnificent," "expensive," "elegant," and "delicate." Drawn in by the luxurious aura of orientalizing sumptuousness, he used Blessington to dramatize his own ideals of British refinement, to style himself as a connoisseur of female beauty, of interiors, of clothing, and as an apostle of aestheticism. Moreover, his description of the solitary evening also contains erotic undercurrents: anything may develop between the solitary hostess with the hand on her book and her visitor. Female reading, much debated in the nineteenth century, was seen as educating but also as morally endangering, especially the reading of fiction, which Blessington herself produced so copiously. The hand on the book, the slight physical contact, hints at readiness to engage with the imaginary erotic encounters offered by novels but also a possible willingness to leave the book behind in order to act out this very encounter with her visitor, before the backdrop of an interior that denotes oriental splendor, erotic transgression, and lascivious opportunities. Willis's fascination ran contrary to all doctrinal church teaching he had previously been exposed to, but under the influence of English dandyism and the aesthete's fascination with the beautiful, he overcompensated. That they were joined by a fellow dandy, D'Orsay, lets the encounter appear more refined to an American readership, who was unaware of the scandalous rumors. *Fraser's Magazine*, which promoted the celebrity cult, was quick to joke about Willis's enthusiasm by calling him "Countess-smit."[70] Willis mentioned her in several of his articles about London and frequented her salon during his stay.[71] By presenting Blessington as a member of the English upper class while ignoring her marginalization, Willis provided a newly emerging urban elite in New York with a model for manners and style.[72] Willis did not realize or did not wish to realize to what extent Lady Blessington and D'Orsay were on the fringe rather than in the center of the bon ton. Apparently, he took them to be at the very heart of the capital's fashionable society and sold these intimate encounters as authentic tête-a-têtes with Britain's social elite to his American readership.

His fascination with English salons found another outlet in a verse narrative in *ottava rima* after Byron's *Don Juan,* entitled *Lady Jane: A Humorous Novel in Rhyme* (1844),[73] which one American paper immediately decried as "aristocratic shilling literature."[74] The tale is a turbulent yet slightly incoherent triangular love affair initiated in a salon context. The central woman character, Lady Jane, visits the Countess of Pasibleu to obtain advice on her love life. Literally translated, "Pasibleu" means "not quite so blue" and alludes to the fact that a new generation of women writers (like Blessington or Norton) wrote novels and poems that were popular but could hardly be deemed intellectual reading matter. If contemporary reviews identify the Countess Pasibleu as the notorious Caroline Norton (e.g., one review in *Graham's American Monthly Magazine*),[75] whose scandalous love affair with the Prime Minister, Lord Melbourne, shaped the perception of her for decades, this literary character nevertheless closely resembles Blessington, too. The identification of Willis's salonnière-cum-procuress with the two hostesses and editors is supported by names of guests (Canto II, stanzas XIV–XVII)[76] one could meet in Blessington's and Norton's entourage. The name of the Countess contains yet another allusion because blue was one of Blessington's favorite colors, especially when it came to clothes. Both Blessington and Norton, likewise Letitia Landon, all three contributors to and editors of annuals, marketed their scandals quite deliberately and successfully.[77] Since the scandal surrounding Norton's and Melbourne's affair reached its climax in 1836, roughly at the time when Willis socialized with Blessington's friends, he may well have had both women in mind when inventing the morally dubious yet rather stimulating character of the Countess Pasibleu, whom he introduces in yet another oriental setting:

> And drapery, gold-broider'd in Stamboul,
> Closed the extremity in lieu of door:
> This the page lifted, and disclosed to view
> The boudoir of the Countess Pasibleu.
>
> It was a small pavilion lined with pink,—
> Mirrors and silk all, save the door and the sky-light,
> The latter of stain'd glass. (You would not think
> How juvenescent is a rosy high light!)
> Upon the table were seen pen and ink.
> (Canto I, from stanzas XXVII and XXVIII)[78]

This is another instance of how a hostess and intellectual woman is set in an orientalizing scene with erotic overtones. The reader is invited into the innermost sanctum of a learned, a reading, and writing woman. The anxieties evoked by intellectual women were thus channelled into visions of erotic possibilities. The lack of a conventional door, the page, the visual qualities of the scene (silk, the colors gold and pink), and the artifice all connote a mock-oriental surrounding designed to entice the visitor. The satire is obvious: only artifice, namely colored glass, can produce the rosy hue on her skin, the sign of youth that ought to make her desirable. In other words: she is a fake sexual object, whose awareness of the London publishing scene, which she has conquered in quasi-Napoleonic fashion, unmasks her as a skilled literary tradeswoman. It seems that Willis's original fascination had given way to a more skeptical attitude, which was possibly informed by envy or rivalry, or maybe by gossip.

Another satirical reaction to Blessington's circle is Edgar Allan Poe's short text "Lionizing" (1835), which takes Willis's journalism about Blessington as a model,[79] caricatures the visitors of "the Duchess of Bless-my-soul," and reveals the hollowness of the supposedly sparkling salon conversation:

> The Duchess of Bless-my-soul was sitting for her portrait. The Marchioness of So-and-so was holding the Duchess's poodle. The Earl of This-and-that was flirting with her salts, and His Royal Highness of Touch-me-not was standing behind her chair. I merely walked towards the artist, and held up my proboscis.
> "O beautiful!"—sighed the Duchess of Bless-my-soul.
> "O pretty!"—lisped the Marchioness of So-and-so.
> "Horrible!"—groaned the Earl of This-and-that.
> "Abominable!"—growled his Highness of Touch-me-not.[80]

Unlike in the horror tales, here, the social satire prevails. The narrator is first cheered because of his impressive nose but soon has to suffer the degrading experience that the new "lion" is someone with no nose at all. The fascination with body parts and mutilation—a nose is shot off—is typical of Poe. Lionizing, it seems, is a vain affair. If Willis admired British upper-class lifestyle and refinement, Poe, who occasionally used aristocratic props and genealogies to flesh out his morbid plots, avowed his skepticism in the face of luxuries, conversation, and taste. Nevertheless, his early pieces also testify to a fascination with British topics and with the cult of celebrity. He followed Willis in as far as he mistook Blessington's salon sociability as a specimen of aristocratic culture, yet if Willis found the tête-a-tête with the reading Countess irresistable, Poe's narrator merely participates in an exchange of commonplaces about his proboscis, his nose, which of course is also a phallic symbol. The erotically tinged intimacy has given way to crude allusions to the sexual undercurrents, yet without any of the fascination encapsulated in Willis's article. The examples of Willis and Poe show how salon conversations can expand in space and time, from Blessington's chats with Byron in Genoa in 1823 to the publication of her *Conversations* in London between 1832 and 1834, to Willis's desire for an authentic tête-a-tête in London and the subsequent articles in New York in 1835, to Poe's satire about salon conversation, also printed in 1835.

Moreover, this case study throws light on how a salonnière's international reputation was forged. The contact with Willis was one reason behind the fame Blessington enjoyed in America,[81] where her novels and keepsakes were sold, partly in the original, partly as reprints. Henry Wikoff, an American author, took "a Philadelphia edition of some of her works" to Gore House.[82] Lydia Sigourney, who had visited Blessington at Gore House, wrote to her in 1842: "I have seen with great admiration your *Keepsake* and *Book of Beauty* for the present year, which are embellishing the center tables of some of our aristocracy," and "Are you aware how much your novel of 'Meredith' is admired in these United States?"[83] Library catalogs list a number of American editions of her novels, especially by publishers in Philadelphia. Before the advent of international copyright law, such reprints had an ambivalent status: they enhanced a writer's reputation but also reduced profit because most of these reprints were pirated editions for which no or hardly any royalties were paid. A letter by her London publisher Longman of 1843 informs Blessington of an American offer "for the early sheets" of her forthcoming novel *Meredith*, which Longman declined because the sum of five pounds seemed inappropriate.[84] A letter by Dickens, fuming about American publishers' reluctance to stop the unauthorized reprinting,[85] shows that copyright questions were among the concerns debated in her salon.

Blessington arrived, however, at an agreement with the German publisher Tauchnitz in Leipzig. Even before international copyright came into force, the Anglophile Tauchnitz, who reprinted best-selling English-language books, particularly novels, for the continental market, came up with an innovative scheme: he paid royalties to British authors (instead of pirating them) and declared that his reprints were not to be sold in Britain or the colonies. In exchange, he often got early sheets and could do the reprinting before any of his competitors.[86] Since his offers were attractive, many of Blessington's novels exist in Tauchnitz editions. Moreover, some of her works were translated into German and French. Readers outside Britain, drawn to her novels as expressions of fashionable Anglomania, must have regarded her predominantly as an aristocratic woman, not as an outsider. A German review of *Strathern* praised "her high social station,"[87] falling into the same trap as Willis, who rendered her a mediator of English style.

Chapter 7

The Countess of Blessington as Writer and Editor

When Lady Oriel and Mrs. Forrester, two characters in Blessington's novel *The Repealers*, visit the London opera, Lady Oriel, an experienced socialite, and her sister-in-law, who has just arrived from rural Ireland, discuss who else of renown is present:

> The lady leaving the box next Lady Ridney's, is the authoress of, what shall I say, half the popular novels of the day, among which there is not a single failure; her books give you all the sparkle of fashionable life, without any of its inanity, and her fecundity of imagination is as extraordinary as her facility of language; she appears never to tire herself, and certainly never tires her readers, for she is always brilliant and often profound. (R 2: 229–230)

This pen portrait exemplifies how Marguerite Blessington, who boldly published her own books under the name "the Countess of Blessington," envisioned the ideal woman writer: successful, tasteful, admired, in the midst of a society whose chronicler and stylish entertainer she was. The unnamed authoress—Catherine Gore, according to Michael Sadleir[1]—is no solitary Romantic genius, no "trumpet of a prophecy"[2] in the style of Shelley. The woman in the opera mirrors Blessington's ideal view of herself as a socialite-cum-writer: the production and reception of her novels, travelogues, and keepsakes was closely linked to her activities as *salonnière*. She could not possibly conceive of writing without socializing, without conversations. But as, unlike male authors such as Charles Dickens, she never worked from an office, she had to negotiate her contacts through invitations and evening entertainments.³ The following chapter will look at Blessington as a travel writer, writer of and character in silver-fork novels, and editor of keepsakes; it will show to what extent her literary and sociable activities were interconnected. That she provided accounts of London society with foreign settings, ranging from Italy to Ireland, heightened her aura as a classy harbinger of cosmopolitan style.

Sociable Idlers in Italy

The main source of Blessington's Italian period is her travelogue *The Idler in Italy*, two volumes published in 1839, followed by a third in 1840, probably named in imitation of Samuel Johnson's weekly series of essays called *The Idler* (1758–1760).⁴ The self-ironic title, a comment on the playful lack of purpose of her journey, suggests that indulgence rather than efficiency and industry were the prevailing moods, although the travelers themselves do not convey the impression that dolce far niente or well-cultivated ennui were their main pleasures. A review in the *New Monthly Magazine* even defends the author against charges of laziness: "Two volumes...prove that her ladyship was constantly and variously employed."⁵ Blessington's decision to publish a travelogue on Italy ten years after her return was probably motivated by pecuniary needs. The number of editions and reprints alone testifies to the success of *The Idler in Italy* and its sequel, *The Idler in France* (1841), which were each issued in a second edition by Colburn and reprinted in English by Galignani (Paris) and Baudry (Paris), who were both catering to English travelers on the continent but also making money from reimporting such print products into Britain, a practice facilitated by a loophole in copyright law.⁶ Moreover, both travelogues were reprinted, if not pirated, by the Philadelphia publishers Carey and Hart.⁷ That nearly all of these second editions and reprints appeared in the year of the books' first publication or shortly afterwards shows that they were attractive to their readers for several reasons: First of all, the "Countess of Blessington," known through her *Conversations of Lord Byron*, several novels, and her editorial work, was already a celebrity. Second, part of *The Idler in Italy* covers the period of her encounters with Byron. Third, the genre of travel writing, particularly about Italy, was very popular among travelers in search of cultural guidebooks.⁸ The reviews about *The Idler in Italy* devote little space to critical comments and quote intensely to give the reader a flavor.⁹ If many travel writers chose either the journal or the epistolary form, both of which allowed for a synthesis of factual description and personalized accounts, Mary Berry combined the two, while Blessington published a revised journal. That the keeping of a travel journal was customary can be seen from Lady Holland, who did not intend to see her observations in print. Although the gap between Blessington's stay in Italy in the 1820s and the publication of *The Idler* in 1839 seems huge, that between Berry's first Italian journey in the 1780s and the posthumous publication of her *Journals* in 1865 is still larger. Blessington's descriptions of landscape, architecture, classical sites, and local ambience are far more elaborate than Berry's and Lady Holland's, maybe because Blessington could turn to a tradition of female travel writing about Italy, which rendered her more self-confident. Among the topics this subchapter concerns itself with are the details of Blessington's journey, her self-fashioning as a social and cultural authority, the all-pervading theatricality she finds in Italy, her rendering of domesticity—deemed particularly relevant in women's travel writing—and the literariness of her text.

Blessington's traveling companions, her fellow idlers, remain shadowy in her publication. The Blessington entourage was originally made up of Lady and Lord Blessington, her sister Mary Ann Power, and Alfred D'Orsay. Further traveling *habitués* joined for parts of the trip, like her other sister Ellen (Mrs. Home Purves), her five children, and her companion, Charles Manners-Sutton, speaker of the House of Commons, or the young architect Charles Mathews, whom Lord Blessington employed to make plans for a fancy castle at Mountjoy, which, however, never materialized. Mathews's autobiography,[10] which covers part of the Italian trip, adds information about the travelers' interaction. Onlookers probably would have characterized the Blessington entourage, which Sadleir fittingly labeled "the Blessington circus,"[11] as luxurious travelers. They did not stay in one place. Among the major stations described in *The Idler in Italy* were, in chronological order, Paris, Geneva, Lyons, Vienne, Avignon, Nice, Genoa, Lucca, Florence, Rome, Naples, Rome, Pisa, and Rome, whereas *The Idler in France* concentrates on Paris. As Naples was the city where they stayed longest, for nearly three years, it receives the most attention in the travelogue and is also the focus of this section. For the majority of English travelers in search of classical lore, art history, and church history, Rome was the principal Italian city. Naples, however, opened the possibility of excursions to places of striking scenery such as Amalfi, Sorento, Capri, and Mount Vesuvius, or to the archeological excavation sites of Pompeii and Herculaneum. Unlike her husband, Lady Blessington was an avid visitor of places of interest.

A letter from Mathews to his mother written in 1824 details the daily routine: after breakfast, the company engaged in daily sightseeing, provided the weather was suitable.[12]

Many descriptions in *The Idler* focus on her large circle of acquaintances, through which Blessington renders herself a social and cultural authority. Among the first people she mentions in her Neapolitan journal are the most authoritative ones in terms of social status, namely the royal family (I 2: 72–73). Among her guests were local Italian nobility, other (mostly English) travelers, for example, Henry Edward Fox (Lady Holland's son), churchmen like the Archbishop of Tarentum, naval officers, scholars, and writers.[13] It is noteworthy that throughout the years in Italy, the Blessington entourage encountered the same set of people in a variety of surroundings so that one criterion for the definition of a salon, the set of regular visitors, is met. As in London, Blessington's salon failed to gain the acceptance of many Englishwomen, most of whom were abroad because they accompanied their husbands. The sections about Naples enumerate nearly only male visitors. Merely a handful of women who belonged to the local nobility were among those who visited. Among her regular guests were the scholars William Gell, William Drummond, and Richard Keppel Craven. Gell's meticulous study *Pompeiana* was the first account of Pompeii in English and went into several editions.[14] Craven published a number of books, among them *A Tour Through the Southern Provinces of the Kingdom of Naples* (1821) and *Excursions in the Abruzzi and Northern Provinces of Naples* (1838).[15] Drummond was a classicist with a declared interest in lost civilizations like Assyria and Babylon. By showing to the 1839 reader that she had continuously surrounded herself with eminent classical scholars, Blessington enhanced her own cultural authority. If Kathryn Walchester remarks that female travelers were usually less enthusiastic about sites of classical antiquity,[16] Blessington proves the opposite: she visited Pompeii and Herculaneum accompanied by Gell, thereby enlisting the most competent authority available as her own and her readers' cicerone.

One major textual strategy in travel writing about Italy is "intensification," as Chloe Chard has shown, which often works through hyperbole and allegory.[17] Blessington repeatedly used this method in descriptions of interaction, for example, of the conversations that were central to all activities:

> I have rarely met so gifted a person as Sir William Drummond, who dined with us yesterday. To a profound erudition in classical lore, he joins a great variety of other knowledge, being an adept in modern

literature, mineralogy, chemistry, and astronomy. The treasures of his capacious mind are brought into action in his conversation, which is at once erudite, brilliant, and playful. (I 2: 111–112)

The image of "treasures" denotes the value Blessington ascribed to his conversation. If Drummond excelled at her dinners through "flashes" of imagination, Gell, prone to ridiculing, emerges as "a laughing philosopher" (112, 113). *The Idler* not only chronicles the communal sightseeing but also praises the quality of interaction, the combination of playfulness, learning, and the ability to perform oneself. Most days were spent outside in surroundings brimming with history:

> Every step in the environs of Naples is pregnant with classical associations, and the pleasure of exploring such scenery is greatly enhanced by the companionship of those whose minds are so highly cultivated, and enriched by learning, that the view of places to which a classical interest is attached awakens in them invaluable stores of erudition to delight their associates. (188)

Tourism, conversation, learning, and delight fuse into one intense emotional experience.[18] Sightseeing opens spaces of creativity, which occasion spontaneous performances like the citation of the poem in the midst of ruins mentioned in chapter 1 of this study.

Blessington's sociability is mirrored by an all-pervasive theatricality, which is embedded into the Italian ambience, where ordinary people and nobility, musicians and poets, even priests and congregations perform continuously in an atmosphere that is histrionic per se. This spectacular quality of the Italian experience is highly visible in the streets of Naples ("the appearance of a fête," 119–120), during religious events like the annually staged miracle of St. Januarius, the exhibition of a vial of a martyred saint's blood, which becomes liquid during mass (144–148),[19] a fête on the water by the King of Naples (224–226), or the grotesque yearly display of bodies in Santa Chiara (263–269). The description of the King's fête possesses the fairy-tale-like intensity of a dream, in which visual and acoustic pleasures create sensory delight:

> A rich stream of music announced the coming of the royal pageant; and proceeded from a gilded barge, to which countless lamps were attached, giving it, when seen at a distance, the appearance of a vast shell of topaz, floating on a sea of sapphire. It was filled with musicians, attired in the most glittering liveries; and every stroke of the oars kept time to the music, and sent forth a silvery light from the water which they rippled. (225)

The comparison with gemstones ("topaz," "sapphire"), the invocation of gold and silver, the visual effect ("glittering") all carry connotations of the precious. This performance continuously creates values, albeit ephemeral ones. If, according to Tzvetan Todorov, journeys and the narratives about them partake in the material and spiritual dimensions, then the spiritual aspect Blessington continuously foregrounds is the gain of a momentary happiness that is fed through human encounters and the intensity of perception.[20]

If not touring the environs of Naples, Blessington resided in the Palazzo Belvedere.[21] Women travel writers often took more interest in domestic arrangements than male travelers. One of the attractions of *The Idler in Italy* is the glamour it presents even on the domestic level, sometimes putting the readers, most of whom did not command over as huge a fortune as Lord Blessington, into the position of the butler peeping through the keyhole of the rich and the powerful. Although the Palazzo was more expensive to rent than a comparable place in London, Lady Blessington did not worry about additional expense, called in an upholsterer, and acquired more furniture. The walls were already hung with valuable paintings, some by Rubens or Salvator Rosa. "Besides five *salons de réception* on the principal floor, the palace contains a richly decorated chapel and sacristy, a large *salle-de-billard*, and several suites of bed and dressing-rooms" (76). Despite its splendor, the mistress of the house occasionally complained about lack of English homeliness: "Notwithstanding that we do not miss the warmth of a fire, we greatly miss the appearance of that truly English focus of comfort" (155). Like other travelogues, *The Idler in Italy* often contrasts the familiar with the foreign, usually to the advantage of the more exciting foreign. In another passage, Blessington compares the different systems of household management and praises the Neapolitan method (76–77).

The grand and stylish Palazzo Belvedere was also the place where Blessington's theatrical sociability occurred. Mathews described the "saloon," the representative room in the Palazzo, where much of the indoors communication took place:

> In one corner of the large saloon stood Lady Blessington's table, laden with books and writings; Count D'Orsay's in another, equally adorned with literary and artistic litter. Miss Power's and mine completed the arrangement, while Lord Blessington strolled and chatted from one to the other, and then dived into his own sanctum, where he divided his time between fresh architectural schemes for his castle in the air, and the novel of "De Vavasour," on which he was busily engaged.[22]

The layout of the room and the creative use of space mirror the principle of conversation. Every participant has his or her own sphere, but mutual intercourse is possible at all times in an atmosphere of ease, as the ironic tone denotes. The fantastic space of this "castle in the air," an allusion to Lord Blessington's architectural plans in Ireland, symbolically mirrors the ephemeral quality of this salon, which consisted of a series of verbal performances and was never stationary, a creative space in which individuals performed. Unlike the French salons of the seventeenth and eighteenth centuries, Blessington's sociability did not occur in one fixed and permanent location, and it is this lack of determinacy that enlivened intellectual exchange.

Like other travel narratives, Blessington's *Idler in Italy* relates to earlier literary texts about the Italian experience. Many passages are a monument not only to Byron but also to her friendship with him, as the two-page advertisement of the *Conversations* that prefaces Colburn's second edition shows.[23] The section about Genoa, the textual basis of her previously published *Conversations of Lord Byron*, chronicles her encounters with him in 1823 but in fact repeats and adds to the information conveyed in her earlier publication. The section about Naples returns to Byron when Blessington receives the "melancholy intelligence" of his death (207). A subsequent dinner on board the yacht Bolivar, which Byron had sold to the Earl of Blessington, "in the cabin where Byron wrote much of his Don Juan" (217), evokes further memories. By the late 1830s, Byron's *Childe Harold*, especially Canto IV, which was dedicated to Italy, had emerged as a major "cultural model" for travelers.[24] Guidebooks and travelogues frequently quoted Byron in descriptions of places he had visited, for example, Rome and Venice, to convey an authenticity that the popular imagination linked to the poet's emotional experience. In her passages about Rome, Blessington quotes from Canto IV several times: her introduction to the eternal city displays stanza 78, Byron's address to the "lone mother of dead empires," while the descriptions of the coliseum by moonlight and the pantheon receive additional splendor by being presented through Byron's eyes.[25] Other places remind her of other writers: Florence, for example, evokes associations with Dante and Milton. On the whole, however, Blessington's Italian travelogue arranges a series of successful human rather than literary encounters. Among the last places she visited in Italy before moving on to France was Leghorn with its English cemetery, where she found Tobias Smollett's grave. Although Smollett had furnished the English reader with a much-read travelogue, it was not the literary model that interested her but the memory of the "delight" he had caused. The cemetery contained yet another grave: that of a woman, "the victim of sorrow," the "living martyr to sensibility" (304), as the inscription on her tombstone, prepared by herself, explains. Like other tourists, Blessington was unable to refrain from smiling and commented that so much tragic self-fashioning "prove[d] incontestibly that the deceased was an Hibernian" (305), that is, Irish, like Blessington herself.

IRISHNESS: FEMALE IDYLLS AND AN IRISHWOMAN ON THE LOOSE

Blessington published her novel *The Repealers* more than a decade after she had last set foot in Ireland. After marrying the Earl of Blessington, she only returned once when the couple visited Mountjoy for their honeymoon, but otherwise she steered clear of her native land, which, however, rendered her luxurious lifestyle up to 1829 possible and provided her with a more moderate income during her widowhood. Maybe her comparatively low social status before her second marriage or unpleasant memories of the three months she had been forced to spend with Captain Farmer as a 15-year-old contributed to her apparent lack of enthusiasm. In her fiction, however, she revisited Ireland several times. Two novels, her first and her last, *The Repealers* (1833) and *Country Quarters* (1850), have some Irish locations, while minor Irish characters figure in other texts, sometimes stereotyped to the point of grotesque exaggeration, like the crude Mrs. MacLaurin in *Strathern* (1845). Blessington's *Grace Cassidy; or, The Repealers*, presumably her first novel, three volumes published by Bentley, alternates between settings in Ireland and London and begins in the year 1832 (R 1: 99). Of all her texts about Ireland, it is the most pronounced in terms of Anglo-Irish political issues, which it combines with several stories of courtship, marriage, scandal, and financial ruin. One plot describes the lives of two simple Irish cottagers, Grace and Jim, and their neighbors, while the other plots focus on the local aristocracy and various London socialites. The section that is set in London is only loosely connected to the Irish cottagers' story. Like Blessington's fictions of Italy, her texts about Ireland contain elements of travel writing through their portrayals of landscape and of the local population. As Ireland did not fully belong to Britain but was not really abroad either, it constituted a special case.[26] The success of novels like Lady Morgan's (Sydney Owenson's) *The Wild Irish Girl* (1806) and Maria Edgeworth's *The Absentee* (1812) testifies to an interest in the fictionalization of Irish national questions.[27]

Blessington's title alludes to current political conflicts treated in the novel. The "Repealers" were a loosely structured group of activists who wanted a repeal of the Union between Britain and Ireland, established in 1801. Further topics are the role of the churches, types of landlords, estate management, and neglect, to which the reader is introduced in the first chapters through Grace's constant arguments with her husband Jim, who believes in the Repealers' cause, until, at the end of the novel, she has finally dissuaded him. The Repealers are linked to "The Liberator" Daniel O'Connell, whom Blessington unflatteringly names "O'Blarney" and "The Agitator," an Irish political leader, who had fought for Catholic Emancipation (1829) and then campaigned for a repeal of the Union. Although his tactics were largely peaceful, some sectarian groups and individuals resorted to violence to further the political aims they were sharing with him.[28] In the 1832 election, the Repealers, who mostly had a nonaristocratic background, played a role although they were not a party in the strict sense.[29] A fairly negative portrait of the Repealers' violent potential appears in Baron D'Haussez' survey *Great Britain in 1833*, which devotes an entire section to Ireland and describes the Repealers' alleged activities:

> From time to time conflicts take place, for which the payment of tithes forms the pretext: some are killed; burnings of houses ensue; peaceable inhabitants are murdered in cowardly manner on the high road, if the popular rage has been excited against them: vengeance thus glutted, turns itself towards another point.[30]

Baron D'Haussez, a French politician who had gone into exile after the July Revolution of 1830, was among the guests of Blessington's salon in the early 1830s.[31] He may have shared his understandable animosity against insurgents of all sorts with his hostess, who, although she tried to allure Liberals into her salon, took a fairly conservative attitude toward Irish issues. If D'Haussez' analysis considers Ireland's extreme poverty as a major problem, he nevertheless also casts the Irish as culprits: in his view, they are simple, gifted without using their talents, revengeful, inclined to drink, inconstant, passionate, and hasty.[32] In this, he came very close to Blessington's own judgment: "All who know Ireland are aware, that in proportion to the exuberance of imagination in her sons, is the deficiency of reason and judgment" (R 1: 24). Stereotypical characterizations, likewise anecdotes about funny, inebriated, violent, and zealous Irishmen and Irishwomen, appear throughout her novel.

Jim, Grace's husband, is one such case: he is increasingly attracted to the Repealers' ideas and actions, from which his wife tries to dissuade him. In episodes that consist of large chunks of dialogue, the rational Grace refutes Jim's intoxication through highly emotional and unreasonable political ideas. Blessington resorts to dialect—a strategy also used by Dickens in *Hard Times*—to authenticate the local ambience:

> [Jim:] "But if we had liberty it would be quite a different thing, and that's what I want."
>
> [Grace:] "And what's liberty, Jim dear, for I can't rightly make out what you mane?"
>
> [Jim:] "Why, liberty, cuishlamachree, manes to do everything we like ourselves, and hinder everyone else from doing it. It also manes to prevent every mother's soul in Ireland from going to church, and making them go to mass, whether they like it or no. Wouldn't this be a great day for the Irish, Grace? And all this will happen, if we only vote for Repealers, pay no tithes, and always keep repeating that the English are the cause of all our troubles." (13–14)

Jim's explanations, which work from the assumption that the Irish are "slaves" and the English their "tyrants" (48), are not only too simple but threaten individual and social peace: his false ideal of liberty envisions the enforcement of Catholic worship. Blessington's novel as well as D'Haussez' study sketch a negative picture of a Catholic church, which in their opinion adds to the overall neglect and is incapable of fulfilling any function, neither leading individuals to salvation nor contributing to community building. Jim is part of what the narrator calls "the ignorant multitude" (23), a phrase reminiscent of the infamous "swinish multitude,"[33] by which Edmund Burke equated the lower classes with the Revolutionary mob in France. That the Repealers lack moral fiber, humanity, in fact, any sense of justice is laid open at the end of the novel when they turn on their own people: When Patrick Mahoney, a neighbor of Jim and Grace's, who has been imprisoned after the murder of a policeman, of which he is innocent, is released at the instigation of Mr. Forrester, a former Colonel of the army, he quits the Repealers and rejects the money they have collected for him, thereby eliciting bouts of meaningless violence: "From the moment Mahoney refused the aid of the Repealers, he became a marked man with them; his horse was houghed, his cow maimed, his pigs killed, and his garden, that spot which had been the pride and pleasure of poor Mary, was uprooted" (R 3: 213). However, help arrives through the Protestant parson and the landlord, who alleviate the Repealers' brutality.

Blessington's novel contrasts two Irelands: one is violent and rebellious, the other is beautiful, simple, and humane. Grace embodies the latter, not only because she eventually keeps her husband away from the Repealers but also because she works hard to keep her cottage clean, grows flowers in her garden, and produces superior eggs, cream-cheese, and honey, which receive praise from her landlady. In her preference for work, order, and cleanliness, she follows in the footsteps of the resident landlord and landlady Mr. and Mrs. Desmond, who invest in their property to create a "progressive state of improvement" (R 1: 92). Their gardener supplies everyone with seeds and plants, the cottages on their land are well-built, have glass windows as well as gardens, and the laborers are taught to make dairy products (89–92). Mrs. Desmond gives their tenants "a taste for cleanliness, and the power of enjoying it" (89). While order and natural simplicity make a meaningful whole, the rural idyll reflects individual benevolence. The choice of the good landlord's name, Desmond, alludes to Lady Blessington's own family: her mother claimed to have descended from the first Earl of Desmond (MA 1: 12). The altruistic Desmond serves as a foil to the obnoxious Lord and Lady Abberville, who promote their own interests at the cost of anyone else and spend far less time in Ireland than the Desmonds. Both the Desmonds and the Abbervilles are criticized harshly by the Repealers; but if the Abberville mansion is burnt down at the end of the third volume, Springmount, the Desmonds' residence, is saved due to Grace's courageous intervention. Although the novel praises the beneficial deeds of resident landlords, it does not heap much blame on absent owners, because absenteeism, according to Desmond, is partly brought about by the "Agitator" O'Connell and his Repealers (R 3: 168), who interfere with the " reciprocity of benefits between landlord and tenant" (169), which Desmond attempts to realize on his estate.[34]

Parallel to these political events and debates, a more positive image of Ireland emerges, built on tradition and on the beauty of its unspoilt landscape. During a marital argument, Jim suddenly praises "the elegance and grandeur of this poor counthry in ould times, when people came flocking from all parts of the world to larn knowledge in Ireland" (R 1: 48). Involuntarily, he resurrects this old Ireland as an alterative to the community created (or rather run down) by the Repealers, who drive even good landlords away. When the Desmonds, the Oriels, and the Forresters leave London and travel to Ireland in the last part of the novel, Blessington, author of several travelogues, presents a beautiful country. The *"bon-hommie*, and ease of manners of the Irish nobility," their "cheerfulness," and "warmth of heart" (R 3: 167) receive praise. Moreover, Ireland's striking scenery conforms to the aesthetics of the sublime, the beautiful, and the picturesque: "Perhaps there is nothing in Ireland more beautiful than the entrance to Lismore. The fine bridge, and the picturesque castle above it, which overhangs the river at a height that makes the head grow dizzy to look down it" (189), or, in a description of Killarney: "The magnificent woods, fine mountains, and admirable lakes spread out like vast mirrors reflecting them" (246). Lord and Lady Oriel, visitors from England, are full of admiration. Although texts about Ireland, unlike travel writing on Italy, do not usually abound with sites universally known and desired such as the coliseum at moonlight, Blessington skillfully marketed her native land, rarely renowned for tourist qualities. One dominant feature of her Irish landscape descriptions is the use of images of clarity and purity, sometimes in connection with water. This physical purity reflects the moral purity attainable through understanding Ireland.

Apart from its political debates as well as several love plots, *The Repealers* is also a roman à clef that contains many thinly disguised allusions to politicians, writers, and members of fashionable society. Blessington herself prepared a key for Bentley.[35] The Duke of Lismore is the Duke of Devonshire, Sir Robert Neil is the politician Sir Robert Peel, the "Agitator" O'Blarney is the "Liberator" O'Connell, etcetera. Sadleir assumes that Lord and Lady Abberville, who are among the most unpleasant characters of the entire novel, are in all likelihood Lord and Lady Charleville, who did not recognize Lady Blessington as an equal.[36] Blessington inscribed herself into the novel not only through the name Desmond, fraught with positive associations, but also by making Desmond remember Lord Mountjoy as a "friend of his early youth" and "the model on which he had formed himself" (R 1: 176–177). As Desmond is 59 in 1832, a reader familiar with Irish families would know that Blessington probably had the recently deceased Earl's father in mind. Blessington's own husband had spent much but not all of his life as an absentee landlord. Before he married her, he was famous for his theatricals at Mountjoy. Madden stresses that Lord Blessington had always been pro-Catholic (MA 1: 50), even traveled to London in 1829 only to vote in favor of Catholic Emancipation (139). His visit to the Earl's surviving Irish tenants in 1854 made them recall his kindness as a landlord: "However much in need he might stand of money, he would not suffer them to be pressed for rent, to be proceeded against or ejected" (63). Lord and

Lady Blessington's luxurious life, however, was only possible through the wealth that was continuously flowing out of Ireland. Lady Blessington, the author, Irish herself, ended up in a rather peculiar position: She was justifying English economic interests and politics in Ireland. Struggling for social recognition herself, she had no wish to promote public understanding for the Irish poor or to denounce the exploitation of Ireland. Her stance was that the Irish should be peaceful. It is contradictory that Blessington tried to turn her salon into a "rallying point" for the Liberals, as the painter Benjamin Haydon phrased it, while openly taking such a conservative stance on Irish questions. A review in the *New Monthly Magazine*, otherwise favorably disposed toward her, criticized her: "She falls into what we must be allowed to term the drawing-room error of confounding the political Liberal with the predatory Whiteboy; and she makes the eloquence of O'Connell the main cause of all the crimes of the midnight murderer and the dastard house-burner."[37] *The Athenaeum*, in contrast, expressed more sympathy for her representation of the "reign of terror" in Ireland.[38] By presenting her countrymen as irrational and the English as reasonable, she was—to use the vocabulary of postcolonial criticism—"Othering" herself.[39] Blessington adapts the colonizer's gaze to justify English rule in Ireland.

Her novel *Country Quarters*, posthumously published in 1850, is less overtly concerned with political questions and even shows a certain fondness for Ireland and its rustic sociability. Blessington, who had spent part of her girlhood in the garrison town of Clonmel, nostalgically returned to the social entertainments and flirtations between local girls and officers.[40] The plot centers on courtship and marriage, like much of Blessington's fiction. In the end, several couples—Irish and Anglo-Irish matches—emerge. As the Anglo-Irish Union of 1801 was occasionally depicted in terms of conjugal imagery,[41] the novel juxtaposes individual and political unions. By far the most interesting character is Honor O'Flaherty, repeatedly referred to as a "wild" girl due to her habit of "quizzing," that is, of making fun of the men. Honor's queer (and queenly) behavior finds at least partial justification through her genealogy, her descent from an "ould and grand family."[42] The self-confident and outspoken Honor, who defies custom by eloping, is eventually educated to be more rational and more wifely through her English husband. This story, reminiscent of the author's own geographical and biographical journey, implies that Blessington had made an uneasy peace with her past.

Another Irish character appears in *Strathern* (1845), a Mrs. MacLaurin, who, like Blessington herself, comes from a nonaristocratic

Irish background; she elicits laughter though her vulgarity and her unveiled greed. The social rise of this former servant is only possible through two advantageous marriages. Despite her remarkable rudeness, her malapropisms, and her lack of tact, she gradually works her way into good society. The novel conventionally ends on a series of happy coincidences that unite the couples, yet final closure is defied by the uncouth Irishwoman, who, through the convenient death of her husband's elder brother, has advanced to the position of marchioness and, after traveling through Italy and France, arrives in London to enter good society. As this is the only strand of the plot left open at the end, and as her rise is unstoppable, further details of her progress are left to the reader's imagination. She is the ultimate threat to all good behavior and mirrors Blessington's own anxieties, who felt that her origin was one reason for her exclusion from the circles of the *bon ton*. Yet the widowed MacLaurin also constitutes a revenge fantasy because, unlike the widowed Blessington, she is extremely wealthy and therefore has to be admitted to all circles regardless of her manners and her origin. Her journey to London, where she will claim her heritage, is a highly symbolic act. In the language of postcolonial theory, this is an intrusion of the "Other," now nightmarishly rich and powerful, into the colonizer's own heartland, which reverses the role Blessington had assigned to the Irish in *The Repealers*.

London Society in Blessington's Silver-Fork Novels

Blessington's own ambivalent attitude toward London society surfaces in her silver-fork novels. It was William Hazlitt's essay "The Dandy School" (1827), which coined the derogatory term "silver fork" by ridiculing novelists who enthused about insignificant details of aristocratic lifestyle such as the supposed consumption of fish only with silver forks.[43] Silver-fork novels, decried as trivial and ephemeral, are often thinly disguised romans à clef and deal with fashionable society. They were *en vogue* in the 1820s and 1830s, then fell into oblivion, and were only considered as relevant by later critics because they influenced writers like Thackeray, who parodied them in *Vanity Fair* (1847–1848). A recent return of academic interest has manifested itself in several studies and an edition of six such silver-fork novels by Harriet Devine Jump.[44] Among the genre's acknowledged classics rank Thomas Henry Lister's *Granby* (1826), Marianne Spencer Hudson's *Almack's* (1827), Bulwer's *Pelham* (1828), and Letitia Landon's *Romance and Reality* (1831). Caroline

Lamb's *Glenarvon* can be considered a precursor. Other writers of silver-fork fiction are Catherine Gore, the young Benjamin Disraeli, Lady Stepney, and Blessington. If some of her novels, like *The Victims of Society* (1837), deal with fashionable society throughout, others, like *The Repealers*, only contain some episodes or strands of plot that zoom in on the manners and mannerisms of the bon ton. As authors of silver-fork novels often belonged to fashionable society or lived at least on its fringe, these novelists found that they might write about acquaintances one month and figure in their novels the following month, like Blessington herself, who not only authored society novels but appeared in them as a character: Lady Stepastray in Rosina Bulwer's *Cheveley* (1839) is a crossbreed between Lady Stepney and Blessington. Such society novels are not only intertextual but stand in a highly dialogic relationship to one another, are in fact part of an extended salon conversation because the people who meet at dinners, balls, and other sociable events encounter one another again on the printed page. Real-life habitués fictionalize one another and react to each other's written fantasies, inside and outside the literary texts.

Silver-fork novels are formula fiction, share a set of thematic and stylistic features, and contain at least some of the following plot elements: courtship, love matches, defiance of parental authority, elopements, unhappy marriages, love affairs, duels, intrigue, blackmail, scandal, neglected children, disinheritance, or unexpected inheritance. Among the stock characters are the dandy, the heiress, the loving but helpless parent, the unfaithful lover, the revengeful ex-lover, the exploited innocent, and the faded beauty. As readers expected gossip and a close-up of the social elite's manners, the lack of a convincing plot would not necessarily work as a deterrent, although reviewers frequently demanded more coherent stories.[45] Many authors of silver-fork novels combined melodrama and pathos on the one hand and a high moral tone on the other. If Rosina Bulwer basked in the tragic suffering of her innocent heroine, she also aimed to expose vice and make sure that her readership knew who was to blame (her husband!), both on the printed page and outside the confines of fiction.

Another key feature of the silver-fork genre is a brand of realism that pays attention to luxurious details such as expensive clothes, jewelry, food served at dinners (hence the "silver fork"), interior decorations, and carriages. The characters move around fashionable London locations: They live in Grosvenor Square and frequent Almack's, gentlemen have their Club, and Regent Street and Hyde Park are places where friends and rivals meet.[46] The lords and ladies move through a series of social rites like presentation at court, balls, dinners, or less formal meetings in a box at the opera. Contemporary figures appear, sometimes disguised by slightly altered names; current political events such as the Irish question in *The Repealers* are referred to. Sometimes, keys uncovering the protagonists' identities were published shortly after the novels. To many a middle-class reader, the frisson or rather illusion of participating in upper-class life, the voyeurism of peeping through an aristocratic keyhole, and the celebration of social exclusiveness were major attractions. That Blessington explicitly mentioned her authorship was a skillful marketing ploy. Colburn, who published most silver-fork novels, was a specialist in the marketing of real as well as fictional celebrities and puffed his books through his magazines, where they usually received raving reviews. Despite their genuine pathos, silver-fork novels often contain satirical elements as well, especially in their critique of the society they celebrate, thus prefiguring later literary satires like *Vanity Fair*. Most of Blessington's short stories and novels possess at least some features of the silver-fork genre, for example, her first collection, *The Magic Lantern* (1822), her Irish novel *The Repealers* (1833), which is partly set in London, and her epistolary novel *The Victims of Society* (1837).

The short texts of *The Magic Lantern*, cheeky descriptions of London society, which pay attention to luxurious detail and fashionable conversation, are early examples of Blessington's satirical style.[47] The slim volume, which first appeared in 1822 and went into a second edition in 1823, contains four sketches of a good society that marginalized Blessington, who in turn took revenge by portraying its follies. "The Auction," "The Park," "The Tomb," and "The Italian Opera" all explore popular activities in which men and women of fashion engaged, for example, the visiting of Egyptian Hall in Piccadilly, where ancient artifacts were on display in 1821–1822.[48] "The Tomb" describes a panorama of visitors, among them fashionable ladies, whose ignorance and narrow-mindedness surpasses everybody else's:

> Oh! pray do look at the female ornaments, exclaimed one of the ladies, did you ever see such horrid things? Only fancy any woman of taste wearing them: well, I declare those same Egyptians must have been dreadfully vulgar, and the women must have looked hideously when adorned in such finery. How surprised they would have been at seeing Wirgman's beautiful trinkets, or the sweet tasteful jewellery at Howel and James's.[49]

Blessington presents the women of the bon ton as incapable of understanding another culture; they are parochial, self-centered, and their unwillingness to recognize the achievements of an ancient culture corresponds to their failure to attribute value to anything beyond their immediate surroundings. The hub of their world is London's elite, its tastes, and its fashions, while deviations can only serve as objects of derision. Maybe Blessington, who was Irish and no aristocrat by birth, felt like an Egyptian, interesting to look at but never able to truly please. Although Irishness is no topic in *The Magic Lantern*, the stories occasionally raise the question of how outsiders felt in top Regency circles, which were by no means the polite society as they are sometimes idealized but rather, as its chronicler Venetia Murray declared, an "impolite society."[50]

In *The Repealers*, Blessington returned to her critique of the bon ton. One of the strands of the plot, which are barely linked to one another, is set in fashionable London. Mr. Forrester's sister, the recently and happily married yet naive Lady Oriel, had struck up a friendship with the ill-reputed Lord Delmore, is wrongly rumored to be his mistress, suffers ostracism, yet is eventually reintegrated into her circles. Blessington uses the Oriel subplot to zoom into the nature of scandalmongering, from which she herself had been suffering so much. At one point in the novel, the slander becomes so powerful that it threatens to undermine the Oriels' otherwise happy marriage. It is a prestigious invitation to the Duchess of Heaviland's (the Duchess of Northumberland's) house that restores Lady Oriel's reputation and ensures that she remains inside the circles of the bon ton. The Duchess is "unaffected," not under the influence of "cliques," stands "proudly aloof from the crowd" and has no desire to lead the fashionable world (R 2: 215). In other words, she believes in a different set of values and ignores gossip, while her elite circle consists of habitués who are—for a change—pleasant and well-mannered. Blessington's criticism of slander concerns attitudes as well as people. Sadleir suggests that the scandalmongering and obnoxious Lady Abberville is Lady Charleville, another Irishwoman and rivaling salonnière, and that the stereotyping she undergoes in *The Repealers* is a punishment for her participation in the 1831 witch hunt against Blessington. This makes sense, because Lady Charleville knew the deceased Lord Blessington's stepmother, who cultivated a strong dislike for the nobody her son had married.[51] The novel also lays open the role of a hostile press that eagerly collects and publicizes all instances of real and imagined misconduct. After her own exposure to nasty rumors and attacks in the press, it is hardly surprising that Blessington chose to unmask the machinations that led to ruinous slander. Moreover, she seems to have made a strategic attempt to ingratiate herself with at least some leading figures in society. As an elaborate key by Sadleir gives the information on who is who, the names of the other society women on whom she heaps praise are traceable. The Countess of Guernsey, her old rival Lady Jersey, appears as "brilliant and sparkling," possesses "great personal charms," and "high spirits" (245), while Lady Augusta Garing (Lady Baring) is "celestial" (258).[52] Moreover, during a visit at the opera, a pantheon of female beauty and talent is sketched: Landon, Rosina Bulwer, and Gore receive enthusiastic praise (223–230).[53] Some society episodes have a very loose storyline and were probably added because the readership expected glamorous locations: great aristocratic houses, receptions, balls, the opera, shopping in Regent Street, or London's gentlemanly clubs; bailiffs in search of Lord Delmore finally encounter the indebted aristocrat outside White's. Peace and harmony are only found at the end of the novel, in rural Ireland. The question arises how such novels are to be read. If, from an aesthetic viewpoint, they lack coherence, to the 1833 reader they offered a medley of political debate, insider information about fashionable life, a travelogue—the mixture expected from a good magazine or an evening's conversation.

Unlike *The Repealers*, Blessington's novel *The Victims of Society* is no roman à clef but also harshly criticizes good society, combining biting satire with melodrama. The novel tells of an imprudent marriage, into which the 16-year-old Augusta enters. While her beauty, admired throughout London, helps her succeed in society, she realizes that she cannot love her husband, the vain Lord Annandale, and soon falls in love with the more serious-minded Lord Nottingham. Through the machinations of a false friend, Caroline Montressor, the scandal is made public, and Lord Annandale seeks a court trial to divorce his supposedly unfaithful wife Augusta, who tragically dies from a broken heart. Lord Annandale now asks the scheming Caroline to marry him, yet she in turn becomes the victim of a former lover's intrigues, is blackmailed, breaks down, and dies, too. *The Victims of Society* is an epistolary novel with several male and female correspondents, whose letters present contrasting views.[54] The main character, Lady Augusta Vernon, stands between two older friends, two types of women, Mary, Countess of Delaward, and Caroline Montressor, who are her main correspondents. Mary possesses all Victorian virtues avant la lettre: she is benevolent, serious, never judges hastily, ignores gossip, and proves to be a faithful friend, who has no qualms about visiting Augusta after her downfall. The scheming, manipulative Caroline on the other hand, spoilt by her reading of French literature, is a bad influence, for example, when she advises the inexperienced

Augusta on her relationship with Annandale: "That he should *admire* you greatly is very desirable, because it will ensure your empire over him."[55] To Caroline, who considers Mary's "principles" to be mere "prejudices,"[56] all relationships between men and women are power games, while love is to be avoided at all cost. The epistolary form allows a juxtaposition of several contrasting images of femininity. Mary recommends that Augusta should avoid Caroline, who in turn advises Augusta to steer clear of Mary. Although the unprincipled Caroline, who alerts Annandale to his wife's supposed infidelity, is clearly marked out as a morally devious character, her worldly-wise views of love and marriage prove to be true at the end of the novel: if Augusta had avoided emotional involvement, if she had never fallen in love first with Annandale and then with Nottingham, she would still be alive. Yet her demise is the precondition for the success of Caroline's ambitions, who had plotted to become Annandale's wife. Once Caroline has succeeded, remorse, that is, emotions she cannot control, as Augusta could not control her feelings, catch up with her and spoil her triumph. Moreover, it is now her turn to be punished through an application of her own principles: through greed and machinations, her diabolic ex-lover, a male version of Caroline's own ruthless self, destroys her.

The sequence of events is much more coherent than in *The Repealers*, although the story, especially the women's deaths from emotional crises, seems not too likely. Moreover, the intrigues can only be followed by the reader because Caroline pours out her heart every time she writes a letter to the Marquise de Villeroi, her friend in France—a highly unlikely course of action. Yet the story is well-developed. Embedded anecdotes about acquaintances who suffer similar fates, for example, the French couple whose lives are ruined by envy, mirror the main plot. As the epistolary form allows introspection, Caroline, Mary, and Augusta are psychologically more convincing than some of Blessington's earlier characters.

The Victims of Society possesses many features of the silver-fork genre: fashionable places are evoked, luxury items appear, like the diamonds presented to Mary. Although strictly speaking no roman à clef, *The Victims of Society* alludes to contemporary events. The trial that Annandale wants bears resemblance to the trial of Caroline Norton in 1836, who was reputed to be the Prime Minister's, Lord Melbourne's, mistress.[57] The famous court hearing came to nothing because the witnesses were considered unreliable. The point Blessington was making in defense of another woman was that accusations of sexual misconduct might be unfounded and the result of intrigues, that those who spread rumors did so because they wanted to remove rivals, improve their own position, and benefit materially. Unlike in real life, in Blessington's novel, all intrigues are eventually laid open. With the death of the Marquise de Villeroi, Caroline's French confidante and correspondent, who melodramatically kills herself with an overdose of laudanum, the letters Caroline had written are discovered by the Marquise's aunt, who announces that she will send them to Augusta's parents so that they can see how their daughter died. Despite the tragic deaths, this ending resounds on a hopeful note, namely the idea that intrigues can be uncovered, that reputations can be restored, even if only posthumously. To Blessington, who had suffered from scandal, from anonymous attacks, from social exclusion due to supposed sexual misconduct, such a utopian resolution may have appeared desirable.[58]

Blessington not only authored silver-fork novels but also appeared as a literary character in several such works. In *Godolphin* (1833), Edward Bulwer used her as a model for Constance, who marries the wealthy Earl of Erpingham and establishes a successful salon: "In her *salons*, the measures of her party were discussed: in her *boudoir* (it was whispered that) they were arranged."[59] After Erpingham's death in Rome (which parallels Lord Blessington's sudden demise in Paris), she becomes Godolphin's wife and gains power through her sociable activities. In *The Victims of Society*, a letter by the sober Mary to her friend Augusta, who has recently arrived in London, recommends suitable friends: "Lady Erpingham is also a charming person."[60] This reference to Lady Erpingham—the only one in the novel—is a conspiratorial wink at Bulwer, her habitué. Blessington also figures as a minor character in *Cheveley* (1839) as Lady Stepastray.[61] *Cheveley*, a roman à clef and Rosina Bulwer's first novel, caricatures Edward Bulwer and his friends at a time when the Bulwer marriage had already broken down. In 1836, Rosina and Edward separated, and in 1838 she lost custody over her children. If the uncaring Lord De Clifford alias Bulwer is presented as a domestic tyrant who mistreats his wife Julia, Rosina Bulwer probably meant to publicize Edward Bulwer's conduct toward his wife and family. De Clifford and his companions, the baddies, are Whigs. The novel constitutes a fundamental critique of Whig lifestyle and Whig beliefs, which Rosina Bulwer unmasked as hypocritical. After De Clifford's death, Julia, now wiser, marries the right man: Cheveley, a Tory. Salon sociability of the kind cultivated by Blessington emerges as vain and superficial. Willis, who appears under the ridiculous name of "Rufus Snobguess," is part of Lady Stepastray's "perfect menagerie of lions."[62] This negative typecasting on the printed page corresponds to the bad opinion Rosina Bulwer held of her husband's friend in real life: her letters insultingly call the hostess "the Old harridan Blessington" and decry her influential circle as "the Blessington Bellows."[63] Such textual evidence proves that when reading silver-fork novels, one needs to consider the conversations that surrounded the books as well as their authors' friends and enemies. Conversations and the texts they react to are inextricably linked. As silver-fork novels are like a huge web with its own intricacies, its sociable infrastructure should be considered in a textual analysis.

THE *BOOK OF BEAUTY* AND OTHER KEEPSAKES

It is Blessington's continuous work for the keepsakes, yearly gift books, in which the interconnection between sociable activities and literary production is most clearly discernible. The editing of annuals such as the *Book of Beauty* provided her with additional income and status but was only possible through her activities as salonnière. Of all her literary endeavors, it was probably the most profitable and the most sociable but probably also the most time-consuming. For more than a decade, Blessington edited *Heath's Book of Beauty* (1834–1850) and *The Keepsake* (1841–1850) while also occasionally contributing to other annuals. If, for a long time, academic criticism has simply ignored annuals, maybe because they were considered ephemeral, maybe because women were among their editors and contributors, a recent upsurge of interest has led to a number of studies, websites, and even an edition.[64]

Such yearly gift books, which went by the generic name of keepsakes, were carefully produced, marketed on a huge scale, and expensive to buy. They catered for a huge readership and were sold not only in Britain but also in the colonies and in America, where they were rather popular, as Lydia Sigourney declared in a letter to Blessington.[65] The annual gift books were renowned not so much for the quality of the literary texts but for their illustrations, and even famous poets would stoop down to writing poetry for a given image, presumably because the editors offered a lot of money. The fees could vary: If the famous literary tycoon Sir Walter Scott received the huge sum of £ 500 for four stories that appeared in the 1829 *Keepsake*,[66] Mrs. Crosland alias Camilla Toulmin, an unknown writer, who eventually contributed to numerous keepsakes, was initially paid merely £ 9 for a story.[67] The article "The Annuals of Former Days" in *The Bookseller*, dating from 1858, a time when the keepsakes were already out of fashion, gives a detailed survey of the financial calculations on which the production and the sale of keepsakes were based, taking the year 1829 as an example. Referring to S. C. Hall as an authority, the entire proceeds of the sale of annuals for 1829 are given as £ 90,000, with £ 50,000 as expenses, £ 10,000 as publishers' profits, and £ 30,000 as retailers' profits. Authors and editors received £ 6,000 all in all.[68] The annuals had to be completed for publication by July, usually appeared in December, and were intended as gifts for Christmas and the New Year.[69] On January 1, 1836, Victoria, the future Queen, then 16 years old, listed her presents in her diary:

> Received from my dear Mamma a very pretty shawl, 2 handkerchiefs, 'The Flowers of Loveliness' (a sort of large annual), 'The Biblical Keepsake,' 'Friendship's Offering,' a book called 'Tyrol' with beautiful views of that fine country, 3 very pretty New Year's wishes, the Gotha Almanack and a very little Almanack...Read in 'The Flowers of Loveliness.' They are poems by the Countess of Blessington and are extremely pretty.[70]

An annual such as the *Flowers of Loveliness* was considered as suitable and safe reading for a young woman of 16 years but also as an elegant gift. The mere possession of such a book raised the owner's status. In *Middlemarch*, Rosamond Vincy, aspiring to a higher social position, receives the latest *Keepsake* as a gift, which indicates that she is at the height of fashion: "He [Mr. Ned Plymdale] had brought the last 'Keepsake,' the gorgeous water-silk publication which marked modern progress at that time."[71] This is an anachronism because the episode in *Middlemarch* is set in 1830, whereas Blessington, whom Rosamond mentions, probably was not contributing to annuals at that time and only edited her first *Book of Beauty* in 1833, that is, for the year 1834.[72] Yet the passage testifies to the impact of this publication, which the superficial Rosalind cherishes. When Fifine, the French maid in *Vanity Fair*, departs with stolen goods, she takes "six gilt Albums, Keepsakes, and Books of Beauty" with her, which mirror her former mistress's pretentious lifestyle.[73] The titles of annuals were *Forget Me Not, Fisher's Drawing Room Scrap Book*, or *The Bijou*, emphasizing an aesthetics of the everyday, the minute, and the domestic, sometimes also stressing the valuable.

The compilation of a keepsake involved a lot of work for Blessington, whose niece, Miss Power, seems to have helped with the correspondence. As women could not run offices the way male authors did, they had to establish contacts and negotiate contributions in the contexts of their sociable circles,[74] hence the need to keep up an extensive and expensive social life. Terence Hoagwood and Kathryn Ledbetter even argue that Blessington's bankruptcy was at least in part related to her "expensive business practices."[75] The list of contributors, whose names appear in the tables of contents to Blessington's annuals, sometimes overlapped with that of her dinner guests and correspondents. Thus, her keepsakes reflected her sociable circle. Among her regular contributors were Benjamin Disraeli, Thomas Moore, Letitia Landon, Mrs. S. C. Hall, Edward Bulwer, Henry F. Chorley, Barry Cornwall, William Thackeray, Walter Savage Landor—in short, Blessington displayed the guests of her salon in her books. Nathaniel Parker Willis also contributed to several British annuals, some of which were edited by Blessington. Less-known writers such as Mrs. Crosland found that contributing helped her to become part of the London literary scene. Since the illustrations were central to the keepsakes, authors could be asked to contribute by "writing to a plate," as Mrs. Crosland explained.[76] When, in one instance, she was unsure how to proceed because the plate she had been sent was merely the outline of a portrait, she asked friends for advice, visited the Countess of Blessington, obtained "a more advanced sketch," and eventually had her contribution published: "Some lines of mine on a lady's portrait appeared in the *Book of Beauty* for 1843."[77] Since a large readership with a fair amount of spending power had to be satisfied, the interaction between editor and contributor was intense. In September 1848, Thackeray wrote to Blessington: "I send my lady a little sketch wh[ich] I hope will be suitable for the pages of the Keepsake. If there is one phrase in it wh[ich][78] may call a blush upon any cheek, (and perhaps there is) I will be happy to expunge the same and replace it or amend it." Writing for the keepsakes would retain an author's name in circulation. It meant recognition for those who were already well established, but it could also be a good starting point for a literary career. Moreover, it brought additional income. Blessington herself contributed stories and poems to her own annuals as well as to those edited by others. She was not alone in using her social networks to attract prestigious contributors; Norton, Landon, and other hostesses followed similar strategies. Male writers, especially novelists, who feared competition from these women, often reacted with condescension. Although Thackeray himself later contributed to annuals several times in the 1840s and 1850s, his article "A Word on the Annuals" (1837) voices unease about the keepsakes' aesthetic and moral standards: "They tend to encourage bad taste in the public, bad engraving, and worse painting," and "the idea of the picture is coarse, mean, and sensual—the execution of it no better,"[79] thus criticizing an image in *Flowers of Loveliness* for 1838, edited by Landon. *Heath's Book of Beauty* for 1840 (published in 1839) is a good example of the politics of selection and arrangement.[80] Blessington had already edited the *Book of Beauty* several times before and selected the usual mixture of stories, poems, and illustrations. If some annuals were dedicated to a theme, the *Book of Beauty* for 1840 incorporated texts on all topics, mostly fiction: ghost stories, unhappy love stories, a historical narrative about Titian in Venice, and fictitious dialogues. Poems celebrate women's beauty, motherhood, and the nation, describe stereotypical social encounters, mythological characters like Ariadne, or nature. Among the nonfictional texts are travel writing and reflections on marriage customs in foreign lands. If some texts are set on the British Isles, others turn to remote locations: Germany, France, Spain, Italy, Russia, Turkey, and Egypt. Tales about life in cities such as Venice and Paris are juxtaposed with narratives set in rural areas. Characters whom the readers might encounter in everyday life, such as a coquettish young woman at a ball, appear alongside much more exotic figures like a pasha's cast-off wife. Some of them eat bread, others drink or consume opium; they go traveling, dancing, walking; they gamble, duel, kill; they flirt, love desperately, die from grief. Many texts sport stereotypical figures (the rake, the wronged innocent) and the corresponding patterns of behavior a reader would expect. In short, the *Book of Beauty* for 1840 offered the usual array of characters, locations, themes, moods, which, like other similar selections, appealed to a large and predominantly female readership. Since the annuals were fairly expensive, their readers were mostly middle-class, yet the galleries of aristocratic women they displayed testify to their function of providing fantasies of social climbing,[81] hence their appeal to a literary character such as Rosamond.

The selection of texts in this as well as in other annuals aimed to provide safe and noncontroversial reading matter. Like Victorian novels, they both confirm and subvert stereotypes of femininity. *Heath's Book of Beauty* for 1840 provides implicit yet contradictory comments on women's status in society and on social norms. In "The Jilt" by "Miss Louisa H. Sheridan," a young woman, Miss St. John, is introduced, who does not wish to marry quickly and talks about her plans with some confidence.[82] However, she receives punishment for her boldness when she realizes that society wrongly believes her to be a coquette, a "jilt," that is, a woman with too much cunning and too much knowledge about men and sexuality, and she is excluded from the social circles in which she would like to move. Disobeying social norms is dangerous, yet sticking to the rules does not guarantee success either. Some women characters are completely unselfish and sacrifice themselves, yet to no avail: they achieve neither joy nor riches, and neither marriage nor solitude leads to lasting happiness. "The Improvident: A Tale" by "Captain Daniel, Coldstream Guards" relates how an irresponsible husband, Albert, ruins his own prospects and destroys his marriage through gambling and overspending.[83] Eventually, he elopes with another's wife, slays his rival in a duel, is dismissed from the army, and, after another killing, is caught, sentenced to death, and executed. His suffering, innocent wife Géraldine, loyal throughout, even helps him to escape from prison in her own clothes while staying behind herself, yet she cannot save him from his impending fate. After his death, she dies too—in other words, as society has no room for single women, Géraldine is conveniently hushed up and shoved off the stage. In "The Lottery of Life" by "R. Bernal, M. P.," a young Englishman of moderate means, Marston, rejects the poor woman he loves, the Frenchwoman Eugénie, whom he first met in the Père Lachaise cemetery, and embarks on an unhappy marriage with a rich heiress, whom he finally leaves to find his first love once again.[84] Fatally wounded in the Revolution of 1830, he is taken to the *Hôtel Dieu*, dies in Eugénie's arms, and is buried at the Père Lachaise cemetery. The mere choice of location for their first encounter indicates that this love is bound to remain infertile, both in a physical and in a spiritual sense. The entire story reeks of meaningless sacrifice, both on his and on her side. The poems that are printed between the stories also adhere to conventional images of femininity: "Stanzas" by "Mrs. Torre Holme," a poem about an orphaned young woman, whose mother had died immediately after giving birth to her, idealizes sacrificial motherhood. The melodramatic tone is typical of the style of poetry found in many keepsakes:

> My Heart instructed me, and nobly taught
> The chain that binds us Death cannot decay;
> By God's own hand its holy links were wrought:
> My mother! *mine*—though only for a day—
> An orphan on this earth I look above
>   Confiding in thy love.[85]

In "The Wife to the Wooer" by "Sir E. Lytton Bulwer, Bart.," a woman rejects a suitor in favor of her husband, thus demonstrating marital fidelity.[86] That the contributors' names contain references to their social station adds to the respectability of the *Book of Beauty*. Social order is not questioned but confirmed.

However, on another level, *Heath's Book of Beauty*, like other annuals, contains strong undercurrents that enable women to read in an escapist fashion. Bulwer's poem about the attempted seduction of a married woman is printed with the instruction "for music" so that the emotional side of the response can receive additional emphasis. The poem and its musical setting may lead a female reader to fantasize about seduction ("the love you press so blindly") without having to expose herself to its emotional, social, and financial risks.[87] A further example: "A Leaf from the Pilgrim's Scrap-Book" by Isabella Romer, set in Constantinople, tells the story of the disastrous marriage between a loyal man and the pasha's cast-off wife.[88] Although the story transports the stereotype of the ever-nagging wife, it also invites the reader to fantasize about the sexual promiscuity embodied by the wife, who is passed on from one husband to another. Such visions of the orient as the location of erotic and sensuous encounters outside the British norms of acceptable marital behavior appear in other annuals, too. Likewise, the illustrations may add to the sensuous undercurrents.[89] *Heath's Book of Beauty* for 1840 contains 12 plates with representations of aristocratic women, some of whom are shown with bare shoulders, very low necklines, jewels, and expensive clothes. They do not conform to Victorian standards of feminine modesty, on the contrary, they are the visual embodiment of the erotic undercurrents one encounters in some of the tales. It is important to note that the fashion of bare shoulders is a relic of the Napoleonic age, a sensuous, even immodest anachronism, which, however, seems to have offered possibilities of identification.[90] If Janice Radway's research has shown that late twentieth-century women readers of contemporary romance benefit from their escapist reading because they secure their own space and at least temporarily refuse the domestic demands placed on them,[91] the same can be said about mid-nineteenth-century women readers, whom the tales and illustrations of annuals invite to daydream, to shirk the strict notions of female modesty and decency, likewise their maternal and marital duties, at least for a short time, without, however, forcing them to risk a scandalous exposition of their own bodies as "extra-domestic," to use Kristin Flieger Samuelian's term.[92]

As a contributor, Blessington herself toyed with escapist readings, for example, in her four-page poem "Francesca Foscari,"[93] which appeared in the *Keepsake* for 1837 and links her own literary production to Byron's oeuvre. Like Byron's historical play *The Two Foscari* (1821), the poem is set in Venice. Here as in a number of other poems, Blessington imitates some key stylistic features of Byron's: the focus on one doomed character, the melodramatic suffering, the fragmentary form, and the Mediterranean setting. The poem is accompanied by an illustration (after a drawing by Meadows) of the heroine, who is reclining on a seat. A closer look reveals that the woman's dress is unbuttoned around the breasts. Thus, the image offers an erotic and sensuous invitation and the possibility of an escapist reading. The melancholy poem depicts an extremely passive woman, whose suffering for love causes her death, hardly the kind of enterprising personality who, like Blessington, would travel to foreign shores. Moreover, Francesca Foscari must die after her betrothed has been killed in a duel because—again—there is no space for a single woman who lives outside the confines of patriarchy:

> Soon as Francesca heard the fatal tale
> Her reason fled, and ere a month had pass'd,
> She slept beside her mother in the tomb.[94]

The literary texts in the keepsakes embody an odd balance between Victorian propriety and adherence to the norms of respectability on the one hand and erotic promise on the other. It is striking that not only Blessington but also other female editors of annuals—Landon and Norton—had tarnished reputations. One can consider such offerings of erotic readings as an invitation to be a subversive reader. Maybe it is time not to save calumniated women from the bad-mouthing they undoubtedly had to suffer but to value their skillful and subversive use of sensuous undercurrents. At least for a while, Blessington, Norton, and Landon seem to have been rather successful at marketing the scandals in their lives and found financial rewards that would otherwise have been unavailable to them.[95]

* * *

Society beauty without society's approval, notorious outcast, victim of slander, celebrity writer, hostess to male "lions," popular conversationalist—the Countess of Blessington had no choice but to stand in the limelight. It seems that after a long phase of suffering from the rumors that were attached to her name, she began to market her public persona accordingly. Despite the financial breakdown at the end of her life, she was a successful literary businesswoman, who skillfully marketed her novels, keepsakes, and her reputation.

Chapter 8

Epilogue

In an ideal world, *salonnières* would be friends to create a communal culture of female conversation and learning. Mary Berry, Lady Holland, and the Countess of Blessington were aware of one another but did not cooperate as hostesses, on the contrary, they were at best ignoring one another, at worst involved in fierce competitions over territory and guests. Although their tireless activities did improve the world of sociable encounters, they did not dream of improving it together. Still, the modest Strawberry, Old Madagascar, and the Countess of Cursington resemble one another at least in some respects. All three experienced an early immersion into the conversational culture of the continent through their journeys to France and Italy, where they explored real, emotional, and intellectual spaces and made contacts relevant to their later activities as London hostesses. Even if they did not befriend one another, their networks included guests like the poet Thomas Moore, who frequented all three circles (and cracked jokes about them all). The three women enjoyed books, although the extent of their reading is not evenly documented. Even some political interests ran parallel. If Holland House was a center of the Whigs and of the Fox cult, Berry at least read and politely praised Fox ("so much thought, and so many new views of things," 1808, JCB 2: 350–351), or wrote about Russell, the Whig martyr, while her friend Damer gave a bust of Fox to Napoleon. Blessington attracted some politicians and liberal thinkers to her library-salon.

All three were deeply engaged in literary activities, inviting writers, reviewers, publishers, and editors, thus creating unique circles that furthered literary careers like that of Joanna Baillie, Lord Byron, Nathaniel Parker Willis, or Charles Dickens, even if the initial stages (as the example of Byron shows) might be tempestuous; sometimes the inspiration provided was involuntary, as in the case of Caroline Lamb's *Glenarvon*. All three women wrote. Lady Holland's writing, her journals and correspondence, prove that she was an astute observer and a witty commentator, yet—busily engaged in the *Edinburgh Review*—she did not wish to figure as a writer for a wider reading audience. Blessington, in contrast, boldly published as "the Countess of Blessington," using the notoriety she had acquired to market her novels, keepsakes, and reminiscences of Byron. Berry takes up a position between these two: she deliberately wrote for a larger audience, but since she did not put her name to her books, only her circles knew of her authorship.

The question arises of how "blue" they were, at a time when the term "bluestocking" was somewhere between joke and insult. They followed the bluestocking ideals in varying degrees. The rational and learned Berry, who ventured onto the male territory of historiography and drama, resembles the bluestockings most closely in her output. Blessington, in contrast, primarily wrote to entertain, not to educate, and had the fewest problems with the disreputable genre of the novel. Lady Holland was least blue of all three. To a certain extent, she took up the classical female role and was in charge of hospitality and of conversation. However, her involvement in huge collaborative efforts like the *Edinburgh Review* and the attempts to put Spain back onto the political and cultural map shows that she was very capable at moving things, ideas, people, and print products. It was her apparent lack of feminine modesty that her guests, who profited from her energetic input, found most remarkable. All three salonnières maneuvered at the intersection of the public and the private spheres, creating a sociable sphere of visiting and conversation, a sphere to which they gave inspiration but which they also ruled with an iron hand.

Reputation was a key factor. Berry presumably had the fewest problems, yet remained an author without a name of her own, maybe because of the disastrous reception of *Fashionable Friends* in Drury Lane. Blessington, in contrast, experienced most exposure to malicious slander, yet eventually began to market such stereotyping. Lady Holland also had attracted scandalous gossip through her divorce but, in the long run, was the object of another kind of problematic reputation: the witch, the slave-owner, and the imperious "centurion." Her diaries and letter, however, let the reader look at a very different person, sensitive and open-minded. The gossip around her has the quality of insider jokes, signaling that those who were able to tell anecdotes about her belonged to the inner circle of one of London's cultural hothouses. What remains? The answer is: a lot more work that can be done about women and their circles. Soon after these three withdrew from organizing sociable encounters, nostalgic retrospects like Perry's *Reminiscences* set in. Yet, what is worse, like the earlier bluestockings, these salonnières not only disappeared from the limelight but were more or less forgotten: Berry possibly because she had not put her name to her writing, Blessington, who had no serious literary executor after her death, and Lady Holland, who did not publish during her lifetime. If salon research is a huge jigsaw puzzle, many more pieces can be gathered from journals, correspondences, novels, and travelogues to complete more and even bigger pictures.

NOTES

1 TRADITIONS AND THEORIES

1. Dena Goodman, *The Republic of Letters: A Cultural History of the French Enlightenment* (Ithaca: Cornell University Press, 1994); Petra Wilhelmy-Dollinger, *Die Berliner Salons. Mit kulturhistorischen Spaziergängen* (Berlin: de Gruyter, 2000); Barbara Hahn, *Die Jüdin Pallas Athene. Auch eine Theorie der Moderne* (Berlin: Berlin Verlag, 2002), 75–98. Some ideas sketched in this introductory chapter have been developed in Susanne Schmid, "Lady Blessington und die Salons der englischen Romantik," in *Subversive Romantik*, ed. Volker Kapp, Helmuth Kiesel, Klaus Lubbers, and Patricia Plummer (Berlin: Duncker & Humblot, 2004), 153–164; Susanne Schmid, "Gespräch, Geselligkeit und Einsamkeit um 1800," in *Trianqulärer Transfer: Großbritannien, Frankreich und Deutschland um 1800*, ed. Sandra Pott and Sebastian Neumeister, special issue of *Germanisch-Romanische Monatsschrift* 56 (2006): 45–58, here 45–48; Schmid, "Einleitung: Einsamkeit und Geselligkeit um 1800," "The Countess of Blessington and the English Romantic Salon," in *Einsamkeit und Geselligkeit um 1800*, ed. Susanne Schmid (Heidelberg: Winter, 2008), 7–16, 95–109, here 95–99. My thanks go to Duncker & Humblot and to Winter for permission to reuse these.
2. Jerome J. McGann, *The Romantic Ideology: A Critical Investigation* (Chicago: University of Chicago Press, 1983), 59.
3. Marc Fumaroli, "Conversation," in *Rethinking France: Les Lieux de mémoire*, ed. Pierre Nora, vol. 3 (Chicago: University of Chicago Press, 2009), 275–342, here 275; Marc Fumaroli, "La Conversation," in *Lieux de mémoire*, ed. Pierre Nora, vol. 3/2 (Paris: Gallimard, 1992), 679–743, here 679.
4. Marc Augé, *Non-Places: An Introduction to Supermodernity,* 2nd ed. (London: Verso, 2008), 64. My thanks go to Ann Gardiner (Lugano) for pointing out this reference.
5. Chauncey Brewster Tinker, *The Salon and English Letters: Chapters on the Interrelations of Literature and Society in the Age of Johnson* (New York: Macmillan, 1915); Deborah Heller, "Bluestocking Salons and the Public Sphere," *Eighteenth-Century Life* 22 (1998): 59–82.

6. Tinker, *Salon and English Letters,* 42–80, 134–141.
7. Goodman, *Republic of Letters;* Jolanta T. Pekacz, *Conservative Tradition in Pre-Revolutionary France: Parisian Salon Women* (New York: Lang, 1999).
8. Pekacz, *Conservative Tradition,* 20–28.
9. A recent study contests this claim: Steven Kale, *French Salons: High Society and Political Sociability from the Old Regime to the Revolution of 1848* (Baltimore: Johns Hopkins University Press, 2004).
10. Elizabeth C. Goldsmith, *"Exclusive Conversations": The Art of Interaction in Seventeenth-Century France* (Philadelphia: University of Philadelphia Press, 1988), 1–9.
11. Ann T. Gardiner, "Salons, Society, and Solitude chez Madame de Staël," in Schmid, *Einsamkeit und Geselligkeit um 1800,* 53–66, here 55–56; Wilhelmy-Dollinger, *Berliner Salons,* 29–30. Both Gardiner and Wilhelmy-Dollinger trace the use of the word "salon" denoting the institution. On the nineteenth-century view of the pre-Revolutionary salon, see Duncan McColl Chesney, "The History of the History of the Salon," *Nineteenth-Century French Studies* 36 (2007): 94–108.
12. Lawrence E. Klein, "The Figure of France: The Politics of Sociability in England, 1660–1715," *Yale French Studies* 92 (1997): 30–45, here 37; on the wider context of the exemplary nature as well as supposed dangers of French manners, see Michèle Cohen, *Fashioning Masculinity: National Identity and Language in the Eighteenth Century* (London: Routledge, 1996).
13. *The Spectator* 15 (March 17, 1711), 45 (April 21, 1711), in *The Spectator,* vol. 1, 2nd ed. (London: Buckley and Tonson, 1713): 56–59, 170–173, here 58, 172.
14. Hannah More, "Thoughts on Conversation," in *Essays on Various Subjects, Principally Designed for Young Ladies* (London: Wilkie and Cadell, 1777), 37–62. More advocates women's silence (42).
15. Paula Finden, "Translating the New Science: Women and the Circulation of Knowledge in Enlightenment Italy," *Configurations* 3 (1995): 167–206. Finden describes several case studies.
16. Samuel Hoole, "Letter VII. Mr. Ralph P-. to To John C-. Esq.: A Conversatione," in *Modern Manners: In a Series of Familiar Epistles* (London: Faulder, 1781), 59–72.
17. John Leon Lievsay, "Notes on *The Art of Conversation* (1738)," *Italica* 17 (1940): 58–63.
18. Gerhard Kurz, "Das Ganze und das Teil. Zur Bedeutung der Geselligkeit in der ästhetischen Diskussion um 1800," in *Kunst und Geschichte im Zeitalter Hegels,* ed. Christoph Jamme, with the assistance of Frank Völkel (Hamburg: Meiner, 1996), 91–113.
19. Hahn, *Die Jüdin Pallas Athene,* 75–98, voices skepticism about this practice. Wilhelmy-Dollinger, *Berliner Salons,* 29–44, provides a thorough examination of the term "salon" as well as of the institution in Germany.

NOTES 179

20. A notable exception is Roberto Simanowski, Horst Turk, and Thomas Schmidt, eds., *Europa—ein Salon? Beiträge zur Internationalität des literarischen Salons* (Göttingen: Wallstein, 1999).
21. Gillen D'Arcy Wood, *Romanticism and Music Culture in Britain, 1770–1840: Virtue and Virtuosity* (Cambridge: Cambridge University Press, 2010), 180–214; Schmid, "The Countess of Blessington and the English Romantic Salon," 104–107; Susanne Schmid, "The Countess of Blessington: Reading as Intimacy, Reading as Sociability," *The Wordsworth Circle* 39 (2008): 88–93.
22. Thomas N. Baker, *Sentiment and Celebrity: Nathaniel Parker Willis and the Trials of Literary Fame* (New York: Oxford University Press, 1999), 67.
23. Almut Otto and Thomas Schmidt, "'Ilm-Athen' oder 'Deutsches Babel'? Der Salon der Ottilie von Goethe zwischen Weltläufigkeit und Provinzialisierung," in *Europa—ein Salon? Beiträge zur Internationalität des literarischen Salons*, ed. Roberto Simanowski, Horst Turk, and Thomas Schmidt (Göttingen: Wallstein, 1999), 161–189.
24. *The Life of Charles James Mathews Chiefly Autobiographical, With Selections from His Correspondence and Speeches*, ed. Charles Dickens, 2 vols. (London: Macmillan, 1879), 1: 109–120.
25. George Gordon Byron, "The Blues: A Literary Eclogue," in *Complete Poetical Works*, ed. Jerome J. McGann, 7 vols. (Oxford: Clarendon Press, 1980–1993), 6: 296–308, here 302; see also Gillian Russell, "Spouters or Washerwomen: The Sociability of Romantic Lecturing," in *Romantic Sociability: Social Networks and Literary Culture in Britain 1770–1840*, ed. Gillian Russell and Clara Tuite (Cambridge: Cambridge University Press, 2002), 123–144, here 134–137.
26. Nicole Pohl and Betty A. Schellenberg, "Introduction: A Bluestocking Historiography," in *Reconsidering the Bluestockings*, ed. Nicole Pohl and Betty A. Schellenberg (San Marino: Huntington Library, 2003), 1–19; here 5.
27. Richard Polwhele, *The Unsex'd Females: A Poem* [American reprint] (New York: Cobbett, 1800); 7. Elizabeth Eger, "The Bluestocking Legacy," in *Brilliant Women*, ed. Elizabeth Eger and Lucy Peltz (New Haven: Yale University Press, 2008), 126–150, here 126–128.
28. Sylvia Harcstark Myers, *The Bluestocking Circle: Women, Friendship, and the Life of the Mind in Eighteenth-Century England* (Oxford: Clarendon Press, 1990); Gary Kelly, general ed., *Bluestocking Feminism: Writings of the Bluestocking Circle, 1738–1785*, 6 vols. (London: Pickering and Chatto, 1999), especially Kelly's "General Introduction: Bluestocking Feminism and Writing in Context," in Kelly, *Bluestocking Feminism*, 1: ix–liv; Eger and Peltz, *Brilliant Women*, is the catalogue to an exhibition in the National Portrait Gallery; for a detailed bibliography see Janice Blathwayt, "A Bluestocking Bibliography," in Pohl and Schellenberg, *Reconsidering the Bluestockings*, 39–57; Elizabeth Eger, *Bluestockings: Women of*

Reason from Enlightenment to Romanticism (Basingstoke: Palgrave Macmillan, 2010).
29. Pohl and Schellenberg, "Introduction," 3–5; Myers, *The Bluestocking Circle*, 6–7.
30. William Roberts, *Memoirs of the Life and Correspondence of Mrs. Hannah More*, vol. 1 (London: R. B. Seeley, 1834), 209; also mentioned in Heller, "Bluestocking Salons," 81.
31. Hannah More, *Florio: A Tale for Fine Gentlemen and Fine Ladies: and, The Bas Bleu; or, Conversation: Two Poems* (London: Cadell, 1786), 84–85, ll. 276–281.
32. Kelly, "General Introduction," xlviii.
33. Harriet Guest, "Hannah More and Conservative Feminism," in *British Women's Writing in the Long Eighteenth Century: Authorship, Politics and History*, ed. Jennie Batchelor and Cora Kaplan (Basingstoke: Palgrave Macmillan, 2005), 158–170.
34. For the roast rabbit see a letter by Elizabeth Montagu to Elizabeth Carter (November 24, 1759), in *Elizabeth Montagu*, ed. Elizabeth Eger, vol. 1 of Kelly, *Bluestocking Feminism*, 150–153, here 151; on the relationship between Carter and Montagu, see Susan Staves, *A Literary History of Women's Writing in Britain, 1660–1789* (Cambridge: Cambridge University Press, 2006), 315.
35. See for example *The Magic Lantern* (1822) or the remarks about Lady Jersey that she puts into Byron's mouth in *Conversations of Lord Byron* (1832–1833); Marguerite Blessington, *The Magic Lantern; or, Sketches of Scenes from the Metropolis* (London: Longman, Hurst, Rees, Orme, and Brown, 1822); *Lady Blessington's Conversations of Lord Byron*, ed. Ernest J. Lovell (Princeton: Princeton University Press, 1969). For an analysis see chapters 6 and 7.
36. Caroline Lamb, *Glenarvon*, ed. Paul Douglass, vol. 1 of *The Works of Caroline Lamb*, ed. Paul Douglass and Leigh Wetherall Dickson, 3 vols. (London: Pickering and Chatto, 2009), 87; for an analysis of this passage, see Susanne Schmid, "Holland House and Mary Berry's Drawing-Room: Salons, *Salonnières* and Writers," *The Wordsworth Circle* 35 (2004): 77–80.
37. Paula R. Feldman, "Introduction," in *The Keepsake for 1829*, ed. Frederic Mansel Reynolds (London: Hurst, Chance, & Co., 1828; reprint Peterborough: Broadview, 2006), 7–25, here 19. On the note see Newton Crosland, *Rambles Round My Life: An Autobiography (1819–1896)* (London: Allen, 1898), 346–347.
38. Terence Allan Hoagwood and Kathryn Ledbetter, *"Colour'd Shadows": Contexts in Publishing, Printing, and Reading Nineteenth-Century British Women Writers* (New York: Palgrave Macmillan, 2005), 47–73; Schmid, "The Countess of Blessington: Reading as Intimacy, Reading as Sociability."
39. On the public sphere see James Van Horn Melton, *The Rise of the Public in Enlightenment Europe* (Cambridge: Cambridge University

Press, 2001); Jürgen Habermas, *The Structural Transformation of the Public Sphere: An Inquiry into a Category of Bourgeois Society* [1962] (Cambridge: Polity Press, 1989); Elizabeth Eger, Charlotte Grant, Clíona Ó Gallchoir, and Penny Warburton, eds., *Women, Writing and the Public Sphere, 1700–1830* (Cambridge: Cambridge University Press, 2001); on coffeehouse sociability see Markman Ellis, *The Coffee-House: A Cultural History* (London: Phoenix, 2005); Brian Cowan, *The Social Life of Coffee: The Emergence of the British Coffeehouse* (New Haven: Yale University Press, 2005); Susanne Schmid, "'Hodge-Podge' of Unreason or the 'Citizens Academy'? The London Coffee-House, 1652–1800," *Das Achtzehnte Jahrhundert* 32 (2008): 62–73.

40. For a selection of criticism, see J. A. Downie, "Public and Private: The Myth of the Bourgeois Public Sphere," in *A Concise Companion to the Restoration and Eighteenth Century*, ed. Cynthia Wall (Oxford: Blackwell, 2005), 58–79; Van Horn Melton, *The Rise of the Public in Enlightenment Europe*, 1–15; Lawrence E. Klein, "Gender and the Public/Private Distinction in the Eighteenth Century: Some Questions About Evidence and Analytic Procedure," *Eighteenth-Century Studies* 29 (1995): 97–109. The following is a systematic survey of the use of the terms "public" and "private": Jeff Weintraub, "The Theory and Politics of the Public/Private Distinction," in *Public and Private in Thought and Practice: Perspectives on a Grand Dichotomy*, ed. Jeff Weintraub and Krishan Kumar (Chicago: University of Chicago Press, 1997), 1–42.

41. Linda K. Kerber lists a number of examples relating to American history, Linda K. Kerber, "Separate Spheres, Female World, Woman's Place: The Rhetoric of Women's History," in *No More Separate Spheres! A Next Wave American Studies Reader*, ed. Cathy N. Davidson and Jessamyn Hatcher (Durham: Duke University Press, 2002), 29–65. For a critique see also Joan B. Landes, "The Public and the Private Sphere: A Feminist Reconsideration," in *Feminists Read Habermas: Gendering the Subject of Discourse*, ed. Johanna Meehan (New York: Routledge, 1995), 91–116; Carole Pateman, *The Disorder of Women: Democracy, Feminism and Political Theory* (Cambridge: Polity Press, 1989), 118–140. The problems arising from the shifting meanings of "public" and "private" may partly be caused by the English translation of Habermas, who uses different words for each of these concepts in the German original.

42. Klein, "Gender and the Public/Private Distinction," 103–104.

43. Ibid., 104.

44. Lawrence E. Klein, "Gender, Conversation and the Public Sphere in Early Eighteenth-Century England," in *Textuality and Sexuality: Reading Theories and Practices*, ed. Judith Still and Michael Worton (Manchester: Manchester University Press, 1993), 100–115, here 102.

45. Amanda Vickery, *The Gentleman's Daughter: Women's Lives in Georgian England* (New Haven: Yale University Press, 1998), 7, 196; C. Dallett Hemphill, *Bowing to Necessities: A History of Manners in America, 1620–1860* (New York: Oxford University Press, 1999), 182.
46. Homi Bhabha, "The Third Space: Interview with Homi Bhabha," in *Identity, Community, Culture, Difference*, ed. Jonathan Rutherford (London: Lawrence & Wishart, 1990), 207–221; Vickery, *The Gentleman's Daughter*, 196; Harriet Guest, *Small Change: Women, Learning, Patriotism, 1750–1810* (Chicago: University of Chicago Press, 2000), 11. Guest uses the term "third site."
47. Gillian Russell and Clara Tuite, eds., *Romantic Sociability: Social Networks and Literary Culture in Britain, 1770–1840* (Cambridge: Cambridge University Press, 2002).
48. Gillian Russell, *Women, Sociability and Theatre in Georgian London* (Cambridge: Cambridge University Press, 2007), 9.
49. Lawrence E. Klein, *Shaftesbury and the Culture of Politeness: Moral Discourse and Cultural Politics in Early Eighteenth-Century England* (Cambridge: Cambridge University Press, 1994).
50. Stephen Copley, "Commerce, Conversation and Politeness in the Early Eighteenth-Century Periodical," *British Journal for Eighteenth-Century Studies* 18 (1995): 63–77, here 66–67; Jon Mee, *Conversable Worlds: Literature, Contention, and Community 1762 to 1830* (Oxford: Oxford University Press, 2011), 37–80.
51. On the distinction between "old" and "new" types of London sociability, see Peter Clark, *British Clubs and Societies, 1500–1800: The Origins of an Associational World* (Oxford: Clarendon Press, 2000), 27, 39, 191–192, and Russell, *Women, Sociability and Theatre*, 9–10; for further examples see Venetia Murray, *High Society in the Regency Period, 1788–1830* (London: Penguin, 1999).
52. Maura A. Henry, "The Making of Elite Culture," in *A Companion to Eighteenth-Century Britain*, ed. H. T. Dickinson (Oxford: Blackwell, 2002), 311–328.
53. Roy Porter, *English Society in the Eighteenth Century* (London: Penguin, rev. ed. 1991), 83.
54. Jeffrey N. Cox, *Poetry and Politics in the Cockney School: Keats, Shelley, Hunt and Their Circle* (Cambridge: Cambridge University Press, 1998); James McKusick, ed., *Joseph Johnson: Essays Mostly Delivered at the Wordsworth-Coleridge Association*, special issue of *The Wordsworth Circle* 23 (2002): 90–122; Dafydd Moore, "Patriotism, Politeness and National Identity in the South West of England in the Late Eighteenth Century," *English Literary History* 76 (2009): 739–762, here 739.
55. Russell, *Women, Sociability and Theatre*, 97, uses this distinction to describe the Pantheon.
56. Augé, *Non-Places*, 64.

NOTES 183

57. Klein employs both of these criteria to define the public sphere, see Klein, "Gender and the Public/Private Distinction," 104.
58. For introductions to this concept and its applications, see Erving Goffman, *The Presentation of Self in Everyday Life* (Garden City: Doubleday, 1959); James Loxley, *Performativity* (London: Routledge, 2007); Tracy C. Davis and Thomas Postlewait, eds., *Theatricality* (Cambridge: Cambridge University Press, 2003); Elin Diamond, ed., *Performance and Cultural Politics* (London: Routledge, 1996); Janelle Reinelt, "The Politics of Discourse: Performativity Meets Theatricality," *SubStance* 98/99 (2002): 201–215; Susanne Bach, *Theatralität und Authentizität zwischen Viktorianismus und Moderne. Romane von Henry James, Thomas Hardy, Oscar Wilde und Wilkie Collins* (Tübingen: Narr, 2006), 12–84. The following studies investigate the link between language and action: Angela Esterhammer, *The Romantic Performative: Language and Action in British and German Romanticism* (Stanford: Stanford University Press, 2000), and Angela Esterhammer, *Romanticism and Improvisation, 1750–1850* (Cambridge: Cambridge University Press, 2008).
59. Elin Diamond, "Introduction," in Diamond, *Performance and Cultural Politics*, 1–12, here 1.
60. Joel Haefner, "The Romantic Scene(s) of Writing," in *Re-Visioning Romanticism: British Women Writers, 1776–1837*, ed. Carol Shiner Wilson and Joel Haefner (Philadelphia: University of Pennsylvania Press, 1994), 256–273, here 260.
61. Russell and Tuite, "Introducing Romantic Sociability," in Russell and Tuite, *Romantic Sociability*, 1–23, here 15.
62. Stephen Greenblatt, *Renaissance Self-Fashioning: From More to Shakespeare* (Chicago: University of Chicago Press, 1980).
63. On the tension between authenticity and theatricality, see Bach, *Theatralität und Authentizität*, 13–17.
64. *Life of Charles James Mathews*, 1: 124–125.
65. Ibid., 1: 141.
66. Roger Chartier, *Cultural History: Between Practices and Representations* (Ithaca: Cornell University Press, 1988).
67. Reinelt, "The Politics of Discourse," 202.
68. Wolf Lepenies uses the term "Langeweile" ("boredom") in Wolf Lepenies, *Melancholie und Gesellschaft. Mit einer neuen Einleitung: Das Ende der Utopie und die Wiederkehr der Melancholie* (Frankfurt am Main: Suhrkamp, 1998), 56.
69. It is also used elsewhere by Moore, who thus situates himself in the tradition of Roman satire (TMJ 1: 80).
70. R. R. Madden, *The Literary Life and Correspondence of the Countess of Blessington*, 3 vols. (London: Newby, 1855; reprint New York: AMS Press, 1973).

71. The Blessington Papers, collection of autographs, 6 vols., The Pforzheimer Collection, The New York Public Library, Pforz MS; Blessington, autograph letters, The Berg Collection, The New York Public Library; Blessington, Correspondence of the Countess of Blessington, 1834–1855, Princeton University Library, C 0147. My thanks go to these institutions for providing access.
72. Harriet Devine Jump, general ed., *Silver Fork Novels, 1826–1841*, 6 vols. (London: Pickering and Chatto, 2005).
73. Kelly, "General Introduction," xxxv.
74. Mary Berry, *A Comparative View of the Social Life of England and France, from the Restoration of Charles the Second to the French Revolution* (London: Longman, Rees, Orme, Brown, and Green, 1828), and *Social Life in England and France, from the French Revolution in 1789 to that of July 1830* (London: Longman, Rees, Orme, Brown, and Green, 1831).
75. Rosina Bulwer, *Cheveley; or, The Man of Honour*, ed. Marie Mulvey-Roberts, vol. 5 of Jump, *Silver Fork Novels, 1826–1841*.
76. Lamb, *Glenarvon*, 86.
77. Henry F. Chorley, *The Authors of England: A Series of Medallion Portraits of Modern Literary Characters* (London: Tilt, 1838).
78. Peter Burke, *What is Cultural History?*, 2nd ed. (Cambridge: Polity Press, 2008); Peter Burke, "Cultural History," in *The Sage Handbook of Cultural Analysis*, ed. Tony Bennett and John Frow (Los Angeles: Sage, 2008), 107–125.
79. William Hazlitt, "On the Conversation of Authors," in *The Complete Works of William Hazlitt*, ed. P. P. Howe, 21 vols. (London: Dent and Sons, 1930–1934), 12: 24–44, here 31.

2 Mary Berry and Her British Spaces

1. William Thackeray, *The Four Georges*, in *The Works of William Makepeace Thackeray*, 24 vols. (London: Smith, Elder, & Co., 1879), 23: 5–116, here 5. For a very brief summary on the Berrys, see Susanne Schmid, "Holland House and Mary Berry's Drawing-Room: Salons, *Salonnières* and Writers," *The Wordsworth Circle* 35 (2004): 77–80, here 79–80.
2. JCB 1: 9–10, 384; BP 3–11; WL 11: xxii, xxvi–xxix.
3. On Walpole's legacy see WL 11, xxvi–xxviii; Sarah Markham, "Mary Berry on the Death of Horace Walpole," *Notes and Queries* 223 (1978): 65–67.
4. JCB 2: 1–5, 294; BP 135–195, 286–287.
5. *The Collected Letters of Joanna Baillie*, ed. Judith Bailey Slagle, 2 vols. (Madison: Fairleigh Dickinson University Press / London: Associated University Presses, 1999), 1: 156–157.
6. Anonymous, "*England and France: A Comparative View*," *The Quarterly Review* 75 (March 1845): 485–496, here 485.

7. Sandra Adickes, *The Social Quest: The Expanded Vision of Four Women Travelers in the Era of the French Revolution* (New York: Lang, 1991), 127.
8. *Extracts from the Journals and Correspondence of Miss Berry from the Year 1783 to 1852* [1865], ed. Theresa Lewis, 2nd ed., 3 vols. (London: Longmans, Green, and Co., 1866).
9. A selection of the correspondence between Walpole and Berry, based on the Yale edition, is Virginia Surtees, ed., *The Grace of Friendship: Horace Walpole and the Misses Berry* (Norwich: Michael Russell, 1995).
10. Theresa Lewis, *Lives of the Friends and Contemporaries of Lord Chancellor Clarendon: Illustrative Portraits in His Gallery*, 3 vols. (London: Murray, 1852).
11. *The Berry Papers: Being the Correspondence Hitherto Unpublished of Mary and Agnes Berry (1763–1852)*, ed. Lewis Melville (London: Lane, 1914).
12. Lord Hartington (William George Spencer Cavendish, Duke of Devonshire), letter to Mary Berry (January 30, 1803), BM Add. MSS. 37726 f. 22. The letter is reprinted in BP 223–225 and JCB 2: 235–236.
13. *The Diary of Joseph Farington*, ed. Kenneth Garlick, Angus MacIntyre, and Kathryn Cave, 16 vols. (New Haven: Yale University Press, 1978–1984), 2: 571 (June 5, 1796).
14. Charles Pigott, *The Female Jockey Club, or a Sketch of the Manners of the Age* (London: Eaton, 1794), 202.
15. *The Works of Horatio Walpole, Earl of Orford*, ed. Mary Berry, 5 vols. (London: Robinson and Edwards, 1798), reprint ed. Peter Sabor (London: Pickering and Chatto, 1999).
16. *Letters of the Marquise du Deffand to the Hon. Horace Walpole*, ed. Mary Berry, 4 vols. (London: Longman, Hurst, Rees, and Orme, 1810).
17. Mary Berry, *The Fashionable Friends; a Comedy, in Five Acts* (London: Ridgway, 1802). References to *The Two Martins* are in JCB 2: 477, 501.
18. Mary Berry, *A Comparative View of the Social Life of England and France, from the Restoration of Charles the Second to the French Revolution* (London: Longman, Rees, Orme, Brown, and Green, 1828), and *Social Life in England and France, from the French Revolution in 1789 to that of July 1830* (London: Longman, Rees, Orme, Brown, and Green, 1831). On women and historiography see D. R. Woolf, "A Feminine Past? Gender, Genre, and Historical Knowledge in England, 1500–1800," *The American Historical Review* 102 (1997): 645–679, here 649.
19. Mary Berry, *Some Account of the Life of Rachael Wriothesley Lady Russell Followed by a Series of Letters* (London: Longman, Hurst, Rees, Orme, and Brown, 1819).
20. Benjamin Disraeli, *Vivian Grey*, ed. Michael Sanders (London: Pickering and Chatto, 2004), 146.

21. Marcie Frank, "Horace Walpole's Family Romances," *Modern Philology* 100 (2003): 417–435.
22. George E. Haggerty, "The Strawberry Committee," in *Horace Walpole's Strawberry Hill*, ed. Michael Snodin, with the assistance of Cynthia Roman (New Haven: Yale University Press, 2009), 80–81. This catalogue accompanied the exhibition "Horace Walpole and Strawberry Hill" at the Victoria and Albert Museum (London) in 2010, providing comprehensive material on Walpole's collections and his self-fashioning.
23. Jill Campbell, "'I am No Giant': Horace Walpole, Heterosexual Incest, and Love among Men," *The Eighteenth Century* 39 (1998): 238–260, here 243.
24. Kevin Rogers, "Walpole's Gothic: Creating a Fictive History," in Snodin, with the assistance of Roman, *Horace Walpole's Strawberry Hill*, 59–73, here 63.
25. Dianne S. Ames, "Strawberry Hill: Architecture of the 'as if,'" *Studies in Eighteenth-Century Culture* 8 (1979): 351–363.
26. Horace Walpole, *Reminiscences Written by Mr Walpole in 1778 for the Amusement of Miss Mary and Miss Agnes Berry*, ed. Paget Toynbee (Oxford: Clarendon Press, 1924); for the catalogue and the dedication see JCB 1: 193.
27. Thomas Babington Macaulay, "*Letters of Horace Walpole, Earl of Orford, to Horace Mann,*" *Edinburgh Review* 58 (October 1833), 227–258; her defense is printed in an 1840 edition of Walpole's letters: M[ary] B[erry], "Advertisement to the Letters Addressed to the Miss Berrys," in *The Letters of Horace Walpole, Earl of Orford*, ed. Mary Berry, 6 vols. (London: Bentley, 1840), 6: vii–xx.
28. William N. Free, "Walpole's Letters: The Art of Being Graceful," in *The Familiar Letter in the Eighteenth Century*, ed. Howard Anderson, Philip B. Daghlian, and Irvin Ehrenpreis (Lawrence: The University of Kansas Press, 1968), 165–185.
29. Patricia Meyer Spacks, *Gossip* (New York: Knopf, 1985), 15.
30. Clare Brant, *Eighteenth-Century Letters and British Culture* (Basingstoke: Palgrave Macmillan, 2006), 273; on letters see also Roger Chartier, Alain Boureau, and Cécile Dauphin, *Correspondence: Models of Letter-Writing from the Middle Ages to the Nineteenth Century* (Cambridge: Polity Press, 1997).
31. The letter is also printed in WL 34: 22–26.
32. For a detailed description of the epistolary exchange, see Yvonne Louise Matthews, "The Relationship of Horace Walpole and Mary and Agnes Berry," unpubl. PhD thesis (Beaumont: Lamar University, 1986).
33. Joanna Baillie, letter to [John Lewis] Mallet [?1842–1843], in *Further Letters of Joanna Baillie*, ed. Thomas McLean (Madison: Fairleigh Dickinson University Press, 2010), 220–221.
34. The poem is also reprinted in WL 34: 26.

35. Richard D. Altick, "Mr. Cambridge Serenades the Berry Sisters," *Notes and Queries* 183 (1942): 158–161.
36. The poem is also reprinted in WL 11: 2–3.
37. Maggie Lane, *Jane Austen and Food* (London: Hambledon Press, 1995), 146.
38. Also reprinted in WL 11: 12.
39. Walpole, letter to Mary Berry (January 9, 1791), autograph letter, Pierpont Morgan Library, MA 494.41. My thanks go to the Pierpont Morgan Library for permission to quote.
40. Some publications give 1748 as the year of birth, but the *Oxford Dictionary of National Biography* gives it as 1749; Alison Yarrington, "Damer [neé Conway], Anne Seymour," *Oxford Dictionary of National Biography* (Oxford: Oxford University Press, 2004–).
41. Percy Noble, *Anne Seymour Damer: A Woman of Art and Fashion, 1748–1828* (London: Kegan Paul, Trench, Trübner, and Co., 1908), 75–83; see also Alison Yarrington, "The Female Pygmalion: Anne Seymour Damer, Allan Cunningham and the Writing of a Woman Sculptor's Life," *The Sculpture Journal* 1 (1997): 32–44; Susan Benforado, "Anne Damer (1748–1828), Sculptor," unpubl. PhD thesis (Albuquerque: University of New Mexico, 1986).
42. Noble, *Damer*, 211.
43. Horace Walpole, *Anecdotes of Painting in England*, 4th ed., 4 vols. (London: Dodsley, 1796), 4: xi–xii.
44. Cynthia Roman, "The Art of Lady Diana Beauclerk: Horace Walpole and Female Genius," in Snodin, with the assistance of Roman, *Horace Walpole's Strawberry Hill*, 155–169.
45. Noble, *Damer*, 77.
46. Farington, *Diary*, 1: 171, 5: 1848, 8: 2936.
47. Andrew Elfenbein, *Romantic Genius: The Prehistory of a Homosexual Role* (New York: Columbia University Press, 1999), 91–124; Emma Donoghue, "'Random Shafts of Malice?': The Outings of Anne Damer," in *Lesbian Dames: Sapphism in the Long Eighteenth Century*, ed. John C. Beynon and Caroline Gonda (Farnham: Ashgate, 2010), 127–146.
48. William Combe, *The First Of April: or, The Triumphs of Folly* (London: Bew, 1777).
49. Anonymous, *A Sapphick Epistle, from Jack Cavendish to the Honourable and Most Beautiful Mrs. D***** (London: Smith, [?1778]), 14. The name Jack Cavendish is a pseudonym; see Donoghue, "Random Shafts of Malice?," 129–131. Donoghue establishes 1778 as the year of print.
50. Charles Pigott, *The Whig Club: or, A Sketch of Modern Patriotism* (London: Crosby, 1794), 91; see Donoghue, "Random Shafts of Malice?," 140–141.
51. Farington, *Diary*, 3: 1048.

52. Jonathan David Gross, "Introduction," in Anne Seymour Damer, *Belmour: A Modern Edition* (Evanston: Northwestern University Press, 2011), xvii–l, here xxxix, xxi. On "haunting" as part of the formulaic nature of Gothic, see Terry Castle, *The Female Thermometer: Eighteenth-Century Culture and the Invention of the Uncanny* (New York: Oxford University Press, 1995), 123.
53. Damer, *Belmour*, 24.
54. Walpole seems occasionally to have referred to her as a "wife," too (WL 37: 428).
55. Noble, *Damer*, 164.
56. My thanks go to The Lewis Walpole Library, Yale University, for providing me with a reproduction of this drawing, which is held there. The name "Cosway" is written underneath, yet it is no longer attributed to him. On Richard Cosway, who painted Damer several times, see Stephen Lloyd, *Richard and Maria Cosway: Regency Artists of Taste and Fashion*, with essays by Roy Porter and Aileen Ribeiro (Edinburgh: Scottish National Portrait Gallery, 1995), 61, 117, 118, 122.
57. Damer, Notebooks, autographs, 4 vols., 1: 5, LWL Mss Vol. 64. Courtesy of The Lewis Walpole Library, Yale University.
58. Damer, Notebooks, 1: 73. Courtesy of The Lewis Walpole Library, Yale University.
59. Emma Donoghue, *Life Mask* (Orlando: Harcourt, 2004). Donoghue makes very accurate use of eighteenth-century sources. See also Eibhear Walshe, "'A Different Story to Tell': The Historical Novel in Contemporary Irish Lesbian and Gay Writing," in *Facing the Other*, ed. Borbála Faragó and Moynagh Sullivan (Cambridge: Cambridge Scholars Publishing, 2008), 137–149. On same-sex desire and the bluestockings, see Susan S. Lanser, "Bluestocking Sapphism and the Economies of Desire," in *Reconsidering the Bluestockings*, ed. Nicole Pohl and Betty A. Schellenberg (San Marino: Huntington Library, 2003), 257–275.
60. A large body of recent criticism has opened the Romantic canon to include drama, especially women's drama: Catherine Burroughs, ed., *Women in British Romantic Theatre: Drama, Performance, and Society, 1790–1840* (Cambridge: Cambridge University Press, 2000); Catherine Burroughs, *Closet Stages: Joanna Baillie and the Theater Theory of British Romantic Women Writers* (Philadelphia: University of Pennsylvania Press, 1997); Thomas C. Crochunis, ed., *Joanna Baillie: Romantic Dramatist; Critical Essays* (London: Routledge, 2004); David Worrall, *The Politics of Romantic Theatricality, 1787–1832: The Road to the Stage* (Basingstoke: Palgrave Macmillan, 2007); Betsy Bolton, *Women, Nationalism, and the Romantic Stage: Theatre and Politics in Britain, 1780–1800* (Cambridge: Cambridge University Press, 2001); Frederick Burwick, *Playing to the Crowd: London Popular Theatre, 1780–1830* (New York: Palgrave Macmillan, 2011). For two contrasting views on the status of women dramatists, especially Joanna Baillie, see Donkin's

and Cox's articles: Ellen Donkin, "Joanna Baillie vs. the Termites Bellicosus," in *Getting into the Act: Women Playwrights in London, 1776–1829* (London: Routledge, 1995), 159–183; Jeffrey N. Cox, "Baillie, Siddons, Larpent: Gender, Power, and Politics in the Theatre of Romanticism," in Burroughs, *Women in British Romantic Theatre*, 23–47, here 29. A good introductory survey is Gillian Russell, "Private Theatricals," in *The Cambridge Companion to British Theatre, 1730–1830*, ed. Jane Moody and Daniel O'Quinn (Cambridge: Cambridge University Press, 2007), 191–203. This subchapter is also published as an article: Susanne Schmid, "Mary Berry's *Fashionable Friends* (1801) on Stage," *The Wordsworth Circle* 43 (2012): 172–177. My thanks go *The Wordsworth Circle* for the permission to reproduce it.

61. Bolton, *Women, Nationalism, and the Romantic Stage*, 33.
62. Burroughs, "'A Reasonable Woman's Desire': The Private Theatrical and Joanna Baillie's *The Tryal*," in Crochunis, *Joanna Baillie*, 187–205, here 188.
63. Sybil Rosenfeld, *Temples of Thespis: Some Private Theatres and Theatricals in England and Wales, 1700–1820* (London: Society for Theatre Research, 1978).
64. Burroughs, "A Reasonable Woman's Desire," 187.
65. Russell, "Private Theatricals," 191.
66. *Collected Letters of Joanna Baillie*, ed. Slagle; *Further Letters of Joanna Baillie*, ed. McLean.
67. *Collected Letters of Joanna Baillie*, ed. Slagle, 1: 158–159, 163, 164, 168.
68. Judith Bailey Slagle, "Joanna Baillie Through Her Letters," in *Collected Letters of Joanna Baillie*, ed. Slagle, 1: 1–23, here 3.
69. Judith Bailey Slagle, "Sisters—Ambition and Compliance: The Case of Mary and Agnes Berry and Joanna and Agnes Baillie," in *Woman to Woman: Female Negotiations During the Long Eighteenth Century*, ed. Carolyn D. Williams, Angela Escott, and Louise Duckling (Newark: University of Delaware Press, 2010), 79–97.
70. On Berry's interest in theater, see also Burroughs, *Closet Stages*, 67–73.
71. Baillie cited in Slagle, "Joanna Baillie Through Her Letters," 11.
72. Noble, *Damer*, 96–106; Andrew Elfenbein, "Lesbian Aestheticism on the Eighteenth-Century Stage," *Eighteenth-Century Life* 25 (2001): 1–16.
73. This painting was recently acquired by the National Portrait Gallery (London); National Portrait Gallery, "Gallery launches actress portraits show..." (www.npg.org.uk/about/press/gallery-launches-actress-portraits-show...-and-acquire-rare-picture-of-society-beauties-as-macbeths-witches.php).
74. Thomas McLean, "Introduction," in *Further Letters of Joanna Baillie*, ed. McLean, 21–29, here 24; Joanna Baillie, "To the Reader," in *The Family Legend: A Tragedy*, 2nd ed. (Edinburgh: Ballantyne & Co., 1810), v–xiii, here v.

75. The Margravine of Anspach rewrote Schiller's *Robbers* for her production; see Burwick, *Playing to the Crowd*, 105.
76. Mrs. Cornwell Barron-Wilson, *Memoirs of Miss Mellon, Afterwards Duchess of St. Albans*, 2 vols. (London: Remington and Co, 1886), 1: 243.
77. Ibid.
78. Anonymous, "Brighton, August 6," *Courier and Evening Gazette* 2491 (August 8, 1800): [3]. Another example is the following poem: M. T., "Fashionable Friends," *The Weekly Entertainer* 24 (611) (October 27, 1794): 340.
79. Elfenbein, "Lesbian Aestheticism," 12.
80. Ibid., 13.
81. Ibid., 2.
82. Cabinet, "Private Theatricals at Strawberry Hill," *The Lady's Monthly Museum* 8 (January 1802): 60; Anonymous, "Private Theatricals," *The Monthly Mirror* 12 (December 1801): 426–427; Noble, *Damer*, 170–171.
83. Anonymous, "Private Theatricals," 427.
84. The print is (wrongly?) dated "November, 1800."
85. Noble, *Damer*, 171–172.
86. Anonymous, "Art. 18. *The Fashionable Friends*," *The British Critic* 20 (December 1802): 677; Anonymous, "The Drama," *The Monthly Magazine* 14 (1802): 600; Anonymous, "Theatre," *The Universal Magazine* 110 (April 1802): 298; Anonymous, "*The Fashionable Friends*," *The Poetical Register* 2 (January 1803): 453; Anonymous, "Art. 37. *The Fashionable Friends*," *The Critical Review* 36 (November 1802): 353–355.
87. Berry, *The Fashionable Friends*, 3.

3 Mary Berry as a Learned Woman: Out of the Closet

1. Hannah More, "Thoughts on Conversation," in *Essays on Various Subjects, Principally Designed for Young Ladies* (London: Wilkie and Cadell, 1777), 37–62, here 37.
2. On women's education see Roy Porter, *Enlightenment: Britain and the Creation of the Modern World* (London: Penguin, 2000), 339–363; Michèle Cohen, *Fashioning Masculinity: National Identity and Language in the Eighteenth Century* (London: Routledge, 1996), 64–78.
3. Tobias Smollett, *The Adventures of Roderick Random*, ed. Paul-Gabriel Boucé (Oxford: Oxford University Press, 1999), 217–218.
4. Mary Berry appears in *The Reading Experience Database (RED), 1450–1945*, both as reader and writer (www.open.ac.uk/Arts/RED/).
5. On panoramas see Markman Ellis, "'Spectacles within doors': Panoramas of London in the 1790s," *Romanticism* 14 (2008): 133–148.

NOTES 191

6. Kate Perry, *Reminiscences of a London Drawing-Room* (London: privately printed, c. 1860).
7. William Hazlitt, "My First Acquaintance with Poets," *The Liberal* 2 (1823): 23–46; see also Jeffrey C. Robinson, "Hazlitt's 'My First Acquaintance with Poets': The Autobiography of a Cultural Critic," *Romanticism* 6 (2000): 178–194.
8. On cards see Janet E. Mullin, "'We Had Carding': Hospitable Card Play and Polite Domestic Sociability among the Middling Sort in Eighteenth-Century England," *Journal of Social History* 42 (2009): 989–1008.
9. Sandra Adickes, *The Social Quest: The Expanded Vision of Four Women Travelers in the Era of the French Revolution* (New York: Lang, 1991), 113.
10. Martineau is merely mentioned once, in a letter by Westmacott to Berry in BP 415.
11. Rictor Norton, *Mistress of Udolpho: The Life of Ann Radcliffe* (London: Leicester University Press, 1999), 229–230; Harriet Martineau, *Autobiography*, ed. Linda H. Peterson (Peterborough: Broadview, 2007), 281–282.
12. Kristin Flieger Samuelian, *Royal Romances: Sex, Scandal, and Monarchy in Print, 1780–1821* (New York: Palgrave Macmillan, 2010).
13. Martineau, *Autobiography*, 282.
14. See also Adickes, *The Social Quest*, 120.
15. Katherine Turner, *British Travel Writers in Europe, 1750–1800: Authorship, Gender and National Identity* (Aldershot: Ashgate, 2001), 127; see also Katherine Turner, "Women's Travel Writing, 1750–1830," in *The History of British Women's Writing, 1750–1830*, ed. Jacqueline M. Labbe, vol. 5 of *The History of British Women's Writing* (Basingstoke: Palgrave Macmillan, 2010), 47–60.
16. Brian Dolan, *Ladies of the Grand Tour* (London: Flamingo, 2002). Dolan repeatedly mentions the Berrys.
17. John Wilton-Ely, "'Classic Ground': Britain, Italy, and the Grand Tour," *Eighteenth-Century Life* 28 (2004): 136–165, here 157. For women's writing about Italy, see Kathryn Walchester, *"Our Own Fair Italy": Nineteenth Century Women's Travel Writing and Italy 1800–1844* (Bern: Lang, 2007).
18. Adickes, *The Social Quest*, 3.
19. The following volume contains reproductions of Agnes's watercolors: Bianca Riccio, ed., with the assistance of Sabina De Vito, Francesco Leone, and Lisa Roscioni, *Mary Berry un' inglese in Italia: Diari e corrispondenza dal 1783 al 1823. Arte personaggi e società* (Rome: Ugo Bozzi, 2002).
20. Elizabeth A. Bohls, *Women Travel Writers and the Language of Aesthetics, 1716–1818* (Cambridge: Cambridge University Press, 1995), 2.
21. On representations of the spectacular in travel writing about Italy, see Chloe Chard, *Pleasure and Guilt on the Grand Tour: Travel Writing*

and Imaginative Geography, 1600–1830 (Manchester: Manchester University Press, 1999), 126–172.
22. See Jonathan White, *Italian Cultural Lineages* (Toronto: University of Toronto Press, 2007), 176–217. White explains that "Italy's Romantic reputation" (176) was influenced by Sismondi, who diagnosed a cultural and political decline and named the Catholic Church as one major cause. Berry, who met Sismondi in 1823 (JCB 3: 342), did not adopt his other points of criticism (breakdown of the family, education, legislation) but seems to have shared some of his anti-Catholicism.
23. Susan Staves, *A Literary History of Women's Writing in Britain, 1660–1789* (Cambridge: Cambridge University Press, 2006), 286–361.
24. Ibid., 304.
25. See also Peter Sabor, "Introduction," in *The Works of Horatio Walpole, Earl of Orford*, ed. Mary Berry, 5 vols. (London: Robinson and Edwards, 1798), reprint ed. Peter Sabor (London: Pickering and Chatto, 1999), 1: ix–xxxi, here xxii–xxviii.
26. *The Quarterly Review* names her as the author of the 1844 edition: Anonymous, "*England and France: A Comparative View*," *The Quarterly Review* 75 (March 1845): 485–496, here 485.
27. See chapter 2.
28. Anonymous, "Preface by the Editor," in *The Works of Horatio Walpole, Earl of Orford*, ed. Mary Berry, 1: v–xx, here xix.
29. Nicholas D. Smith, *The Literary Manuscripts and Letters of Hannah More* (Farnham: Ashgate, 2008), 59.
30. On the psychological side of the edition, see Laura Mandell, "Producing Hate in 'Private' Letters: Horace Walpole, Mary Hays," *European Romantic Review* 17 (2006): 169–177.
31. Mary Berry, "Preface," in *Letters of the Marquise du Deffand to the Hon. Horace Walpole*, ed. Mary Berry, 4 vols. (London: Longman, Hurst, Rees, and Orme, 1810), 1: v–lxv, here xxix. For a friendly review see Anonymous, "*Letters of the Marquise du Deffand to the Honourable Horace Walpole*," *Edinburgh Review* 17 (February 1811): 290–311. A more negative review is: Anonymous, "*Letters of the Marquise Du Deffand to the Hon. Horace Walpole*," *The Monthly Review* 65 (1811): 28–36.
32. Staves, *Literary History*, 289.
33. Ibid.
34. D. R. Woolf, "A Feminine Past? Gender, Genre, and Historical Knowledge in England, 1500–1800," *The American Historical Review* 102 (1997): 645–679, here 648–649.
35. Hannah More, *Strictures on the Modern System of Female Education*, 2 vols. (London: Cadell and Davies, 1799), 1: 105; see also Woolf, "A Feminine Past?," 669.
36. Lois G. Schwoerer, *Lady Rachel Russell: "One of the Best of Women"* (Baltimore: Johns Hopkins University Press, 1988), xx.

37. Mary Berry, *Some Account of the Life of Rachael Wriothesley Lady Russell Followed by a Series of Letters* (London: Longman, Hurst, Rees, Orme, and Brown, 1819), 25–26.
38. One of Catharine Macaulay's innovations had been the systematic use of manuscripts; see Staves, *Literary History*, 328.
39. For a review see Anonymous, "Some Account of the Life of Rachael Wriothesley, Lady Russell," *The British Review* 16, no. 32 (1820): 459–474.
40. Elizabeth Eger, *Bluestockings: Women of Reason from Enlightenment to Romanticism* (Basingstoke: Palgrave Macmillan, 2010), 121–162. See also Catherine Gallagher, *Nobody's Story: The Vanishing Acts of Women Writers in the Marketplace, 1670–1820* (Oxford: Clarendon Press, 1994). Mary Robinson's game with pseudonyms, though motivated by other reasons, is another example that highlights the problems of female authorship around 1800; see Daniel Robinson, *The Poetry of Mary Robinson: Form and Fame* (New York: Palgrave Macmillan, 2011).

4 Holland House and Lady Holland

1. *The Creevey Papers: A Selection from the Correspondence and Diaries of the Late Thomas Creevey, M. P. Born 1768–Died 1838*, ed. Herbert Maxwell, 2 vols. (London: Murray, 1903–1904), 2: 58.
2. On the representation of cats and misogyny, see Robert Darnton, *The Great Cat Massacre and Other Episodes in French Cultural History* (New York: Vintage, 1985), 75–104.
3. *Creevey Papers*, 2: 269.
4. Giles Stephen Holland Fox-Strangways, Earl of Ilchester, *The Home of the Hollands, 1605–1820* (London: Murray, 1937), 6; Derek Hudson, *Holland House in Kensington* (London: Davies, 1967), 5. Unless otherwise indicated, I have followed Ilchester's and Hudson's histories of the house.
5. Hudson, *Holland House*, 20; Ilchester, *Home of the Hollands*, 32.
6. *The Life and Letters of Lord Macaulay*, ed. George Otto Trevelyan, 2 vols. (London: Longmans, Green, and Co., 1876), 1: 207.
7. Ibid., 1: 208.
8. See, for example, *Creevey Papers*, 2: 231, 311.
9. Hudson, *Holland House*, 53, 57.
10. Lepenies uses the term "Langeweile" ("boredom") in Wolf Lepenies, *Melancholie und Gesellschaft. Mit einer neuen Einleitung: Das Ende der Utopie und die Wiederkehr der Melancholie* (Frankfurt am Main: Suhrkamp, 1998), 56.
11. L. J. Gorton, "The Holland House Papers and Their History," *The British Museum Quarterly* 29 (1965): 71–78. For the location of further manuscripts, see Hudson, *Holland House*, 136.

12. Henry Richard Fox, Lord Holland, *Memoirs of the Whig Party During My Time*, ed. Henry Edward Fox, Lord Holland, 2 vols. (London: Longman, Brown, Green, and Longmans, 1852–1854); Henry Richard Fox, Lord Holland, *Foreign Reminiscences* [1850], ed. Henry Edward Fox, Lord Holland, 2nd ed. (London: Longman, Brown, Green, and Longmans, 1851).
13. Princess Marie Liechtenstein, *Holland House*, 2 vols. (London: Macmillan, 1874). For a comment on its style and accuracy, see Hudson, *Holland House*, 115.
14. Henry Richard Fox, Lord Holland, *Further Memoirs of the Whig Party, 1807–1821*, ed. Earl of Ilchester (London: Murray, 1905); *The Journal of Elizabeth, Lady Holland (1791–1811)*, ed. Earl of Ilchester, 2 vols. (London: Longmans, Green, and Co., 1908); *The Spanish Journal of Elizabeth Lady Holland*, ed. Earl of Ilchester (London: Longmans, Green, and Co., 1910); *The Journal of the Hon. Edward Fox (Afterwards Fourth and Last Lord Holland), 1818–1830*, ed. Earl of Ilchester (London: Butterworth, 1923); *Elizabeth, Lady Holland to Her Son, 1821–1845*, ed. Earl of Ilchester (London: Murray, 1946); Earl of Ilchester, *The Home of the Hollands*; Earl of Ilchester, *Chronicles of Holland House, 1820–1900* (London: Murray, 1937); see also Hudson, *Holland House*, 122.
15. *The Holland House Diaries, 1831–1840: The Diary of Henry Richard Vassall Fox, Third Lord Holland, with Extracts from the Diary of Dr John Allen*, ed. Abraham D. Kriegel (London: Routledge & Kegan Paul, 1977).
16. Richard Brent, *Liberal Anglican Politics: Whiggery, Religion, and Reform, 1830–1841* (Oxford: Clarendon Press, 1987); William Anthony Hay, *The Whig Revival, 1808–1830* (Basingstoke: Palgrave Macmillan, 2005); Peter Mandler, *Aristocratic Government in the Age of Reform: Whigs and Liberals, 1830–1852* (Oxford: Clarendon Press, 1990); Ian Newbould, *Whiggery and Reform, 1830–41: The Politics of Government* (Stanford: Stanford University Press, 1990).
17. Leslie Mitchell, *Holland House* (London: Duckworth, 1980); Leslie Mitchell, *The Whig World, 1760–1837* (London: Hambledon and London, 2005).
18. Mitchell, *Whig World*, 1, 3.
19. Ibid., 12.
20. Despite their predilection for the town, Whigs also embraced the pastoral mode: Joe Bord, *Science and Whig Manners: Science and Political Style in Britain, c. 1790–1850* (Basingstoke: Palgrave Macmillan, 2009), 102–134.
21. Anonymous, "Art. II. De Buonaparte, et des Bourbons...Par F. A. de Chateaubriand," *The British Critic* 2 (July 1814): 22–33, here 33; for the reference and contexts of Francophilia as well as anti-French sentiment, see Gerald Newman, "Anti-French Propaganda and British Liberal Nationalism in the Early Nineteenth Century: Suggestions

Toward a General Interpretation," *Victorian Studies* 18 (1975): 385–418, here 398–399, 408, 411.
22. Abraham D. Kriegel, "Liberty and Whiggery in Early Nineteenth-Century England," *The Journal of Modern History* 52 (1980): 253–278.
23. Mitchell, *Whig World*, 122.
24. *Life and Letters of Macaulay*, 1: 209.
25. *Correspondence of Mr. Joseph Jekyll with His Sister-in-Law, Lady Gertrude Sloane Stanley, 1818–1838*, ed. Algernon Bourke (London: Murray, 1894), 176.
26. *Letters of Harriet Countess Granville, 1810–1845*, ed. F. Leveson Gower, 3rd ed., 2 vols. (London: Longmans, Green, and Co., 1894).
27. The standard biography, based on the above-mentioned editions and studies, is Sonia Keppel, *The Sovereign Lady: A Life of Elizabeth, Third Lady Holland, with Her Family* (London: Hamish Hamilton, 1974); for a brief survey see C. J. Wright, "Fox, Elizabeth Vassall," *Oxford Dictionary of National Biography* (Oxford: Oxford University Press, 2004–).
28. Ilchester, *Home of the Hollands*, 133.
29. On the financial details see Ilchester, *Home of the Hollands*, 143–145; Keppel, *Sovereign Lady*, 74.
30. In order to retain influence over her youngest, Harriet, she pretended that the baby had died in Italy and even staged a mock funeral to mislead her husband. However, she handed the child over to him in 1799; see EHJ 1: 263–266.
31. This period is covered by her *Spanish Journal*, which Ilchester published separately.
32. Keppel, *Sovereign Lady*, 349.
33. The most accurate and detailed information on Lord Holland's life is to be gained from Ilchester, *Home of the Hollands;* for a brief survey see C. J. Wright, "Fox [*later* Vassall], Henry Richard," *Oxford Dictionary of National Biography* (Oxford: Oxford University Press, 2004–).
34. Lord Holland, *Memoirs of the Whig Party*, 1: 3; Ilchester, *Home of the Hollands*, 112.
35. Lord Holland, *Memoirs of the Whig Party*, 1: 55.
36. Ilchester, *Home of the Hollands*, 148; Henry Richard Fox, Lord Holland, *The Opinions of Lord Holland as Recorded in the Journals of the House of Lords from 1797 to 1841*, ed. D. C. Moylan (London: Ridgway, 1841).
37. Henry Richard Fox, Lord Holland, *Some Account of the Life and Writings of Lope Felix de Vega Carpio* (London: Longman, Hurst, Rees, and Orme, 1806). A revised edition appeared in 1817.
38. James N. McCord Jr., "Taming the Female Politician in Early Nineteenth-Century England: John Bull *versus Lady Jersey," Journal*

of Women's History 13 (2002): 31–53. The article treats the Queen Caroline affair.
39. Henry Holland, *Recollections of Past Life* (London: Longmans, Green, and Co., 1872), 228–229; see also Lloyd Sanders, *The Holland House Circle* (New York: Putnam's Sons, 1908), 62–63.
40. Brian Dolan, *Ladies of the Grand Tour* (London: Flamingo, 2002), 104–121, 261–267.
41. Keppel notes her wild traveling and her disregard for comfort during her first journeys on the continent in the 1790s and points out that her style of traveling had changed by 1802 when she was older, had gone through numerous births, and was accompanied by two "delicate" children; see Keppel, *Sovereign Lady,* 122.
42. While Lady Blessington's *Idler to Italy* devotes a long passage to the miracle of St. Januarius in Naples, Lady Holland's *Journal* only mentions it in passing and finds a scientific explanation; see chapter 7.
43. For a summary of the Spanish involvement of Holland House, see Mitchell, *Holland House,* 217–239, and Diego Saglia, *Poetic Castles in Spain: British Romanticism and Figurations of Iberia* (Amsterdam: Rodopi, 2000), 26–32.
44. John-David Lopez, "The British Romantic Reconstruction of Spain," unpubl. PhD thesis (Los Angeles: UCLA, 2008), 3–4; Saglia, *Poetic Castles in Spain,* 11.
45. Saglia, *Poetic Castles in Spain,* 11.
46. Lopez, "British Romantic Reconstruction," 5
47. Lord Holland, *Foreign Reminiscences,* 68.
48. Mitchell, *Holland House,* 223.
49. Ibid., 226.
50. Ibid., 223.
51. Ibid., 231.
52. Clare Brant, *Eighteenth-Century Letters and British Culture* (Basingstoke: Palgrave Macmillan, 2006), 273; Roger Chartier, Alain Boureau, and Cécile Dauphin, *Correspondence: Models of Letter-Writing from the Middle Ages to the Nineteenth Century* (Cambridge: Polity Press, 1997); see chapter 2. The text of Lady Holland's *Spanish Journal* is not complete, as Ilchester's comment shows: "I have omitted or shortened the less important details as much as possible" (SJ v).
53. Bruce W. Wardropper, "An Early English Hispanist," *Bulletin of Spanish Studies* 24 (1947): 259–268.
54. Mitchell, *Holland House,* 231–235; Saglia, *Poetic Castles in Spain,* 29–30; Keppel, *Sovereign Lady,* 220; Nanora Sweet, "'Hitherto Closed to British Enterprise': Trading and Writing the Hispanic World Circa 1815," *European Romantic Review* 8 (1997): 139–147.
55. George Ticknor, *Life, Letters, and Journals,* 2 vols. (London: Sampson Low, Marston, Searle, & Rivington, 1876), 1: 264. On comparing the German Romantic writer Ludwig Tieck's and Holland's Spanish

collections, Ticknor felt that Tieck's was better, though none of the two was as good as his own (Ticknor, *Life, Letters, and Journals*, 1: 457).
56. TMJ 4: 1734. On the library, its books, and manuscripts, see Liechtenstein, *Holland House*, 2: 173–201.
57. George Gordon Byron, *Childe Harold's Pilgrimage*, vol. 2 of *Complete Poetical Works*, ed. Jerome J. McGann (Oxford: Clarendon Press, 1980), 42. The stanza was intended to follow after l. 890. On *Childe Harold* and Spain, see Saglia, *Poetic Castles in Spain*, 125–141.
58. For Byron's attack on Holland House in *English Bards and Scotch Reviewers* as well as his further involvement with the Holland House circle, see chapter 5.
59. Ilchester, *Home of the Hollands*, 243.
60. N. B. Penny, "The Whig Cult of Fox in Early Nineteenth-Century Sculpture," *Past and Present* 70 (1976): 94–105, here 101. On Holland House and the Fox cult, see also Mitchell, *Holland House*, 39–60.
61. Kriegel, "Liberty and Whiggery," 254.
62. Mitchell, *Holland House*, 44.
63. *Elizabeth, Lady Holland to Her Son*, 46.
64. See also Michael Sadleir, *Blessington-d'Orsay: A Masquerade* [1933] (London: Folio Society, 1983), 42.
65. Newman, "Anti-French Propaganda and British Liberal Nationalism," 390, 388.
66. For a summary see Mitchell, *Holland House*, 240–268; Mitchell, *Whig World*, 77–97.
67. Mitchell, *Whig World*, 88.
68. Keppel, *Sovereign Lady*, 117.
69. Ilchester, *Home of the Hollands*, 185. In May 1815, Anne Damer presented Napoleon with a bust of Fox; see Percy Noble, *Anne Seymour Damer: A Woman of Art and Fashion, 1748–1828* (London: Kegan Paul, Trench, Trübner, and Co., 1908), 211; see also chapter 2.
70. Lord Holland, *Foreign Reminiscences*, 191–192; Ilchester, *Home of the Hollands*, 188, 190.
71. Stuart Semmel, *Napoleon and the British* (New Haven: Yale University Press, 2004).
72. *The Opinions of Lord Holland*, 86–87; Mitchell, *Holland House*, 260.
73. Keppel, *Sovereign Lady*, 217.
74. For this and other gifts, see Keppel, *Sovereign Lady*, 221–226; Lord Holland, *Foreign Reminiscences*, 197–198.
75. *Creevey Papers*, 2: 39; Mitchell, *Holland House*, 260. Examples are: Anonymous, "Art VIII. *Facts Illustrative of the Treatment of Napoleon Buonaparte in St Helena...*," *Edinburgh Review* 32 (July 1819): 148–170; John Allen, "Art. IX. *Letters from St. Helena. By William Warden*," *Edinburgh Review* 27 (December 1816): 459–492.

76. *Life and Letters of Macaulay*, 1: 213–214; for the Greek text see Liechtenstein, *Holland House*, 1: 183.
77. Lord Holland, *Foreign Reminiscences*, 188–191; Semmel, *Napoleon and the British*, 219–220.
78. Keppel, *Sovereign Lady*, 254; Ilchester, *Chronicles of Holland House*, 17. On the relic-collecting see also Semmel, *Napoleon and the British*, 226.
79. See also Schmid, "Holland House and Mary Berry's Drawing-Room," *The Wordsworth Circle* 35 (2004): 77–80, here 77.
80. TMJ 2: 476; Thomas Moore, "To Lady Holland on Napoleon's Legacy of a Snuff-Box," *Poetical Works*, ed. A. D. Godley (Oxford: Oxford University Press, 1915), 717. For the poems see Keppel, *Sovereign Lady*, 226–227.
81. Lord Carlisle, "To Lady Holland, on the Legacy of a Snuff-Box, Left to Her by Buonaparte," *The Gentleman's Magazine* 91 (1821): 457–458.
82. Byron, "Napoleon's Snuff-Box," in *Complete Poetical Works*, 6: 512.
83. Julia M. Wright, "'All the Fire-Side Circle': Irish Women Writers and the Sheridan-Lefanu Coterie," *Keats-Shelley Journal* 55 (2006): 63–72, here 65; on improvisation see Angela Esterhammer, *Romanticism and Improvisation, 1750–1850* (Cambridge: Cambridge University Press, 2008), 1–58; for the Romantic poets as a coterie or a circle, see Jeffrey N. Cox, *Poetry and Politics in the Cockney School: Keats, Shelley, Hunt and Their Circle* (Cambridge: Cambridge University Press, 1998), 1–15.
84. *Life and Letters of Macaulay*, 1: 214. Holland's inscription is in Liechtenstein, *Holland House*, 1: 181; Luttrell's reply is ibid., 1: 182–183, for the chapter on the grounds, see ibid., 1: 166–196.
85. Ibid., 1: 134; for the subsequent printing see Ilchester, *Chronicles of Holland House*, 283–284.
86. Matthew Lewis, *The Monk*, ed. Howard Anderson (Oxford: Oxford University Press, 1998), 313.
87. *Life and Letters of Macaulay*, 1: 211.
88. On upper-class speech and the deliberate use of archaisms in the nineteenth century, see K. C. Phillipps, *Language and Class in Victorian England* (Oxford: Blackwell, 1984), 27–35.

5 THE HOLLAND HOUSE SET

1. Saba Holland, *A Memoir of the Reverend Sydney Smith, by His Daughter, Lady Holland: With a Selection from His Letters*, ed. Mrs. Austen, 3rd ed., vol. 1 (London: Longman, Brown, Green, and Longmans, 1855), 409.
2. Lloyd Sanders, *The Holland House Circle* (New York: Putnam's Sons, 1908), 164, 220, 246. Ilchester's two volumes on the history of Holland House and Hudson's study mix the biographical with the

anecdotal. Leslie Mitchell's seminal study, *Holland House* (London: Duckworth, 1980), organizes its material by people and themes.
3. Patricia Meyer Spacks, *Gossip* (New York: Knopf, 1985), 15.
4. Ibid., 4.
5. Giles Stephen Holland Fox-Strangways, Earl of Ilchester, *The Home of the Hollands, 1605–1820* (London: Murray, 1937), 166. The Dinner Books run until 1875.
6. *The Life and Letters of Lord Macaulay*, ed. George Otto Trevelyan, 2 vols. (London: Longmans, Green, and Co., 1876), 1: 205.
7. Ibid., 1: 235.
8. *The Greville Memoirs, 1814–1860*, ed. Lytton Strachey and Roger Fulford, 8 vols. (London: Macmillan, 1938), 2: 331.
9. Leslie Mitchell, *The Whig World, 1760–1837* (London: Hambledon and London, 2005), 25.
10. *The Creevey Papers: A Selection from the Correspondence and Diaries of the Late Thomas Creevey, M. P. Born 1768–Died 1838*, ed. Herbert Maxwell, 2 vols. (London: Murray, 1903–1904), 1: xvi–xviii. Not all of the individuals listed belonged to the inner circle of Holland House.
11. Sanders, *Holland House Circle*, 108–118, 206, 217, 292; EHJ 2: 55.
12. *The Diary of Joseph Farington*, ed. Kenneth Garlick, Angus MacIntyre, and Kathryn Cave, 16 vols. (New Haven: Yale University Press, 1978–1984), 12: 4342.
13. Lady Holland's diary entry on Rumford's personal history, previous achievements, and current status testifies to her interest in her visitors (EHJ 1: 206–208). On scientists in Whig contexts, see also Joe Bord, *Science and Whig Manners: Science and Political Style in Britain, c. 1790–1850* (Basingstoke: Palgrave Macmillan, 2009).
14. *The Diary of Benjamin Robert Haydon*, ed. Willard Bissell Pope, 5 vols. (Cambridge/MA: Harvard University Press, 1960–1963), 5: 498.
15. *Creevey Papers*, 2: 231.
16. Ibid., 2: 311. On the dinner hours see Ilchester, *Home of the Hollands*, 250–251.
17. *The Greville Memoirs*, 2: 331.
18. Elizabeth Vassall Fox, Lady Holland, *Elizabeth, Lady Holland to Her Son, 1821–1845*, ed. Giles Stephen Holland Fox-Strangways, Earl of Ilchester (London: Murray, 1946), 3.
19. *Life and Letters of Macaulay*, 1: 267; see also Derek Hudson, *Holland House in Kensington* (London: Davies, 1967), 87.
20. Mitchell, *Holland House*, 33.
21. *Creevey Papers*, 2: 155–156.
22. Mitchell, *Whig World*, 12.
23. Gerald Newman, "Anti-French Propaganda and British Liberal Nationalism in the Early Nineteenth Century: Suggestions Toward a General Interpretation" *Victorian Studies* 18 (1975): 385–418, here 415.

24. An in-depth analysis of the *Edinburgh Review* is beyond the scope of this study; see Biancamaria Fontana, *Rethinking the Politics of Commercial Society: The* Edinburgh Review *1802–1832* (Cambridge: Cambridge University Press, 1985); George Pottinger, *Heirs of the Enlightenment: Edinburgh Reviewers and Writers 1800–1830* (Edinburgh: Scottish Academic Press, 1992); Massimiliano Demata and Duncan Wu, eds., *British Romanticism and the* Edinburgh Review (Basingstoke: Palgrave Macmillan, 2002); Mark Schoenfield, *British Periodicals and Romantic Identity: The "Literary Lower Empire"* (New York: Palgrave Macmillan, 2009); for the ties between Scotland and Holland House, see Mitchell, *Holland House*, 172–195.
25. William Christie, *The* Edinburgh Review *in the Literary Culture of Romantic Britain* (London: Pickering and Chatto, 2009), 42.
26. See, for example, *The "Pope" of Holland House: Selections from the Correspondence of John Whishaw and His Friends, 1813–1840*, ed. Lady Seymour (London: Fisher Unwin, 1906), 59–60, 139, 173, 189.
27. On Jeffrey, the Whigs, and Holland House, see Philip Flynn, *Francis Jeffrey* (Newark: University of Delaware Press, 1978), 95–108.
28. *Creevey Papers*, 1: 205.
29. John Allen, "Art. IX. *Letters from St. Helena.* By William Warden," *Edinburgh Review* 27 (December 1816): 459–492; Ilchester, *Home of the Hollands*, 326; see chapter 4.
30. Princess Marie Liechtenstein, *Holland House*, 2 vols. (London: Macmillan, 1874), 2: 142–147.
31. Thomas Babington Macaulay, "Art. VII. *The Opinions of Lord Holland*," *Edinburgh Review* 73 (July 1841): 560–568.
32. *Creevey Papers*, 2: 162. On Rogers see Avery F. Gaskins, "Samuel Rogers: A Revaluation," *The Wordsworth Circle* 16 (1985): 146–149; Ellis Roberts, *Samuel Rogers and His Circle* (London: Methuen, 1910).
33. Kate Perry, *Reminiscences of a London Drawing-Room* (London: privately printed, c. 1860), 8.
34. *Recollections of the Table-Talk of Samuel Rogers. Porsoniana*, 2nd ed. (London: Moxon, 1856), 95, 28, 58.
35. Samuel Rogers, *Italy: A Poem* (London: Cadell, 1830). On the illustrations see J. R. Hale, "Samuel Rogers the Perfectionist," *Huntington Library Quarterly* 25 (1961): 61–67.
36. *The "Pope" of Holland House*, 42.
37. [James Mackintosh], "Art. II. *Poems*, by Samuel Rogers," *Edinburgh Review* 22 (October 1813): 32–50, here 50.
38. Donald Weeks, "Samuel Rogers: Man of Taste," *Publications of the Modern Language Association* 62 (1947): 472–486.
39. *Table-Talk of Samuel Rogers*, 278–280.
40. Ibid., 89.
41. Joseph J. Firebaugh, "Samuel Rogers and American Men of Letters," *American Literature* 13 (1942): 331–345.

42. Liechtenstein, *Holland House*, 1: 157. See also Hesketh Pearson, *The Smith of Smiths, Being the Life, Wit and Humour of Sydney Smith*, with a new introduction by Richard Ingrams (London: Hogarth Press, 1984).
43. *The Greville Memoirs*, 5: 87. This passage is a short obituary on Allen. On the Whigs as "unbelievers," see Mitchell, *Whig World*, 117–134.
44. *Table-Talk of Samuel Rogers*, 288.
45. *The Letters of Sydney Smith*, ed. Nowell C. Smith, 2 vols. (Oxford: Clarendon Press, 1953): 1: 109.
46. Ibid., 1: 331.
47. For a collection of his articles, see *The Works of the Reverend Sydney Smith, Including His Contributions to the* Edinburgh Review, 2 vols. (London: Longman, Brown, Green, Longmans, and Roberts, 1859).
48. Sanders, *Holland House Circle*, 206; see also Susanne Schmid, "Holland House and Mary Berry's Drawing-Room: Salons, *Salonnières* and Writers," *The Wordsworth Circle* 35 (2004): 77–80, here 78–79.
49. Thomas Moore, *Memoirs of the Life of the Right Honourable Richard Brinsley Sheridan*, 2nd ed., 2 vols. (London: Longman, Hurst, Rees, Orme, Brown, and Green, 1825).
50. Ronan Kelly, *Bard of Erin: The Life of Thomas Moore* (Dublin: Penguin, 2008), 362–368, 404–415; TMJ 2: 466.
51. *Letters and Journals of Byron: With Notices of His Life*, ed. Thomas Moore, 2 vols. (London: Murray, 1830).
52. *The Journal of the Hon. Edward Fox (Afterwards Fourth and Last Lord Holland), 1818–1830*, ed. Earl of Ilchester (London: Butterworth, 1923), 162. Lady Holland's letters mention the memoirs and Moore's biography: *Elizabeth, Lady Holland to Her Son*, 28, 109.
53. See also Schmid, "Holland House and Mary Berry's Drawing-Room," 78.
54. *Life and Letters of Macaulay*, 1: 213; Ilchester, *Home of the Hollands*, 274.
55. William Christie, "Running With the English Hares and Hunting With the Scotch Bloodhounds," *The Byron Journal* 25 (1997): 23–43; Jane Stabler, "Against Their Better Selves: Byron, Jeffrey and the *Edinburgh*," in *British Romanticism and the* Edinburgh Review, ed. Massimiliano Demata and Duncan Wu (Basingstoke: Palgrave Macmillan, 2002), 146–167.
56. Henry Brougham, "ART II. *Hours of Idleness: A Series of Poems, Original and Translated*. By George Gordon, Lord Byron, a Minor," *Edinburgh Review* 11 (January 1808): 285–289.
57. George Gordon Byron, *English Bards and Scotch Reviewers*, in *Complete Poetical Works*, ed. Jerome J. McGann, 7 vols. (Oxford: Clarendon Press, 1980–1993), 1: 227–264, here 246, ll. 540–559.
58. See also a letter to John Becher in BLJ 1: 157 (February 26, 1808).
59. See chapter 4.
60. Schoenfield, *British Periodicals and Romantic Identity*, 138.

61. Stabler, "Against Their Better Selves," 151–156.
62. Benita Eisler, *Byron: Child of Passion, Fool of Fame* (New York: Knopf, 1999), 307–330.
63. Eisler, *Byron*, 370–371; BLJ 2: 191–226.
64. For further events see Ilchester, *Home of the Hollands*, 263–280.
65. Paul Douglass, "The Madness of Writing: Lady Caroline Lamb's Byronic Identity," *Pacific Coast Philology* 34 (1999): 53–71, here 53. For a survey see also Paul Douglass, "Introduction," in *Glenarvon*, ed. Paul Douglass, vol. 1 of *The Works of Caroline Lamb*, ed. Paul Douglass and Leigh Wetherall Dickson, 3 vols. (London: Pickering and Chatto, 2009), xxvii–xliv.
66. Caroline Lamb, letter to Lady Holland (before April 16 [or 11?], 1811), in *The Whole Disgraceful Truth: Selected Letters of Lady Caroline Lamb*, ed. Paul Douglass (New York: Palgrave Macmillan, 2006), 62–64.
67. Paul Douglass, *Lady Caroline Lamb: A Biography* (New York: Palgrave Macmillan, 2004), 63.
68. Lamb, *The Whole Disgraceful Truth*, 62–74.
69. Douglass, *Lady Caroline Lamb*, 102.
70. *Table-Talk of Samuel Rogers*, 233.
71. John Clubbe, "*Glenarvon* Revised—and Revisited," *The Wordsworth Circle* 10 (1979): 205–217.
72. Peter W. Graham, "Fictive Biography in 1816: The Case of *Glenarvon*," *The Byron Journal* 19 (1991): 53–68.
73. For stage productions see Frederick Burwick, *Playing to the Crowd, London Popular Theatre, 1780–1830* (New York: Palgrave Macmillan, 2011), 71–79.
74. Lamb, *Glenarvon*, 86.
75. Ibid., 87.
76. Ibid.
77. Ria Grimbergen and Paul Douglass, "On a Special Copy of Caroline Lamb's *Glenarvon* Recently Discovered in the Koninklijke Bibliotheek," *The Byron Journal* 37 (2009): 151–160, here 154.
78. Lamb, *Glenarvon*, 88.
79. Malcolm Kelsall, "The Byronic Hero and Revolution in Ireland: The Politics of *Glenarvon*," *The Byron Journal* 9 (1981): 4–19, here 14.
80. Lamb, *Glenarvon*, 88.
81. Ibid., 346.
82. *Creevey Papers*, 1: 255.

6 The Countess of Blessington as Hostess

1. P. G. Patmore, "Personal Recollections of the Late Lady Blessington," *Bentley's Miscellany* 26 (1849): 162–175, here 162.

NOTES 203

2. Michael Sadleir, *Blessington-d'Orsay: A Masquerade* [1933] (London: Folio Society, 1983), 38.
3. *Correspondence of Mr. Joseph Jekyll with His Sister-in-Law, Lady Gertrude Sloane Stanley, 1818–1838*, ed. Algernon Bourke (London: Murray, 1894), 272.
4. Unless otherwise indicated, details of Blessington's biography have been taken from Sadleir and Madden. See also Susanne Schmid, "Lady Blessington und die Salons der englischen Romantik," in *Subversive Romantik*, ed. Volker Kapp, Helmuth Kiesel, Klaus Lubbers, and Patricia Plummer (Berlin: Duncker & Humblot, 2004), 153–164, here 158–160; Susanne Schmid "The Countess of Blessington and the English Romantic Salon," in *Einsamkeit und Geselligkeit um 1800*, ed. Susanne Schmid (Heidelberg: Winter, 2008), 95–109, here 99–101.
5. Venetia Murray, *High Society in the Regency Period, 1788–1830* (London: Penguin, 1999), 134–156, here 136.
6. See Hawkins on their collaboration, Ann R. Hawkins, "Marguerite, Countess of Blessington, and L. E. L. (Letitia Elizabeth Landon): Evidence of a Friendship," *ANQ: A Quarterly Journal of Short Articles, Notes and Reviews* 16 (2003): 27–32. See also chapter 7 on the *Keepsake*.
7. This is Sadleir's suggestion, who does not believe that Lady Blessington and D'Orsay had sexual intercourse; Sadleir, *Blessington-d'Orsay*, 54.
8. On the representation of scandalous womanhood, the family, and the female body, see Kristin Flieger Samuelian, *Royal Romances: Sex, Scandal, and Monarchy in Print, 1780–1821* (New York: Palgrave Macmillan, 2010).
9. Patmore, "Personal Recollections," 169.
10. William Jerdan, *Autobiography*, 4 vols. (London: Hall, 1852–1853), 4: 321; see also MA 1: 277.
11. Nathaniel Parker Willis, "Pencillings by the Way," *New-York Mirror* 12 (April 18, 1835): 332; see also Sadleir, *Blessington-d'Orsay*, 196.
12. Marguerite Blessington, *The Magic Lantern; or, Sketches of Scenes from the Metropolis* (London: Longman, Hurst, Rees, Orme, and Brown, 1822); Marguerite Blessington, *Sketches and Fragments* (London: Longman, Hurst, Rees, Orme, and Brown, 1822); Marguerite Blessington, *Journal of a Tour through the Netherlands to Paris, in 1821* (London: Longman, Hurst, Rees, Orme, and Brown, 1822); Marguerite Blessington, *Rambles in Waltham Forest: A Stranger's Contribution to the Triennial Sale for the Benefit of the Wanstead Lying-In Charity* (London: Cox, 1827). Her friends probably knew of her authorship. Jerdan's autobiograhy states that some of her first anonymously published prose texts appeared in the *Literary Gazette* he edited (Jerdan, *Autobiography*, 3: 277–278). For her publications see Ann R. Hawkins and Jeraldine R. Kraver, "List of Author's Works,"

"Appendix A: Blessington's Ephemera," in Marguerite Blessington, *The Victims of Society*, ed. Ann R. Hawkins and Jeraldine R. Kraver, vol. 4 of *Silver Fork Novels, 1826–1841*, ed. Harriet Devine Jump, 6 vols. (London: Pickering and Chatto, 2005), xxxi–xxxvi, 285–291.
13. Alison Adburgham, *Silver Fork Society: Fashionable Life and Literature from 1814 to 1840* (London: Constable, 1983); Matthew Whiting Rosa, *The Silver-Fork School: Novels of Fashion Preceding* Vanity Fair (New York: Columbia University Press, 1936). For a detailed analysis see chapter 7.
14. Marguerite Blessington, *Grace Cassidy; or, The Repealers*, 3 vols. (London: Bentley, 1833); Marguerite Blessington, *The Two Friends*, 3 vols. (London: Saunders and Otley, 1835); Marguerite Blessington, *The Confessions of an Elderly Gentleman* (London: Longman, Rees, Orme, Brown, Green, and Longman, 1836); Marguerite Blessington, *The Victims of Society*, 3 vols. (London: Saunders and Otley, 1837); Marguerite Blessington, *The Confessions of an Elderly Lady* (London: Longman, Orme, Brown, Green, and Longmans, 1838); Marguerite Blessington, *The Governess*, 2 vols. (London: Longman, Orme, Brown, Green, and Longmans, 1839); Marguerite Blessington, *Meredith*, 3 vols. (London: Longman, Brown, Green, and Longmans, 1843); Marguerite Blessington, *Strathern; or, Life at Home and Abroad. A Story of the Present Day*, 4 vols. (London: Colburn, 1845); Marguerite Blessington, *The Memoirs of a Femme de Chambre*, 3 vols. (London: Bentley, 1846); Marguerite Blessington, *Marmaduke Herbert; or, The Fatal Error. A Novel Founded on Fact*, 3 vols. (London: Bentley, 1847); Marguerite Blessington, *Country Quarters; A Novel*, 3 vols. (London: Shoberl, 1850). Besides, she edited the following novel: Barbara Hemphill, *Lionel Deerhurst; or, Fashionable Life Under the Regency*, ed. Marguerite Blessington, 3 vols. (London: Bentley, 1846).
15. Marguerite Blessington, *The Idler in Italy*, 2nd ed., 2 vols. (London: Colburn, 1839), a third volume appeared in 1840; *The Idler in France*, 2 vols. (London: Colburn, 1841).
16. Marguerite Blessington, "The Auction," in *The Magic Lantern*, 3–17.
17. Margaret Power, "Memoir of the Countess of Blessington," in Marguerite Blessington, *Country Quarters*, 1: iii-xxiii.
18. Henry Brougham, letter to Marguerite Blessington (November 28, 1843), Correspondence of the Countess of Blessington, 1834–1855, Princeton University Library, C0147, Folder 2, AM 12757.
19. Alfred Morrison, ed., *The Collection of Autograph Letters and Historical Documents (Second Series 1882–1893): The Blessington Papers* (London: privately printed, 1895). I have looked at a number of letters in the Pforzheimer Collection of the New York Public Library (The Blessington Papers, collection of autographs, 6 vols., The Pforzheimer Collection, New York Public Library, Pforz MS; Blessington, autograph letters, The

Berg Collection, New York Public Library) and in Princeton University Library (Blessington Correspondence, C 0147). Morrison's edition also contains some letters already printed by Madden. If Madden sometimes abbreviates them, Morrison has them in their full length.
20. J. Fitzgerald Molloy, *The Most Gorgeous Lady Blessington*, 2 vols. (London: Downey & Co., 1896), 1: 23.
21. Henry F. Chorley, *Authors of England: A Series of Medallion Portraits of Modern Literary Characters* (London: Tilt, 1838), 34–36.
22. Anonymous, "No. XXXIV. Gallery of Literary Characters: Countess of Blessington," *Fraser's Magazine* 7 (March 1833): 267; on the gallery see Judith L. Fisher, "'In the Present Famine of Anything Substantial': *Fraser's* 'Portraits' and the Construction of Literary Celebrity; or, 'Personality, Personality Is the Appetite of the Age,'" *Victorian Periodicals Review* 39 (2006): 97–135. Sometimes, such collections only featured women. This tradition of juxtaposing especially biographies of "Women Worthies," as Natalie Zemon Davis ironically put it, can be traced back to the Middle Ages; see Natalie Zemon Davis, "'Women's History' in Transition: The European Case," *Feminist Studies* 3 (1976): 83–103, here 83. The British model for such galleries of "Women Worthies" is George Ballard's *Memoirs of Several Ladies of Great Britain* (1752), a compendium of exemplary educated women, for which Ballard enlisted the support of bluestocking Hester Chapone; see Ruth Perry, "George Ballard's Biographies of Learned Ladies," in *Biography in the Eighteenth Century*, ed. J. D. Browning (New York: Garland, 1980), 85–111.
23. *Lady Blessington's Conversations of Lord Byron*, ed. Ernest J. Lovell (Princeton: Princeton University Press, 1969). The original book appeared as *Conversations of Lord Byron with the Countess of Blessington* (London: Bentley, 1834). The most detailed piece of criticism to date is Lovell's introduction (3–114); see also Harriet Jump, "Marguerite Blessington, Teresa Guiccioli, and the Writing of the *Conversation with Byron*," *The Byron Journal* 31 (2003): 51–60; Julian North, "Self-Possession and Gender in Romantic Literary Biography," in *Romantic Biography*, ed. Arthur Bradley and Alan Rawes (Aldershot: Ashgate, 2003), 109–138; see also Schmid, "Lady Blessington," 160–162; Schmid, "The Countess of Blessington and the English Romantic Salon," 101–104; Susanne Schmid, "Gespräch, Geselligkeit und Einsamkeit um 1800," in *Trianqulärer Transfer: Großbritannien, Frankreich und Deutschland um 1800*, ed. Sandra Pott and Sebastian Neumeister, special issue of *Germanisch-Romanische Monatsschrift* 56 (2006): 45–58, here 53–55.
24. For a survey see Claudia Schmölders, ed., *Die Kunst des Gesprächs. Texte zur Geschichte der europäischen Konversationstheorie* (München: dtv, 1979); Claudia Henn-Schmölders, "Ars conversationis. Zur Geschichte des sprachlichen Umgangs," *arcadia* 10 (1975): 16–33; Peter N. Miller,

Peiresc's Europe: Learning and Virtue in the Seventeenth Century (New Haven: Yale University Press, 2000), 49–75; Peter Burke, *The Art of Conversation* (Cambridge: Polity Press, 1993).
25. Karin Ehler and Martin Mulsow, "Gespräche über Grammatik und Civilité. Multifunktionalität von sprachdidaktischen Dialogen bei François de Fenne (1690) und Pierre François Roy (1693)," *Romanische Forschungen* 107 (1995): 314–342.
26. Rosemarie Zeller, "Die Rolle der Frauen im Gesprächspiel und in der Konversation," in *Geselligkeit und Gesellschaft im Barockzeitalter*, ed. Wolfgang Adam, with the assistance of Knut Kiesant, Winfried Schulze, and Christoph Strosetzki, 2 vols. (Wiesbaden: Harrassowitz, 1997), 1: 531–541, here 534–536.
27. Walter Savage Landor, *Imaginary Conversations*, ed. Charles G. Crump, 6 vols. (London: Dent, 1909).
28. J. L. Austin, *How to Do Things with Words: The William James Lectures Delivered at Harvard University in 1955* (Cambridge/MA: Harvard University Press, 1962), 3–4.
29. Ernest J. Lovell, "Introduction," in Thomas Medwin, *Conversations of Lord Byron*, ed. Ernest J. Lovell (Princeton: Princeton University Press, 1966), vii–xiv.
30. Clara Tuite, "Tainted Love and Romantic Literary Celebrity," *English Literary History* 74 (2007): 59–88, here 71; Sarah Bradford, *Disraeli* (New York: Stein & Day, 1982), 31; Benjamin Disraeli, *Letters. Volume One: 1815–1834*, ed. J. A. W. Gunn, John Matthews, Donald M. Schurman, and M. G. Wiebe (Toronto: University of Toronto Press, 1982), no. 74.
31. Sadleir, *Blessington-d'Orsay*, 171–172; Samuel Carter Hall, *Retrospect of a Long Life: From 1815 to 1883* (New York: Appleton and Company, 1883), 367.
32. For the question of gendered gossip in the *Conversations*, see North, "Self-Possession and Gender," 113, 126–134.
33. Caroline Lamb's description in *Lady Morgan's Memoirs: Autobiography, Diaries and Correspondence*, ed. William Dixon, 2nd ed., 2 vols. (London: Allen, 1863), 2: 200.
34. For details see Sadleir, *Blessington-d'Orsay*, 123–129, 140–166.
35. Anonymous, "The Magazines," *Examiner* 1275 (July 8, 1832): 435; Anonymous, "*Conversations of Lord Byron*," *The Metropolitan Magazine* 9 (January 1834): 6–7, here 6. Occasionally, the question of authenticity was raised, for example, in Anonymous, "*Journal of Conversations with Lord Byron*," *The Literary Gazette* 881 (December 7, 1833): 775.
36. Ernest J. Lovell, "Introduction," in *Lady Blessington's Conversations of Lord Byron*, 93.
37. Mark Parker, *Literary Magazines and British Romanticism* (Cambridge: Cambridge University Press, 2000), 1.
38. Deborah Wynne, *The Sensation Novel and the Victorian Family Magazine* (Basingstoke: Palgrave, 2001), 3.

NOTES 207

39. Marguerite Blessington, "Journal of Conversations with Lord Byron. No. IV," *New Monthly Magazine* 35 (October 1832): 305–319.
40. Thomas Jefferson Hogg, "Percy Bysshe Shelley at Oxford," *New Monthly Magazine* 35 (October 1832): 321–330, here 326.
41. M., "Private Hints to a Juvenile Physician," *New Monthly Magazine* 35 (October 1832): 359–364, here 360.
42. Edward Bulwer Lytton, *England and the English* [1833], ed. Standish Meacham (Chicago: University of Chicago Press, 1970), 96; see also Schmid, "The Countess of Blessington and the English Romantic Salon," 95.
43. K. C. Phillipps, *Language and Class in Victorian England* (Oxford: Blackwell, 1984), 38. The fashionable Whig circles, in contrast, were reputed to have a culture of sparkling conversation, partly because they cultivated the French connection. See Leslie Mitchell, *The Whig World, 1760–1837* (London: Hambledon and London, 2005), 83.
44. Patmore, "Personal Recollections," 172.
45. Henry Crabb Robinson, *Diary, Reminiscences, and Correspondence,* ed. Thomas Sadler, 2nd ed., 3 vols. (London: Macmillan, 1869), 3: 12; Mrs. Newton Crosland (Camilla Toulmin), *Landmarks of a Literary Life, 1820–1892* (London: Low, Marston, & Company, 1893), 103.
46. Sadleir, *Blessington-d'Orsay,* 212–213.
47. See ibid., 136.
48. Crosland, *Landmarks of a Literary Life,* 101–102. On the interior of Gore House, see Nick Foulkes, *Last of the Dandies: The Scandalous Life and Escapades of Count D'Orsay* (London: Little, Brown, 2003), 285–295.
49. Crosland, *Landmarks of a Literary Life,* 98; Patmore, "Personal Recollections," 170.
50. Anonymous, "Gore House: By an American Traveller," *The New Monthly Magazine and Humorist* 86 (1849): 135–151, here 150.
51. Anonymous, "Sale of the Countess of Blessington's Effects," *The Times* (May 17 1849), 7.
52. *Correspondence of Mr. Joseph Jekyll,* 269.
53. Ibid., 272.
54. Ibid., 285.
55. Sadleir, *Blessington-d'Orsay,* 132–135; *Correspondence of Mr. Joseph Jekyll,* 297–301.
56. Gillen D'Arcy Wood, *Romanticism and Music Culture in Britain, 1770–1840: Virtue and Virtuosity* (Cambridge: Cambridge University Press, 2010), 196–197. Wood links Liszt's marginalization in London's society to the fact that he attended Blessington's salon.
57. *The Diary of Benjamin Robert Haydon,* ed. Willard Bissell Pope, 5 vols. (Cambridge/MA: Harvard University Press, 1960–1963), 4: 197; see also Lovell, "Introduction," in *Lady Blessington's Conversations of Lord Byron,* 25.

58. William Archer Shee, *My Contemporaries, 1830–1870* (London: Hurst and Blackett, 1893), 97.
59. Ibid., 98.
60. Hall, *Retrospect of a Long Life*, 369.
61. *Correspondence of Mr. Joseph Jekyll*, 290.
62. *The Diary of Benjamin Haydon*, 4: 263–266, 270–271; see also Lovell, "Introduction," in *Lady Blessington's Conversations of Lord Byron;* Anonymous, "Gore House: By an American Traveller." As the mid-nineteenth century was the age of the voluminous realist novel with lively dialogues, it is not surprising that detailed accounts of dialogues found their way into print, yet their reliability is questionable. The further removed in time they are, the less likely they are to be anywhere near an exact transcript. Diary entries like Haydon's, who sometimes sketched his conversations, are more reliable than obituaries or nostalgic essays.
63. Fisher, "'In the Present Famine,'" 99; Nicholas Dames, "Brushes with Fame: Thackeray and the Work of Celebrity," *Nineteenth-Century Literature* 56 (2001): 23–51, here 33.
64. Lewis Melville, *William Makepeace Thackeray* (New York: Doubleday, Doran, & Company, 1928), 314.
65. See also Schmid, "The Countess of Blessington and the English Romantic Salon," 104–107; Susanne Schmid, "The Countess of Blessington: Reading as Intimacy, Reading as Sociability," *The Wordsworth Circle* 39 (2008), 88–93, here 88–90.
66. Willis, "Pencillings by the Way," *New-York Mirror* (March 7, 1835) 281.
67. Homi Bhabha, "Of Mimicry and Man: The Ambivalence of Colonial Discourse," in *The Location of Culture* (London: Routledge, 1994), 85–92; Sandra Tomc, "Restyling an Old World: Nathaniel Parker Willis and Metropolitan Fashion in the Antebellum United States," *Representations* 85 (2004): 98–124, here 99.
68. Thomas N. Baker, *Sentiment and Celebrity: Nathaniel Parker Willis and the Trials of Literary Fame* (New York: Oxford University Press, 1999), 13–38.
69. Nathaniel Parker Willis, *Pencillings by the Way*, 3 vols. (London: John Macrone, 1835); on the reprints see Baker, *Sentiment and Celebrity*, 231.
70. Anonymous, "Regina's Maids of Honour," *Fraser's Magazine* 13 (January 1836): 80.
71. Baker, *Sentiment and Celebrity*, 61–85; Willis, "Pencillings by the Way," *New-York Mirror* 12 (March 7, 14, 21, 28; April 4, 11, 18, 25, 1835): 281, 292, 297, 308, 316, 324, 332, 340–341.
72. On the developing celebrity cult in America, see Baker, *Sentiment and Celebrity*, 86–114.
73. Nathaniel Parker Willis, *Lady Jane: A Humorous Novel in Rhyme* [1844], in *The Poems, Sacred, Passionate, and Humorous*, 6th ed. (New York: Clark & Austin, 1845), 263–331.

74. Anonymous, "Chit-Chat of New York: From the Correspondence of the National Intelligencer," *The New Mirror* 2 (January 27, 1844): 269–271, here 269.
75. Anonymous, "*The Poems, Sacred, Passionate, and Humorous,* of Nathaniel Parker Willis," *Graham's American Monthly Magazine of Literature, Art, and Fashion* 26 (1844): 44–47.
76. Willis, *Lady Jane*, 301–302.
77. Terence Allan Hoagwood and Kathryn Ledbetter, "*Colour'd Shadows*": *Contexts in Publishing, Printing, and Reading Nineteenth-Century British Women Writers* (New York: Palgrave Macmillan, 2005), 47–73; Harriet Devine Jump, "'The False Prudery of Public Taste': Scandalous Women and the Annuals, 1820–1850," in *Feminist Readings of Victorian Popular Texts: Divergent Femininities*, ed. Emma Liggins and Daniel Duffy (Aldershot: Ashgate, 2001), 1–17.
78. Willis, *Lady Jane*, 272.
79. On Poe and Willis see Sandra Tomc, "Poe and His Circle," in *The Cambridge Companion to Edgar Allan Poe*, ed. Kevin J. Hayes (Cambridge: Cambridge University Press, 2002), 21–41.
80. Edgar Allan Poe, "Lionizing," in *Tales and Sketches, 1831–1842*, vol. 2 of *Collected Works of Edgar Allan Poe*, ed. Thomas Ollive Mabbott (Cambridge/MA: Belknap Press, 1978), 172–177, here 174; Richard P. Benton, "Poe's 'Lionizing': A Quiz on Willis and Lady Blessington," *Studies in Short Fiction* 5 (1968): 239–244.
81. Sadleir, *Blessington-d'Orsay*, 199–200.
82. Henry Wikoff, *The Reminiscences of an Idler* (New York: Fords, Howard & Hulbert, 1880), 475.
83. Morrison, *Blessington Papers*, 208–209.
84. Ibid., 160.
85. Ibid., 42–43.
86. William B. Todd and Ann Bowden, *Tauchnitz International Editions in English 1841–1955: A Bibliographical History* (New York: Bibliographical Society of America, 1988).
87. In German: "Ihre hohe gesellschaftliche Stellung," Anonymous, "Literarische Notiz aus England. Lady Blessington," *Blätter für Literarische Unterhaltung* 125 (1845): 504.

7 The Countess of Blessington as Writer and Editor

1. According to Sadleir, this passage describes Catherine Gore; Michael Sadleir, *Blessington-d'Orsay: A Masquerade* [1933] (London: Folio Society, 1983), 182.
2. Percy Bysshe Shelley, "Ode to the West Wind," in *Complete Poetical Works*, ed. Thomas Hutchinson (Oxford: Oxford University Press, 1971), 577–579, here 579, l. 69.

3. Terence Allan Hoagwood and Kathryn Ledbetter, *"Colour'd Shadows": Contexts in Publishing, Printing, and Reading Nineteenth-Century British Women Writers* (New York: Palgrave Macmillan, 2005), 84.
4. Samuel Johnson, "The Idler" and "The Adventurer," ed. W. J. Bate, John M. Bullitt, and L. F. Powell, vol. 2 of *The Works of Samuel Johnson* (New Haven: Yale University Press, 1963).
5. Anonymous, "The Idler in Italy," *New Monthly Magazine and Humorist* 55 (1839): 418–423.
6. Susanne Schmid, *Shelley's German Afterlives, 1814–2000* (New York: Palgrave Macmillan, 2007), 23–24.
7. In 1979, an abbreviated version of Blessington's *Idler in Italy* appeared: *Lady Blessington at Naples*, ed. Edith Clay, with an introduction by Harold Acton (London: Hamish Hamilton, 1979).
8. See Kathryn Walchester, *"Our Own Fair Italy": Nineteenth Century Women's Travel Writing and Italy 1800–1844* (Bern: Lang, 2007), 12. This study treats women's travelogues about Italy: Mariana Starke's *Letters from Italy* (1800), Charlotte Eaton's *Rome in the Nineteenth Century* (1820), Lady Morgan's *Italy* (1821), Anna Jameson's *Diary of an Ennuyée* (1826), and Mary Shelley's *Rambles in Germany and Italy* (1844).
9. Among the laudatory reviews are Anonymous, "The Idler in Italy," *The Literary Examiner* 1622 (March 3, 1839): 132–133; Anonymous, "The Idler in Italy, Vol. III," *The Literary Gazette* 1248 (December 19, 1840): 810–811; Anonymous, "The Idler in Italy," *The Athenaeum* 592 (March 2, 1839): 165–168.
10. *The Life of Charles James Mathews, Chiefly Autobiographical, With Selections from His Correspondence and Speeches*, ed. Charles Dickens, 2 vols. (London: Macmillan, 1879), 1: 77–165.
11. Sadleir, *Blessington-d'Orsay*, 63.
12. *Life of Charles James Mathews*, 1: 146.
13. For list of guests in Naples, see MA 1: 113–114. The friendship Blessington struck up with Walter Savage Landor in Florence led to an exchange of poems and letters; see John F. Mariani, "The Letters of Walter Savage Landor to Marguerite Countess of Blessington," unpubl. PhD thesis (New York: Columbia University, 1973). The Pforzheimer collection holds a copy. Landor and Blessington stayed friends after her return to London; see John F. Mariani, "Lady Blessington's 'Ever Obliged Friend and Servant, W. S. Landor': A Study of Their Literary Relationship," *The Wordsworth Circle* 7 (1976): 17–30. Fox's diary repeatedly makes unfriendly comments about her, for example: "The whole family bore me to extinction...She [Blessington] writes on life and manners. I wish she would acquire some of the latter before she criticises...She forces herself into the correspondence or acquaintance of all who have (unhappily for them) acquired any sort of fame." See *The Journal of the Hon. Edward Fox (Afterwards Fourth and Last Lord Holland), 1818–1830*, ed. Earl of

Ilchester (London: Butterworth, 1923), 204. Fox also voiced disgust about the marriage between Harriet and D'Orsay.
14. William Gell and John P. Gandy, *Pompeiana: The Topography, Edifices, and Ornaments of Pompeii* (London: Rodwell and Martin, 1817–1819).
15. Richard Keppel Craven, *A Tour Through the Southern Provinces of the Kingdom of Naples* (London: Rodwell and Martin, 1821); Richard Keppel Craven, *Excursions in the Abruzzi and Northern Provinces of Naples*, 2 vols. (London: Bentley, 1838).
16. Walchester, *"Our Own Fair Italy"*, 17.
17. Chloe Chard, *Pleasure and Guilt on the Grand Tour: Travel Writing and Imaginative Geography, 1600–1830* (Manchester: Manchester University Press, 1999), 40–83.
18. Gabriella Di Martino, "Motions and Emotions in a Lady Traveller's Writing," in *The Language of Public and Private Communication in a Historical Persepective*, ed. Nicholas Brownlees, Gabriella Del Lungo, and John Denton (Newcastle: Cambridge Scholars, 2010), 100–115.
19. Lady Holland devotes only a few lines to this event, EHJ 1: 21–22.
20. Tzvetan Todorov, "The Journey and Its Narratives," in *Transports: Travel, Pleasure, and Imaginative Geography, 1600–1830*, ed. Chloe Chard and Helen Langdon (New Haven: Yale University Press, 1996), 287–296, here 289.
21. Sadleir, *Blessington-d'Orsay*, 93–95.
22. *Life of Charles James Mathews*, 1: 95; see also Sadleir, *Blessington-d'Orsay*, 94.
23. A first edition available through the Bodleian Library in Oxford does not have this advertisement. As the success of Blessington's travel narrative was probably related to the Byron factor, Colburn may have decided to foreground the poet in the second edition.
24. Peter J. Manning, "Childe Harold in the Marketplace: From Romaunt to Handbook," *Modern Language Quarterly* 52 (1991): 170–190, here 187.
25. See I 2: 47, George Gordon Byron, *Childe Harold's Pilgrimage*, vol. 2 of *Complete Poetical Works*, ed. Jerome J. McGann (Oxford: Clarendon Press, 1980), 150 (*Canto* IV, stanza 78); I 2: 49, Byron, *Childe Harold*, 2: 172–173 (*Canto* IV, stanzas 143, 144); I 2: 54, Byron, *Childe Harold*, 2: 173–174 (*Canto* IV, stanzas 146, 147).
26. For an analysis of *The Repealers*, see Riana O'Dwyer, "Travels of a Lady of Fashion: The Literary Career of Lady Blessington (1789–1849)," in *New Contexts: Re-Framing Nineteenth-Century Irish Women's Prose*, ed. Heidi Hansson (Cork: Cork University Press, 2008), 35–54, here 45–53.
27. Miranda Burgess, "The National Tale and Allied Genres, 1770s–1840s," in *The Cambridge Companion to the Irish Novel*, ed. John Wilson Foster (Cambridge: Cambridge University Press, 2006),

39–59; Vera Kreilkamp, "The Novel of the Big House," in Foster, *Cambridge Companion to the Irish Novel*, 60–77; James H. Murphy, *Irish Novelists and the Victorian Age* (Oxford: Oxford University Press, 2011), especially 27–44.
28. J. H. Whyte, "The Age of Daniel O'Connell (1800–47)," in *The Course of Irish History*, ed. T. W. Moody and F. X. Martin (Cork: Mercier Press, 1967), 248–262.
29. J. H. Whyte, "Daniel O'Connell and the Repeal Party," *Irish Historical Studies* 11 (1959): 297–316.
30. Baron D'Haussez, *Great Britain in 1833* (Philadelphia: Mielke, 1833), 222–240, here 223. This book was originally published by Bentley (London).
31. P. G. Patmore, "Personal Recollections of the Late Lady Blessington," *Bentley's Miscellany* 26 (1849): 162–175, here 175.
32. D'Haussez, *Great Britain in 1833*, 237. On representations of the Irish character in the early nineteenth century, see William H. A. Williams, *Tourism, Landscape, and the Irish Character: British Travel Writers in Pre-Famine Ireland* (Madison: University of Wisconsin Press, 2008), 117–121.
33. Edmund Burke, *Reflections on the Revolution in France* (London: Dodsley, 1790), 117.
34. Absenteeism was a frequent topic in nineteenth-century Irish novels; see Kreilkamp, "The Novel of the Big House," 63–64.
35. Royal A. Gettmann, *A Victorian Publisher: A Study of the Bentley Papers* (Cambridge: Cambridge University Press, 1960), 64. I have not seen this key, yet Sadleir has his own in Sadleir, *Blessington-d'Orsay*, 307.
36. Sadleir, *Blessington-d'Orsay*, 178–180.
37. Anonymous, "*The Repealers*," *New Monthly Magazine* 38 (August 1833): 466–468, here 466.
38. Anonymous, "*The Repealers*," *The Athenaeum* 294 (June 15, 1833): 372–373, here 373.
39. Gayatri Chakravorty Spivak, "The Rani of Simur: An Essay in Reading the Archives," in *Europe and Its Other: Proceedings of the Essex Conference on the Sociology of Literature*, ed. Francis Barker, Peter Hulme, et al., 2 vols. (Colchester: University of Essex, 1985), 1: 128–151.
40. On the biographical side of *Country Quarters*, see O'Dwyer, "Travels of a Lady of Fashion," 37–38.
41. Kathryn J. Kirkpatrick, "Introduction," in Maria Edgeworth, *Castle Rackrent*, ed. George Watson (Oxford: Oxford University Press, 1995), vii–xxxvi, here xxxv.
42. Marguerite Blessington, *Country Quarters; A Novel*, 3 vols. (London: Shoberl, 1850), 2: 51.
43. William Hazlitt, "The Dandy School," in *The Complete Works of William Hazlitt*, ed. P. P. Howe, 21 vols. (London: Dent and Sons, 1930–1934), 20: 143–149, here 146.

44. Winifred Hughes, "Silver Fork Writers and Readers: Social Contexts of a Best Seller," *NOVEL: A Forum on Fiction* 25 (1992): 328–347; Ellen Miller Casey, "'The Aristocracy and Upholstery': The Silver Fork Novel," in *A Companion to Sensation Fiction*, ed. Pamela K. Gilbert (Malden: Blackwell Wiley, 2011), 13–25; Harriet Devine Jump, "General Introduction," in Thomas Henry Lister, *Granby: A Novel*, ed. Clare Bainbridge, vol. 1 of Jump, *Silver Fork Novels, 1826–1841*, ix–xxii; Muireann O'Cinneide, *Aristocratic Women and the Literary Nation, 1832–1867* (Basingstoke: Palgrave Macmillan, 2008); Tamara S. Wagner, ed., *Silver-Fork Fiction and Its Literary Legacies*, special issue of *Women's Writing* 16 (2009): 181–364; Alison Adburgham, *Silver Fork Society: Fashionable Life and Literature from 1814 to 1840* (London: Constable, 1983); Matthew Whiting Rosa, *The Silver-Fork School: Novels of Fashion Preceding* Vanity Fair (New York: Columbia University Press, 1936).
45. On typical narrative patterns see O'Cinneide, *Aristocratic Women and the Literary Nation*.
46. Edward Copeland, "Crossing Oxford Street: Silverfork Geopolitics," *Eighteenth-Century Life* 25 (2001): 116–134; Edward Copeland, "Opera and the Great Reform Act: Silver Fork Fiction, 1822–1842," in *Opera and Nineteenth-Century Literature*, ed. Nicholas Halmi, special issue of *Romanticism on the Net* 34–35 (2004) (www.erudit.org/revue/ron/2004/v/n34-35/009440ar.html). The latter article also treats Blessington.
47. See also Susanne Schmid, "Lady Blessington und die Salons der englischen Romantik," in *Subversive Romantik*, ed. Volker Kapp, Helmuth Kiesel, Klaus Lubbers, and Patricia Plummer (Berlin: Duncker & Humblot, 2004), 153–164, here 160.
48. Anthony Sattin, *Lifting the Veil: British Society in Egypt, 1768–1956* (London: Dent, 1988), 42–43.
49. Marguerite Blessington, "The Tomb," in *The Magic Lantern; or, Sketches of Scenes from the Metropolis* (London: Longman, Hurst, Rees, Orme, and Brown, 1822), 39–51, here 48.
50. Venetia Murray, *High Society in the Regency Period, 1788–1830* (London: Penguin, 1999), 1.
51. Sadleir, *Blessington-d'Orsay*, 132–133, 179–181; MA 1: 165–166.
52. Ibid., 179.
53. Ibid., 181–182. Sadleir suggests these attributions.
54. For an analysis see Ann R. Hawkins and Jeraldine R. Kraver, "Introduction," in Marguerite Blessington, *Victims of Society*, ed. Ann R. Hawkins and Jeraldine R. Kraver, vol. 4 of *Silver Fork Novels, 1826–1841*, ed. Harriet Devine Jump, 6 vols. (London: Pickering and Chatto, 2005), vii–xxvi, here xxii–xxvi; O'Cinneide, *Aristocratic Women and the Literary Nation*, 56–59.
55. Marguerite Blessington, *Victims of Society*, ed. Ann R. Hawkins and Jeraldine R. Kraver, vol. 4 of Jump, *Silver Fork Novels, 1826–1841*, 23.

56. Ibid., 11.
57. Randall Craig, *The Narratives of Caroline Norton* (New York: Palgrave Macmillan, 2009).
58. The reviews were favorable, for example, Anonymous, "The Victims of Society," *Monthly Magazine* 23 (May 1837): 542–545; Anonymous, "The Victims of Society," *The Metropolitan Magazine* 19 (May 1837): 1–4; Anonymous, "The Victims of Society," *The Athenaeum* 494 (April 15, 1837): 260.
59. Edward Bulwer Lytton, *Godolphin: A Novel*, ed. Harriet Devine Jump, vol. 3 of Jump, *Silver Fork Novels, 1826–1841*, 102. On similarities between some of his literary characters and the Blessington *entourage*, see Harriet Devine Jump, "Introduction," in Bulwer, *Godolphin*, ix–xxii, here xix–xx.
60. Blessington, *Victims of Society*, 108.
61. For passages alluding to Blessington and her circle, see Rosina Bulwer, *Cheveley; or, The Man of Honour*, ed. Marie Mulvey-Roberts, vol. 5 of Jump, *Silver Fork Novels, 1826–1841*, 324–331, 335–336, 357, 370–372. Lady Stepstray is a mixture of Blessington and Stepney. Here, as in other romans à clef, real-life and fictitious characters do not always stand in a one-to-one relationship to one another.
62. Rosina Bulwer, *Cheveley*, 325.
63. *The Collected Letters of Rosina Bulwer Lytton*, ed. Marie Mulvey-Roberts with the assistance of Steve Carpenter, 3 vols. (London: Pickering and Chatto, 2008), 1: 210, 208.
64. See Paula R. Feldman, "Introduction," "Bibliography," in *The Keepsake for 1829*, ed. Frederic Mansel Reynolds (London: Hurst, Chance, & Co., 1828; reprint Peterborough: Broadview, 2006), 7–25, 27–32, for a list of websites; Cindy Dickinson, "Creating a World of Books, Friends, and Flowers: Gift Books and Inscriptions, 1825–60," *Winterthur Portfolio* 31 (1996): 53–66; Ann R. Hawkins, "Marguerite, Countess of Blessington, and L.E.L. (Letitia Elizabeth Landon): Evidence of a Friendship," *ANQ: A Quarterly Journal of Short Articles, Notes and Reviews* 16 (2003): 27–32; Ann R. Hawkins, "'Formed with Curious Skill': Blessington's Negotiation of the 'Poetess' in *Flowers of Loveliness*," *Romanticism on the Net* 29–30 (2003) (www.erudit.org/revue/ron/2003/v/n29–30/007721ar.html); Hoagwood and Ledbetter, "*Colour'd Shadows*"; Harriet Devine Jump, "'The False Prudery of Public Taste': Scandalous Women and the Annuals, 1820–1850," in *Feminist Readings of Victorian Popular Texts: Divergent Femininities*, ed. Emma Liggins and Daniel Duffy (Aldershot: Ashgate, 2001), 1–17; Jill Rappoport, "Buyer Beware: The Gift Poetics of Letitia Elizabeth Landon," *Nineteenth-Century Literature* 58 (2004): 441–473. Among a number of websites, these have been particularly useful: Katherine D. Harris, *Forget Me Not: A Hypertextual Archive* (www.orgs.muohio.edu/anthologies/FMN/); Harry E. Hootman, *British Annuals and Giftbooks* (www.britannuals.com). This subchapter extends part of the

NOTES

following article: Susanne Schmid, "The Countess of Blessington: Reading as Intimacy, Reading as Sociability," *The Wordsworth Circle* 39 (2008): 88–93, here 91–92.

65. See chapter 6.
66. Feldman, "Introduction," 18.
67. Newton Crosland, *Rambles Round My Life: An Autobiography (1819–1896)* (London: Allen, 1898), 356. Mrs. Crosland worked her way up to become subeditor of *Friendship's Offering* and received "liberal remuneration" (356). On her contributions and income, see Crosland, *Rambles Round My Life*, 345–357.
68. Anonymous, "The Annuals of Former Days," *The Bookseller* 1 (November 29, 1858): 493–499, here 493.
69. On the July date see Mrs. Newton Crosland, *Landmarks of a Literary Life, 1820–1892* (London: Low, Marston, & Company, 1893), 96.
70. *Queen Victoria's Journals: Lord Esher's Typescripts*, 2: 8–10, here 9 (January 1, 1836) (www.queenvictoriasjournals.org/search/display-ItemFromId.do?FormatType=fulltextimgsrc&QueryType=articles&ItemID=18360101&volumeType=ESHER). On gifting patterns see Paula R. Feldman, "Women, Literary Annuals, and the Evidence of Inscriptions," *Keats-Shelley Journal* 55 (2006): 54–62.
71. George Eliot, *Middlemarch: A Study of Provincial Life*, ed. Gregory Maertz (Peterborough: Broadview, 2004), 235, 237 [chapter 27].
72. Kathleen Gilbert, "Rosamond and Lady Blessington: Another *Middlemarch* Anachronism," *Notes and Queries* 27 (1980): 527–528.
73. William Makepeace Thackeray, *Vanity Fair: A Novel without a Hero*, ed. John Carey (London: Penguin, 2001), 637 [chapter 55]; Vanessa Warne, "Thackeray Among the Annuals: Morality, Cultural Authority and the Literary Annual Genre," *Victorian Periodicals Review* 39 (2006): 158–178, here 161.
74. Hoagwood and Ledbetter, *"Colour'd Shadows"*, 83–84.
75. Ibid., 86.
76. Crosland, *Landmarks of a Literary Life*, 97–98.
77. Ibid., 98–99; the poem is Camilla Toulmin, "On the Portrait of Mrs. Burr," in *Heath's Book of Beauty, 1843,* ed. Marguerite Blessington (London: Longman, Rees, Orme, Brown, Green, and Longmans, 1842), 210–211. (www.britannuals.com/mes/mespl–2.php?siteID=britannuals&pageref=21).
78. Thackeray, "To Lady Blessington, September 1848," in *Letters and Private Papers,* ed. Gordon N. Ray, 4 vols. (Cambridge, MA: Harvard University Press, 1945–1946), 2: 426.
79. Thackeray, "A Word on the Annuals," *Fraser's Magazine* 16 (1837): 757–763, here 757, 761.
80. *Heath's Book of Beauty, 1840,* ed. Marguerite Blessington (London: Longman, Orme, Brown, Green, and Longmans, 1839). As the books were published shortly before Christmas, the *Book of Beauty* for 1840 appeared in 1839.

81. Warne, "Thackeray Among the Annuals," 161.
82. Louisa H. Sheridan, "The Jilt," in Blessington, *Heath's Book of Beauty, 1840*, 83–96.
83. Captain Daniel, "The Improvident: A Tale," in Blessington, *Heath's Book of Beauty, 1840*, 139–164.
84. R. Bernal, "The Lottery of Life," in Blessington, *Heath's Book of Beauty, 1840*, 14–43.
85. Torre Holme, "Stanzas," in Blessington, *Heath's Book of Beauty, 1840*, 203–204, here 204, ll. 41–42.
86. Edward Bulwer Lytton, "The Wife to the Wooer," in Blessington, *Heath's Book of Beauty, 1840*, 11–12.
87. Ibid., here 11, l. 2.
88. Isabella Romer, "A Leaf from the Pilgrim's Scrap-Book," in Blessington, *Heath's Book of Beauty, 1840*, 62–80.
89. Hoagwood and Ledbetter, *"Colour'd Shadows"*, 95–124.
90. Ibid., 103–104.
91. Janice Radway, *Reading the Romance: Women, Patriarchy, and Popular Literature* (London: Verso, 1984).
92. On the example of Queen Caroline's scandalous body as an "extra-domestic" body, see Kristin Flieger Samuelian, *Royal Romances: Sex, Scandal, and Monarchy in Print, 1780–1821* (New York: Palgrave Macmillan, 2010), 133.
93. Marguerite Blessington, "Francesca Foscari," in *The Keepsake for 1837*, ed. Emmeline Stuart Wortley (London: Longman, Rees, Orme, Brown, Green, and Longman, 1836), 43–46.
94. Ibid., 46.
95. Hoagwood and Ledbetter call this use of scandal a "commodity," see *"Colour'd Shadows"*, 56–73.

Works Cited

Adburgham, Alison. *Silver Fork Society: Fashionable Life and Literature from 1814 to 1840.* London: Constable, 1983.
Adickes, Sandra. *The Social Quest: The Expanded Vision of Four Women Travelers in the Era of the French Revolution.* New York: Lang, 1991.
Allen, John. "Art. IX. *Letters from St. Helena.* By William Warden." *Edinburgh Review* 27 (December 1816): 459–492.
Altick, Richard D. "Mr. Cambridge Serenades the Berry Sisters." *Notes and Queries* 183 (1942): 158–161.
Ames, Dianne S. "Strawberry Hill: Architecture of the 'as if.'" *Studies in Eighteenth-Century Culture* 8 (1979): 351–363.
Anonymous. "The Annuals of Former Days." *The Bookseller* 1 (November 29, 1858): 493–499.
———. "Art VIII. *Facts Illustrative of the Treatment of Napoleon Buonaparte in St Helena...,*" *Edinburgh Review* 32 (July 1819): 148–170.
———. "Art. 18. *The Fashionable Friends.*" *The British Critic* 20 (December 1802): 677.
———. "Art. 37. *The Fashionable Friends.*" *The Critical Review* 36 (November 1802): 353–355.
———."Art. II. *De Buonaparte, et des Bourbons... Par F. A. de Chateaubriand.*" *The British Critic* 2 (July 1814): 22–33.
———. "Brighton, August 6." *Courier and Evening Gazette* 2491 (August 8, 1800): [3].
———. "Chit-Chat of New York: From the Correspondence of the National Intelligencer." *The New Mirror* 2 (January 27, 1844): 269–271.
———. "*Conversations of Lord Byron.*" *The Metropolitan Magazine* 9 (January 1834): 6–7.
———. "The Drama." *The Monthly Magazine* 14 (1802): 600.
———. "*England and France: A Comparative View.*" *The Quarterly Review* 75 (March 1845): 485–496.
———. "The Fashionable Friends." *The Poetical Register* 2 (January 1803): 453.
———. "Gore House: By an American Traveller." *The New Monthly Magazine and Humorist* 86 (1849): 135–151.
———. "*The Idler in Italy.*" *The Athenaeum* 592 (March 2, 1839): 165–168.
———. "*The Idler in Italy.*" *The Literary Examiner* 1622 (March 3, 1839): 132–133.

Anonymous. "*The Idler in Italy.*" *New Monthly Magazine and Humorist* 55 (1839): 418–423.
———. "*The Idler in Italy*, Vol. III." *The Literary Gazette* 1248 (December 19, 1840): 810–811.
———. "*Journal of Conversations with Lord Byron.*" *The Literary Gazette* 881 (December 7, 1833): 775.
———. "Letters of the Marquise Du Deffand to the Hon. Horace Walpole." *The Monthly Review* 65 (1811): 28–36.
———. "Letters of the Marquise du Deffand to the Honourable Horace Walpole." *Edinburgh Review* 17 (February 1811): 290–311.
———. "Literarische Notiz aus England. Lady Blessington." *Blätter für Literarische Unterhaltung* 125 (1845): 504.
———. "The Magazines." *Examiner* 1275 (July 8, 1832): 435.
———. "No. XXXIV. Gallery of Literary Characters: Countess of Blessington." *Fraser's Magazine* 7 (March 1833): 267.
———. "*The Poems, Sacred, Passionate, and Humorous, of Nathaniel Parker Willis.*" *Graham's American Monthly Magazine of Literature, Art, and Fashion* 26 (1844): 44–47.
———. "Preface by the Editor." In *The Works of Horatio Walpole, Earl of Orford*, ed. Mary Berry. 5 vols. London: Robinson and Edwards, 1798. Reprint ed. Peter Sabor. London: Pickering and Chatto, 1999, 1:v–xx.
———. "Private Theatricals." *The Monthly Mirror* 12 (December 1801): 426–427.
———. "Regina's Maids of Honour." *Fraser's Magazine* 13 (January 1836): 80.
———. "*The Repealers.*" *The Athenaeum* 294 (June 15, 1833): 372–373.
———. "*The Repealers.*" *New Monthly Magazine* 38 (August 1833): 466–468.
———. "Sale of the Countess of Blessington's Effects." *The Times* (May 17, 1849), 7.
———. *A Sapphick Epistle, from Jack Cavendish to the Honourable and Most Beautiful Mrs. D*****. London: Smith, [?1778].
———. "Some Account of the Life of Rachael Wriothesley, Lady Russell." *The British Review* 16, no. 32 (1820): 459–474.
———. "Theatre." *The Universal Magazine* 110 (April 1802): 298.
———. "The Victims of Society." *The Athenaeum* 494 (April 15, 1837): 260.
———. "The Victims of Society." *Monthly Magazine* 23 (May 1837): 542–545.
———. "The Victims of Society." *The Metropolitan Magazine* 19 (May 1837): 1–4.
Augé, Marc. *Non-Places: An Introduction to Supermodernity*. 2nd ed. London: Verso, 2008.
Austin, J. L. *How to Do Things with Words: The William James Lectures Delivered at Harvard University in 1955*. Cambridge, MA: Harvard University Press, 1962.
Bach, Susanne. *Theatralität und Authentizität zwischen Viktorianismus und Moderne. Romane von Henry James, Thomas Hardy, Oscar Wilde und Wilkie Collins*. Tübingen: Narr, 2006.

Works Cited

Baillie, Joanna. *The Collected Letters of Joanna Baillie*, ed. Judith Bailey Slagle. 2 vols. Madison: Fairleigh Dickinson University Press / London: Associated University Presses, 1999.

———. *Further Letters of Joanna Baillie*, ed. Thomas McLean. Madison: Fairleigh Dickinson University Press, 2010.

———. "To the Reader." In *The Family Legend: A Tragedy*. 2nd ed. Edinburgh: Ballantyne & Co., 1810, v–xiii.

Baker, Thomas N. *Sentiment and Celebrity: Nathaniel Parker Willis and the Trials of Literary Fame*. New York: Oxford University Press, 1999.

Barron-Wilson, Mrs. Cornwell. *Memoirs of Miss Mellon, Afterwards Duchess of St. Albans*. 2 vols. London: Remington and Co, 1886.

Benforado, Susan. "Anne Damer (1748–1828), Sculptor," unpubl. PhD thesis, University of New Mexico, Albuquerque, 1986.

Benton, Richard P. "Poe's 'Lionizing': A Quiz on Willis and Lady Blessington." *Studies in Short Fiction* 5 (1968): 239–244.

Bernal, R. "The Lottery of Life." In *Heath's Book of Beauty, 1840*, ed. Marguerite Blessington. London: Longman, Orme, Brown, Green, and Longmans, 1839, 14–43.

Berry, Mary. "Advertisement to the Letters Addressed to the Miss Berrys." In *The Letters of Horace Walpole, Earl of Orford*, ed. Mary Berry. 6 vols. London: Bentley, 1840, 6:vii–xx.

———. *A Comparative View of the Social Life of England and France, from the Restoration of Charles the Second to the French Revolution*. London: Longman, Rees, Orme, Brown, and Green, 1828.

———. *A Comparative View of Social Life in England and France, from the Restoration of Charles the Second to the Present Time, to Which Are Now First Added the Lives of the Marquise Du Deffand and of Rachael Lady Russell—Fashionable Friends, a Comedy, &c. A New Edition*. 2 vols. London: Bentley, 1844.

———. *Extracts from the Journals and Correspondence of Miss Berry from the Year 1783 to 1852* [1865], ed. Theresa Lewis. 2nd ed. 3 vols. London: Longmans, Green, and Co., 1866.

———. *The Fashionable Friends; a Comedy, in Five Acts*. London: Ridgway, 1802.

———. "Preface." In *Letters of the Marquise du Deffand to the Hon. Horace Walpole*, ed. Mary Berry. 4 vols. London: Longman, Hurst, Rees, and Orme, 1810, 1:v–lxv.

———. *Social Life in England and France, from the French Revolution in 1789 to that of July 1830*. London: Longman, Rees, Orme, Brown, and Green, 1831.

———. *Some Account of the Life of Rachael Wriothesley Lady Russell Followed by a Series of Letters*. London: Longman, Hurst, Rees, Orme, and Brown, 1819.

The Berry Papers: Being the Correspondence Hitherto Unpublished of Mary and Agnes Berry (1763–1852), ed. Lewis Melville. London: Lane, 1914.

Bhabha, Homi. "Of Mimicry and Man: The Ambivalence of Colonial Discourse." In *The Location of Culture*. London: Routledge, 1994, 85–92.

———. "The Third Space: Interview with Homi Bhabha." In *Identity, Community, Culture, Difference*, ed. Jonathan Rutherford. London: Lawrence & Wishart, 1990, 207–221.

Blathwayt, Janice. "A Bluestocking Bibliography." In *Reconsidering the Bluestockings*, ed. Nicole Pohl and Betty A. Schellenberg. San Marino: Huntington Library, 2003, 39–57.

Blessington, Marguerite Gardiner, Countess of. "The Auction." In *The Magic Lantern; or, Sketches of Scenes from the Metropolis*. London: Longman, Hurst, Rees, Orme, and Brown, 1822, 3–17.

———. Autograph letters, The Berg Collection, New York Public Library.

———. *The Confessions of an Elderly Gentleman*. London: Longman, Rees, Orme, Brown, Green, and Longman, 1836.

———. *The Confessions of an Elderly Lady*. London: Longman, Orme, Brown, Green, and Longmans, 1838.

———. *Conversations of Lord Byron with the Countess of Blessington*. London: Bentley, 1834.

———. Correspondence of the Countess of Blessington, 1834–1855. Princeton University Library, C 0147.

———. *Country Quarters; A Novel*. 3 vols. London: Shoberl, 1850.

———. "Francesca Foscari." In *The Keepsake for 1837*, ed. Emmeline Stuart Wortley. London: Longman, Rees, Orme, Brown, Green, and Longman, 1837, 43–46.

———. *The Governess*. 2 vols. London: Longman, Orme, Brown, Green, and Longmans, 1839.

———. *Grace Cassidy; or, The Repealers*. 3 vols. London: Bentley, 1833.

———. *The Idler in France*. 2 vols. London: Colburn, 1841.

———. *The Idler in Italy*. 2nd ed. 2 vols. London: Colburn, 1839.

———. *The Idler in Italy*, vol. 3. London: Colburn, 1840.

———. *Journal of a Tour through the Netherlands to Paris, in 1821*. London: Longman, Hurst, Rees, Orme, and Brown, 1822.

———. "Journal of Conversations with Lord Byron. No. IV." *New Monthly Magazine* 35 (October 1832): 305–319.

———. *Lady Blessington at Naples*, ed. Edith Clay, with an introduction by Harold Acton. London: Hamish Hamilton, 1979.

———. *Lady Blessington's Conversations of Lord Byron*, ed. Ernest J. Lovell. Princeton: Princeton University Press, 1969.

———. *The Magic Lantern; or, Sketches of Scenes from the Metropolis*. London: Longman, Hurst, Rees, Orme, and Brown, 1822.

———. *Marmaduke Herbert; or, The Fatal Error. A Novel Founded on Fact*. 3 vols. London: Bentley, 1847.

———. *The Memoirs of a Femme de Chambre*. 3 vols. London: Bentley, 1846.

———. *Meredith*. 3 vols. London: Longman, Brown, Green, and Longmans, 1843.
———. *Rambles in Waltham Forest: A Stranger's Contribution to the Triennial Sale for the Benefit of the Wanstead Lying-In Charity*. London: Cox, 1827.
———. *Sketches and Fragments*. London: Longman, Hurst, Rees, Orme, and Brown, 1822.
———. *Strathern; or, Life at Home and Abroad. A Story of the Present Day*. 4 vols. London: Colburn, 1845.
———. "The Tomb." In *The Magic Lantern*, 39–51.
———. *The Two Friends: A Novel*. 3 vols. London: Saunders and Otley, 1835.
———. *The Victims of Society*. 3 vols. London: Saunders and Otley, 1837.
———. *The Victims of Society*, ed. Ann R. Hawkins and Jeraldine R. Kraver. vol. 4 of *Silver Fork Novels, 1826–1841*. General ed. Harriet Devine Jump. 6 vols. London: Pickering and Chatto, 2005.
The Blessington Papers, collection of autographs, 6 vols. The Pforzheimer Collection. New York Public Library, Pforz MS.
Bohls, Elizabeth A. *Women Travel Writers and the Language of Aesthetics, 1716–1818*. Cambridge: Cambridge University Press, 1995.
Bolton, Betsy. *Women, Nationalism, and the Romantic Stage: Theatre and Politics in Britain, 1780–1800*. Cambridge: Cambridge University Press, 2001.
Bord, Joe. *Science and Whig Manners: Science and Political Style in Britain, c. 1790–1850*. Basingstoke: Palgrave Macmillan, 2009.
Bradford, Sarah. *Disraeli*. New York: Stein & Day, 1982.
Brant, Clare. *Eighteenth-Century Letters and British Culture*. Basingstoke: Palgrave Macmillan, 2006.
Brent, Richard. *Liberal Anglican Politics: Whiggery, Religion, and Reform, 1830–1841*. Oxford: Clarendon Press, 1987.
Brougham, Henry. "ART II. Hours of Idleness: A Series of Poems, Original and Translated. By George Gordon, Lord Byron, a Minor." *Edinburgh Review* 11 (January 1808): 285–289.
———. Letter to Marguerite Blessington (November 28, 1843). Blessington Correspondence, Princeton University, Box C0147, Folder 2, AM 12757.
Bulwer Lytton, Edward. *England and the English* [1833], ed. Standish Meacham. Chicago: University of Chicago Press, 1970.
———. *Godolphin: A Novel*, ed. Harriet Devine Jump, vol. 3 of Jump, *Silver Fork Novels, 1826–1841*.
———. "The Wife to the Wooer." In Blessington, *Heath's Book of Beauty, 1840*, 11–12.
Bulwer, Rosina. *Cheveley; or, The Man of Honour*, ed. Marie Mulvey-Roberts, vol. 5 of Jump, *Silver Fork Novels, 1826–1841*.
———. *The Collected Letters of Rosina Bulwer Lytton*, ed. Marie Mulvey-Roberts with the assistance of Steve Carpenter. 3 vols. London: Pickering and Chatto, 2008.

Burgess, Miranda. "The National Tale and Allied Genres, 1770s–1840s." In *The Cambridge Companion to the Irish Novel*, ed. John Wilson Foster. Cambridge: Cambridge University Press, 2006, 39–59.

Burke, Edmund. *Reflections on the Revolution in France*. London: Dodsley, 1790.

Burke, Peter. *The Art of Conversation*. Cambridge: Polity Press, 1993.

———. "Cultural History." In *The Sage Handbook of Cultural Analysis*, ed. Tony Bennett and John Frow. Los Angeles: Sage, 2008, 107–125.

———. *What is Cultural History?* 2nd ed. Cambridge: Polity Press, 2008.

Burroughs, Catherine B. *Closet Stages: Joanna Baillie and the Theater Theory of British Romantic Women Writers*. Philadelphia: University of Pennsylvania Press, 1997.

———. "'A Reasonable Woman's Desire': The Private Theatrical and Joanna Baillie's *The Tryal*." In *Joanna Baillie: Romantic Dramatist; Critical Essays*, ed. Thomas C. Crochunis. London: Routledge, 2004, 187–205.

———, ed. *Women in British Romantic Theatre: Drama, Performance, and Society, 1790–1840*. Cambridge: Cambridge University Press, 2000.

Burwick, Frederick. *Playing to the Crowd: London Popular Theatre, 1780–1830*. New York: Palgrave Macmillan, 2011.

Byron, George Gordon. "The Blues: A Literary Eclogue." In *Complete Poetical Works*, ed. Jerome J. McGann. 7 vols. Oxford: Clarendon Press, 1980–1993, 6:296–308.

———. *Byron's Letters and Journals*, ed. Leslie A. Marchand. 12 vols. London: Murray, 1974–1982.

———. *Childe Harold's Pilgrimage*, vol. 2 of *Complete Poetical Works*.

———. *English Bards and Scotch Reviewers*. In *Complete Poetical Works*, 1:227–264.

———. *Letters and Journals of Byron: With Notices of His Life*, ed. Thomas Moore. 2 vols. London: Murray, 1830.

———. "Napoleon's Snuff-Box." In *Complete Poetical Works*, 6:512.

Cabinet. "Private Theatricals at Strawberry Hill." *The Lady's Monthly Museum* 8 (January 1802): 60.

Campbell, Jill. "'I am No Giant': Horace Walpole, Heterosexual Incest, and Love among Men." *The Eighteenth Century* 39 (1998): 238–260.

Carlisle, Lord. "To Lady Holland, on the Legacy of a Snuff-Box, Left to Her by Buonaparte." *The Gentleman's Magazine* 91 (1821): 457–458.

Casey, Ellen Miller. "'The Aristocracy and Upholstery': The Silver Fork Novel." In *A Companion to Sensation Fiction*, ed. Pamela K. Gilbert. Malden: Blackwell Wiley, 2011, 13–25.

Castle, Terry. *The Female Thermometer: Eighteenth-Century Culture and the Invention of the Uncanny*. New York: Oxford University Press, 1995.

Chard, Chloe. *Pleasure and Guilt on the Grand Tour: Travel Writing and Imaginative Geography, 1600–1830*. Manchester: Manchester University Press, 1999.

Chartier, Roger. *Cultural History: Between Practices and Representations*. Ithaca: Cornell University Press, 1988.

Chartier, Roger, Alain Boureau, and Cécile Dauphin. *Correspondence: Models of Letter-Writing from the Middle Ages to the Nineteenth Century*. Cambridge: Polity Press, 1997.
Chesney, Duncan McColl. "The History of the History of the Salon." *Nineteenth-Century French Studies* 36 (2007): 94–108.
Chorley, Henry F. *The Authors of England: A Series of Medallion Portraits of Modern Literary Characters*. London: Tilt, 1838.
Christie, William. *The Edinburgh Review in the Literary Culture of Romantic Britain*. London: Pickering and Chatto, 2009.
———. "Running with the English Hares and Hunting with the Scotch Bloodhounds." *The Byron Journal* 25 (1997): 23–43.
Clark, Peter. *British Clubs and Societies, 1500–1800: The Origins of an Associational World*. Oxford: Clarendon Press, 2000.
Clubbe, John. "*Glenarvon* Revised—and Revisited." *The Wordsworth Circle* 10 (1979): 205–217.
Cohen, Michèle. *Fashioning Masculinity: National Identity and Language in the Eighteenth Century*. London: Routledge, 1996.
Combe, William. *The First of April: or, The Triumphs of Folly*. London: Bew, 1777.
Copeland, Edward. "Crossing Oxford Street: Silverfork Geopolitics." *Eighteenth-Century Life* 25 (2001): 116–134.
———. "Opera and the Great Reform Act: Silver Fork Fiction, 1822–1842." In *Opera and Nineteenth-Century Literature*, ed. Nicholas Halmi. Special issue of *Romanticism on the Net* 34–35 (2004). www.erudit.org/revue/ron/2004/v/n34-35/009440ar.html.
Copley, Stephen. "Commerce, Conversation and Politeness in the Early Eighteenth-Century Periodical." *British Journal for Eighteenth-Century Studies* 18 (1995): 63–77.
Cowan, Brian. *The Social Life of Coffee: The Emergence of the British Coffeehouse*. New Haven: Yale University Press, 2005.
Cox, Jeffrey N. "Baillie, Siddons, Larpent: Gender, Power, and Politics in the Theatre of Romanticism." In *Women in British Romantic Theatre: Drama, Performance, and Society, 1790–1840*, ed. Catherine Burroughs. Cambridge: Cambridge University Press, 2000, 23–47.
———. *Poetry and Politics in the Cockney School: Keats, Shelley, Hunt and Their Circle*. Cambridge: Cambridge University Press, 1998.
Craig, Randall. *The Narratives of Caroline Norton*. New York: Palgrave Macmillan, 2009.
Craven, Richard Keppel. *Excursions in the Abruzzi and Northern Provinces of Naples*. 2 vols. London: Bentley, 1838.
———. *A Tour Through the Southern Provinces of the Kingdom of Naples*. London: Rodwell and Martin, 1821.
Creevey, Thomas. *The Creevey Papers: A Selection from the Correspondence and Diaries of the Late Thomas Creevey, M. P. Born 1768–Died 1838*, ed. Herbert Maxwell. 2 vols. London: Murray, 1903–1904.
Crochunis, Thomas C., ed. *Joanna Baillie: Romantic Dramatist; Critical Essays*. London: Routledge, 2004.

Crosland, Mrs. Newton (Camilla Toulmin). *Landmarks of a Literary Life, 1820–1892*. London: Low, Marston, & Company, 1893.
———. "On the Portrait of Mrs. Burr." In *Heath's Book of Beauty, 1843*, ed. Marguerite Blessington. London: Longman, Rees, Orme, Brown, Green, and Longmans, 1842, 210–211.
Crosland, Newton. *Rambles Round My Life: An Autobiography (1819–1896)*. London: Allen, 1898.
Damer, Anne Seymour. *Belmour: A Modern Edition*, ed. Jonathan David Gross. Evanston: Northwestern University Press, 2011.
———. Notebooks, autographs, 4 vols. The Lewis Walpole Library, Yale University, LWL Mss Vol. 64.
Dames, Nicholas. "Brushes with Fame: Thackeray and the Work of Celebrity." *Nineteenth-Century Literature* 56 (2001): 23–51.
Daniel, Captain. "The Improvident: A Tale." In Blessington, *Heath's Book of Beauty, 1840*, 139–164.
Darnton, Robert. *The Great Cat Massacre and Other Episodes in French Cultural History*. New York: Vintage, 1985.
Davis, Natalie Zemon. "'Women's History' in Transition: The European Case." *Feminist Studies* 3 (1976): 83–103.
Davis, Tracy C., and Thomas Postlewait, eds. *Theatricality*. Cambridge: Cambridge University Press, 2003.
Demata, Massimiliano, and Duncan Wu, eds. *British Romanticism and the Edinburgh Review*. Basingstoke: Palgrave Macmillan, 2002.
Di Martino, Gabriella. "Motions and Emotions in a Lady Traveller's Writing." In *The Language of Public and Private Communication in a Historical Persepective*, ed. Nicholas Brownlees, Gabriella Del Lungo, and John Denton. Newcastle: Cambridge Scholars, 2010, 100–115.
Diamond, Elin. "Introduction." In *Performance and Cultural Politics*, ed. Elin Diamond. London: Routledge, 1996, 1–12.
———, ed. *Performance and Cultural Politics*. London: Routledge, 1996.
Dickinson, Cindy. "Creating a World of Books, Friends, and Flowers: Gift Books and Inscriptions, 1825–60." *Winterthur Portfolio* 31 (1996): 53–66.
Disraeli, Benjamin. *Benjamin Disraeli: Letters. Volume One: 1815–1834*, ed. J. A. W. Gunn, John Matthews, Donald M. Schurman, and M. G. Wiebe. Toronto: University of Toronto Press, 1982.
———. *Vivian Grey*, ed. Michael Sanders. London: Pickering and Chatto, 2004.
Dolan, Brian. *Ladies of the Grand Tour*. London: Flamingo, 2002.
Donkin, Ellen. "Joanna Baillie vs. the Termites Bellicosus." In *Getting into the Act: Women Playwrights in London, 1776–1829*. London: Routledge, 1995, 159–183.
Donoghue, Emma. *Life Mask*. Orlando: Harcourt, 2004.
———. "'Random Shafts of Malice?': The Outings of Anne Damer." In *Lesbian Dames: Sapphism in the Long Eighteenth Century*, ed. John C. Beynon and Caroline Gonda. Farnham: Ashgate, 2010, 127–146.

WORKS CITED

Douglass, Paul. "Introduction." In *Glenarvon*, ed. Paul Douglass, vol. 1 of *The Works of Caroline Lamb*, ed. Paul Douglass and Leigh Wetherall Dickson. 3 vols. London: Pickering and Chatto, 2009, xxvii–xliv.

———. "The Madness of Writing: Lady Caroline Lamb's Byronic Identity." *Pacific Coast Philology* 34 (1999): 53–71.

———. *Lady Caroline Lamb: A Biography*. New York: Palgrave Macmillan, 2004.

Downie, J. A. "Public and Private: The Myth of the Bourgeois Public Sphere." In *A Concise Companion to the Restoration and Eighteenth Century*, ed. Cynthia Wall. Oxford: Blackwell, 2005, 58–79.

Du Deffand, Marie de Vichy Chamrond. *Letters of the Marquise du Deffand to the Hon. Horace Walpole*, ed. Mary Berry. 4 vols. London: Longman, Hurst, Rees, and Orme, 1810.

Eger, Elizabeth. "The Bluestocking Legacy." In *Brilliant Women*, ed. Elizabeth Eger and Lucy Peltz. New Haven: Yale University Press, 2008, 126–150.

———. *Bluestockings: Women of Reason from Enlightenment to Romanticism*. Basingstoke: Palgrave Macmillan, 2010.

Eger, Elizabeth, Charlotte Grant, Clíona Ó Gallchoir, and Penny Warburton, eds. *Women, Writing and the Public Sphere, 1700–1830*. Cambridge: Cambridge University Press, 2001.

Ehler, Karin, and Martin Mulsow. "Gespräche über Grammatik und Civilité. Multifunktionalität von sprachdidaktischen Dialogen bei François de Fenne (1690) und Pierre François Roy (1693)." *Romanische Forschungen* 107 (1995): 314–342.

Eisler, Benita. *Byron: Child of Passion, Fool of Fame*. New York: Knopf, 1999.

Elfenbein, Andrew. "Lesbian Aestheticism on the Eighteenth-Century Stage." *Eighteenth-Century Life* 25 (2001): 1–16.

———. *Romantic Genius: The Prehistory of a Homosexual Role*. New York: Columbia University Press, 1999.

Eliot, George. *Middlemarch: A Study of Provincial Life*, ed. Gregory Maertz. Peterborough: Broadview, 2004.

Ellis, Markman. *The Coffee-House: A Cultural History*. London: Phoenix, 2005.

———. "'Spectacles within doors': Panoramas of London in the 1790s." *Romanticism* 14 (2008): 133–148.

Esterhammer, Angela. *Romanticism and Improvisation, 1750–1850*. Cambridge: Cambridge University Press, 2008.

———. *The Romantic Performative: Language and Action in British and German Romanticism*. Stanford: Stanford University Press, 2000.

Farington, Joseph. *The Diary of Joseph Farington*, ed. Kenneth Garlick, Angus MacIntyre, and Kathryn Cave. 16 vols. New Haven: Yale University Press, 1978–1984.

Feldman, Paula R. "Bibliography." In *The Keepsake for 1829*, ed. Frederic Mansel Reynolds. London: Hurst, Chance, & Co., 1828; reprint Peterborough: Broadview, 2006, 27–32.

---. "Introduction." In Reynolds, *The Keepsake for 1829*, 7–25.
---. "Women, Literary Annuals, and the Evidence of Inscriptions." *Keats-Shelley Journal* 55 (2006): 54–62.
Finden, Paula. "Translating the New Science: Women and the Circulation of Knowledge in Enlightenment Italy." *Configurations* 3 (1995): 167–206.
Firebaugh, Joseph J. "Samuel Rogers and American Men of Letters." *American Literature* 13 (1942): 331–345.
Fisher, Judith L. "'In the Present Famine of Anything Substantial': *Fraser's* 'Portraits' and the Construction of Literary Celebrity; or, 'Personality, Personality Is the Appetite of the Age.'" *Victorian Periodicals Review* 39 (2006): 97–135.
Flynn, Philip. *Francis Jeffrey*. Newark: University of Delaware Press, 1978.
Fontana, Biancamaria. *Rethinking the Politics of Commercial Society: The Edinburgh Review 1802–1832*. Cambridge: Cambridge University Press, 1985.
Foulkes, Nick. *Last of the Dandies: The Scandalous Life and Escapades of Count D'Orsay*. London: Little, Brown, 2003.
Frank, Marcie. "Horace Walpole's Family Romances." *Modern Philology* 100 (2003): 417–435.
Free, William N. "Walpole's Letters: The Art of Being Graceful." In *The Familiar Letter in the Eighteenth Century*, ed. Howard Anderson, Philip B. Daghlian, and Irvin Ehrenpreis. Lawrence: University of Kansas Press, 1968, 165–185.
Fumaroli, Marc. "Conversation." In *Rethinking France: Les Lieux de mémoire*, ed. Pierre Nora, vol. 3. Chicago: University of Chicago Press, 2009, 275–342.
---. "La Conversation." In *Lieux de mémoire*, ed. Pierre Nora. vol. 3/2 Paris: Gallimard, 1992, 679–743.
Gallagher, Catherine. *Nobody's Story: The Vanishing Acts of Women Writers in the Marketplace, 1670–1820*. Oxford: Clarendon Press, 1994.
Gardiner, Ann T. "Salons, Society, and Solitude chez Madame de Staël." In *Einsamkeit und Geselligkeit um 1800*, ed. Susanne Schmid. Heidelberg: Winter, 2008, 53–66.
Gaskins, Avery F. "Samuel Rogers: A Revaluation." *The Wordsworth Circle* 16 (1985): 146–149.
Gell, William, and John P. Gandy. *Pompeiana: The Topography, Edifices, and Ornaments of Pompeii*. London: Rodwell and Martin, 1817–1819.
Gettmann, Royal A. *A Victorian Publisher: A Study of the Bentley Papers*. Cambridge: Cambridge University Press, 1960.
Gilbert, Kathleen. "Rosamond and Lady Blessington: Another *Middlemarch* Anachronism." *Notes and Queries* 27 (1980): 527–528.
Goffman, Erving. *The Presentation of Self in Everyday Life*. Garden City: Doubleday, 1959.
Goldsmith, Elizabeth C. *"Exclusive Conversations": The Art of Interaction in Seventeenth-Century France*. Philadelphia: University of Philadelphia Press, 1988.

Goodman, Dena. *The Republic of Letters: A Cultural History of the French Enlightenment.* Ithaca: Cornell University Press, 1994.
Gorton, L. J. "The Holland House Papers and Their History." *The British Museum Quarterly* 29 (1965): 71–78.
Graham, Peter W. "Fictive Biography in 1816: The Case of *Glenarvon*." *The Byron Journal* 19 (1991): 53–68.
Granville, Harriet. *Letters of Harriet Countess Granville, 1810–1845,* ed. F. Leveson Gower, 3rd ed. 2 vols. London: Longmans, Green, and Co., 1894.
Greenblatt, Stephen. *Renaissance Self-Fashioning: From More to Shakespeare.* Chicago: University of Chicago Press, 1980.
Greville, Charles Cavendish Fulke. *The Greville Memoirs, 1814–1860,* ed. Lytton Strachey and Roger Fulford. 8 vols. London: Macmillan, 1938.
Grimbergen, Ria, and Paul Douglass. "On a Special Copy of Caroline Lamb's *Glenarvon* Recently Discovered in the Koninklijke Bibliotheek." *Byron Journal* 37 (2009): 151–160.
Gross, Jonathan David. "Introduction." In Anne Seymour Damer, *Belmour: A Modern Edition,* ed. Jonathan Gross. Evanston: Northwestern University Press, 2011, xvii–l.
Guest, Harriet. "Hannah More and Conservative Feminism." In *British Women's Writing in the Long Eighteenth Century: Authorship, Politics and History,* ed. Jennie Batchelor and Cora Kaplan. Basingstoke: Palgrave Macmillan, 2005, 158–170.
———. *Small Change: Women, Learning, Patriotism, 1750–1810.* Chicago: University of Chicago Press, 2000.
Habermas, Jürgen. *The Structural Transformation of the Public Sphere: An Inquiry into a Category of Bourgeois Society* [1962]. Cambridge: Polity Press, 1989.
Haefner, Joel. "The Romantic Scene(s) of Writing." In *Re-Visioning Romanticism: British Women Writers, 1776–1837,* ed. Carol Shiner Wilson and Joel Haefner. Philadelphia: University of Pennsylvania Press, 1994, 256–273.
Haggerty, George E. "The Strawberry Committee." In *Horace Walpole's Strawberry Hill,* ed. Michael Snodin with the assistance of Cynthia Roman. New Haven: Yale University Press, 2009, 80–81.
Hahn, Barbara. *Die Jüdin Pallas Athene. Auch eine Theorie der Moderne.* Berlin: Berlin Verlag, 2002.
Hale, J. R. "Samuel Rogers the Perfectionist." *Huntington Library Quarterly* 25 (1961): 61–67.
Hall, Samuel Carter. *Retrospect of a Long Life: From 1815 to 1883.* New York: Appleton and Company, 1883.
Harris, Katherine D. *Forget Me Not: A Hypertextual Archive.* www.orgs.muohio.edu/anthologies/FMN/.
Hartington, Lord (William George Spencer Cavendish, Duke of Devonshire). Letter to Mary Berry (January 30, 1803), BM Add. MSS. 37726 f. 22.

Haussez, Charles Lemercier de Longpré. *Great Britain in 1833*. Philadelphia: Mielke, 1833.

Hawkins, Ann R. "'Formed with Curious Skill': Blessington's Negotiation of the 'Poetess' in *Flowers of Loveliness*." *Romanticism on the Net* 29–30 (2003). www.erudit.org/revue/ron/2003/v/n29-30/007721ar.html.

———. "Marguerite, Countess of Blessington, and L.E.L. (Letitia Elizabeth Landon): Evidence of a Friendship." *ANQ: A Quarterly Journal of Short Articles, Notes and Reviews* 16 (2003): 27–32.

Hawkins, Ann R., and Jeraldine R. Kraver. "Introduction." In Marguerite Blessington, *Victims of Society*, ed. Ann R. Hawkins and Jeraldine R. Kraver, vol. 4 of Jump, *Silver Fork Novels, 1826–1841*, vii–xxvi.

Hay, William Anthony. *The Whig Revival, 1808–1830*. Basingstoke: Palgrave Macmillan, 2005.

Haydon, Benjamin Robert. *The Diary of Benjamin Robert Haydon*, ed. Willard Bissell Pope. 5 vols. Cambridge, MA: Harvard University Press, 1960–1963.

Hazlitt, William. "The Dandy School." In *The Complete Works of William Hazlitt*, ed. P. P. Howe. 21 vols. London: Dent and Sons, 1930–1934, 20:143–149.

———, "My First Acquaintance with Poets." *The Liberal* 2 (1823): 23–46.

———. "On the Conversation of Authors." In *Complete Works*, 12:24–44.

Heath's Book of Beauty, 1840, ed. Marguerite Blessington. London: Longman, Orme, Brown, Green, and Longmans, 1839.

Heller, Deborah. "Bluestocking Salons and the Public Sphere." *Eighteenth-Century Life* 22 (1998): 59–82.

Hemphill, Barbara. *Lionel Deerhurst; or, Fashionable Life Under the Regency*, ed. Marguerite Blessington. 3 vols. London: Bentley, 1846.

Hemphill, C. Dallett. *Bowing to Necessities: A History of Manners in America, 1620–1860*. New York: Oxford University Press, 1999.

Henn-Schmölders, Claudia. "Ars conversationis. Zur Geschichte des sprachlichen Umgangs." *arcadia* 10 (1975): 16–33.

Henry, Maura A. "The Making of Elite Culture." In *A Companion to Eighteenth-Century Britain*, ed. H. T. Dickinson. Oxford: Blackwell, 2002, 311–328.

Hoagwood, Terence Allan, and Kathryn Ledbetter. *"Colour'd Shadows": Contexts in Publishing, Printing, and Reading Nineteenth-Century British Women Writers*. New York: Palgrave Macmillan, 2005.

Hogg, Thomas Jefferson. "Percy Bysshe Shelley at Oxford." *New Monthly Magazine* 35 (October 1832): 321–330.

Holland, Elizabeth Vassall Fox, Lady. *Elizabeth, Lady Holland to Her Son, 1821–1845*, ed. Giles Stephen Holland Fox-Strangways, Earl of Ilchester. London: Murray, 1946.

———. *The Journal of Elizabeth, Lady Holland (1791–1811)*, ed. Earl of Ilchester. 2 vols. London: Longmans, Green, and Co., 1908.

———. *The Spanish Journal of Elizabeth Lady Holland*, ed. Earl of Ilchester. London: Longmans, Green, and Co., 1910.

Holland, Henry. *Recollections of Past Life.* London: Longmans, Green, and Co., 1872.
Holland, Henry Edward Fox, Lord. *The Journal of the Hon. Edward Fox (Afterwards Fourth and Last Lord Holland), 1818–1830,* ed. Earl of Ilchester. London: Butterworth, 1923.
Holland, Henry Richard Fox, Lord. *Foreign Reminiscences* [1850], ed. Henry Edward Lord Holland. 2nd ed. London: Longman, Brown, Green, and Longmans, 1851.
———. *Further Memoirs of the Whig Party, 1807–1821,* ed. Earl of Ilchester. London: Murray, 1905.
———. *The Holland House Diaries, 1831–1840: The Diary of Henry Richard Vassall Fox, Third Lord Holland, with Extracts from the Diary of Dr John Allen,* ed. Abraham D. Kriegel. London: Routledge & Kegan Paul, 1977.
———. *Memoirs of the Whig Party During My Time,* ed. Henry Edward Fox, Lord Holland. 2 vols. London: Longman, Brown, Green, and Longmans, 1852–1854.
———. *The Opinions of Lord Holland as Recorded in the Journals of the House of Lords from 1797 to 1841,* ed. D. C. Moylan. London: Ridgway, 1841.
———. *Some Account of the Life and Writings of Lope Felix de Vega Carpio.* London: Longman, Hurst, Rees, and Orme, 1806.
Holland, Saba. *A Memoir of the Reverend Sydney Smith, by His Daughter, Lady Holland: With a Selection from His Letters,* ed. Mrs. Austen. 3rd ed., vol. 1. London: Longman, Brown, Green, and Longmans, 1855.
Holme, Torre. "Stanzas." In Blessington, *Heath's Book of Beauty, 1840,* 203–204.
Hoole, Samuel. "Letter VII. Mr. Ralph P-. to To John C-. Esq.: A Conversatione." In *Modern Manners: In a Series of Familiar Epistles.* London: Faulder, 1781, 59–72.
Hootman, Harry E. *British Annuals and Giftbooks.* www.britannuals.com.
Hudson, Derek. *Holland House in Kensington.* London: Davies, 1967.
Hughes, Winifred. "Silver Fork Writers and Readers: Social Contexts of a Best Seller." *NOVEL: A Forum on Fiction* 25 (1992): 328–347.
Ilchester, Giles Stephen Holland Fox-Strangways, Earl of. *Chronicles of Holland House, 1820–1900.* London: Murray, 1937.
———. *The Home of the Hollands, 1605–1820.* London: Murray, 1937.
Jekyll, Joseph. *Correspondence of Mr. Joseph Jekyll with His Sister-in-Law, Lady Gertrude Sloane Stanley, 1818–1838,* ed. Algernon Bourke. London: Murray, 1894.
Jerdan, William. *Autobiography.* 4 vols. London: Hall, 1852–1853.
Johnson, Samuel. *"The Idler" and "The Adventurer,"* ed. W. J. Bate, John M. Bullitt, and L. F. Powell, vol. 2 of *The Works of Samuel Johnson.* New Haven: Yale University Press, 1963.
Jump, Harriet. "Marguerite Blessington, Teresa Guiccioli, and the Writing of the *Conversation with Byron.*" *The Byron Journal* 31 (2003): 51–60.
Jump, Harriet Devine. "'The False Prudery of Public Taste': Scandalous Women and the Annuals, 1820–1850." In *Feminist Readings of Victorian*

Popular Texts: Divergent Femininities, ed. Emma Liggins and Daniel Duffy. Aldershot: Ashgate, 2001, 1–17.

———. "General Introduction." In Thomas Henry Lister, *Granby: A Novel,* ed. Clare Bainbridge, vol. 1 of Jump, *Silver Fork Novels, 1826–1841,* ix–xxii.

———. "Introduction." In Edward Bulwer, *Godolphin,* ed. Jump, vol. 3 of Jump, *Silver Fork Novels, 1826–1841,* ix–xxii.

———, general ed. *Silver Fork Novels, 1826–1841.* 6 vols. London: Pickering and Chatto, 2005.

Kale, Steven. *French Salons: High Society and Political Sociability from the Old Regime to the Revolution of 1848.* Baltimore: Johns Hopkins University Press, 2004.

Kelly, Gary, general ed. *Bluestocking Feminism: Writings of the Bluestocking Circle, 1738–1785.* 6 vols. London: Pickering and Chatto, 1999.

———. "General Introduction: Bluestocking Feminism and Writing in Context." In Kelly, *Bluestocking Feminism,* 1:ix–liv.

Kelly, Ronan. *Bard of Erin: The Life of Thomas Moore.* Dublin: Penguin, 2008.

Kelsall, Malcolm. "The Byronic Hero and Revolution in Ireland: The Politics of *Glenarvon.*" *The Byron Journal* 9 (1981): 4–19.

Keppel, Sonia. *The Sovereign Lady: A Life of Elizabeth, Third Lady Holland, with Her Family.* London: Hamish Hamilton, 1974.

Kerber, Linda K. "Separate Spheres, Female World, Woman's Place: The Rhetoric of Women's History." In *No More Separate Spheres! A Next Wave American Studies Reader,* ed. Cathy N. Davidson and Jessamyn Hatcher. Durham: Duke University Press, 2002, 29–65.

Kirkpatrick, Kathryn J. "Introduction." In Maria Edgeworth, *Castle Rackrent,* ed. George Watson. Oxford: Oxford University Press, 1995, vii–xxxvi.

Klein, Lawrence E. "The Figure of France: The Politics of Sociability in England, 1660–1715." *Yale French Studies* 92 (1997): 30–45.

———. "Gender and the Public/Private Distinction in the Eighteenth Century: Some Questions About Evidence and Analytic Procedure." *Eighteenth-Century Studies* 29 (1995): 97–109.

———. "Gender, Conversation and the Public Sphere in Early Eighteenth-Century England." In *Textuality and Sexuality: Reading Theories and Practices,* ed. Judith Still and Michael Worton. Manchester: Manchester University Press, 1993, 100–115.

———. *Shaftesbury and the Culture of Politeness: Moral Discourse and Cultural Politics in Early Eighteenth-Century England.* Cambridge: Cambridge University Press, 1994.

Kreilkamp, Vera. "The Novel of the Big House." In *The Cambridge Companion to the Irish Novel,* ed. John Wilson Foster. Cambridge: Cambridge University Press, 2006, 60–77.

Kriegel, Abraham D. "Liberty and Whiggery in Early Nineteenth-Century England." *Journal of Modern History* 52 (1980): 253–278.

Kurz, Gerhard. "Das Ganze und das Teil. Zur Bedeutung der Geselligkeit in der ästhetischen Diskussion um 1800." In *Kunst und Geschichte im*

Zeitalter Hegels, ed. Christoph Jamme, with the assistance of Frank Völkel. Hamburg: Meiner, 1996, 91–113.
Lamb, Caroline. *Glenarvon*, ed. Paul Douglass, vol. 1 of *The Works of Caroline Lamb*, ed. Paul Douglass and Leigh Wetherall Dickson. 3 vols. London: Pickering and Chatto, 2009.
———. *The Whole Disgraceful Truth: Selected Letters of Lady Caroline Lamb*, ed. Paul Douglass. New York: Palgrave Macmillan, 2006.
Landes, Joan B. "The Public and the Private Sphere: A Feminist Reconsideration." In *Feminists Read Habermas: Gendering the Subject of Discourse*, ed. Johanna Meehan. New York: Routledge, 1995, 91–116.
Landor, Walter Savage. *Imaginary Conversations*, ed. Charles G. Crump. 6 vols. London: Dent, 1909.
Lane, Maggie. *Jane Austen and Food*. London: Hambledon Press, 1995.
Lanser, Susan S. "Bluestocking Sapphism and the Economies of Desire." In Pohl and Schellenberg, *Reconsidering the Bluestockings*, 257–275.
Lepenies, Wolf. *Melancholie und Gesellschaft. Mit einer neuen Einleitung: Das Ende der Utopie und die Wiederkehr der Melancholie*. Frankfurt am Main: Suhrkamp, 1998.
Lewis, Matthew. *The Monk*, ed. Howard Anderson. Oxford: Oxford University Press, 1998.
Lewis, Theresa. *Lives of the Friends and Contemporaries of Lord Chancellor Clarendon: Illustrative Portraits in His Gallery*. 3 vols. London: Murray, 1852.
Liechtenstein, Marie, Princess. *Holland House*. 2 vols. London: Macmillan, 1874.
Lievsay, John Leon. "Notes on *The Art of Conversation* (1738)." *Italica* 17 (1940): 58–63.
Lloyd, Stephen. *Richard and Maria Cosway: Regency Artists of Taste and Fashion*, with essays by Roy Porter and Aileen Ribeiro. Edinburgh: Scottish National Portrait Gallery, 1995.
Lopez, John-David. "The British Romantic Reconstruction of Spain," unpubl. PhD thesis, UCLA, Los Angeles, 2008.
Lovell, Ernest J. "Introduction." In *Lady Blessington's Conversations of Lord Byron*, ed. Ernest J. Lovell. Princeton: Princeton University Press, 1969, 3–114.
———. "Introduction." In Thomas Medwin, *Conversations of Lord Byron*, ed. Ernest J. Lovell. Princeton: Princeton University Press, 1966, vii–xiv.
Loxley, James. *Performativity*. London: Routledge, 2007.
M. "Private Hints to a Juvenile Physician." *New Monthly Magazine* 35 (October 1832): 359–364.
M. T. "Fashionable Friends." *The Weekly Entertainer* 24 (611) (October 27, 1794): 340.
Macaulay, Thomas Babington. "Art. VII. *The Opinions of Lord Holland*." *Edinburgh Review* 73 (July 1841): 560–568.
———. "Letters of Horace Walpole, Earl of Orford, to Horace Mann." *Edinburgh Review* 58 (October 1833): 227–258.
———. *The Life and Letters of Lord Macaulay*, ed. George Otto Trevelyan. 2 vols. London: Longmans, Green, and Co., 1876.

Mackintosh, James. "Art. II. *Poems,* by Samuel Rogers." *Edinburgh Review* 22 (October 1813): 32–50.
Madden, R. R. *The Literary Life and Correspondence of the Countess of Blessington.* 3 vols. London: Newby, 1855; repr., New York: AMS Press, 1973.
Mandell, Laura. "Producing Hate in 'Private' Letters: Horace Walpole, Mary Hays." *European Romantic Review* 17 (2006): 169–177.
Mandler, Peter. *Aristocratic Government in the Age of Reform: Whigs and Liberals, 1830–1852.* Oxford: Clarendon Press, 1990.
Manning, Peter J. "Childe Harold in the Marketplace: From Romaunt to Handbook." *Modern Language Quarterly* 52 (1991): 170–190.
Mariani, John F. "Lady Blessington's 'Ever Obliged Friend and Servant, W. S. Landor': A Study of Their Literary Relationship." *The Wordsworth Circle* 7 (1976): 17–30.
———. "The Letters of Walter Savage Landor to Marguerite Countess of Blessington," unpubl. PhD thesis, Columbia University, New York, 1973.
Markham, Sarah. "Mary Berry on the Death of Horace Walpole." *Notes and Queries* 223 (1978): 65–67.
Martineau, Harriet. *Autobiography,* ed. Linda H. Peterson. Peterborough: Broadview, 2007.
Mathews, Charles James. *The Life of Charles James Mathews, Chiefly Autobiographical, With Selections from His Correspondence and Speeches,* ed. Charles Dickens. 2 vols. London: Macmillan, 1879.
Matthews, Yvonne Louise. "The Relationship of Horace Walpole and Mary and Agnes Berry," unpubl. PhD thesis, Lamar University, Beaumont, 1986.
McCord Jr., James N. "Taming the Female Politician in Early Nineteenth-Century England: John Bull *versus Lady Jersey.*" *Journal of Women's History* 13 (2002): 31–53.
McGann, Jerome J. *The Romantic Ideology: A Critical Investigation.* Chicago: University of Chicago Press, 1983.
McKusick, James, ed. *Joseph Johnson: Essays Mostly Delivered at the Wordsworth-Coleridge Association.* Special issue of *The Wordsworth Circle* 23 (2002): 90–121.
McLean, Thomas. "Introduction." In *Further Letters of Joanna Baillie,* ed. Thomas McLean. Madison: Fairleigh Dickinson University Press, 2010, 21–29.
Mee, Jon. *Conversable Worlds: Literature, Contention, and Community 1762 to 1830.* Oxford: Oxford University Press, 2011.
Melton, James Van Horn. *The Rise of the Public in Enlightenment Europe.* Cambridge: Cambridge University Press, 2001.
Melville, Lewis. *William Makepeace Thackeray.* New York: Doubleday, Doran, & Company, 1928.
Miller, Peter N. *Peiresc's Europe: Learning and Virtue in the Seventeenth Century.* New Haven: Yale University Press, 2000.

Mitchell, Leslie. *Holland House*. London: Duckworth, 1980.

———. *The Whig World, 1760–1837*. London: Hambledon and London, 2005.

Molloy, J. Fitzgerald. *The Most Gorgeous Lady Blessington*. 2 vols. London: Downey & Co., 1896.

Montagu, Elizabeth. *Elizabeth Montagu*, ed. Elizabeth Eger, vol. 1 of Kelly, *Bluestocking Feminism*.

Moore, Dafydd. "Patriotism, Politeness, and National Identity in the South West of England in the Late Eighteenth Century." *English Literary History* 76 (2009): 739–762.

Moore, Thomas. *The Journal of Thomas Moore*, ed. Wilfred S. Dowden. 6 vols. Newark: University of Delaware Press, 1983–1991.

———. *Memoirs of the Life of the Right Honourable Richard Brinsley Sheridan*. 2nd ed. 2 vols. London: Longman, Hurst, Rees, Orme, Brown, and Green, 1825.

———. "To Lady Holland on Napoleon's Legacy of a Snuff-Box." *Poetical Works*, ed. A. D. Godley. Oxford: Oxford University Press, 1915, 717.

More, Hannah. *Florio: A Tale for Fine Gentlemen and Fine Ladies: and, The Bas Bleu; or, Conversation: Two Poems*. London: Cadell, 1786.

———. *Strictures on the Modern System of Female Education*. 2 vols. London: Cadell and Davies, 1799.

———. "Thoughts on Conversation." In *Essays on Various Subjects, Principally Designed for Young Ladies*. London: Wilkie and Cadell, 1777, 37–62.

Morgan, Sydney. *Lady Morgan's Memoirs: Autobiography, Diaries and Correspondence*, ed. William Dixon. 2nd ed. 2 vols. London: Allen, 1863.

Morrison, Alfred, ed. *The Collection of Autograph Letters and Historical Documents (Second Series 1882–1893): The Blessington Papers*. London: Privately printed, 1895.

Mullin, Janet E. "'We Had Carding': Hospitable Card Play and Polite Domestic Sociability among the Middling Sort in Eighteenth-Century England." *Journal of Social History* 42 (2009): 989–1008.

Murphy, James H. *Irish Novelists and the Victorian Age*. Oxford: Oxford University Press, 2011.

Murray, Venetia. *High Society in the Regency Period, 1788–1830*. London: Penguin, 1999.

Myers, Sylvia Harcstark. *The Bluestocking Circle: Women, Friendship, and the Life of the Mind in Eighteenth-Century England*. Oxford: Clarendon Press, 1990.

National Portrait Gallery. "Gallery launches actress portraits show..." www.npg.org.uk/about/press/gallery-launches-actress-portraits-show... -and-acquire-rare-picture-of-society-beauties-as-macbeths-witches.php.

New Monthly Magazine 34–39 (1832–1833).

Newbould, Ian. *Whiggery and Reform, 1830–41: The Politics of Government*. Stanford: Stanford University Press, 1990.

Newman, Gerald. "Anti-French Propaganda and British Liberal Nationalism in the Early Nineteenth Century: Suggestions Toward a General Interpretation." *Victorian Studies* 18 (1975): 385–418.

Noble, Percy. *Anne Seymour Damer: A Woman of Art and Fashion, 1748–1828*. London: Kegan Paul, Trench, Trübner, and Co., 1908.

North, Julian. "Self-Possession and Gender in Romantic Literary Biography." In *Romantic Biography*, ed. Arthur Bradley and Alan Rawes. Aldershot: Ashgate, 2003, 109–138.

Norton, Rictor. *Mistress of Udolpho: The Life of Ann Radcliffe*. London: Leicester University Press, 1999.

O' Cinneide, Muireann. *Aristocratic Women and the Literary Nation, 1832–1867*. Basingstoke: Palgrave Macmillan, 2008.

O' Dwyer, Riana. "Travels of a Lady of Fashion: The Literary Career of Lady Blessington (1789–1849)." In *New Contexts: Re-Framing Nineteenth-Century Irish Women's Prose,* ed. Heidi Hansson. Cork: Cork University Press, 2008, 35–54.

Otto, Almut, and Thomas Schmidt. "'Ilm-Athen' oder 'Deutsches Babel'? Der Salon der Ottilie von Goethe zwischen Weltläufigkeit und Provinzialisierung." In *Europa–ein Salon? Beiträge zur Internationalität des literarischen Salons,* ed. Roberto Simanowski, Horst Turk, and Thomas Schmidt. Göttingen: Wallstein, 1999, 161–189.

Parker, Mark. *Literary Magazines and British Romanticism*. Cambridge: Cambridge University Press, 2000.

Pateman, Carole. *The Disorder of Women: Democracy, Feminism and Political Theory*. Cambridge: Polity Press, 1989.

Patmore, P. G. "Personal Recollections of the Late Lady Blessington." *Bentley's Miscellany* 26 (1849): 162–175.

Pearson, Hesketh. *The Smith of Smiths, Being the Life, Wit and Humour of Sydney Smith,* with a new introduction by Richard Ingrams. London: Hogarth Press, 1984.

Pekacz, Jolanta T. *Conservative Tradition in Pre-Revolutionary France: Parisian Salon Women*. New York: Lang, 1999.

Penny, N. B. "The Whig Cult of Fox in Early Nineteenth-Century Sculpture." *Past and Present* 70 (1976): 94–105.

Perry, Kate. *Reminiscences of a London Drawing-Room*. London: Privately printed, c. 1860.

Perry, Ruth. "George Ballard's Biographies of Learned Ladies." In *Biography in the Eighteenth Century,* ed. J. D. Browning. New York: Garland, 1980, 85–111.

Phillipps, K. C. *Language and Class in Victorian England*. Oxford: Blackwell, 1984.

Pigott, Charles. *The Female Jockey Club, or a Sketch of the Manners of the Age*. London: Eaton, 1794.

———. *The Whig Club: or, A Sketch of Modern Patriotism*. London: Crosby, 1794.

Poe, Edgar Allan. "Lionizing." In *Tales and Sketches, 1831–1842*, vol. 2 of *Collected Works of Edgar Allan Poe*, ed. Thomas Ollive Mabbott. Cambridge, MA: Belknap Press, 1978, 172–177.
Pohl, Nicole, and Betty A. Schellenberg. "Introduction: A Bluestocking Historiography." In Pohl and Schellenberg, *Reconsidering the Bluestockings*, 1–19.
———, eds. *Reconsidering the Bluestockings*. San Marino: Huntington Library, 2003.
Polwhele, Richard. *The Unsex'd Females: A Poem* [American reprint]. New York: Cobbett, 1800.
Porter, Roy. *English Society in the Eighteenth Century*. Rev. ed. London: Penguin, 1991.
———. *Enlightenment: Britain and the Creation of the Modern World*. London: Penguin, 2000.
Pottinger, George. *Heirs of the Enlightenment: Edinburgh Reviewers and Writers 1800–1830*. Edinburgh: Scottish Academic Press, 1992.
Power, Margaret. "Memoir of the Countess of Blessington." In Marguerite Blessington, *Country Quarters: A Novel*. 3 vols. London: Shoberl, 1850, 1:iii–xxiii.
Queen Victoria's Journals: Lord Esher's Typescripts. Entry of January 1, 1836, 2:8–10. www.queenvictoriasjournals.org/search/displayItemFromId.do?FormatType=fulltextimgsrc&QueryType=articles&ItemID=18360101&volumeType=ESHER.
Radway, Janice. *Reading the Romance: Women, Patriarchy, and Popular Literature*. London: Verso, 1984.
Rappoport, Jill. "Buyer Beware: The Gift Poetics of Letitia Elizabeth Landon." *Nineteenth-Century Literature* 58 (2004): 441–473.
The Reading Experience Database (RED), 1450–1945. www.open.ac.uk/Arts/RED/.
Reinelt, Janelle. "The Politics of Discourse: Performativity Meets Theatricality." *SubStance* 98/99 (2002): 201–215.
Riccio, Bianca, ed., with the assistance of Sabina De Vito, Francesco Leone, and Lisa Roscioni. *Mary Berry un' inglese in Italia: Diari e corrispondenza dal 1783 al 1823. Arte personaggi e società*. Rome: Ugo Bozzi, 2002.
Roberts, Ellis. *Samuel Rogers and His Circle*. London: Methuen, 1910.
Roberts, William. *Memoirs of the Life and Correspondence of Mrs. Hannah More*, vol. 1. London: R. B. Seeley, 1834.
Robinson, Daniel. *The Poetry of Mary Robinson: Form and Fame*. New York: Palgrave Macmillan, 2011.
Robinson, Henry Crabb. *Diary, Reminiscences, and Correspondence*, ed. Thomas Sadler. 2nd ed. 3 vols. London: Macmillan, 1869.
Robinson, Jeffrey C. "Hazlitt's 'My First Acquaintance with Poets': The Autobiography of a Cultural Critic." *Romanticism* 6 (2000): 178–194.
Rogers, Kevin. "Walpole's Gothic: Creating a Fictive History." In Snodin, with the assistance of Roman, *Horace Walpole's Strawberry Hill*, 59–73.

Rogers, Samuel. *Italy: A Poem*. London: Cadell, 1830.
———. *Recollections of the Table-Talk of Samuel Rogers. Porsoniana*. 2nd ed. London: Moxon, 1856.
Roman, Cynthia. "The Art of Lady Diana Beauclerk: Horace Walpole and Female Genius." In Snodin, with the assistance of Cynthia Roman, *Horace Walpole's Strawberry Hill*, 155–169.
Romer, Isabella. "A Leaf from the Pilgrim's Scrap-Book." In Blessington, *Heath's Book of Beauty, 1840*, 62–80.
Rosa, Matthew Whiting. *The Silver-Fork School: Novels of Fashion Preceding Vanity Fair*. New York: Columbia University Press, 1936.
Rosenfeld, Sybil. *Temples of Thespis: Some Private Theatres and Theatricals in England and Wales, 1700–1820*. London: Society for Theatre Research, 1978.
Russell, Gillian, and Clara Tuite. "Introducing Romantic Sociability." In *Romantic Sociability: Social Networks and Literary Culture in Britain, 1770–1840*, ed. Gillian Russell and Clara Tuite. Cambridge: Cambridge University Press, 2002, 1–23.
———, eds. *Romantic Sociability: Social Networks and Literary Culture in Britain, 1770–1840*. Cambridge: Cambridge University Press, 2002.
Russell, Gillian. "Private Theatricals." In *The Cambridge Companion to British Theatre, 1730–1830*, ed. Jane Moody and Daniel O'Quinn. Cambridge: Cambridge University Press, 2007, 191–203.
———. "Spouters or Washerwomen: The Sociability of Romantic Lecturing." In Russell and Tuite, *Romantic Sociability*, 123–144.
———. *Women, Sociability and Theatre in Georgian London*. Cambridge: Cambridge University Press, 2007.
Sabor, Peter. "Introduction." In *The Works of Horatio Walpole, Earl of Orford*, ed. Mary Berry. 5 vols. London: Robinson and Edwards, 1798. Reprint ed. Peter Sabor. London: Pickering and Chatto, 1999, 1:ix–xxxi.
Sadleir, Michael. *Blessington-d'Orsay: A Masquerade* [1933]. London: Folio Society, 1983.
Saglia, Diego. *Poetic Castles in Spain: British Romanticism and Figurations of Iberia*. Amsterdam: Rodopi, 2000.
Samuelian, Kristin Flieger. *Royal Romances: Sex, Scandal, and Monarchy in Print, 1780–1821*. New York: Palgrave Macmillan, 2010.
Sanders, Lloyd. *The Holland House Circle*. New York: Putnam's Sons, 1908.
Sattin, Anthony. *Lifting the Veil: British Society in Egypt, 1768–1956*. London: Dent, 1988.
Schmid, Susanne. "The Countess of Blessington and the English Romantic Salon." In Schmid, *Einsamkeit und Geselligkeit um 1800*, 95–109.
———. "The Countess of Blessington: Reading as Intimacy, Reading as Sociability." *The Wordsworth Circle* 39 (2008): 88–93.
———. "Einleitung: Einsamkeit und Geselligkeit um 1800." In Schmid, *Einsamkeit und Geselligkeit um 1800*, 7–16.

———, ed. *Einsamkeit und Geselligkeit um 1800*. Heidelberg: Winter, 2008.

———. "Mary Berry's *Fashionable Friends* (1801) on Stage." *The Wordsworth Circle* 43 (2012): 172–177.

———. "Gespräch, Geselligkeit und Einsamkeit um 1800." In *Triangulärer Transfer: Großbritannien, Frankreich und Deutschland um 1800*, ed. Sandra Pott and Sebastian Neumeister. Special issue of *Germanisch-Romanische Monatsschrift* 56 (2006): 45–58.

———. "'Hodge-Podge' of Unreason or the 'Citizens Academy'? The London Coffee-House, 1652–1800." *Das Achtzehnte Jahrhundert* 32 (2008): 62–73.

———. "Holland House and Mary Berry's Drawing-Room: Salons, *Salonnières* and Writers." *The Wordsworth Circle* 35 (2004): 77–80.

———. "Lady Blessington und die Salons der englischen Romantik." In *Subversive Romantik*, ed. Volker Kapp, Helmuth Kiesel, Klaus Lubbers, and Patricia Plummer. Berlin: Duncker & Humblot, 2004, 153–164.

———. *Shelley's German Afterlives, 1814–2000*. New York: Palgrave Macmillan, 2007.

Schmölders, Claudia, ed. *Die Kunst des Gesprächs. Texte zur Geschichte der europäischen Konversationstheorie*. München: dtv, 1979.

Schoenfield, Mark. *British Periodicals and Romantic Identity: The "Literary Lower Empire."* New York: Palgrave Macmillan, 2009.

Schwoerer, Lois G. *Lady Rachel Russell: "One of the Best of Women."* Baltimore: Johns Hopkins University Press, 1988.

Semmel, Stuart. *Napoleon and the British*. New Haven: Yale University Press, 2004.

Seymour, Elizabeth, ed. *The "Pope" of Holland House: Selections from the Correspondence of John Whishaw and His Friends, 1813–1840*. London: Fisher Unwin, 1906.

Shee, William Archer. *My Contemporaries, 1830–1870*. London: Hurst and Blackett, 1893.

Shelley, Percy Bysshe. "Ode to the West Wind." In *Complete Poetical Works*, ed. Thomas Hutchinson. Oxford: Oxford University Press, 1971, 577–579.

Sheridan, Louisa H. "The Jilt." In Blessington, *Heath's Book of Beauty, 1840*, 83–96.

Simanowski, Roberto, Horst Turk, and Thomas Schmidt, eds. *Europa–ein Salon? Beiträge zur Internationalität des literarischen Salons*. Göttingen: Wallstein, 1999.

Slagle, Judith Bailey. "Joanna Baillie Through Her Letters." In *Collected Letters of Joanna Baillie*, ed. Judith Bailey Slagle. 2 vols. Madison: Fairleigh Dickinson University Press / London: Associated University Presses, 1999, 1–23.

———. "Sisters—Ambition and Compliance: The Case of Mary and Agnes Berry and Joanna and Agnes Baillie." In *Woman to Woman: Female Negotiations During the Long Eighteenth Century*, ed. Carolyn D. Williams, Angela Escott, and Louise Duckling. Newark: University of Delaware Press, 2010, 79–97.

Smith, Nicholas D. *The Literary Manuscripts and Letters of Hannah More.* Farnham: Ashgate, 2008.
Smith, Sydney. *The Letters of Sydney Smith,* ed. Nowell C. Smith. 2 vols. Oxford: Clarendon Press, 1953.
———. *The Works of the Reverend Sydney Smith: Including His Contributions to the Edinburgh Review.* 2 vols. London: Longman, Brown, Green, Longmans, and Roberts, 1859.
Smollett, Tobias. *The Adventures of Roderick Random,* ed. Paul-Gabriel Boucé. Oxford: Oxford University Press, 1999.
Snodin, Michael, ed., with the assistance of Cynthia Roman. *Horace Walpole's Strawberry Hill.* New Haven: Yale University Press, 2009.
Spacks, Patricia Meyer. *Gossip.* New York: Knopf, 1985.
The Spectator, vol. 1. 2nd ed. London: Buckley and Tonson, 1713.
Spivak, Gayatri Chakravorty. "The Rani of Simur: An Essay in Reading the Archives." In *Europe and Its Other: Proceedings of the Essex Conference on the Sociology of Literature,* ed. Francis Barker, Peter Hulme, et al. 2 vols. Colchester: University of Essex, 1985, 1:128–151.
Stabler, Jane. "Against Their Better Selves: Byron, Jeffrey and the *Edinburgh.*" In *British Romanticism and the* Edinburgh Review, ed. Massimiliano Demata and Duncan Wu. Basingstoke: Palgrave Macmillan, 2002, 146–167.
Staves, Susan. *A Literary History of Women's Writing in Britain, 1660–1789.* Cambridge: Cambridge University Press, 2006.
Surtees, Virginia, ed. *The Grace of Friendship: Horace Walpole and the Misses Berry.* Norwich: Michael Russell, 1995.
Sweet, Nanora. "'Hitherto Closed to British Enterprise': Trading and Writing the Hispanic World Circa 1815." *European Romantic Review* 8 (1997): 139–147.
Thackeray, William Makepeace. *The Four Georges.* In *The Works of William Makepeace Thackeray.* 24 vols. London: Smith, Elder, & Co., 1879, 23:5–116.
———. *The Letters and Private Papers of William Makepeace Thackeray,* ed. Gordon N. Ray. 4 vols. Cambridge, MA: Harvard University Press, 1945–1946.
———. *Vanity Fair: A Novel without a Hero,* ed. John Carey. London: Penguin, 2001.
———. "A Word on the Annuals." *Fraser's Magazine* 16 (December 1837): 757–763.
Ticknor, George. *Life, Letters, and Journals.* 2 vols. London: Sampson Low, Marston, Searle, & Rivington, 1876.
Tinker, Chauncey Brewster. *The Salon and English Letters: Chapters on the Interrelations of Literature and Society in the Age of Johnson.* New York: Macmillan, 1915.
Todd, William B., and Ann Bowden. *Tauchnitz International Editions in English 1841–1955: A Bibliographical History.* New York: Bibliographical Society of America, 1988.

Todorov, Tzvetan. "The Journey and Its Narratives." In *Transports: Travel, Pleasure, and Imaginative Geography, 1600–1830*, ed. Chloe Chard and Helen Langdon. New Haven: Yale University Press, 1996, 287–296.

Tomc, Sandra. "Poe and His Circle." In *The Cambridge Companion to Edgar Allan Poe*, ed. Kevin J. Hayes. Cambridge: Cambridge University Press, 2002, 21–41.

———. "Restyling an Old World: Nathaniel Parker Willis and Metropolitan Fashion in the Antebellum United States." *Representations* 85 (2004): 98–124.

Tuite, Clara. "Tainted Love and Romantic Literary Celebrity." *English Literary History* 74 (2007): 59–88.

Turner, Katherine. *British Travel Writers in Europe, 1750–1800: Authorship, Gender and National Identity*. Aldershot: Ashgate, 2001.

———. "Women's Travel Writing, 1750–1830." In *The History of British Women's Writing, 1750–1830*, ed. Jacqueline M. Labbe, vol. 5 of *The History of British Women's Writing*. Basingstoke: Palgrave Macmillan, 2010, 47–60.

Vickery, Amanda. *The Gentleman's Daughter: Women's Lives in Georgian England*. New Haven: Yale University Press, 1998.

Wagner, Tamara S., ed. *Silver-Fork Fiction and Its Literary Legacies*. Special issue of *Women's Writing* 16 (2009): 181–364.

Walchester, Kathryn. *"Our Own Fair Italy": Nineteenth Century Women's Travel Writing and Italy 1800–1844*. Bern: Lang, 2007.

Walpole, Horace. *Anecdotes of Painting in England*. 4th ed. 4 vols. London: Dodsley, 1796.

———. Letter to Mary Berry (January 9, 1791), autograph letter, Pierpont Morgan Library, MA 494.41.

———. *Reminiscences Written by Mr Walpole in 1778 for the Amusement of Miss Mary and Miss Agnes Berry*, ed. Paget Toynbee. Oxford: Clarendon Press, 1924.

———. *The Works of Horatio Walpole, Earl of Orford*, ed. Mary Berry. 5 vols. London: Robinson and Edwards, 1798. Reprint ed. Peter Sabor. London: Pickering and Chatto, 1999.

———. *The Yale Edition of Horace Walpole's Correspondence*, ed. W. S. Lewis. 48 vols. New Haven: Yale University Press, 1937–1983.

Walshe, Eibhear. "'A Different Story to Tell': The Historical Novel in Contemporary Irish Lesbian and Gay Writing." In *Facing the Other*, ed. Borbála Faragó and Moynagh Sullivan. Cambridge: Cambridge Scholars Publishing, 2008, 137–149.

Wardropper, Bruce W. "An Early English Hispanist." *Bulletin of Spanish Studies* 24 (1947): 259–268.

Warne, Vanessa. "Thackeray Among the Annuals: Morality, Cultural Authority and the Literary Annual Genre." *Victorian Periodicals Review* 39 (2006): 158–178.

Weeks, Donald. "Samuel Rogers: Man of Taste." *Publications of the Modern Language Association* 62 (1947): 472–486.

Weintraub, Jeff. "The Theory and Politics of the Public/Private Distinction." In *Public and Private in Thought and Practice: Perspectives on a Grand Dichotomy*, ed. Jeff Weintraub and Krishan Kumar. Chicago: University of Chicago Press, 1997, 1–42.
White, Jonathan. *Italian Cultural Lineages*. Toronto: University of Toronto Press, 2007.
Whyte, J. H. "The Age of Daniel O'Connell (1800–47)." In *The Course of Irish History*, ed. T. W. Moody and F. X. Martin. Cork: Mercier Press, 1967, 248–262.
———. "Daniel O'Connell and the Repeal Party." *Irish Historical Studies* 11 (1959): 297–316.
Wikoff, Henry. *The Reminiscences of an Idler*. New York: Fords, Howard & Hulbert, 1880.
Wilhelmy-Dollinger, Petra. *Die Berliner Salons. Mit kulturhistorischen Spaziergängen*. Berlin: de Gruyter, 2000.
Williams, William H. A. *Tourism, Landscape, and the Irish Character: British Travel Writers in Pre-Famine Ireland*. Madison: University of Wisconsin Press, 2008.
Willis, Nathaniel Parker. *Lady Jane: A Humorous Novel in Rhyme* [1844]. In *The Poems, Sacred, Passionate, and Humorous*. 6th ed. New York: Clark & Austin, 1845, 263–331.
———. "Pencillings by the Way." *New-York Mirror* 12 (March 7, 14, 21, 28; April 4, 11, 18, 25, 1835): 281, 292, 297, 308, 316, 324, 332, 340–341.
———. *Pencillings by the Way*. 3 vols. London: John Macrone, 1835.
Wilton-Ely, John. "'Classic Ground': Britain, Italy, and the Grand Tour." *Eighteenth-Century Life* 28 (2004): 136–165.
Wood, Gillen D' Arcy. *Romanticism and Music Culture in Britain, 1770–1840: Virtue and Virtuosity*. Cambridge: Cambridge University Press, 2010.
Woolf, D. R. "A Feminine Past? Gender, Genre, and Historical Knowledge in England, 1500–1800." *The American Historical Review* 102 (1997): 645–679.
Worrall, David. *The Politics of Romantic Theatricality, 1787–1832: The Road to the Stage*. Basingstoke: Palgrave Macmillan, 2007.
Wright, C. J. "Fox, Elizabeth Vassall." *Oxford Dictionary of National Biography*. Oxford: Oxford University Press, 2004–.
———. "Fox [*later* Vassall], Henry Richard." *Oxford Dictionary of National Biography*. Oxford: Oxford University Press, 2004–.
Wright, Julia M. "'All the Fire-Side Circle': Irish Women Writers and the Sheridan-Lefanu Coterie." *Keats-Shelley Journal* 55 (2006): 63–72.
Wynne, Deborah. *The Sensation Novel and the Victorian Family Magazine*. Basingstoke: Palgrave, 2001.
Yarrington, Alison. "Damer [*neé* Conway], Anne Seymour." *Oxford Dictionary of National Biography*. Oxford: Oxford University Press, 2004–.

———. "The Female Pygmalion: Anne Seymour Damer, Allan Cunningham and the Writing of a Woman Sculptor's Life." *The Sculpture Journal* 1 (1997): 32–44.

Zeller, Rosemarie. "Die Rolle der Frauen im Gesprächspiel und in der Konversation." In *Geselligkeit und Gesellschaft im Barockzeitalter*, ed. Wolfgang Adam, with the assistance of Knut Kiesant, Winfried Schulze, and Christoph Strosetzki. 2 vols. Wiesbaden: Harrassowitz, 1997, 1:531–541.

Index

This index lists names and literary works.

Addison, Joseph, 5, 173
Adickes, Sandra, 59
Ailesbury, Lady, 38
Allen, John, 76, 84, 98, 99, 102, 103, 104, 105, 106, 107, 108, 110, 115
American Monthly Magazine, 138
Ames, Dianne S., 31
Anne, Queen, 23
"The Annuals of Former Days," 165–66
Anspach, Margravine of, 42, 43
Antonio, 108
Archbishop of Tarentum, 148
Ashe, Thomas, *Travels in America*, 53
The Athenaeum, 157
Augé, Marc, 14
Austen, Jane, 9, 29, 41, 53, 65
  Mansfield Park, 41

Baillie, Joanna, 2, 10, 25, 26, 27, 32, 40–43, 44, 48, 49, 53, 54, 58, 67, 68, 173
  Basil, 42
  Constantine Paleologus, 41
  De Montfort, 42
  The Family Legend, 26, 41, 43, 58
  Plays on the Passions, 42, 44
  The Tryal, 41
Bailllie, Agnes, 42
Barbauld, Anna Laetitia, 66
Baring, Lady, 162
Bartolini, Lorenzo, 54
Baudry (publ.), 146
Beaumont, Lady, 58

Beaumont, Sir Godfrey, 58
Bedford, Duke of, 68
Belloy, Pierre-Laurent, *Gabrielle de Vergy*, 86
Bernal, R., "The Lottery of Life," 169
Berry, Agnes, 2, 4, 10, 17, 18, 23–25, 30–33, 35, 42, 48, 52, 55, 57, 59, 60, 61, 62, 74, 92, 99, 135, 136
Berry, Mary, 1, 2, 3, 4, 6, 10, 11, 16, 17, 18, 19, 20, 23–69, 74, 80, 82, 83, 92, 99, 101, 104, 117, 119, 120, 124, 135, 136, 147, 173–75
  "Advertisement," 27, 66
  A Comparative View of the Social Life of England and France, 18, 29, 68–69
  Fashionable Friends, 16, 20, 29, 40–49, 69, 174
  Journals and Correspondence, 6, 17, 23, 25–28, 32–35, 38, 39, 42, 48, 51–68, 147, 173
  Life of Lady Russell, 20, 29, 53, 66, 67–68, 101
  Social Life in England and France, 18, 29, 69
  The Two Martins, 29, 49
  editor of Mme du Deffand's *Letters*, 29, 65–67, 68
  editor of Walpole's *Works*, see Walpole, *Works*
The Berry Papers, 23, 38, 42, 48, 49, 53, 58, 59
Berry, Robert, 24, 25, 31, 48, 51, 52, 58, 59, 60, 65, 66

Index

Berry, William, 29
Bertrand, Henri-Gratien, Count of, 91
Bessborough, Lady, 100, 113
Bhabha, Homi, 13, 138
Bible, 85
The Biblical Keepsake, 166
The Bijou, 166
Blake, William, 55
Blanco White, José María, 87
   Letters from Spain by Don Leucadio Doblado, 87
Blessington, Charles John Gardiner, Lord Mountjoy, Earl of Blessington, 10, 119–23, 125, 129, 131, 134–36, 147, 150–51, 156–57, 161, 164
   De Vavasour, 150
Blessington, Marguerite, Countess of (née Power), 1, 2, 3, 4, 7, 10, 11, 14–20, 80, 82, 89, 99, 117, 119–71, 173–75
   "The Auction," 124, 160
   The Confessions of an Elderly Gentleman, 123
   The Confessions of an Elderly Lady, 123
   Conversations of Lord Byron, 1, 15, 18, 20, 120, 123, 124, 126–32, 135, 137, 142, 146, 151
   Country Quarters, 123, 124, 152, 157
   "Francesca Foscari," 170–71
   The Governess, 123
   The Idler in France, 123–24, 146, 147
   The Idler in Italy, 1, 20, 123–24, 146–52
   "The Italian Opera," 160
   Journal of a Tour through the Netherlands to Paris, 123
   The Magic Lantern, 123, 160–61
   Marmaduke Herbert, 123
   The Memoirs of a Femme de Chambre, 123
   Meredith, 123, 142
   "The Park," 160
   Rambles in Waltham Forest, 123
   The Repealers, 123, 145, 152–58, 161–62
   Sketches and Fragments, 123
   Strathern, 152, 157–58
   "The Tomb," 160–61
   The Two Friends, 123
   The Victims of Society, 18, 123, 159, 160, 162–64
Bohls, Elizabeth A., 63
Book of Beauty, 3, 20, 124, 142, 165–71
The Bookseller, 165
Borrow, George, 17
Brant, Clare, 31
Brougham, Henry Lord, 58, 71–72, 103, 105, 110, 124
Bruce, Lady, 83
Bryant, William Cullen, 105
Bulwer Lytton, Edward, 122, 123, 125, 127, 135, 159, 164, 167
   England and the English, 133
   Godolphin, 164
   Pelham, 139, 158
   "The Wife to the Wooer," 169–70
Bulwer, Rosina, 162
   Cheveley, 19, 159, 164–65
Buonaparte, Lucien, 91
Buonaparte, *see* Napoleon
Burke, Edmund, 154
Burn, Mr. and Mrs., 55
Burnet, Gilbert, *History*, 80
Burney, Fanny, 36, 40, 65
Burroughs, Catherine, 40
Bury, Charlotte, Lady, 122
Byron, George Gordon, Lord, 2, 3, 8, 10, 14, 17, 19, 20, 28, 29, 37, 42, 52, 53, 59, 72, 91, 92, 98, 100, 105, 107, 108–16, 120, 121, 125, 126–32, 134, 136, 138, 139, 142, 146, 151, 173, 174
   "The Blues: A Literary Eclogue," 7–8
   The Bride of Abydos, 111, 112

Childe Harold, 84, 87, 88, 100, 111, 112, 113, 151
The Corsair, 111
Don Juan, 84, 112, 114, 140, 151
English Bards and Scotch Reviewers, 88, 109–12, 115
The Giaour, 112
Hours of Idleness, 109–10
Lara, 53
memoirs, 108, 127
The Two Foscari, 170–71
Byron, Lady, 52, 110, 129, 131

Calderón, Pedro, 86
Cambridge, Richard Owen, 33
Campbell, Thomas, 125
 The Pleasures of Hope, 136
Canning, George, 2, 95, 121, 133
Canova, Antonio, 54, 91
Carey and Hart (publ.), 146
Carlisle, Earl of, "To Lady Holland, on the Legacy of a Snuff-Box, Left to Her by Buonaparte," 91–92
Carlisle, Lady (G.), 28
Caroline of Brunswick, Princess of Wales, 26, 36, 58–59, 67
Carter, Elizabeth, 8, 10
Castiglione, Baldassare, *Il Libro del Cortegiano,* 126
Castlereagh, Viscount, 121, 133, 135
Catalani, Angelica, 58
Catherine II, Empress of Russia, 86
Chaos, 7
Chapone, Hester, 8
Chard, Chloe, 148
Charleville, Lady, 135, 156, 161
Charleville, Lord, 156
Chartier, Roger, 16
Cholm(e)ley, Mrs., 55, 58
Chorley, Henry F., 167
 The Authors of England: A Series of Medallion Portraits, 19, 125
Christie, William, 103
Cicero, 105

Clark, Peter, 13
Cohen, Michèle, 5
Colburn, Henry, 87, 114, 127, 146, 151, 160
Coleridge, Samuel Taylor, 55–56, 125
Colman, George, 136
Combe, William, *The First of April: or, The Triumphs of Folly,* 36
Constant, Benjamin, 132
Conway, Anne Seymour, *see* Damer, Anne Seymour
Conway, Henry Seymour, 31, 35, 39
 False Appearances, 47
Cook, James, 80
Cooper, Anthony Ashley, *see* Shaftesbury, Third Earl of
Cooper, James Fenimore, 105
Cork, Lady, 56, 135
Cornwall, Barry, 167
Cowper, Lord, 53
Cradock, Mr., 76
Craven, Richard Keppel, 27, 58
 Excursions in the Abruzzi and Northern Provinces of Naples, 58
 A Tour Through the Southern Provinces of the Kingdom of Naples, 58
Creevey, Mrs., 116
Creevey, Thomas, 71, 72, 74, 78, 101, 102, 103, 104
 The Creevey Papers, 71, 72, 99, 116
The Critical Review, 49
Crosland, Mrs. Newton (Camilla Toulmin), 11, 15, 133, 134, 136, 138, 165, 167

D'Albany, Countess of, 83
Damer, Anne Seymour (née Conway), 10, 20, 24–31, 35–44, 46–49, 54, 55, 58, 61, 173
 Belmour, 29, 37–38
 notebooks, 28, 35, 38–40

Damer, John, 35
Daniel, Captain, "The Improvident: A Tale," 169
Dante, Alighieri, 151
Darwin, Erasmus, *The Botanic Garden*, 34
D'Aulnoy, Marie-Catherine, 9
De Balzac, Honoré, 53
De Cervantes, Miguel, *Don Quixote*, 86
De Coigny, Mme, 55
De Deffand, Marquise, 4, 29, 65–67
De Fenne, François, *Entretiens familiers pour les Amateurs de la Langue Françoise*, 126
De Jovellanos, Gaspar Melchor, 87
De Lespinasse, Julie, 4
De Luines, Duchesse, 57
De Montaigne, Michel, 80
   Essais, 53
De Montholon, Charles, 91
De Peñafiel, Marqués, 86
De Rambouillet, Marquise, 4
De Sismondi, Léonard Simonde, *History of the Italian Republics in the Middle Ages*, 64
De Staël, Germaine, 27, 51, 58, 100, 105, 129–30, 131, 132
   Delphine, 53, 107
De Ulloa, Francisco, 80
Derby, Earl of, 36, 37
Devonshire, Georgiana Cavendish, Duchess of, 23, 25, 43, 75, 100
Devonshire, Rachel Cavendish, Duchess of, 68
Devonshire, William Cavendish, Fifth Duke of, 28, 59
Devonshire, William Cavendish, Second Duke of, 68
Devonshire, William Cavendish, Sixth Duke of, 28, 54, 57, 59, 66, 68, 156
D'Haussez, Baron, *Great Britain in 1833*, 153, 154
Diamond, Elin, 15

Dickens, Charles, 100, 135, 142, 145, 173
   Hard Times, 154
Digby, Lord, 83
Dinner Books, 73, 74, 90, 98, 99, 101
Disraeli, Benjamin, 123, 127, 135, 159, 167
   Vivian Grey, 29
Dolan, Brian, 60, 82
Donegal, Lady, 58
Donoghue, Emma, 36, 38, 39
   Life Mask, 40
D'Orsay, Alfred Count of, 7, 121, 122, 131, 138, 139, 147, 150
Douglass, Paul, 113
Downie, J. A., 12
Drummond, William, 148, 149
Dumont, Etienne, 93, 105

Edgeworth, Maria, *The Absentee*, 152
Edinburgh Review, 3, 19, 20, 31, 66, 72, 91, 98–107, 109–11, 115–16, 174
Edwards, J., 54
Eger, Elizabeth, 9, 69
Eldon, Lord, 99
Elfenbein, Andrew, 36, 38, 39, 47
Eliot, George, *Middlemarch*, 166
Erskine, Thomas, 99, 106
El Espagnol, 87
Examiner, 125, 131

Farington, Joseph, 28, 36, 37
Farmer, Maurice St. Leger, Captain, 120, 121, 125, 152
Farren, Elizabeth, 36, 37, 40, 43
Fawkener, Mr., 48
Ferguson, Robert (Agnes Berry's cousin), 25
Ferguson, Robert (Robert Berry's uncle), 24, 60
Fisher's Drawing Room Scrap Book, 166
Flowers of Loveliness, 166, 168
Fonblanque, Albany, 125, 135
Fontana, Biancamaria, 103

Forget Me Not, 166
Fox, Caroline, 74, 78
Fox, Charles James, 23, 35, 36, 73, 76, 79, 89, 90, 94, 99, 105, 110, 117, 173
   History of the Reign of James II, 90
Fox, Henry Richard, Third Baron Holland, see Holland, Henry Richard, Third Baron
Fox, Henry, First Baron Holland, 72, 73
Fox, Stephen, Second Baron Holland, 72, 73
Frank, Marcie, 30
Fraser's Magazine, 125, 139
Friendship's Offering, 166
Fumaroli, Marc, 2

G., see Lady Carlisle
Galignani (publ.), 146
Gardiner, Harriet, 121, 131
Gardner, Daniel, 43
Gay, John, 23
Gell, William, 27, 28, 58, 148, 149
Gell, William, and John P. Gandy, *Pompeiana*, 148
The Gentleman's Magazine, 91
Geoffrin, Marie-Thérèse, 4
George I, 23
George III, 23, 36
George IV, 43, 58, 90
Godwin, William, *St. Leon*, 53
Goethe, Ottilie von, 7
Goffman, Erving, 15
Goldsmith, Elizabeth C., 5
Goodman, Dena, 4
Gore, Catherine, 145, 159
Gotha Almanack, 166
Gow (Scotch fiddler), 58
Graham's American Monthly Magazine, 140
Granville, Countess of, 77, 100
Granville, Lord, 79
Grattan, Mr., 57
Grattan, Thomas, 122
Greenblatt, Stephen, 15

Greffulhe, M., 56
Greville, Charles, 99, 101
Grey, Charles, Earl of, 73, 94, 99
Griffith, Elizabeth, 69
Gross, Jonathan, 37, 38
Guazzo, Stefano, *La Civil conversatione*, 6
Guiccioli, Teresa, Countess, 136

Habermas, Jürgen, 11, 12
Haefner, Joel, 15
Hall, Mrs. S. C., 136, 167
Hall, Samuel Carter, 127, 136, 166
Hardwicke, Lady, 58
Harrington, Lady, 135
Harsdörffer, Georg Philipp, *Frauenzimmer Gesprächsspiele*, 126
Hartington, Lord, see Devonshire, William Cavendish, Sixth Duke of
Haydon, Benjamin, 100, 135, 136, 157
Hazlitt, William, "The Dandy School," 158
   "On the Conversation of Authors," 21
   "My First Acquaintance with Poets," 55–56
Hearne, Samuel, 80
Heath, Charles, 11, 122
Heath's Book of Beauty, see *Book of Beauty*
Heller, Deborah, 3
Hemans, Felicia, 125
   England and Spain, 84
Hemphill, C. Dallett, 13
Herz, Henriette, 7
Hoagwood, Terence, 167
Hobhouse, Benjamin, 99
Hobhouse, John, 132
Hogarth, William, 46
Hogg, Thomas Jefferson, *The Life of Shelley*, 132
Holland, Henry, 81, 117

Holland, Henry Edward, Fourth
    Baron, 108, 112, 113, 148
  *The Journal of the Hon. Edward
    Fox (Afterwards Fourth and
    Last Lord Holland),
    1818–1830,* 74, 108
Holland, Henry Richard Fox, Third
    Baron, 8, 13, 16, 71–117
  Foreign Reminiscences, 74
  *Further Memoirs of the Whig
    Party,* 74
  *The Holland House Diaries,
    1831–1840,* 75
  Life of Lope de Vega, 79, 87, 112
  Memoirs of the Whig Party, 74, 79
  The Opinions of Lord Holland, 79,
    90, 104
Holland, Lady, Elizabeth Vassall
    Fox (also Lady Webster), 3, 4,
    10, 11, 19, 20, 71–117, 130,
    135, 136, 147, 148, 173–75
  *The Journal of Elizabeth, Lady
    Holland (1791–1811),* 74,
    75–78, 80, 81–83, 87, 90,
    93–95, 98, 99, 101, 102,
    103, 147, 174
  *Lady Holland to Her Son,
    1821–1845,* 74, 89
  Spanish Journal, 72, 74, 80, 82,
    84–88, 174
Holme, Torre, Mrs., "Stanzas,"
    169
Home Purves, Ellen,
    see Manners-Sutton, Ellen
Homer, 53, 91
Hoole, Samuel, "A Conversatione," 6
Horace, 104
Horner, Francis, 103
Howard, George, 1
Howard, George, Earl of Carlile
    (G.'s son), 28
Hudson, Derek, 75, 98
Hudson, Marianne Spencer,
    Almack's, 158
Humboldt, Alexander von, 100
Hutton, Charles, 105

Ilchester, Giles Stephen Holland
    Fox-Strangways, Sixth Earl of,
    74, 75, 93, 94, 98
Inchbald, Elizabeth, 40
Irving, Washington, 105

Jeffrey, Francis, 41, 103, 105–7, 110
Jekyll, Joseph, 77, 135, 136
Jenkins, Thomas, Captain, 120
Jerdan, William, 122
Jerningham, Edward, 55
Jersey, Lady, 81, 130, 135, 162
Johnson, Joseph, 14
Johnson, Samuel, 23
  The Idler, 146
Jordan, Dorothy, 49
Jump, Harriet Devine, 18, 158
Juvenal, 80

Kauffmann, Angelica, 36
Keepsake, 11, 18, 124, 136, 142,
    165, 166, 167, 170–71
Kelly, Gary, 8, 9, 18
Kemble, Charles, 49
Kemble, John Philip, 42
Kemble, Mrs., 57
King Charles II, 67
King of Naples, 149–50
King of Sweden, 64
Kirgate, Thomas, 34, 35
Klein, Lawrence E., 5, 12
Klopstock, Friedrich, 94
Kotzebue, August von, *Lovers'
    Vows,* 41, 53
Kriegel, Abraham D., 75

La Fontaine, 80
The Lady's Monthly Museum, 48
Lamb, Caroline (née Ponsonby), 10,
    56, 72, 98, 100, 113–16
  Glenarvon, 10, 19, 20, 72, 98,
    113–16, 117, 159, 174
  A New Canto, 114
Lamb, Charles, 125
Lamb, Elizabeth, Viscountess
    Melbourne, 43

Lamb, William, 114
Landon, Letitia (L. E. L.), 11, 121,
    136, 140, 162, 167, 168, 171
    Romance and Reality, 158
Landor, Walter Savage, 7, 135, 137,
    167
    Imaginary Conversations, 126
Lawrence, Thomas, 58, 119, 121
Lazarillo de Tormes, 80
Ledbetter, Kathryn, 167
Leigh, Augusta, 129
Lennox, Charlotte, 69
    The Female Quixote, 69
Lepenies, Wolf, 16, 74
Leti, Gregorio, *Life of Pope
    Sixtus, V,* 80
Lewis, Matthew ("Monk" Lewis),
    78, 102, 107
    The Monk, 64, 84, 95
Lewis, Theresa, 26
    editor of *Journals and
    Correspondence of Miss Berry,*
    see Berry, *Journals and
    Correspondence*
    *Lives of the Friends and
    Contemporaries of
    Clarendon,* 27
Liechtenstein, Marie, *Holland
    House,* 74, 93
Lieven, Count, 16
Lindsay, Lady Charlotte, 58
Lister, Thomas Henry, *Granby,* 158
Liszt, Franz, 7, 135
The Literary Gazette, 122
Longfellow, Henry Wadsworth, 105
Longman (publ.), 67, 142
Louis Napoleon, 135
Luttrell, Henry, 71, 72, 92, 93, 101
    Advice to Julia, 100

M., "Private Hints to a Juvenile
    Physician," 132
Macaulay, Catherine, *History of
    England,* 67
Macaulay, Thomas Babington, 73,
    75, 76, 93, 95, 99, 100, 101, 109

"Letters of Horace Walpole," 31, 66
"The Opinions of Lord Holland,"
    104
Madden, *The Literary Life and
    Correspondence of the Countess
    of Blessington,* 18, 124–25,
    133, 156
Malthus, Robert, "Essay on the
    Principle of Population," 51, 53
Manners-Sutton, Charles, 135, 147
Manners-Sutton, Ellen, 135, 147
Marie Antoinette, 37, 134
Martial, 17
Martineau, Harriet, 59
Mathews, Charles, 7, 16, 147, 148, 150
Mathews, Mrs. Charles, 121, 136
Meadows, 171
Medwin, Thomas, *Conversations
    of Lord Byron,* 127
Melbourne, Lady, 113, 114
Melbourne, Lord, 74, 140, 163
Mellon, Harriet, 43, 48
    Memoirs of Miss Mellon, 43
Melville, Lewis, 28
The Metropolitan Magazine, 131
Milbanke, Annabella, *see* Lady Byron
Milbanke, Lady, 52
Milton, John, 80, 151
    Paradise Lost, 53, 115
Mitchell, Leslie, 75, 84, 89, 98,
    101, 102
Mitford, Mary Russell, 125
Molloy, J. Fitzgerald, 125
Montagu, Elizabeth, 4, 8, 9, 10, 59, 69
Montagu, Mary Wortley, *Turkish
    Embassy Letters,* 60
The Monthly Mirror, 48
Moore, Thomas, 2, 15, 17, 20, 41,
    53, 58, 72, 74, 88, 89, 93, 99,
    100, 104, 105, 107–9, 110,
    116, 121, 125, 130, 135,
    167, 173
    Journals, 16, 17, 89, 91, 101, 102,
    107–9
    Lalla Rookh, 109
    Memoirs of the Life of Sheridan, 107

More, Hannah, 6, 8, 23, 28, 40, 45, 52, 58, 66, 67
The Bas Bleu, 9
"Bishop Bonner's Ghost," 35
Coelebs in Search of a Wife, 107
Strictures on the Modern System of Female Education, 52
"Thoughts on Conversation," 51
Morgan, Lady (Sydney Owenson), 125, 135, 136, 152
The Wild Irish Girl, 152
The Morning Post, 41
Morrisson, Alfred, 125
Mount Edgcumbe, Earl of, 48
Mountjoy, Lord, *see* Blessington, Lord
Mountjoy, Lord (Blessington's father), 156
Mouravieff-Apostil, Ivan, 86
Murray (publ.), 17, 108
Murray, Venetia, 161
Murray's Handbook, 61
Myers, Sylvia Harcstark, 8

Napoleon, 20, 28, 36, 72, 76, 78, 79, 80, 81, 83, 84, 88–92, 104, 110, 116, 117, 128, 132, 134, 135, 141, 170, 173
Neapolitan Royal Family, 148
Necker, Suzanne, 4
Nelson, Lord, 27, 36
New Monthly Magazine, 87, 126, 127, 129, 132, 133, 135, 146, 157
Newman, Gerald, 102
New-York Mirror, 137–39
Noble, Percy, 49
Nora, Pierre, 2
Northumberland, Duchess of, 161
Norton, Caroline, 11, 122, 140, 163, 167, 171

O'Connell, Daniel, 153, 155, 156, 157
O'Hara, Charles, 25, 38, 46
Orford, Lord, *see* Walpole, Horace
Ossory, Lady, 31–32, 94

Owenson, Sydney, *see* Morgan, Lady
Oxford, Lady, 114

Palmerston, Viscount, 99
Parr, Samuel, 121
Parsons, William, 34
Patmore, P. G., "Personal Recollections of the Late Lady Blessington," 119, 121, 122, 124, 133
Peel, Robert, 156
Pekacz, Jolanta T., 4
Pepys, Sir William, 58
Perry, Kate, *Reminiscences of a London Drawing-Room*, 55, 58, 175
Petty, Henry, 110
Pigott, Charles
The Female Jockey Club, 29
The Whig Club, 36–37
Pinkerton, John, 34
Playfair, John, 27, 105
Poe, Edgar Allan, "Lionizing," 141–42
Polwhele, Richard, *The Unsex'd Females*, 8
Poodle Byng (Byng, Frederick), 58
Pope, 64, 91
Pope, Alexander, translation of Homer, 53, 94
Porchester, Lord, 109
Porter, Roy, 14
Pottinger, George, 103
Power, Edmund, 120
Power, Ellen, 124, 136, 166
Power, Margaret, *see* Blessington, Marguerite, Countess of
Power, Mary Ann, 147, 150
Prince of Wales, *see* George IV
Prince Regent, *see* George IV
Princess of Wales, *see* Caroline of Brunswick
Prior, Matthew, 23

The Quarterly Review, 26
Queensbury, Duchess of, 23

Index

Radcliffe, Ann, 59, 60
Radway, Janice, 170
Rasponi, Count, 112
Rembrandt, 54
Richardson, Samuel, 66
Richmond, Duke of, 42, 43
Robinson, Henry Crabb, 133, 135
Rogers, Samuel, 20, 42, 58, 71, 72, 93, 98, 101, 104–9, 110, 112, 113–14, 115, 121, 135
  Italy, 104–5
  The Pleasures of Memory, 136
  Table-Talk, 104, 106
Romer, Isabella, "A Leaf from the Pilgrim's Scrap-Book," 170
Rosa, Salvator, 62, 150
Roscoe, William, 53
Rosslyn, Lord, 53
Rousseau, Jean Jacques, 53, 63, 80
  Rêveries du promeneur solitaire, 93
Rowlandson, Thomas, 8
Rubens, Peter Paul, 150
Rumford, Count, 100
Russell, Gillian, 13, 15, 40
Russell, John, Lord, 76, 99, 101
Russell, Lady Rachel, 53, 67–68
Russell, William Lord, 67–68, 173

Sadleir, Michael, 119, 125, 134, 145, 147, 156, 161, 162
Samuelian, Kristin Flieger, 170
Sanders, Lloyd, 97, 98
Sapio, Mr., 58
A Sapphick Epistle, from Jack Cavendish to the Honourable and Most Beautiful Mrs. D****, 36
Schoenfield, Mark, 103, 111
Scott, Walter, 26, 42, 53, 54, 58, 67, 99, 110, 125, 165
  Marmion, 53
Sefton, Lord, 102
Seton, Elizabeth, 24
Shaftesbury, Third Earl of (Cooper, Anthony Ashley), 5, 13

Shakespeare, William, 53, 69
  Hamlet, 54
  Lady Macbeth, 43, 86
Sharp, Richard, 101
Shee, William Archer, 136
Shelley, Mary, 88
Shelley, Percy Bysshe, 14, 125, 130, 145
  Alastor, 2
Sheridan, Louisa H., "The Jilt," 168–69
Sheridan, Richard Brinsley, 48, 99, 107–8
  The School for Scandal, 44, 48, 86
Siddons, Sarah, 40, 54
Sigourney, Lydia, 105, 142, 165
Slagle, Judith Bailey, 41
Smith, James, *Rejected Addresses*, 136
Smith, Mrs., 101
Smith, Sydney, 19, 20, 58, 67, 72, 97, 98, 99, 103–9, 110
Smollett, Tobias, 151–52
  Roderick Random, 52
  Travels Through France and Italy, 61
Somerset, Duke of, 102
Sotheby, Mrs., 57
Southey, Robert, 11, 73, 88, 110, 125
  The Cid, 73
Spacks, Patricia Meyer, 31, 98
The Spectator, 6, 13
Star(h)emberg, Prince, 57, 58
Staves, Susan, 65, 67, 81
Steele, Richard, 5
Stepney, Lady, 159
Sterne, Laurence, *Tristram Shandy*, 53
Stillingfleet, Benjamin, 9
Stothard, Thomas, 105, 109
Strawberry Committee, 30
Strawberry Hill Press (publ.), 33, 35
Stuart, Lady Louisa, 58

Talleyrand, Prince, 79
The Tatler, 13
Tauchnitz (publ.), 142–43

Thackeray, William Makepeace, 53, 58, 135, 137, 167
The Four Georges, 23
Vanity Fair, 158
"A Word on the Annuals," 167
Thrale, Hester Lynch, 8, 9
Ticknor, George, 87
Tierney, George, 101
The Times, 41
Tinker, Chauncey Brewster, 3, 8
Titian, 168
Todorov, Tzvetan, 150
Tomc, Sandra, 138
Toulmin, Camilla, *see* Mrs. Newton Crosland
Trevelyan, Hannah, 73, 95
Tuite, Clara, 13, 15

Universal Magazine, 49
Upper Ossory, Lord, 79

Varnhagen, Rahel, 7
Ventini, Sigr., 64
Vesey, Elizabeth, 8, 9
Vickery, Amanda, 12
Victoria, Queen, 99, 166
Virgil, 104
Volney, Constantin-François, *Travels Through Syria and Egypt,* 80
Voltaire, 66, 76, 80, 90

Walchester, Kathryn, 148
Walpole, Horace, Lord Orford, 2, 3, 4, 20, 23–36, 38, 39, 44, 49, 53, 54, 58, 60–63, 65–67, 92, 134
Anecdotes of Painting, 36
The Castle of Otranto, 29–31, 49, 54
correspondence, 26, 27, 30–35, 38, 60, 61–63, 66, 94
A Description of the Villa of Horace Walpole, 31
Reminiscences Written by Mr Walpole in 1778 for the Amusement of Miss Mary and Miss Agnes Berry, 31
Works, 65–66
Walpole, Robert, 58
Warden, William, *Letters from St. Helena,* 104
Webster, Elizabeth Lady, *see* Holland, Lady
Webster, Godfrey, Sir (Lady Holland's first husband), 77, 78
Webster, Godfrey, Sir (Lady Holland's son), 113, 114
Wellington, Duke of, 58, 90
West, Richard, 62
Westmacott, Richard, 99
Whishaw, John (also Wishaw, John), 101, 103, 105
Wikoff, Henry, 142
Wilberforce, William, 108
Wilbraham, Roger, 101
Wilhelmy-Dollinger, Petra, 56
Williams, Helen Maria, 60
Willis, Nathaniel Parker, 7, 19, 105, 120, 122, 137–43, 164, 167, 173
Lady Jane: A Humorous Novel in Rhyme, 140–41
"Pencillings by the Way," 122, 137–40, 142
Pencillings by the Way, 139
Wilton-Ely, John, 60
Wishaw, John, *see* Whishaw, John
Wolff, Joseph, 80
Wollstonecraft, Mary, 8, 26, 52, 60
Wordsworth, Willliam, 55–56, 63, 105, 110, 125
Lyrical Ballads, 2
Wynne, Deborah, 132

CPI Antony Rowe
Chippenham, UK
2019-12-04 13:40